Crusades

Volume 21, 2022

Crusades

Edited by
Jonathan Phillips, Iris Shagrir and Benjamin Z. Kedar,
with Nikolaos G. Chrissis

Crusades

Volume 21, 2022

Published by ROUTLEDGE for the Society for the Study of the Crusades and the Latin East

First published 2022
by Routledge
4 Park Square, Milton Park, Abingdon, Oxon OX14 4RN

and by Routledge
605 Third Avenue, New York, NY 10158

Routledge is an imprint of the Taylor & Francis Group, an informa business

British Library Cataloguing-in-Publication Data
A catalogue record for this book is available from the British Library

ISBN: 978-1-032-37826-8 (hbk)
ISBN: 978-1-003-34212-0 (ebk)

DOI: 10.4324/9781003342120

Typeset in Times New Roman
by N²productions

Printed and bound in Great Britain by
TJ Books Limited, Padstow, Cornwall

CONTENTS

Abbreviations

AA	Albert of Aachen, *Historia Ierosolimitana. History of the Journey to Jerusalem*, ed. and trans. Susan B. Edgington (Oxford, 2007)
AOL	*Archives de l'Orient latin*
Autour	*Autour de la Première Croisade. Actes du colloque de la Society for the Study of the Crusades and the Latin East: Clermont-Ferrand, 22–25 juin 1995*, ed. Michel Balard (Paris, 1996)
Cart Hosp	*Cartulaire général de l'ordre des Hospitaliers de Saint-Jean de Jérusalem, 1100–1310*, ed. Joseph Delaville Le Roulx. 4 vols. (Paris, 1884–1906)
Cart St Sép	*Le Cartulaire du chapitre du Saint-Sépulcre de Jérusalem*, ed. Geneviève Bresc-Bautier, Documents relatifs à l'histoire des croisades 15 (Paris, 1984)
Cart Tem	*Cartulaire général de l'ordre du Temple 1119?–1150. Recueil des chartes et des bulles relatives à l'ordre du Temple*, ed. Guigue A.M.J.A., (marquis) d'Albon (Paris, 1913)
CCCM	Corpus Christianorum. Continuatio Mediaevalis
Chartes Josaphat	*Chartes de la Terre Sainte provenant de l'abbaye de Notre-Dame de Josaphat*, ed. Henri F. Delaborde, Bibliothèque des Écoles françaises d'Athènes et de Rome 19 (Paris, 1880)
Clermont	*From Clermont to Jerusalem: The Crusades and Crusader Societies 1095–1500. Selected Proceedings of the International Medieval Congress, University of Leeds, 10–13 July 1995*, ed. Alan V. Murray. International Medieval Research 3 (Turnhout, 1998)
Crusade Sources	*The Crusades and their Sources: Essays Presented to Bernard Hamilton*, ed. John France and William G. Zajac (Aldershot, 1998)
CS	*Crusade and Settlement: Papers read at the First Conference of the Society for the Study of the Crusades and the Latin East and Presented to R. C. Smail*, ed. Peter W. Edbury (Cardiff, 1985)
CSEL	Corpus Scriptorum Ecclesiasticorum Latinorum
FC	Fulcher of Chartres, *Historia Hierosolymitana (1095–1127)*, ed. Heinrich Hagenmeyer (Heidelberg, 1913)
GF	*Gesta Francorum et aliorum Hierosolimitanorum*, ed. and trans. Rosalind M. T. Hill and Roger Mynors (London, 1962)
GN	Guibert of Nogent, *Dei gesta per Francos*, ed. Robert B. C. Huygens, CCCM 127A (Turnhout, 1996)

Horns	*The Horns of Hattin*, ed. Benjamin Z. Kedar (Jerusalem and London, 1992)
Mansi. *Concilia*	Giovanni D. Mansi, *Sacrorum conciliorum nova et amplissima collectio*
Mayer, *Urkunden*	*Die Urkunden der lateinischen Könige von Jerusalem*, ed. Hans E. Mayer, 4 vols. (Hanover, 2010)
MGH	Monumenta Germaniae Historica
SRG	Scriptores Rerum Germanicarum
SS	Scriptores (in Folio)
MO, 1	*The Military Orders: Fighting for the Faith and Caring for the Sick*, ed. Malcolm Barber (Aldershot, 1994)
MO, 2	*The Military Orders, vol. 2: Welfare and Warfare*, ed. Helen Nicholson (Aldershot, 1998)
MO, 3	*The Military Orders, vol. 3: History and Heritage*, ed. Victor Mallia-Milanes (Aldershot, 2008)
MO, 4	*The Military Orders, vol. 4: On Land and by Sea*, ed. Judi Upton-Ward (Aldershot, 2008)
MO, 5	*The Military Orders, vol. 5: Politics and Power*, ed. Peter W. Edbury (Farnham, 2012)
MO, 6/1	*The Military Orders, Volume 6.1: Culture and Contact in the Mediterranean World*, ed. Jochen Schenk and Mike Carr (London and New York, 2017)
MO, 6/2	*The Military Orders, Volume 6.2: Culture and Contact in Western and Northern Europe*, ed. Jochen Schenk and Mike Carr (London and New York, 2017)
Montjoie	*Montjoie: Studies in Crusade History in Honour of Hans Eberhard Mayer*, ed. Benjamin Z. Kedar, Jonathan Riley-Smith and Rudolf Hiestand (Aldershot, 1997)
Outremer	*Outremer. Studies in the History of the Crusading Kingdom of Jerusalem Presented to Joshua Prawer*, ed. Benjamin Z. Kedar, Hans E. Mayer and Raymond C. Smail (Jerusalem, 1982)
PG	Patrologia Graeca
PL	Patrologia Latina
PPTS	Palestine Pilgrims' Text Society Library
Pringle, *Churches*	Denys Pringle, *The Churches of the Crusader Kingdom of Jerusalem: A Corpus*, 4 vols. (Cambridge, 1993–2009)
RHC	*Recueil des Historiens des Croisades*
Darm	*Documents arméniens*
Lois	*Les assises de Jérusalem*
Oc	*Historiens occidentaux*
Or	*Historiens orientaux*
RHGF	Recueil des Historiens des Gaules et de la France

RIS	Rerum Italicarum Scriptores
NS	New Series
RM	*The* Historia Iherosolimitana *of Robert the Monk*, ed. Damien Kempf and Marcus G. Bull (Woodbridge, 2013)
ROL	*Revue de l'Orient latin*
RRH	Reinhold Röhricht, comp., *Regesta regni hierosolymitani* (Innsbruck, 1893)
RRH Add	Reinhold Röhricht, comp., *Additamentum* (Innsbruck, 1904)
RS	Rolls Series
Setton, *Crusades*	*A History of the Crusades*, general editor Kenneth M. Setton, 2nd edn., 6 vols. (Madison, 1969–89)
WT	William of Tyre, *Chronicon*, ed. Robert B. C. Huygens, with Hans E. Mayer and Gerhard Rösch, CCCM 63–63A (Turnhout, 1986)

Et erit sepulchrum eius gloriosum:
The Impact of Medieval Sibylline Prophecy
on the Origin of the Idea of Crusade

Marco Giardini

École Pratique des Hautes Études, Paris
giardinimarco82@gmail.com

Abstract

The article examines the role of the medieval Sibylline tradition in the development of the idea of crusade at the end of the eleventh century. It compares a set of sources that include references to this prophetic material, with a special focus on Benzo of Alba's Ad Heinricum IV Imperatorem *and Pseudo Alcuin's* Vita Antichristi ad Carolum Magnum. *In particular, this article pursues the following objectives: 1) it examines the impact of the Sibylline prophetic tradition in shaping expectations on the future liberation of the Holy Sepulchre within an eschatological scenario; 2) it analyses the function of this prophetic "proto-crusading" motif as a legitimization tool for the aspirations to universal kingship shared by both German Salian emperors and French Capetian kings; and 3) it highlights the role played by the conquest/liberation of Jerusalem as a pivotal event in the implementation of universal rulership.*

In two of his essays,[1] Carl Erdmann mentioned two prophetic texts dating to the second half of the eleventh century and sharing common intertwining features: both were attributed to Sibylline authorship and both tackled the question of the role of the Roman emperor in the conquest or liberation of the Holy Land within an eschatological framework. The sources in question are a brief mention of a so-called *Cumaean Sibyl*[2] in Benzo of Alba's celebration of the German ruler in his *Ad Heinricum IV imperatorem*;[3] and an adaptation (attributed to Alcuin) of Adso of Montier-en-Der's *De ortu et tempore Antichristi*[4] which includes interpolated

---

[1] Carl Erdmann, "Endkaiserglaube und Kreuzzugsgedanke im 11. Jahrhundert," *Zeitschrift für Kirchengeschichte* 51 (1932): 384–414, here 412; idem, *Die Entstehung des Kreuzzugsgedankens* (Stuttgart, 1935), 279 n. 119.

[2] To be clearly distinguished from a prophetic text that began to circulate under the same authorship during the eleventh century, edited by Erdmann, "Endkaiserglaube," 396–403. On the chronological placement of this *Cumaean Sibyl*, see below, p. 3.

[3] Benzo of Alba, *Ad Heinricum IV Imperatorem Libri VII*, ed. Hans Seyffert, MGH SS rer. Germ. 65 (Hanover, 1996), 142, 144, 146.

[4] See *Vita Antichristi ad Carolum Magnum ab Alcuino edita*, in Adso Dervensis, *De ortu et tempore Antichristi: necnon et tractatus qui ab eo dependunt*, ed. Daniël Verhelst (Turnhout, 1976), 105–28. The original text of Adso is edited in ibid., 20–30. In reality, the Pseudo-Alcuin prophecy does not rely directly on Adso's writing but on one of its first reworkings: the *Descriptio cuiusdam sapientis*

1

excerpts from the original *Sibylla Tiburtina* (in particular the passages concerning the so-called *Vaticinium* of Constans).[5] Whilst there was no controversy over the "pre-crusades" origin of the *Cumaean Sibyl* mentioned by Benzo, on account of its reference in his *Ad Heinricum IV imperatorem*, which was certainly completed by 1085, Erdmann addressed the issue of Pseudo-Alcuin's chronology in order to ascertain whether this text had been written before or after the First Crusade. Although Erdmann seemed inclined to admit a pre-1095 redaction, he did not reach a definitive conclusion.[6] The issue was not only a philological or diplomatic matter: the question is whether Pseudo-Alcuin's work, just like Benzo of Alba's mention of the *Cumaean Sibyl*, contributed to shaping the idea of crusade.[7] If that is the case, what was the impact of the prophetic and eschatological literature (epitomized by the Sibylline tradition) on the crusading movement and ideals?

Benzo of Alba's *Ad Heinricum IV* and the version of Adso's writing attributed to Alcuin (as well as other related sources discussed below) have been evoked as representative testimonies that plans to undertake a military conquest or recovery of Jerusalem, elicited by expectations concerning the figure of the "Last World Emperor," were already present before the First Crusade.[8] Recent scholarship has considerably downplayed this assumption by showing the untenability of Erdmann's position according to which there would have been "regular plan(s) for crusade" as early as the 1060s or 1070s.[9] However, without overstating the impact

---

de Antichristo, probably dating back to the early eleventh century (see Verhelst's introduction to the text in ibid., 33–53). The French origin of Pseudo-Alcuin's text seems to be confirmed not only by its content, as will be shown in the final pages of this article, but also by the fact that all of the most ancient manuscripts conveying it (dating back to the twelfth century) come from France: see ibid., 110–15. For a discussion of this adaptation of Adso's writing, see also Matthew Gabriele, *An Empire of Memory: The Legend of Charlemagne, the Franks, and Jerusalem before the First Crusade* (New York, 2011), 123–25, 127.

[5] See Ernst Sackur, *Sibyllinische Texte und Forschungen* (Halle, 1898), 177–87 (see ibid., 117–77 for a still perceptive commentary on it). The reference book for the history of this text is now Anke Holdenried, *The Sibyl and Her Scribes: Manuscripts and Interpretation of the Latin Sibylla Tiburtina, c. 1050–1500* (Aldershot, 2006). See also, on the first extant manuscript of the prophecy, Anke Holdenried, "Christian Moral Decline: A New Context for the Sibilla Tiburtina (Ms. Escorial &.I.3)," in *Peoples of the Apocalypse: Eschatological Beliefs and Political Scenarios*, ed. Wolfram Brandes, Felicitas Schmieder, and Rebekka Voß (Berlin-Boston, 2016), 321–36; for the previous stages of its composition, see Anke Holdenried, "Many Hands without Design: The Evolution of a Medieval Prophetic Text," *The Mediaeval Journal* 4/1 (2014): 23–42.

[6] See, in particular, Erdmann, "Endkaiserglaube," 412; Erdmann, *Die Entstehung*, 279 n. 119.

[7] See the same question in Daniël Verhelst's introduction to Pseudo-Alcuin's writing in Adso Dervensis, *De ortu*, 109. The editor supports a redaction before the First Crusade.

[8] See Erdmann, "Endkaiserglaube," 403–7; Robert Folz, *Le souvenir et la légende de Charlemagne dans l'Empire germanique médiéval*, 2nd ed. (Geneva, 1973), 139–42; on this subject, see also Federica Monteleone, *Il Viaggio di Carlo Magno in Terra Santa. Un'esperienza di pellegrinaggio nella tradizione europea occidentale*, 2nd ed. (Fasano, 2015), 29–32.

[9] See Anne A. Latowsky, *Emperor of the World: Charlemagne and the Construction of Imperial Authority, 800–1229* (Ithaca and London, 2013), 123, in which the author addresses Erdmann's interpretation of Benzo's writing. It is worth noting that, after Erdmann's seminal works, scepticism on the actual impact of prophetical discourse on the origins of the crusades has been widely dominant among scholars: see for instance Jonathan Riley-Smith, *The First Crusade and the Idea of Crusading*,

of the "Last World Emperor" legend on the military and organizational aspects of the expedition launched in 1096, a more in-depth examination of the eleventh-century prophetic material may lead to a re-evaluation of its role in forging political ideas which paved the way for those religious aspirations that would actually lead to the First Crusade.[10] The aim of the following pages is to re-assess the impact of the abovementioned sources on the origins of the crusading idea.

It is first necessary to introduce some elements of the *Sibylla Tiburtina*, which stands as the major reference source for both texts under discussion, especially the final section of this prophetic writing, devoted to the description of the "Last World Emperor" and his actions during the final stage of world history.

It is not possible here to delve into the complex issue of the dating of this work. It consists of several parts composed in different periods, combined into a single piece at the beginning of the eleventh century. Anke Holdenried[11] has recently identified four different versions of the *Sibylla Tiburtina*, or, better, of the Latin translation of a Greek Sibylline prophecy.[12] The first version, no longer extant, was supposedly composed around 1000 in the Ottonian realm; the second, dating presumably to around 1030, is a reworking of the Ottonian version and is the most frequently transmitted in subsequent transcriptions;[13] the third version was attributed to the Sibyl of Cumae instead of the Tiburtine Sibyl and is an abridged rendering of the previous one (doubts have been raised as to its dating).[14] Finally, a fourth version, consisting of another reworking of the Ottonian Sibyl with additional elements drawn from the Cumaean Sibyl and other eschatological traditions, appeared around 1100.[15]

3rd ed. (London and New York, 2003), esp. 35, where the author maintains that "evidence is not copious enough for us to suppose that eschatological ideas were widespread" during the First Crusade (and tends to reductively dismiss them as "hysteria," without engaging the relevant secondary literature on eleventh- and twelfth-century eschatological production – which was not, however, as abundant as today when the first edition of Riley Smith's book was published in 1986). This position has been considerably re-evaluated: see, for instance, Jay Rubenstein, *Nebuchadnezzar's Dream: The Crusades, Apocalyptic Prophecy, and the End of History* (New York, 2019), esp. 1–98.

[10] The eschatological implications of these "pre-crusading" writings have been generally recognized, but more in relation to the Charlemagne legend rather than the Sibylline tradition in itself (see Folz, *Le souvenir*, 139–42).

[11] Holdenried, *The Sibyl*, 4–5.

[12] Edited and studied in Paul Julius Alexander, *The Oracle of Baalbek: The Tiburtine Sibyl in Greek Dress* (Washington, 1967). See also idem, "Byzantium and the Migration of Literary Works and Motifs: The Legend of the Last Roman Emperor," *Medievalia et humanistica* n.s. 2 (1971): 47–68, and Pier Franco Beatrice, "Das Orakel von Baalbek und die sogenannte Sibyllentheosophie," *Römische Quartalschrift für christliche Altertumskunde und Kirchengeschichte* 92 (1997): 177–89.

[13] It is the version edited by Sackur (see above, n. 5).

[14] Circa 1090 for Carl Erdmann, no later than 1039 for Hannes Möhring, *Der Weltkaiser der Endzeit. Entstehung, Wandel und Wirkung einer tausendjährigen Weissagung* (Stuttgart, 2000), 149–56.

[15] Edited in Bernard McGinn, "Oracular Transformations: The Sibylla Tiburtina in the Middle Ages," in *Sibille e linguaggi oracolari: mito, storia, tradizione. Atti del Convegno, Macerata-Norcia, [20–24] Settembre 1994*, ed. Ileana Chirassi Colombo and Tullio Seppilli (Pisa, 1998), 603–44, here 636–44.

The standard and most widespread version of the *Sibylla Tiburtina* appeared in 1047.[16] Within a few years, as is testified by the wide distribution of its manuscript tradition, it acquired an undisputed authority that led to several reworkings.[17] We focus here mainly on the last section of the *Sibylla Tiburtina*, the so-called *Vaticinium of Constans*, which includes the prediction of a *rex Romanorum et Grecorum*, named Constans, who would establish a universal Christian kingdom for 112 (or 120) years at the end of time, eradicate all unbelief, convert the Jews, and defeat Gog and Magog, before delivering his kingdom to God, thus, leaving room for the short and dreadful dominion of the Antichrist.[18] The *Vaticinium of Constans* is considered one of the most important testimonies of the "Last World Emperor" legend, which was to shape medieval eschatological thinking up to the early modern age, along with Pseudo-Methodius's *Revelationes* and, later on, Adso of Montier-en-Der's references included in his *De ortu et tempore Antichristi*.[19] The influence of these texts and the tradition that derives from them can be readily acknowledged if we consider that their content was to eclipse certain essential apocalyptic aspects derived from the Scriptures, specifically from the *Book of Revelation*.

---

[16]   Madrid, Escorial, ms. & I. 3, coll. 240–42, in Guillermo Antolín, *Catálogo de los códices latinos de la Real Biblioteca del Escorial* (Madrid, 1911), ii. See Holdenried, "Christian Moral Decline;" for the previous stages of its composition, see Holdenried, "Many Hands without Design." 23–42.

[17]   See above, n. 11.

[18]   See Sackur, *Sibyllinische Texte*, 185. There is still much debate on the origins of the *Vaticinium of Constans* and its relations with Syriac prophetic writings (most notably Pseudo-Methodius's *Revelationes*) that considerably influenced Latin eschatological beliefs up to the early modern age. See Gian Luca Potestà, "The Vaticinium of Constans: Genesis and Original Purposes of the Legend of the Last World Emperor," *Millennium-Jahrbuch* 8 (2011): 271–90; Christopher Bonura, "The Man and the Myth: Did Heraclius Know the Legend of the Last Roman Emperor?," *Studia patristica* 62 (2013): 503–14; Bonura, "When Did the Legend of the Last Emperor Originate? A New Look at the Textual Relationship between the Apocalypse of Pseudo-Methodius and the Tiburtine Sibyl," *Viator* 47/3 (2016): 47–100, who both challenge the consensus and propose to antedate Pseudo-Methodius's *Revelationes* to the *Vaticinium of Constans*. For a general overview, see Stephen J. Shoemaker, *The Apocalypse of Empire: Imperial Eschatology in Late Antiquity and Early Islam* (Philadelphia, 2018), 42–63 (supporting a Late Antique origin of the *Vaticinium*).

[19]   For some essential references on Pseudo-Methodius and the *Vaticinium*, see Gerrit J. Reinink, "Die syrischen Wurzeln der mittelalterlichen Legende vom römischen Endkaiser," in *Non Nova, sed Nove. Mélanges de civilisation médiévale dédiés à Willem Noonen*, ed. Martin Gosman and Jaap van Os (Groningen, 1984), 195–209; Reinink, "Pseudo-Methodius und die Legende vom römischen Endkaiser," in *The Use and Abuse of Eschatology in the Middle Ages*, ed. Werner Verbeke, Daniël Verhelst, and Andries Welkenhuysen (Leuven, 1988), 82–111; Reinink, "Pseudo-Methodius: A Concept of History in Response to the Rise of Islam," in *The Byzantine and the Early Islamic Near East I: Problems in the Literary Source Material*, ed. Averil M. Cameron and Lawrence I. Conrad (Princeton, 1992), 149–87; Reinink, "Alexandre et le dernier empereur du monde: Les développements du concept de la royauté chrétienne dans les sources syriaques du septième siècle," in *Alexandre le Grand dans les littératures occidentales et proche-orientales. Actes du Colloque de Paris, 27–29 novembre 1999*, ed. Laurence Harf-Lancner, Claire Kappler, and François Suard (Nanterre, 1999), 149–59; Hannes Möhring, *Der Weltkaiser der Endzeit*; Potestà, "The Vaticinium of Constans;" Potestà, *L'ultimo messia. Profezia e sovranità nel Medioevo* (Bologna, 2014); Lutz Greisiger, *Messias – Endkaiser – Antichrist. Politische Apokalyptik unter Juden und Christen des Nahen Ostens am Vorabend der arabischen Eroberung* (Wiesbaden, 2014). As to Adso's *De ortu*, see below, n. 101, with relevant bibliography.

This is particularly true regarding the representation of the Roman Empire in the eschatological scenario. While in *Revelation* it is portrayed with extremely dark traits,[20] the *Vaticinium of Constans* and Pseudo-Methodius's *Revelationes* assign a positive and even providential function to what was widely acknowledged as the last universal monarchy of the vision of Daniel.[21] This transformation was made possible thanks to the identification, already widespread during the Patristic era, of the Roman Empire with the *katéchon* mentioned in the *Second Letter to the Thessalonians*, the mysterious power that "withholds" the coming of the "Son of Perdition,"[22] that is, the Antichrist, according to an interpretation that became widely popular in the following centuries.[23] As a result, after the Christianization of the Empire, the Roman emperor acquired a central position in salvation history and in the establishment of the kingdom of heaven, to the point of being seen as the ultimate and most convenient "image" (*eikon*) of God on earth.[24]

This "imperial doctrine," combining ancient Augustan models and Christian ideas had been essentially defined by Eusebius of Caesarea, and later became central to the Byzantine imperial idea.[25] It already included certain prophetic elements in the age of Constantine and Justinian, most notably the attribution to the empire of the task of fulfilling the evangelical promise according to which "this gospel of the kingdom will be preached throughout the world as a testimony to all nations, and then the end will come."[26] However, its explicit connection with eschatology would be outlined clearly and extensively only in subsequent centuries, thanks to the wide dissemination of prophetic material included in Pseudo-Methodius's *Revelationes* and the *Vaticinium of Constans*. Both texts ground their prophetic content in the

---

[20] To the point that, according to a famous understanding supported by Irenaeus of Lyon, the "Number of the Beast" could be indicated through numerological interpretation, as "LATEINOS:" see Irenaeus of Lyon, *Adversus Haereses*, 30, 3, in *Ante-Nicene Fathers: The Writings of the Fathers down to AD 325*, i, ed. Alexander Roberts and James Donaldson (Grand Rapids, 1987), 559–60.

[21] See Dan. 2.31–45.

[22] See 2 Thess. 2.6–7.

[23] See Marco Rizzi, "Storia di un inganno (ermeneutico): il *Katéchon* e l'Anticristo nelle interpretazioni del II e III secolo della *Seconda lettera ai Tessalonicesi*," in *Il Katéchon (2Ts 2,6–7) e l'Anticristo. Teologia e politica di fronte al mistero dell'anomia*, ed. Michele Nicoletti (Brescia, 2009): 41–56. See also François Paschoud, "La doctrine chrétienne et l'idéologie impériale romaine," in *L'apocalypse de Jean. Traditions exégétiques et iconographiques, IIIᵉ-XIIIᵉ siècles. Actes du Colloque de la Fondation Hardt, 29 février – 3 mars 1976* (Geneva, 1979), 31–72.

[24] See Frederick Lauritzen, "Eikon tu theu: Imago Dei in Byzantine Imperial Encomia," in *In the Image of God: Foundations and Objections within the Discourse on Human Dignity. Proceedings of the Colloquium at Bologna and Rossena (July 2009) in honour of Pier Cesare Bori*, ed. Alberto Melloni and Riccardo Saccenti (Münster, 2010), 217–26. See also Antonio Carile, "La sacralità rituale dei ΒΑΣΙΛΕΙΣ bizantini," in *Per me reges regnant. La regalità sacra nell'Europa medievale*, ed. Franco Cardini and Monica Saltarelli (Rimini-Siena, 2002), 53–95, at 82.

[25] See Gerhard Podskalsky, *Byzantinische Reichseschatologie* (Munich, 1972). See also Podskalsky, "Marginalien zur byzantinischen Reichseschatologie," *Byzantinische Zeitschrift* 67 (1974): 351–58; Podskalsky, "Politische Theologie in Byzanz zwischen Reichseschatologie und Reichsideologie," in *Cristianità d'Occidente e cristianità d'Oriente (secoli VI–XI): 24–30 aprile 2003*, ii (Spoleto, 2004), 1421–34.

[26] Matt. 24.14.

"imperial doctrine" outlined above, which was to be adopted in Latin Christendom during the Middle Ages.[27]

It is easy to see how these texts could be conceived in the eleventh century as two complementary and consistent accounts of the final stage of world history. Their focus, however, was different. The *Vaticinium*, presents the traits and deeds of the "Last World Emperor" in general terms, only highlighting his chronological placement at the end of time (between a period marked by "sorrow that had never been experienced before"[28] and the final advent of the Antichrist), without reference to the wars he would presumably fight before his enthronement. Conversely, Pseudo-Methodius's *Revelationes*, which had been circulating in the Latin West since the eighth century,[29] provides a more detailed historical framework including the events that would allow the future *Rex Graecorum et Romanorum* to rise from obscurity ("roused as from a drunken stupor like one whom men had thought dead and worthless").[30] In this context, the confrontation with the "Ishmaelites," that is, the Muslims, and the liberation of the Holy Land from their hands, acquired a fundamental importance as the major event preceding the enthronement of the "Last World Emperor."[31]

Thus, the so-called *Cumaean Sibyl*, composed after the second and most widespread version of the *Tiburtina*,[32] may be understood as a conscious conflation of both texts. While following the *Tiburtine Sibyl* both in content and style,[33] the

---

[27] These texts were diffused in the West along very different paths. See Möhring, *Der Weltkaiser*, 17–104, for a comprehensive examination of the origins and first circulation of the *Vaticinium of Constans* included in the *Sibylla Tiburtina* and Pseudo-Methodius's *Revelationes*.

[28] See Sackur, *Sibyllinische Texte*, 184. According to *Tiburtina*, this period is introduced by a *Salicus de Francia B nomine*, who cannot be identified with an historical character (see Erdmann, "Endkaiserglaube," 395 n. 31; Möhring, *Der Weltkaiser*, 33).

[29] See Otto Prinz, "Eine frühe abendländische Aktualisierung der lateinischen Übersetzung des Pseudo-Methodius," *Deutsches Archiv* 41 (1985): 1–23; Möhring, *Der Weltkaiser*, 101–2, 136–43. See also Michael W. Herren, "The *Revelationes* of Pseudo-Methodius in the Eighth Century," in *Felici curiositate: Studies in Latin Literature and Textual Criticism from Antiquity to the Twentieth Century. In Honour of Rita Beyers*, ed. Guy Guldentops, Christian Laes, and Gert Partoens (Turnhout, 2017), 409–18.

[30] English translation in Bernard McGinn, *Visions of the End: Apocalyptic Traditions in the Middle Ages* (New York, 1979), 75.

[31] Jerusalem, however, is mentioned in the *Vaticinium of Constans* only as the location of the Last World Emperor's demise, an event placed between the victory over the *spurcissime gentes, quas Alexander inclusit, Gog videlicet et Magog* and the definitive takeover of Jerusalem by the Antichrist: see Sackur, *Sibyllinische Texte*, 186.

[32] Möhring, *Der Weltkaiser*, 154–56, traces the redaction of this text back to shortly after the redaction of the *Sibyllina*, between 1024 and 1039 (see above, n. 11), thus contesting the latter's dating (during the kingdom of Henry IV) proposed by other scholars such as Erdmann (in "Endkaiserglaube," 401–2) and Alexander, "Diffusion," 71, 99 n. 67. Nevertheless, Möhring shares with Erdmann and, before him, Sackur (*Sibyllinische Forschungen*, 127 n. 2) the belief in the origin of the *Cumaean Sibyl* in Tuscia on account of the laudatory expressions addressed to Boniface of Canossa (presented as *dux in Tuscia per B nomen*). The interest in prophecy nourished by the predecessors of Matilda of Canossa merits a special investigation.

[33] Möhring, *Der Weltkaiser*, 149, considers it a "significantly modified version" of the *Tiburtina*.

Cumaean Sibyl adds details about the future confrontation with the Ishmaelites, details which are clearly drawn from Pseudo-Methodius's *Revelationes*. In particular, it announces a dreadful *rex Salicus de Baiowaria*, "who will come with fury" (*qui veniet cum furore*) and will usher in a period of sorrow "that has never been since the beginning of the world" (*quale non fuit ab inicio mundi*), culminating in the destruction of Rome before the final annihilation of the tyrant.[34] The prophecy affirms that:

> after him [*de illo*], then, a king from Byzantium must come, who will have written on his forehead [that he will be ruler of] the Romans and the Greeks, to claim the kingdom of the Christians; he will subdue the sons of Ishmael and defeat them and uproot the kingdom from the awful yoke of the Saracens. At that time, no one under the sky will be able to overcome the kingdom of the Christians.[35]

After a temporary successful reaction of the Muslims,[36] the ultimate triumph of the Christians is announced:

> After that, the kingdom of the Romans[37] will rise and strike them, and after that there will be peace and the kingdom of the Christians [will endure] up to the time of the Antichrist.[38]

The most remarkable trait of this prophecy is the strong emphasis – particularly interesting with regard to the origins of the idea of crusade – on the victorious outcome of the battle against the "Ishmaelites" (presented as the most notable deed performed by the "Last World Emperor") and the ultimate liberation of Christian believers from the yoke of the Muslims. Aside from Pseudo-Methodius's *Revelationes*, with regard to the lands where Christians live under Muslim domination, it is difficult not to detect in this passage a hint at the historical circumstances in which the *Cumaean Sibyl* was written. If an early composition of this prophecy is accepted, around the

---

[34] The prediction of the *Sibylla Tiburtina* is here maintained rather faithfully, except for a detail: while the *inicium dolorum* is placed under the rule of a *rex Salicus de Francia B nomine*, the *Cumaean* stresses the "German" origin, both in his geographical provenance (de *Baiowaria*) and his character traits (*veniet cum furore* may in fact hint at the *furor Teutonicus* customarily applied to Germans by their enemies: see Möhring, *Der Weltkaiser*, 154). Of course, the original *rex Salicus de Francia* of the *Tiburtina* might refer to a ruler of "German" origin as well, although the epithet may also refer to other non-German dynasties that held the imperial title in the Latin West (for the identification of the four *rex Salici* that appear in the *Tiburtina* with Carolingian rulers, see ibid., 33–35).

[35] In Erdmann, "Endkaiserglaube," 398.

[36] See ibid.

[37] The text is not clear on the identity of the victorious *rex Romanorum*, whether he is different from one who had previously defeated the Muslims or the same. If the first interpretation is correct, the author may be hinting at the dynastic continuity of the first *rex de Bizantio*, so that the attributes of the "Last World Emperor" could be applied to all the members of his dynasty. This possible interpretation should be compared with the hypothesis raised by Hannes Möhring that the words *de illo*, with which the *rex de Bizantio* is introduced (see the abovementioned quotation), may suggest a kinship between this ruler and the previous "Salian" king *de Baiowaria*. See Möhring, *Der Weltkaiser*, 156.

[38] Erdman, "Endkaiserglaube," 398.

third or the fourth decade of the eleventh century, the regions to which the Sibyl alludes may refer to southern Italy – more precisely those regions that were subject to frequent Arab incursions while concurrently being contested by the Byzantine and German empires.[39] Otherwise, in the case of a later composition, at the end of the eleventh century, the author (who may likely be traced among supporters of the dukes of Tuscia, as mentioned above)[40] could not ignore the establishment of Norman rule in areas of southern Italy, which ended Muslim domination and assaults in the region.

In any case, whatever the political situation or the assessment of the Christian-Muslim confrontation in this strategic region may have been, the author of the *Cumaean Sibyl* could not ignore the role that another country under "Ishmaelite" dominion, that is, the Holy Land, had to play in the eschatological drama, as the forerunners of the *Cumaean Sibyl* foretold. In this sense, the "ideal" reference was to be Jerusalem, as in the *Sibylla Tiburtina* and Pseudo-Methodius's *Revelationes*. Indeed, the Holy City is evoked immediately after the final triumph of the "Christian kingdom" over the Saracens:

> After that the king of the Romans will ascend to Jerusalem, to the place of Golgotha and will remove the crown from his head and put it on the holy cross and raise his hands toward the sky and return the kingdom of the Christians to God the Father, and when the holy cross together with the crown of the king will be taken up to heaven. Then the Lord Jesus Christ will come to judge the world through fire.[41]

As Carl Erdmann has observed,[42] the words here are drawn almost *verbatim* from Pseudo-Methodius's *Revelationes*. This is significant because in this apocalyptic account of Syriac origin, the role assigned to Jerusalem (and the Holy Land) in the eschatological scenario was more crucial than in the *Vaticinium of Constans*. Moreover, it was combined with the decisive struggle against the Ishmaelites, an element that was absent in the *Sibylla Tiburtina*. It is also worth noting that in this passage of the *Cumaean Sibyl*, there is no mention of the kingdom of the "Last World Emperor." In fact, the narrative links the victory over the "Ishmaelites" directly to the deposition of the crown on the Cross,[43] that is, according to the *Sibylla Tiburtina*, with the end of the Roman empire and the beginning of the Antichrist's rule. It seems that the focus of the author lies precisely in the clash with the Muslims, a conflict charged with eschatological significance and that would

---

[39] The battle of Cap Colonne of 982 in which the German army was almost annihilated has to be put within this framework. See Dirk Alvermann, "La battaglia di Ottone II contro i Saraceni nel 982," *Archivio storico per la Calabria e la Lucania* 62 (1995): 115–30. See also Karl Joseph Leyser, "The Tenth Century in Byzantine-Western Relationships," in *Relations between East and West in the Middle Ages*, ed. Derek Baker (Edinburgh, 1973), 29–63.

[40] See above, n. 32.

[41] In Erdmann, "Endkaiserglaube," 398.

[42] Ibid.

[43] See the preceding quotation.

find its resolution in Jerusalem. It is likely, therefore, that the choice to interpolate passages from the work attributed to Pseudo-Methodius served to redefine the imperial "mission" from an eschatological point of view: the future candidate for the role of "Last World Emperor" would be recognized as such (*before* the establishment of his rule) not by the mere restoration of the pristine state of the Christian kingdom, as seemed to be the case in the original *Sibylla Tiburtina*, but rather by the protection and restoration of Christian lands currently under the yoke of the Saracens, as in Pseudo-Methodius's *Revelationes*; among these lands, the city of Jerusalem enjoyed special consideration: it was the geographical centre of the world;[44] it was the place in which the redemptive action of Christ took place; and, finally, from a typological perspective, it was the location in which the "messianic" nature of the "Last World Emperor" and his participation in the redemptive mission of Christ was to be fully disclosed.[45]

These "proto-crusading" elements were consistently elaborated by Benzo of Alba in his work *Ad Heinricum IV imperatorem*. Although this text can be considered as a collection of writings composed in different periods (from Henry IV's adolescence in the 1060s up to c. 1085, when the work was finished), thus mirroring different political contexts and preoccupations,[46] it is still possible to identify key tenets that demonstrate the author's fundamental views. Probably its most important characteristic is the apologetic representation of the German "would-be" emperor (Henry's coronation, in fact, did not take place until 1084), who is portrayed in a way that highlights his truly "messianic" traits and his participation in the divine kingship.[47] Aside from expressions that were customarily applied to rulers at the

---

[44] In the original narrative, a typological link between Jerusalem as the centre of the world and the Earthly Paradise as the pristine abode of humankind (an abode that will eventually be restored at the end of time) is set out in a very clear fashion in the *Cave of the Treasures*, one of the main references for Pseudo-Methodius's *Revelationes*: see Alexander Toepel, *Die Adam- und Seth-Legenden im syrischen Buch der Schatzhöhle. Eine quellenkritische Untersuchung* (Leuven, 2006), 76–81, 131–32; see also Marco Giardini, *Figure del regno nascosto. Le leggende del Prete Gianni e delle dieci tribù perdute d'Israele fra Medioevo e prima età moderna* (Florence, 2016), 288–89, with relevant bibliographic references included.

[45] See the works by Gerrit J. Reinink mentioned above at n. 19.

[46] See Latowsky, *Emperor of the World*, 106, 108, 111, 121, 124, 130, where the author observes that neglecting the different phases of composition of the *Ad Heinricum IV* has led to several discrepancies as to the contextualisation of Benzo's discourse. In any case, it seems necessary to admit an intervention by Benzo on his earlier writings, aimed at providing a certain consistency in the final version of his work. A discussion of the prophetic overtones in Benzo's main writing is present also in Matthew Gabriele, *An Empire of Memory*, 112–15. This book provides a valuable collection of sources that enlighten the relationship established over the centuries between the Frankish empire (and subsequently its early French Capetian heir) and the Holy Land. See in particular ibid., 107–28 for a discussion of the prophetic and eschatological tradition on which the sources at the core of the present article were based.

[47] On Benzo's portrait of the emperor, see Percy E. Schramm, *Kaiser, Rom und "Renovatio": Studien zur Geschichte des römischen Erneuerungsgedankens vom Ende des Karolingischen Reiches bis zum Investiturstreit* (Darmstadt, 1957), 258–74; Gottfried Koch, *Auf dem Wege zum Sacrum Imperium* (Berlin, 1972), 42–43, 53, 71–73, 81–82, 105–6, 116–18; Tilman Struve, "Kaisertum und Romgedanke in salischer Zeit," *Deutsches Archiv* 44 (1988): 424–54, here 437–52; Saverio Sagulo, *Ideologia imperiale e analisi politica in Benzone, vescovo d'Alba* (Bologna, 2003). See also Möhring, "Benzo

time, such as the epithet *christus*,[48] Henry is hailed as the *imperator imperatorum*,[49] "whom [God] made in his likeness as second creator among creatures" (*qui eum ad similitudinem sui fecit*[50] *in creaturis humanis alterum creatorem*);[51] moreover, he is the one whom "everyone on earth awaits [...] almost as a redeemer" (*omnis terra expectat [...] quasi redemptorem*)[52] and a true *vicarius Conditoris*.[53]

Evident in these lines, is Benzo's attempt to celebrate his ruler by taking up the *apotheosis* of ancient Roman emperors within a proper Christian framework; this conflation could be performed by means of a close association of the imperial function with the "messianic" dignity, derived from the passages of the New Testament that highlight the *regal* traits of Christ.

In this context, it seems plausible to include the *Cumaean Sibyl* as a primary source of inspiration of this set of ideas. In fact, the *Fourth Eclogue* of Virgil, where the poet attributed the coming of a Golden Age to that prophetess, could have been conceived in Christian reinterpretation as an authoritative source for the association between the Messiah and the emperor in the redemption of humanity and its restoration to the primordial "paradisiacal" condition.[54] In Benzo's *Ad*

---

von Alba und die Entstehung des Kreuzzugsgedankens," in *Forschungen zur Reichs-, Papst- und Landesgeschichte. Peter Herde zum 65. Geburtstag von Freunden, Schülern und Kollegen dargebracht*, ii, ed. Enno Bünz and Karl Borchardt (Stuttgart, 1998), 177–86, reedited with slight modifications in Möhring, *Der Weltkaiser*, 157–65.

[48] See Benzo of Alba, *Ad Heinricum IV*, 1, 4, 118.

[49] Benzo of Alba, *Ad Heinricum IV*, 7, 2, 586. The superlative value of this expression may be a stylistic hint at the epithets *rex regum* and *dominus dominantium*, both attributed to the messianic figure in Rev. 17.14 and 19.16 (see also 1 Tim. 6.15). The passage in which this expression appears, is full of similar superlative epithets. See also Benzo of Alba, *Ad Heinricum IV*, dedicatio, 88. On the use of the emphatic genitive, see Gerd Schäfer, *König der Könige, Lied der Lieder. Studien zum paronomastischen Intensitätsgenitiv* (Heidelberg, 1974).

[50] Speculations on the specifically "regal" interpretation of Gen 2.26, of Byzantine origins (see above, p. 5), seem to resonate here. The image of the ruler made *ad similitudinem Dei* may suggest that the emperor has restored the pristine condition of Adam before the Fall. In fact, the analogy between the king and pre-lapsarian Adam was customary in medieval *specula principum* inspired by Augustinian political theology: see Michel Senellart, *Les arts de gouverner. Du regimen médiéval au concept de gouvernement* (Paris, 1995), 157. This idea may also be related to the description (customary especially in the Byzantine tradition) of the emperor as "icon of God" – that is, the same expression that appears in Gen. 2.26 to define the pristine nature of man: see above, n. 24; and Maria Cristina Carile, "Imperial Icons in Late Antiquity and Byzantium: The Iconic Image of the Emperor between Representation and Presence," *Ikon* 9 (2016): 75–98.

[51] Benzo of Alba, *Ad Heinricum IV*, 1, 8, 172.

[52] Ibid., 140. This passage is followed by a reference to Jesus' entry to Jerusalem, an episode often re-enacted in coronation processions: see Kantorowicz, "The 'King's Advent';" Sergio Bertelli, *The King's Body: Sacred Rituals of Power in Medieval and Early Modern Europe* (Philadelphia, 2003).

[53] Benzo of Alba, *Ad Heinricum IV*, 1, 8, 172. On these attributes, see Schramm, *Kaiser, Rom und Renovatio*, 271–73; Koch, *Auf dem Wege*, 71–73, 81–82; Struve, "Kaisertum," 439, 441, 446–49. For other similar epithets applied to Henry III, father of the dedicatee of Benzo's work, see Folz, *Le souvenir*, 101 n. 26.

[54] On the Christian interpretations of the *Fourth Eclogue*, see Henri Jeanmaire, *Le messianisme de Virgile* (Paris, 1930); Pierre Courcelle, "Les exégèses chrétiennes de la quatrième *Églogue*," *Revue des études anciennes* 59 (1957): 294–309; Steven Benko, "Virgil's Fourth *Eclogue* in Christian Interpretation," *Aufstieg und Niedergang der Römischen Welt* 31/1 (1980): 646–705; *The Virgilian*

Heinricum, the restoration of the state of bliss was made possible precisely by the connection established between the Roman emperor and the messianic dignity (in a way that could suitably reintroduce, at least rhetorically, the ancient "deification of the monarch").[55] Such a link was a privilege that could not be shared by any other human being.[56] Moreover, within the framework of Benzo's specific political preoccupations, this linkage allowed Henry to efficiently counter what he perceived as the emperor's main opposing force, that is the reforming papacy,[57] and fulfil the "messianic promises," understood in a specific "Roman" meaning.[58] It is not surprising, therefore, to see short but perceptive references to the Sibyl in Benzo's major work, albeit in the Christianized form in which they were widely circulating during the eleventh century.[59] It is also significant that in the *Ad Heinricum IV imperatorem*, the "messianic" representation of the emperor is directly associated with some of the traits of the "Last World Emperor" as they appear in the *Vaticinium of Constans*[60] – an eschatological section that the author of the *Cumaean Sibyl* did not include in his narrative (by contrast with the *Sibylla Tiburtina*).[61] It seems therefore possible to assume that for Benzo (and probably for other imperial supporters), attempts were made to merge the traits of the "Last World Emperor's" kingdom of peace and justice, foretold in medieval Sibylline literature, with those of the Virgilian-inspired "Golden Age" handed down by the ancient Sibylline prophecies.

Tradition: The First Fifteen Hundred Years, ed. Jan M. Ziolkowski and Michael C. J. Putnam (New Haven and London, 2008), 487–503.

[55]   On the ancient deification of the emperor, see Giorgio Bonamente, "L'apoteosi degli imperatori nell'ultima storiografia pagana latina," in *Studien zur Geschichte der römischen Spätantike. Festgabe für Professor Johannes Straub*, ed. Evangelos K. Chrysos (Athens, 1989), 19–73; Larry Kreitzer, "Apotheosis of the Roman Emperor," *The Biblical Archaeologist* 53 (1990): 210–19; Leonhard Schumacher, "Zur 'Apotheose' des Herrschers in der Spätantike," in *X Convegno Internazionale in onore di Arnaldo Biscardi* (Naples, 1995), 105–26; Paul Zanker, *Die Apotheose der römischen Kaiser. Ritual und städtische Bühne* (Munich, 2004); Tommaso Gnoli and Federicomaria Muccioli, eds., *Divinizzazione, culto del sovrano e apoteosi tra antichità e Medioevo* (Bologna, 2014). See also Andreas Alföldi, "Der neue Weltherrscher der IV. Ekloge Vergils," *Hermes* 65 (1930): 369–84.

[56]   In fact, the emperor is not actually a "man of flesh," but rather "sent from heaven" (see Benzo of Alba, *Ad Heinricum*, 6, 7, 574).

[57]   Understood as a "horsefly" (*hoestrum*: see the explanation of the Graecism in Struve, "Kaisertum," 446 n. 101) that will be chased away the *eagle* (see Benzo of Alba, *Ad Heinricum* 2, 15, 242). As Tilman Struve suitably remarks ("Kaisertum," 446), the eagle, a bird that shared some essential traits with the phoenix in medieval bestiaries, is associated here with regenerative power. On the reforming papacy in Benzo's opinion, see below, pp. 13–15.

[58]   See the significant sentences in *Ad Heinricum* 6, 4, 550 and 6, 5, 552. See also Struve, "Kaisertum," 448–49.

[59]   According to Möhring, *Der Weltkaiser*, 160–64 (contrary to Edrmann, "Endkaiserglaube," 405–8, Struve, "Kaisertum," 444, and Herbert E. J. Cowdrey, "Pope Gregory VII's 'Crusading' Plans of 1074," in *Outremer*, 27–40, here 30), it is unlikely that the "Cumaean prophecy" reported by Benzo is the same as the one that we have examined above. It is significant that under the same "Sibylline" authority, expectations for a future conquest or annexation of Jerusalem and the Holy Land by imperial hands were circulating in several strands.

[60]   See below, pp. 19–20.

[61]   See Möhring, *Der Weltkaiser*, 155.

The *Cumaean Sibyl*, as reported by Benzo,[62] foretold that, in order to fulfil the task providentially assigned to Henry,[63] the German ruler would settle the matter of Apulia and Calabria, then march eastwards, be crowned in Constantinople, and eventually reach Jerusalem, kiss the Holy Sepulchre and once again be crowned to the glory of God.[64] At this point, his universal dominion would be acknowledged by all nations, for "Babylon will come to Zion astonished, with the desire to lick the dust of his feet."[65] The prediction concludes with the words drawn from the *Book of Isaiah* that had appeared in the *Sibylla Tiburtina*, a sort of distinctive mark of medieval Sibylline literature: "Then, what is written will be fulfilled: And his sepulchre will be glorious" (*Tunc implebitur, quod scriptum est: Et erit sepulchrum eius gloriosum*).[66] The Sepulchre here being clearly identified as the Holy Sepulchre, liberated by the "Last World Emperor" at the end of time.

The steps on Henry's way as the "messianic" ruler towards his accession to world rulership merit special attention. His first task was to solve the issue of Apulia and Calabria. These regions had been mentioned in previous and contemporary prophetic works, very likely in relation to the confrontations between Christians and Muslims in the tenth and eleventh centuries.[67] In particular, the *Sibylla Tiburtina* mentions the occupation of Taranto and Bari by the Muslims, a detail taken up from the *Cumaean Sibyl*,[68] with the addition of the toponyms *Apulia* and "*Pulsaria*."[69] During that time, Bari and Taranto had passed under the rule of the many political powers vying for control of southern Italy. While the *Sibyllina Tiburtina*, written

---

[62] This section is probably to be considered as one of the earliest parts of Benzo's *Ad Heinricum*, to be dated to the 1060s: see Latowsky, *Emperor of the World*, 124.

[63] Celebrations of the universal power assigned to the Roman emperor were widely scattered among members and associates of the imperial chancellery (German and Italian alike), in terms that were largely consistent with the expressions reported in previous lines as well as in other parts of Benzo of Alba's writing (see Struve, "Kaisertum," 424–42), without, however, the same accentuated prophetic overtones. Interestingly enough, the most remarkable affinity with Benzo's eschatological understanding of the imperial power came, some decades earlier, from champions of the papal reform like Petrus Damiani who, during one of the short periods of *concordia* between the Salian rulers and the papacy, linked the restoration of the "Golden Age" with the representation of the monarch as authentic *imago Dei*. See Petrus Damiani, *Epistola* 7, 2, ed. Kurt Reindel, MGH *Die Briefe der deutschen Kaiserzeit* 4, 1 (Munich, 1983), 200–1; see also Hans Peter Laqua, *Traditionen und Leitbilder bei dem Ravennater Reformer Petrus Damiani* (Munich, 1976), 269–70; Struve, "Kaisertum," 430–31. This sharing of similar eschatological conceptions associated with the "Golden Age" by supporters of both the papal reform and the imperial standpoint – regardless of their circumstantial use for rhetorical purposes – merits special attention.

[64] See Benzo of Alba, *Ad Heinricum IV*, 1, 15, 144.

[65] Ibid.

[66] Conflation of passages drawn from Isa. 11.10, Luke 22.37, and Matt. 27.9. In the *Sibylla Tiburtina*, this biblical quotation is included with reference to the general conversion (including that of the Jews) that was to take place during the "Last World Emperor's" kingdom: it is, therefore, consistent with the "proto-crusading" framework outlined by Benzo. See Sackur, *Sibyllinische Texte*, 185.

[67] See Erdmann, *Die Entstehung*, 86–106; Christopher Tyerman, *God's War: A New History of the Crusades* (London, 2006), 54–57.

[68] See Sackur, *Sibyllinische Texte*, 183.

[69] See Erdmann, "Endkaiserglaube," 397.

c. 1030 (and the *Cumaean Sibyl*, not later than 1039 in the event of an earlier redaction) could refer to the ninth-century Muslim rule over Apulia, it is likely that Benzo of Alba was mentioning the liberation of these Apulian cities not from the Muslims but from the Norman rulers who took possession of Apulia and Calabria in 1059, in alliance with the reforming papacy.[70]

Benzo has no kind words for these new rulers of southern Italy who, in other parts of his main work, are equated with the *spurcissimae gentes* whom the *Sibyllina Tiburtina* had assimilated to the apocalyptic Gog and Magog.[71] Just like the unclean peoples of the Bible, the Normans were "peoples from the North," and, for Benzo, represented the worst threat to the imperial aspirations to universal dominion. Benzo's inclusion of Normans in the eschatological scenario outlined by the *Cumaean Sibyl* should be seen in the context of the clash between the empire and the papacy: in this scenario, it was all but natural to extend the "antichristic" traits that the imperial bishop of Alba had often ascribed to Alexander II or Hildebrand (the future Gregory VII)[72] to political and military allies of the papacy.[73] This transposition of political tensions into the apocalyptic discourse is clearly revealed in the letter – included in the *Ad Heinricum IV* – supposedly written by the Byzantine emperor, Constantine Doukas, to the Antipope Honorius II, but likely composed by

---

[70] See Möhring, *Der Weltkaiser*, 34.

[71] See Sackur, *Sibyllinische Texte*, 186. For references to the *spurcicia* of the Normans in Benzo's work, see below, p. 14. On the association of Gog and Magog with the populations that, according to the legendary accounts of Alexander the Great, had been enclosed by the Macedonian ruler, see Andrew Runni Anderson, *Alexander's Gate, Gog and Magog and the Inclosed Nations* (Cambridge, MA, 1932); Andrew Colin Gow, *The Red Jews: Antisemitism in an Apocalyptic Age, 1200–1600* (Leiden, 1995); Emeri J. Van Donzel and Andrea Barbara Schmidt, eds., *Gog and Magog in Early Eastern Christian and Islamic Sources: Sallam's Quest for Alexander's Wall* (Leiden, 2010); Christian Thrue Djurslev, "Revisiting Alexander's Gates against 'Gog and Magog:' Observations on the Testimonies before the Alexander Romance Tradition," in *The Alexander Romance: History and Literature*, ed. Richard Stoneman, Agnieszka Wojciechowska, and Krzysztof Nawotka (Groningen, 2018), 201–14.

[72] Together they are described as the "double-headed Antichrist" against whom the Empire has to stand up (see *Ad Heinricum IV* 3, 19, 322). Because of them, Rome has been turned into Babylon, (ibid., 6, 4, 536), and the end of the world is nigh (see ibid., 6, 2, 522; see also ibid., 3, 2, 276). Hildebrand is vividly portrayed as the Antichrist: see, in particular, the so-called *Descriptio de Prandelli maleficiis et de similibus suis*, in ibid., 6, 6, 560 ("Prandellus" and "Folleprandus" are nicknames applied to Gregory VII by Benzo). The conflict with the reforming papacy is framed as apocalyptic. See also ibid., 6, 2, 524, where "Prandellus" is again called Antichrist; in the following verses, there is a clear reference to the "Son of Perdition" sitting in the temple of God (2 Thess. 2.4), here applied to the Roman Church. For similar apocalyptic references in Benzo's *Ad Heinricum*, see Struve, "Kaisertum," 442–44.

[73] On the political and diplomatic issues posed by the Normans in southern Italy and their wavering relations with the competing powers of the region, see Walther Holtzmann, "Sui rapporti fra Normanni e Papato," *Archivio storico pugliese* 11 (1958): 20–35; Holtzmann, "Papsttum, Normannen und die griechische Kirche," *Miscellanea Bibliothecae Hertzianae* 16 (1961): 69–76; Josef Deér, *Papsttum und Normannen. Untersuchungen zu ihren lehnsrechtlichen und kirchenpolitischen Beziehungen* (Cologne and Vienna, 1972); Cecilie Hollberg, "Ein Kampf um Unteritalien: Normannen, Papsttum und Reich," in *Heiliges Römisches Reich Deutscher Nation 962 bis 1806: altes Reich und neue Staaten 1495 bis 1806*, i, ed. Hans Ottomeyer and Jutta Götzmann (Dresden, 2006), 249–61; Hubert Houben, "Die Normannen und das Papsttum," in *Vom Umbruch zur Erneuerung? Das 11. und beginnende 12. Jahrhundert*, ed. Nicola Karthaus, Jörg Jarnut, and Matthias Wemhoff (Munich, 2006), 47–54.

Benzo himself.[74] Here it is written that the *spurcicia*, explicitly attributed to the Normans,[75] has to be removed,[76] along with that of the pagans, so that "Christian freedom may blossom again, at least at the end of time." Towards this aim a military expedition, jointly organized by Henry IV and Constantine, both identified as legitimate "Roman kings," had to be prepared, so that the removal of the "false Pope" Alexander II, allied with the Normans,[77] would lead to the reunification of Roman Christianity and eventually to the liberation of the Holy Sepulchre.[78]

In his letter, as in previous references to the *Cumaean Sibyl*, several elements are interwoven: Henry's eastward march and his close association with the Byzantine empire, which would eventually be reunited with Latin Christendom;[79] the preliminary inner pacification of Christianity through the removal of papal reformers; the eschatological framing of the wars that have to be fought by Henry;

[74]   Included in Benzo of Alba, *Ad Heinricum IV*, 2, 12, 226, 228. See Johann Friedrich Böhmer and Tilman Struve, eds., *Regesta Imperii*, iii/2 (Cologne and Vienna, 1984), nr. 258. For discussion of it, see Franz Dölger and Peter Wirth, eds., *Regesten der Kaiserkunden des oströmischen Reiches von 565–1453*, ii, 2nd ed. (Munich, 1995), nr. 952; Erdmann, "Endkaiserglaube," 403–5; Telemachos C. Lounghis, *Les ambassades byzantines en Occident depuis la fondation des états barbares jusqu'aux croisades (407–1096)* (Athens, 1980), 233–34; Struve, "Kaisertum," 443, 445 n. 99; Jean Sansterre, "Byzance et son souverain dans les *Libri ad Heinricum IV imperatorem* de Benzo d'Alba," in *'Οπώρα. Studi in onore di Mgr. Paul Canart per il LXX compleanno*, i, ed. Santo Lucà and Lidia Perria (Grottaferrata, 1997), 93–112; Möhring, *Der Weltkaiser*, 161–65.

[75]   It is true that this term may also refer to ideas of "contamination," in particular of holy sites (in the sense that was applied to it, for instance, by Urban II at the Council of Clermont and subsequently taken up by other authors: see Robert the Monk, *Historia Iherosolimitana*, in *RHC Oc*, 3:727–29; Baldric of Bourgueil, *Historia Jerosolimitana*, in *RHC Oc*, 4:12–15, and other examples collected in Jonathan Riley-Smith, "The Idea of Crusading in the Charters of Early Crusaders, 1095–1102," in *Le concile de Clermont de 1095 et l'appel à la croisade. Actes du Colloque Universitaire International de Clermont-Ferrand [23–25 juin 1995]*, [Rome, 1997], 155–66, here 156–57); however, the eschatological framework in which Benzo includes it leaves no doubt as to the assimilation of the Normans to the *spurcissimae gentes* of the *Sibylla Tiburtina*.

[76]   Elsewhere in the *Ad Heinricum IV*, they are called *filii spurcicie* (see 3, 15, 316).

[77]   Their "anti-christic" association is clearly set up in the passage mentioned in the previous note: *Sed prius* (that is the subjugation of Apulia and Calabria) *eradicentur Badaculus et Prandellus* [one of the nicknames for Gregory VII], *qui sunt causa malicie, deinde Normanni, filii spurcicie* (ibid.).

[78]   See ibid., 2, 12, 226.

[79]   Through pacific annexation or subjugation, in the excerpt in the *Cumaean Sibyl*, or through military alliance and religious reconciliation in the alleged letter of Constantine. For references to the Virgilian imperial motif of the peaceful subjugation of nations in Benzo's *Ad Heinricum*, see Latowsky, *Emperor of the World*, 133, 135. See ibid., 115–16, for the appearance of the same motif in the *Exhortatio ad Proceres Regni*, very likely to be ascribed to the same author. See also Percy Ernst Schramm, *Kaiser, Rom und Renovatio*, 257. Hypotheses have been raised that Benzo's vision on the reunification of the two empires (and its messianic overtones) was shared by Emicho of Flonheim and could have inspired his 1096 anti-Jewish undertaking: see Norman Cohn, *The Pursuit of the Millennium: Revolutionary Messianism in Medieval and Reformation Europe and its Bearing on Modern Totalitarian Movements* (London, 1957), 56–57, 390, 453; Jonathan Riley-Smith, "The First Crusade and the Persecution of the Jews," in *Persecution and Toleration*, ed. William J. Sheils (Oxford, 1984), 51–72, here 59; Benjamin Z. Kedar, "Emicho of Flonheim and the Apocalyptic Motif in the 1096 Massacres: Between Paul Alphandéry and Alphonse Dupront," in *Conflict and Religious Conversation in Latin Christendom: Studies in Honour of Ora Limor*, ed. Israel Jacob Yuval and Ram Ben-Shalom (Turnhout, 2014), 87–97, here 94.

and, finally, the liberation of the Holy Sepulchre from the yoke of the infidels as the final task that the German ruler has to carry out in order to fulfil his vocation as "Last World Emperor."[80]

Therefore, the eschatological material that Benzo could easily draw from the medieval Sibylline tradition as well as from Pseudo-Methodius's *Revelationes* was directly related to the contemporary political and religious situation. On this account, the bishop of Alba outlined the order of events: an internal peace within Christianity, defeat of the external "pagan" enemies, epitomized by the liberation of the Holy Sepulchre, and eventual universal extension of the imperial power. This sequence would be standardized in the following centuries with some adaptations but without considerable alterations to the narrative.[81] This chronological sequence accords with the geographical one (southern Italy[82] – Constantinople – Jerusalem) that would mark the fulfilment of Henry's imperial "messianic" vocation: triumph in southern Italy would mean peace within Christendom, through the removal of the "anti-christic" reform papacy and its Norman allies; triumph in Constantinople would signify the reunification of the Roman empire, implicitly foretold by the *Sibylla Tiburtina*, who announced the future advent of a *rex Romanorum et Grecorum*;[83] and finally, triumph over Jerusalem would usher in the ultimate kingdom of peace and justice under the rule of the "Last World Emperor,"

---

[80] On the final stages of Henry as the "Last World Emperor," see the commentary of Folz, *Le souvenir*, 140. See also Sansterre, "Byzance et son empereur," 102, 106.

[81] This scheme can be best observed in the complementary prophecies of the "Third Frederick" and the "Second Charlemagne" that appeared at the end of the thirteenth century in Germany and France, respectively: see Kampers, *Die deutsche Kaiseridee*, 110–53; Reeves, *The Influence of Prophecy: A Study in Joachimism* (Oxford, 1969): 320–92; Möhring, *Der Weltkaiser*, 217–68, 291–310.

[82] As Anne A. Latowsky has observed (*Emperor of the World*, 113), Benzo's words describing the role of Apulia and Calabria in the struggle between the German ruler and his enemies are reminiscent of the representation that Apulia had assumed in Antiquity "as a major theatre of the war in Italy, [that] became symbolic of the larger theme of Rome's struggle to triumph over the dual barbarian worlds of Carthage and the Greeks." The reference here is to Plautus' appellation of Apulia as *terra nostra*, in *Casina* (v. 72, ed. Lindsay 1904); but the same expression, applied to Calabria, appears also in Andrew of Bergamo's account of the Saracen conquest of Bari of 871 and the subsequent attack against the Arabs by Louis II (see Andrew of Bergamo, *Historia*, 14, ed. Waitz, 227) – the same events that were taken up and inscribed in a prophetic discourse by the *Sibylla Tiburtina*. See Lorenzo Lozzi Gallo, *La Puglia nel medioevo germanico. Da Apulia a Pülle/Púl* (Ravenna, 2012), 69.

[83] Roman unity had been strongly affirmed in the alleged letter of Emperor Constantine who supported the idea of an "indivisible bond of *caritas*" between the German and the Byzantine rulers on the ground of their shared Roman origin and "nature" (see Benzo of Alba, *Ad Heinricum IV*, 2, 12, 226). Shortly before, Constantine had stated that it was the Norman presence in southern Italy that was threatening the integrity of Roman wisdom (see ibid.). The reference to the Ottonians and the Greek heritage may well offer a hint at the process of the transmission of Byzantine imperial doctrines to the German empire: see Werner Ohnsorge, "Konstantinopel im politischen Denken der Ottonenzeit," in *Polychronion: Festschrift Franz Dölger zum 75. Geburtstag*, ed. Peter Wirth (Heidelberg, 1966), 388–412; on the references to Otto III in Benzo's writings, see Schramm, *Kaiser, Rom und Renovatio*, 262–63. The same topics are evoked in the letter allegedly sent to Benzo by Pantaleus of Amalfi (see Benzo of Alba, *Ad Heinricum IV*, 2, 7, 212, 214).

accompanied, according to the Sibylline prophecies, with the universal conversion to Christianity and eradication of unbelief.[84]

Another aspect of Benzo's reference to the *Cumaean Sibyl* in his *Ad Heinricum Imperatorem* merits further examination, as it offers a glimpse on the contemporary developments of the "Sibylline" tradition in other parts of Europe. Benzo understands Henry's triumphal march eastward, which extends his authority over Constantinople and Jerusalem, as an imitation of Charlemagne's "pilgrimage,"[85] a tradition circulating in imperial circles since the end of the tenth century,[86] which had been vividly rekindled in France around the time of Benzo's writing. This is particularly evident in some texts written during the reign of Philip I. Our prime source is the *Descriptio qualiter Karolus Magnus*[87] which is centred on the legendary journey of Charlemagne to Constantinople and Jerusalem and his return to his kingdom. The dating of this text has been debated. Joseph Bédier was inclined to trace it back to the early twelfth century, others have dated it to the middle or the last quarter of the eleventh.[88] This question is relevant since it raises the issue of the relationship between this text and the First Crusade: did it contribute to inspiring

---

[84] It is interesting to observe that the same sequence, albeit in very different forms and circumstances, was to appear again in subsequent periods, most notably in the thirteenth century, when the heritage of the Norman kingdom of Sicily would again assume a central role in eschatological expectations, both during the clash between Frederick II and the papacy and, later on, as a part of the "war of prophecies" that was to animate the struggle between the descendants of the Swabian emperor and their Angevin opponents. The expression "war of prophecies" comes from Franz Kampers, *Kaiserprophetieen und Kaisersagen im Mittelalter. Ein Beitrag zur Geschichte der deutschen Kaiseridee* (Munich, 1895), 145. For important references to this use of prophetic material in the struggle between pro-imperial and pro-Angevin factions, see above, n. 81.

[85] The connection between Charlemagne and Henry IV as the "Last World Emperor" is expressed in a rather "theatrical" way in Benzo of Alba, *Ad Heinricum IV*, 6, 7, where the Frankish ruler addresses the Salian as his imitator and even the one who will accomplish what he had left uncompleted. See Folz, *Le souvenir*, 140–41. On the importance of the relics of the Passion in the eleventh-century revivals of the Charlemagne legend attached to the regaining of the Holy Sepulchre and the "Last World Emperor," see below, pp. 17–18.

[86] See Benedict of St. Andrew, *Chronicon*, ed. Giuseppe Zucchetti (Rome, 1920), 112–16; see also Erdmann, *Die Entstehung*, 277; Folz, *Le souvenir*, 135–36; Möhring, *Der Weltkaiser*, 157–58; Gabriele, *An Empire of Memory*, 41–44, 98–99.

[87] The full title is *Descriptio qualiter Karolus Magnus clavum et coronam Domini a Constantinopoli Aquisgrani detulerit qualiterque Karolus Calvus hec ad sanctum Dionysium retulerit*, in *Die Legende Karls des Großen im 11. und 12. Jahrhundert*, ed. Gerhard Rauschen (Leipzig, 1890): 103–25. See also Federica Monteleone, *L'Anonimo di Saint-Denis: Una fortunata storia di reliquie* (Bari, 2012).

[88] For an early-twelfth-century dating, see Joseph Bédier, *Légendes épiques: Recherches sur la formation des chansons de geste*, iv (Paris, 1921), 125–27; see also, more recently, Matthias M. Tischler, "Tatmensch oder Heidenapostel: Die Bilder Karls des Großen bei Einhart und in Pseudo-Turpin," in *Jakobus und Karl der Große: Von Einhards Karlsvita zum Pseudo-Turpin*, ed. Klaus Herbers (Tübingen, 2003), 1–37. For a mid-eleventh-century dating, see Rolf Grosse, "Reliques du Christ et foires de Saint-Denis au XIᵉ siècle," *Revue d'Histoire de l'Église de France* 87 (2001): 357–75. For a dating in the last quarter of the eleventh century (which has been widely maintained), see Gaston Paris, *Histoire poétique de Charlemagne*, 2nd ed. (Paris, 1905): 56; Rauschen, *Die Legende*, 99–100; Folz, *Le souvenir*, 179 n. 111; Léon Levillain, "Essai sur les origines du Lendit," *Revue Historique* 155 (1927): 261–62; more recently, with convincing arguments, Matthew Gabriele, "The Provenance of the *Descriptio qualiter Karolus Magnus*: Remembering the Carolingians in the Entourage of King Philip I (1060–1108) before

the crusading effort or was it influenced by it? When carefully compared with other sources of the 1070s, several hints scattered in the texts allow us to assign its first redaction to about 1079–1080, close to the translation of the Holy Shroud to a new reliquary in the abbey of Sainte-Corneille in Compiègne. Moreover, Philip I, who was present at the relic translation, is known to have performed several other acts that can be detected in the *Descriptio qualiter*'s narrative (such as the restoration of the Lendit fair and attempts to link the Capetian kingship with the Carolingian empire).[89]

Like Benedict's *Chronicon*, this source admits a close connection of the first Frankish ruler both with the emperor of Constantinople and the patriarch of Jerusalem, and, as in Benedict's text, the military effort aimed at liberating the Holy Sepulchre from the yoke of the infidels is understood as the most essential criterion legitimizing the acquisition of the imperial dignity.[90] Moreover, like the account of the monk of Mount Soracte, the *Descriptio qualiter* associates the motifs of the liberation of the Holy Land and the elevation to the imperial dignity with the transfer of relics in the West.

Significantly, this kind of *translatio* of relics is described in similar terms in Benzo of Alba's *Ad Heinricum IV imperatorem*, in the speech that Charlemagne addresses to the Salian ruler,[91] to the extent that a more or less direct knowledge of the *Descriptio qualiter* (or, more likely, of the political currents in which it was grounded) seems reasonable on the part of Benzo.[92] In the French source, however, the translation of relics assumes central importance, whereas the relics are supposed to represent "something visible in our regions which might soften their hearts [of our people] at the mention of the Lord's Passion."[93] In other words, the places to

---

the First Crusade," *Viator* 39/2 (2008): 93–118. See also Gabriele, *An Empire of Memory*, 51–60; Latowsky, *Emperor of the World*, 74–98.

[89] See Gabriele, "Provenance," 112–14.

[90] See Kampers, *Die deutsche Kaiseridee*, 56, and Folz, *Le souvenir*, 136.

[91] See Benzo of Alba, *Ad Heinricum* 1, 17, 152. As in the *Descriptio qualiter*, in Benzo's work, the Western Roman emperor receives the relics of the Passion from the emperor of Constantinople. What is peculiar to Benzo, however, is the reference to the Cross as the Constantinian "sign of the victory" (see Eusebius, *Life of Constantine*, ed. Averil Cameron and Stuart G. Hall [Oxford, 1999], 48–50); in this way, not only was the derivation of Henry's imperial dignity from Constantine strengthened, but also his superiority over the Byzantine emperor was highlighted insofar as the transfer of the relics from East to West presupposed a parallel transfer of power. On these subjects, see also Sansterre, "Byzance et son empereur," 106–8. Interestingly enough, the author of the *Descriptio qualiter* also seems to have resorted to the tradition related to the *Visio Constantini* (see Latowsky, *Emperor of the World*, 81–82).

[92] See, in particular, Latowsky, *Emperor of the World*, 107, 135–37, where Benzo's knowledge of the assumptions conveyed by the *Descriptio qualiter* is tentatively connected with the mediation of the anti-Gregorian archbishop of Reims, Manasses, who took refuge at the Salian court approximately at the time when Benzo composed the Charlemagne speech. See Gabriele, *An Empire of Memory*, 115, for the similarities between Benzo's account and the *Descriptio qualiter*.

[93] *Descriptio qualiter*, 112, translated in Gabriele, "The Provenance," 97. On the role of relics in the *Descriptio qualiter*, see also Anne A. Latowsky, "Charlemagne as Pilgrim? Requests for Relics in the *Descriptio qualiter* and the *Voyage of Charlemagne*," in *The Legend of Charlemagne in the Middle Ages: Power, Faith, and Crusade*, ed. Matthew Gabriele and Jace Stuckey (New York, 2008), 153–67, here 153–59; Latowsky, *Emperor of the World*, 75, 77, 88–91, 135–36.

which these relics are transferred represent a sort of symbolic reproduction of the Holy Land, which the Frankish people were not able to visit at the (legendary) time in which Charlemagne's "armed pilgrimage" took place.[94] A direct (albeit spiritual) relation of the kingdom with the Holy Land is therefore granted by the locations where the relics of the Passion are preserved. Interestingly, these sites are also associated with the most important phases of the transfer of power from Carolingian rulers to the Robertian/Capetian kings in previous centuries: respectively Aix-la-Chapelle, Compiègne (where part of the liturgical objects of Aix-la-Chapelle had been transferred in 876, thus making possible a "partial integration of the aixois heritage"[95] in the Carolingian kingdom of West Francia) and Saint-Denis, ceded to the new *race royale* by Charles the Fat.[96]

The French kingdom was therefore seen as a true heir of the Carolingian empire thanks to its direct association with the Holy Land, made visible both through Charlemagne's "first crusade"[97] and his translation of the relics of the Passion within the Frankish empire. While this intricate weave of legendary motifs was foundational in the shaping of the Charlemagne legend in France,[98] it is remarkable to see it exploited by Benzo of Alba, a most fervent supporter of the German sovereign, that is, of France's foremost competitor for the legacy of the first Frankish "crusading" ruler.

---

[94]   See *Descriptio qualiter*, 112.

[95]   Karl Ferdinand Werner, "Il y a mille ans, les Carolingiens: fin d'une dynastie, début d'un mythe," *Annuaire. Bulletin de la Société de l'Histoire de France* 105 (1991–92): 17–89, here 59.

[96]   Ibid., 60. Interestingly, all of these locations are also burial sites of kings (respectively of Charlemagne himself, of certain Carolingian kings of *Francia Occidentalis* and of Capetians); moreover, all of them are destinations of pilgrimages more or less associated with the Carolingian memory.

[97]   This was a widespread opinion in subsequent centuries as well: see, for instance Alberic of Trois-Fontaines, *Chronicon*, ed. Paul Scheffer-Boichorst, MGH SS 23 (Hannover, 1875), 804; the same idea was suggested by a series of medallions placed on a window of the abbey church of Saint-Denis: see Elizabeth A. R. Brown and Michael W. Cothren, "The Twelfth-Century Crusading Window of the Abbey of Saint-Denis: Praeteritorum enim recordatio futurorum est exhibitio," *Journal of the Warburg and Courtauld Institutes* 49 (1986): 1–38; and Gabriele, "The Provenance," 95.

[98]   Consistent elaborations on the special tie between the French (Capetian) monarchy and the figure of Charlemagne which had emerged in the *Descriptio qualiter* can be observed throughout the twelfth and the thirteenth centuries, and most evidently in several documentary and literary sources produced in (or inspired by) the abbey of Saint-Denis (including the *Chanson de Roland* and the *Historia Karoli Magni et Rotholandi*): see Folz, *Le souvenir*, 214–25; Gabrielle M. Spiegel, *The Chronicle Tradition of Saint-Denis: A Survey* (Brookline, MA, 1979), 30; Brown and Cothren, "The Twelfth-Century Crusading Window," 32; Ludwig Vones, "Heiligsprechung und Tradition: Die Kanonisation Karls des Großen 1165, die Aachener Karlsvita und der Pseudo-Turpin," in Herkens, *Jakobus und Karl der Große*, 89–105; Gabriele, "The Provenance," 103–4; Latowsky, *Emperor of the World*, 220–25; Monteleone, *Il Viaggio di Carlo Magno*, 269–79; Monteleone, *L'Anonimo di Saint-Denis*, 27–35. In this context, it is also appropriate to mention the active role played by the royal chancellery of Philip Augustus in fostering the so-called *Reditus regni ad stirpem Karoli Magni*, in this case by taking up the prophetic material conveyed by both the *Sibylla Tiburtina* and Pseudo-Alcuin's version of Adso's treatise on the Antichrist: see Elizabeth A. R. Brown, "La notion de la légitimité et la prophétie à la cour de Philippe Auguste," in *La France de Philippe Auguste: le temps des mutations. Actes du Colloque International organisé par le C.N.R.S. (Paris, 29 septembre – 4 octobre 1980)*, ed. Robert-Henri Bautier (Paris, 1982), 77–112.

In Benzo, the Charlemagne connection with the Holy Land was directly connected with the Sibylline prophetic tradition; can such a link be observed in the French area as well? The answer is affirmative, as some scholars have observed[99] with reference to the so-called *Vita Antichristi ad Carolum Magnum*, for a long time attributed to Alcuin, but in reality an adaptation of Adso of Montier-en-Der's *De ortu et tempore Antichristi*, composed at approximately the same time as all the other "proto-crusading" sources mentioned in this article were produced.[100]

As is well-known, Adso's treatise on the Antichrist had been dedicated in 954 to Queen Gerberga, wife of the Carolingian king of West Francia, Charles V, and sister of the Saxon king of East Francia, Otto the Great (not yet crowned emperor at that time).[101] It included a short passage on the "Last World Emperor" in which the compiler, while resuming the eschatological concepts derived from Pseudo-Methodius's *Revelationes* and other possible versions of the *Vaticinium of Constans* available at the time,[102] simultaneously provided a new interpretation that would become extremely influential in the following centuries, especially in France. Adso connected the traditional interpretation of the Pauline *katéchon*, identified with the Roman Empire, with the theory of the *translatio imperii*, according to which the fourth and last universal monarchy announced by the prophet Daniel, while persisting until the end of time, had been transferred to the Frankish people.[103] For Adso, therefore, the Roman Empire was being preserved only by Frankish kings so that the "Last World Emperor" (portrayed along the lines of Pseudo-Methodius's

---

[99]   See in particular Edrmann, "Endkaiserglaube," 409–13; Folz, *Le souvenir*, 141–42.

[100]   See *Vita Antichristi ad Carolum Magnum ab Alcuino edita*, in Adso Dervensis, *De ortu*, 105–28.

[101]   On Adso's writing and its doctrinal as well as political implications, see Gian Andri Bezzola, *Das Ottonische Kaisertum in der französischen Geschichtsschreibung des 10. und beginnenden 11. Jahrhunderts* (Graz and Cologne, 1956), 55–64; Robert Konrad, *De ortu et tempore Antichristi. Antichristvorstellung und Geschichtsbild des Abtes Adso von Montier-en-Der* (Kallmünz, 1964); Maurizio Rangheri, "La 'Epistola ad Gerbergam reginam de ortu et tempore Antichristi' di Adsone di Montier-en-Der e le sue fonti," *Studi medievali* 14/2 (1973): 677–732; Danïel Verhelst, "La préhistoire des conceptions d'Adson concernant l'Antichrist," *Recherches de théologie ancienne et médiévale* 40 (1972): 52–103; Bernd Schneidmüller, "Adso von Montier-en-Der und die Frankenkönige," *Trierer Zeitschrift für Geschichte und Kunst des Trierer Landes und seiner Nachbargebiete* 40/1 (1977–78): 189–99; Schneidmüller, *Karolingische Tradition und frühes französisches Königtum. Untersuchungen zur Herrschaftslegitimation der westfränkisch-französischen Monarchie im 10. Jahrhundert* (Wiesbaden, 1979), 61–65; Simon MacLean, "Reform, Queenship and the End of the World in Tenth-Century France: Adso's 'Letter on the Origin and Time of the Antichrist' Reconsidered," *Revue belge de philologie et d'histoire* 86/3–4 (2008): 645–75.

[102]   It is difficult to ascertain whether Adso had actually read these texts or other writings directly inspired by them, and consciously included them within the *doctores* (or *auctores*) *nostri* upon which he declared his reliance (see Adso Dervensis, *De ortu*, 23, 26). On the problem of Adso's sources, see Martin Haeusler, *Das Ende der Geschichte in der mittelalterlichen Weltchronistik* (Cologne and Vienna, 1980), 47–48; Möhring, *Der Weltkaiser*, 146, 332.

[103]   For the idea of the *translatio imperii* during the tenth and eleventh centuries, see Werner Goez, *Translatio imperii. Ein Beitrag zur Geschichte des Geschichtsdenkens und der politischen Theorien im Mittelalter und in der frühen Neuzeit* (Tübingen, 1958); Ulrike Krämer, *Translatio imperii et studii. Zum Geschichts- und Kulturverständnis in der französischen Literatur des Mittelalters und der frühen Neuzeit* (Bonn, 1996), 49–69, where a collection of examples is provided.

Revelationes, including his representation as liberator of Jerusalem) would be necessarily one of them, without a doubt the most illustrious.[104]

As for Pseudo-Alcuin's version, it makes a significant change by interpolating large sections of the *Vaticinium of Constans* within the narrative. Moreover, the author of this reshaped text introduced a small but meaningful modification: instead of reporting the name of *Constans*, the "Last World Emperor's" name in the original *Sibylla Tiburtina*, Pseudo-Alcuin replaced it with just the initial "C.", thus making possible a connection with the supposedly first "crusader king" who was widely associated with the recovery of the Holy Sepulchre, around the time of Benzo of Alba's writing of *Ad Heinricum* and the *Descriptio qualiter* (and maybe also the *Cumaean Sibyl*). Moreover, the combination of the Sibylline *rex Romanorum totius imperii* with the Adsonian *rex Francorum* who *Romanum imperium ex integro tenebit* could not but recall a Frankish king who was supposed to replicate the deeds of Charlemagne (restorer of the empire, pilgrim to and liberator of the Holy Land), or, from a point of view more in line with Pseudo-Methodius, fulfil the task of the "Last World Emperor" through the imitation of the first Frankish emperor. In this case, however, by contrast with Benzo's assumption (who also combined universal imperial aspirations with the memory of Charlemagne), it was the Capetian French ruler who had to be understood as the true heir of the Charlemagne legend attached to the Sibylline prophecy.

If, all in all, "the author of the pseudo-Alcuinian text is influenced by the same currents of ideas" that had inspired Benzo of Alba,[105] we may be faced with the parallel emergence of a prophetic tradition, whose doctrinal assumptions were consciously elaborated in a favourable way by the two competing heirs to the Carolingian empire. The memory of Charlemagne, including his legendary qualities as pilgrim and protector of the Holy Land, was an essential tool of legitimization, which could be connected with the eschatological tradition derived from Pseudo-Methodius's *Revelationes* and the *Sibylla Tiburtina* – both texts that revealed the most profound implications of the Roman imperial dignity. While the sources examined here contribute to "explaining" the sacral foundations on which both German empire and French kingdom were being based, it is noteworthy that this fundamental step in the process of sacralizing the European monarchies[106] could

---

[104] See Adso Dervensis, *De ortu*, 26.

[105] See the introduction to Pseudo-Alcuin's text by Verhelst: ibid., 109.

[106] Ruling dynasties, however, would come to see the crusades as a tool of sacral legitimization only in the following decades (certainly *after* the First Crusade), with the apex of this process likely culminating during the age of Frederick Barbarossa for Germany (see Latowsky, *Emperor of the World*, 139–214) and Philip II Augustus for France (see Latowsky, *Emperor of the World*, 215–50; James Naus, *Constructing Kingship: The Capetian Monarchs of France and the Early Crusades* [Manchester, 2016], 112–40, although "using the participation in the crusades as a way to promote sacred kingship" [ibid., 123] had been strongly supported in France since the age of Suger, as Naus argues in his book. On the role played by Sibylline prophecy as a legitimization tool at the age of Philip Augustus, see Brown, "La notion de la légitimité"). For the general process of sacralization of European monarchies in subsequent centuries, see Ernst H. Kantorowicz, "Mysteries of State: An Absolutist Concept and Its Late Mediaeval Origins," *The Harvard Theological Review* 48/1 (1955): 65–91.

not be carried out without a direct reference to the Holy Land, perceived as the ultimate source of any legitimate authority – even superior to priestly mediation, which, interestingly, is never mentioned in any prophetic texts examined (whether they be traced back to the first centuries of the Christian era or to the eleventh century).

In this sense, it would be tempting to see in the Sibylline prophetic tradition a powerful tool for the emerging of both national identities and the idea of crusade – with the connection between them being based on common eschatological presuppositions.

Itineraria Terrae Sanctae minora IIIA:
A Revised Edition of *Descriptio Ierusalem* (Group E2), based on British Library, Royal MS 6.A.I, fols. 134r–135r

Denys Pringle

Cardiff University
pringlerd@cardiff.ac.uk

Abstract

This short note, representing an addendum to an article that appeared in Crusades *20 (2021), presents a revised edition of a short early-twelfth-century description of Jerusalem. It is based on a twelfth-century manuscript in the British Library (Royal MS 6.A.I, fols. 134r–135r) that was not accessible at the time when the earlier article was written. Besides giving an earlier version of the text than that presented before, this manuscript also sheds further light on the text's early development.*

Introduction

In a recent discussion of some early twelfth-century guides to Frankish Jerusalem, I identified a family of some seventeen early twelfth-century versions of a text that Reinhold Röhricht had referred to as *De Situ Hierusalem* but which, for convenience and in order to avoid confusion with another text known as *De Situ urbis Ierusalem*, I have chosen to call simply *Descriptio Ierusalem*.[1] These texts give a short description of the city of Jerusalem within the first two decades after its fall to the First Crusade in 1099. They are easily recognized by their *incipit*, which in most cases reads: *Ab occidente est introitus Ierusalem per portam David*. The texts of the *Descriptio Ierusalem* may be divided into five separate groups, the last of which (Group E) is distinguished from the others by a copyist's mistake, which resulted in *occidente* being accidentally changed to *oriente*. Four manuscripts may be identified as belonging to Group E:

Cg Cambridge, Gonville and Caius College Library, MS 151, fol. 109r.[2] 13c.

---

[1] Reinhold Röhricht, *Bibliotheca Geographica Palaestinae* (Berlin, 1890), 63, no. 157; Denys Pringle, "Itineraria Terrae Sanctae minora III: Some Early Twelfth-Century Guides to Frankish Jerusalem," *Crusades* 20 (2021): 3–63, at 30–31, 60–63.

[2] Montague Rhodes James, *A Descriptive Catalogue of the Manuscripts in the Library of Gonville and Caius College*, 2 vols. (Cambridge, 1907–8), 1:173, no. 151.

Ch Cheltenham, formerly in Sir Thomas Phillipps's Library, MS 16588. 13c.
      Current whereabouts unknown.[3]
Lr London, British Library, Royal MS 6 A. I, fols. 134–5.[4]   12c.
Oa Oxford, Bodleian Library, MS Ashmole 1280, part V, fols. 107r–v.[5] 13c.

As *Lr* was not accessible at the time when I was working on these texts, owing to the Covid-19 pandemic, and *Ch* still remains lost, my earlier article included parallel editions of only two examples from Group E, *Cg* and *Oa*. The close similarity of *Cg* in all respects other than its *incipit* with another Cambridge manuscript from Group D,[6] however, suggested that the Group E texts had developed from a text related to Group D. At the same time, *Oa* appeared to represent a development of the version in *Cg*, with some material added and a smaller amount omitted. Published extracts from and descriptions of *Lr* suggested that it was similar to *Oa*,[7] but how similar it was not possible to know without seeing the manuscript itself. Since then, however, it has been possible to obtain images of the relevant folios from the British Library.[8] These confirm that the text of *Lr* is virtually identical to *Oa* and support the view that it represents a slightly earlier version of it, in terms both of its textual content and the dating of the manuscript. The main purpose of this short note is therefore to present a new combined edition of *Lr* and *Oa* (henceforth renamed Group E2), based primarily on the former.[9]

---

[3] [Thomas Phillipps] *Catalogus Librorum Manuscriptorum in Bibliotheca D. Thomæ Phillipps, Bart. A.D. 1837* (Middle Hill, Worcestershire, 1837), 321, no. 16588. On the dispersal of the Phillipps Library, see A. N. L. Munby, *The Dispersal of the Phillipps Library*, Phillipps Studies 5 (Cambridge, 1960); Toby Burrows, "Manuscripts of Sir Thomas Phillipps in North American Institutions," *Manuscript Studies* 1/2 (2016): 307–27 (art. 9).

[4] George F. Warner and Julius P. Gibson, *British Museum: Catalogue of Western Manuscripts in the Old Royal and King's Collections*, 4 vols. (London, 1921), 1:126–27.

[5] William Henry Black, *A Descriptive, Analytical and Critical Catalogue of the Manuscripts bequeathed unto the University of Oxford by Elias Ashmole, Esq., M.D., F.R.S.* (Oxford, 1945), cols. 1033–39, no. 1280.

[6] Cambridge, Emmanuel College, MS 143 (II.2.18/CMA 16), fol. 128: Montague Rhodes James, *The Western Manuscripts in the Library of Emmanuel College: A Descriptive Catalogue* (Cambridge, 1904), 116, no. 143.3.

[7] Warner and Gibson, *British Museum: Catalogue of Western Manuscripts in the Old Royal and King's Collections*, 1:126–27; Krijnie N. Ciggaar, "Une Description de Constantinople traduite par un pèlerin anglais," *Revue des études byzantines* 34 (1976), 211–68, at 240.

[8] I am most grateful to the British Library staff for providing these images in difficult circumstances.

[9] Comparison of *Lr* and *Oa* has also exposed some errors in my earlier edition of *Oa*, for which the following corrections may be noted: for *Secus* read *Retro* (para. 2.2), for *lectus* read *locus* (para 3.6), for *genetricis* read *genitricis* (para 4.1), and for *Sanctum Spiritum* read *Spiritum Sanctum* (para 6.10). On p. 25 of the introduction it was also incorrectly stated that "Group B differs from the other versions of the *Descriptio* in making the Holy Sepulchre the first place to be mentioned on entering through David's Gate." This should of course have read "*Templum Domini*," not "Holy Sepulchre."

The Text

The following edition of the text follows *Lr*, with differences that appear in *Oa* noted in the apparatus. Standard contractions are expanded where it is clear from the contraction sign or the grammatical sense what the missing letters would have been. The numbering of paragraphs and sub-sections follows that previously established for all versions of the *Descriptio Ierusalem*. This accounts for the discontinuity in the numbering sequence, when passages of text found in other versions do not appear in the one presented here.

Descriptio Ierusalem (Group E2) (after 1099–c. 1120)

Lr = London, BL, Royal MS 6.A.I, fols. 134r–135r (12c.).

Oa = Oxford, Bodleian Library, MS Ashmole 1280, part V, fols. 107r–v (13c.).

De situ[i] Ierusalem

1. Ab oriente est introitus Ierusalem per portam David.

2.1 Non longe infra civitatem est sepulchrum Domini. Foris in capite ecclesie est medium mundi. Ultra non longe est carcer. Ibique prope est ligatio. Ibique est flagellatio. Ibique est spinea corona coronatus. Ibique spoliatus et vestimenta eius divisa. Ibique in ipso ordine est Calvarie Mons, ubi crucifixus fuit Dominus. 2.2 Subtus est Golgotha, ubi sanguis cecidit per petram scissam. Retro Montis Calvarie est locus, ubi sancta Helena invenit crucem.[ii]

3.1[1] Subterius contra orientem ex alia parte civitatis est Templum Domini, quod Salomon fecit, quattuor portas habens, prima ab oriente, secunda ab occidente, tercia ad meridiem, quarta ab aquilone, que habent significationes quattuor partium[iii] mundi, deforis octo[iv] angulos habens. Per unumquemque angulum duodecim[v] passus voluitur. 3.4 In medio Templi est saxum magnum, circumdatum parietibus, in quo ab uno latere est tabernaculum, ubi est archa federis Domini et virga Aaron et due tabule testamenti et septem candelabra aurea, sicut dixit beatus Paulus,[vi] et mensa et propositio panum, aureum habens thuribulum,[vii] et archa testamenti, in qua urna aurea habens manna. Supraque erat Cherubin glorie.[2] 3.6 Ab alio latere est tabernaculum apertum, per quod omnes ingrediuntur, ubi Dominus sepius[viii] intrabat. Ibi **[134v]** sacrificabat Zacharias quando annunciatus fuit beatus Iohannes. Ibi est

---

[1] Apart from the description of the contents of the Holy of Holies (3.4) and Jesus' words to the woman caught in adultery (3.6), paras. 3 and 4 represent a summarized version of what appears in Peter the Deacon (1137), *Liber de Locis Sanctis*, ed. R. Weber, CCSL 175 (Turnhout, 1965), 95 (sections C.3–4).

[2] The contents of the Holy of Holies are described here as in Paul's letter to the Hebrews 9.2–5.

---

[i]   situ *Lr*] sita *Oa*.

[ii] crucem] *followed by* Domini *Oa*.

[iii] partium *Lr*] parcium *Oa*.

[iv] octo *Lr*] quattuor *Oa*.

[v]   duodecim *Lr*] duodescim *or* duotescim *Oa*.

[vi] Paulus *Lr*] Paulus apostolus *Oa*.

[vii] habens thuribulum *Lr*] habens ~~tabernaculum~~ turibulum *Oa*.

[viii] sepius] *omitted from Oa*.

locus ubi Dominus iacebat et ibi dixit mulieri: *Ubi sunt qui te accusabant?*[3] Et ibi scripsit in terra: *Siquis sine peccato est, mittat in eam lapidem.*[4] 3.7 Super saxum in medio Templi pendet ampulla aurea, in qua est sanguis Christi, cum petra scissa.[5] Extra Templum est locus ubi Zacharias filius Barachie interfectus fuit contra meridiem.

4.1 Non longe est Templum Salomonis. Subtus est cunabulum Christi et balneum eius et lectus genitricis eius. Subtus Templum Domini est Porta Speciosa, in qua Dominus intravit quando sedit super pullum asine et ibi dixit beatus Petrus paralitico:[ix] *Surge, ambula.*[6] 4.2 Contra aquilonem est ecclesia sancte Anne, ubi beata MARIA tribus annis nutrita fuit.[7] Et ibi non longe est Probatica Piscina.

5.1 Foris civitatem contra orientem est vallis Iosaphat, in qua sancta Dei genitrix sepulta fuit ab apostolis. 5.2 Ibidem est Gethsemani, ubi Iudas Salvatorem Iudeis tradidit. Et inde non longe, scilicet quantum iactus lapidis, est locus ubi oravit. 5.3 Superius est mons Oliveti, unde Dominus ascendit in celum, et ibi *Pater Noster* fecit. 5.4 Subterius est[x] Bethania, ubi Dominus resuscitavit Lazarum. 5.5 Per illum montem itur ad Iordanem et in ipsa via est locus ubi Cain[xi] occidit Abel.[8] In planicie est Ierico[xii] et ortus Abrahe. Contra aquilonem mons est ubi Dominus ieunavit XL diebus. Iordanis longe est a Ierico milibus quinque.

6.1 Mons Syon a meridie Ierusalem, ubi **[135r]** migravit sancta MARIA. Ibi est Galilea, ubi Dominus primitus[xiii] apparuit, et ibi est mensa, qua cum discipulis suis cenavit, et ibi dedit Spiritum Sanctum apostolis[xiv] in die Pentecostes. 6.2 Subterius est Gallicantus,[xv] ubi Petro Dominus peccata dimisit, et non longe inde est[xvi] Natatoria Syloe. Ex alia parte est Acheldemach, sepultura peregrinorum.

7.1 Bethleem longe est ab Ierusalem duas leugas,[xvii] ubi Dominus natus fuit, et presepe ubi fuit positus, et puteus, ubi stella apparuit, et ibi centum quadraginta quattuor milia martyres ab Herode interfecti fuerunt. Et ibi est tabula, in qua sancta Maria cum tribus magis requirentibus comedit, et ibi est balneum eius.

---

[3] John 8.10.

[4] Cf. John 8.7.

[5] Cf. Peter the Deacon, CCSL 175:95 (C3): "Super saxum in medio templi pendet candela aurea, in qua est sanguis Christi, qui per petram scissam descendit."

[6] Cf. Acts 3.6.

[7] Cf. *de Nativitate Mariae* 1–6, ed. Constantin von Tischendorf, *Evangelia Apocrypha* (Leipzig, 1876), 113–17; trans. Alexander Roberts and James Donaldson, *The Ante-Nicene Fathers* 8 (New York, 1903), 384–85.

[8] John of Würzburg, c. 1165 (ed. R. B. C. Huygens, CCCM 139 (Turnhout, 1994), 103), following Rorgo Fretellus (Count Rodrigo version, c. 1137: cf. Paris, Bibliothèque nationale de France (BnF), MS latin, 18018, fol. 107vb), locates Cain's murder of Abel in the territory of Damascus, while Innominatus II (c. 1165–75) places it near Hebron (Denys Pringle, "Itineraria Terrae Sanctae Minora II: Innominati II–V and VIII," *Crusades* 19 (2020): 57–108, at 89, para 19.2).

[ix] paralitico] *corr. from* paraclitico *Lr.*

[x]   est] *omitted from Oa.*

[xi] Cain *Lr*] Caim *Oa.*

[xii] Ierico *Lr*] Iherico *Oa.*

[xiii] primitus *Lr*] primus *Oa.*

[xiv] apostolis *Lr*] discipulis *Oa.*

[xv] Gallicantus *Lr*] Gallicanustus *Oa.*

[xvi] est] *followed by* ~~natori~~ *Oa.*

[xvii] leugas *Lr*] leucas *Oa.*

8. De Ierusalem ad flumen Iordanis decem leugas.[xviii] De Ierico autem ad duas leugas[xix] mons excelsus conspicitur, ubi Dominum diabolus temptavit.

IDUS IULII capta est Ierusalem a Latinis. Eodem die Divisio Apostolorum.[xx]

[xviii] decem leugas *Lr*] .xi. leucas *Oa*.

[xix] leugas *Lr*] leucas *Oa*.

[xx] IDUS IULII … Apostolorum *Lr*] omitted from *Oa*.

A Georgian Monk – Steward of a Crusader King: Georgian-Frankish Relations in the Twelfth Century

Mamuka Tsurtsumia

Independent scholar, Tbilisi
mamuka@mkhedari.ge

Abstract

The archives of the Hospitaller Order preserve a twelfth-century document which illuminates a chapter in the relationship between the Eastern Christians and the Hospital. The document has long been known to scholars and has been thoroughly studied, but still raises as many questions as it answers. The present study discusses evidence from Georgian manuscripts produced in the Holy Land, which shed new light on the identities of the persons and locations mentioned. The evidence from these Georgian manuscripts shows that, from the mid-eleventh to the mid-twelfth century, three generations of one Georgian feudal family worked and lived in the Holy Land. It shows that the Shehan monastic complex in Transjordan included the St. Moses Monastery, the settlement named Ara (Hara), and other estates on both banks of the Arnon River (Wadi al-Mujib). Also, contrary to a previous assumption, it is suggested that there was no parish church in Jeham, but rather a Georgian monastery named after Moses. According to the evidence discussed here, King Baldwin II appointed Saba the Georgian as his steward of the Eastern Christian settlement, indicating that royal possessions in Transjordan were established early on in the history of the Latin kingdom, and that the lands of Arnon belonged to the crown and were not included in the lordship of Transjordan. Furthermore, it can be established that the transfer of the Georgian monastery to the Hospital must be dated to the 1140s or the 1150s and that the Georgian monks handed over to the Hospital not only the village, but also the monastery of Shehan.

A twelfth-century charter preserved in the archives of the Order of St. John brings to light an intriguing episode in relations between the Eastern Christians and the Order. The document is familiar to scholars and has been thoroughly studied; its contents are known from three catalogues, two of which were compiled in the sixteenth and one in the eighteenth century.[1] Importantly, however, the document is unknown in its complete form, because only selected parts of it were registered in the abovementioned inventories. The eighteenth-century catalogue was compiled

I would like to thank Professor Hans Eberhard Mayer for his valuable comments on my draft paper. Special thanks also to the editors for their hard work on this paper.

[1] Hans Eberhard Mayer, *Die Kreuzfahrerherrschaft Montréal (Šōbak): Jordanien im 12. Jahrhundert* (Wiesbaden, 1990), 98.

by Jean Raybaud, archivist of the Hospitaller Order.[2] The documents of the Hospital issued in the Holy Land were kept in the priory of Saint-Gilles, France, and were transferred to Malta in 1742 at the request of the Order's Grand Master, Manuel Pinto de Fonseca. Raybaud's inventory includes 378 documents written between 1107 and 1287.[3] Some of these documents no longer survive and are only known today through Raybaud's catalogue. The inventory of documents compiled by him in 1741 under the title *Inventaire des chartes de Syrie* is kept in the Departmental Archives of Bouches-du-Rhône (Marseille).[4]

The document that stands in the centre of this study is the donation of a *casale* to the Knights Hospitaller, first published by Joseph Delaville Le Roulx. In the first volume of the cartularies of the Hospital he provided the French text of Raybaud's inventory.[5] A year later, in 1895, he reprinted the same text with virtually no changes.[6] Delaville Le Roulx dated the document to 1160, relying on Jean Raybaud who placed it between the documents of 1159 and 1160.[7] Röhricht accepted this dating and summarized the document in Latin.[8] It is noteworthy that both Delaville Le Roulx and Röhricht used the inventory entries provided by Raybaud in the eighteenth century.[9] Towards the end of the twentieth century, Hans Eberhard Mayer studied the document thoroughly,[10] and in 2010 he published all the inventory entries and commented upon them.[11]

The entry in the Manosque inventory of 1531–35 (M[1]), which is the fullest, states that the "brothers Joseph and John, the sons of Saba the Georgian,[12] and others named, gave to the Holy Hospital of Jerusalem a casale named in Arabic Bara [Hara], located on the plain under the hill of Saint Moses beyond the river, and the Church of Saint Moses, referred to in Arabic as Jeham, [which they hold] through a privilege [by which] King Baldwin, the second king of the Franks and Jerusalem, gave and confirmed with a seal to Saba, their aforementioned father, the

---

[2] J. Delaville Le Roulx, "Inventaire de pièces de Terre Sainte de l'Ordre de l'Hopital," ROL 3 (1895): 37.

[3] Cart Hosp, 1:XVIII, n. 2.

[4] Cart Hosp, 1:XVIII.

[5] Cart Hosp, 1:210, no. 284: "Donation faite par Joseph et Jean, frères, enfants de Saba, Géorgien, d'un casal appelé en langue arabe 'Hara', situé dans la plaine sous la montagne de S. Moyse, dite en arabe 'Jeham', qui avoit été donnée à leur père par Baudouin, II[e] du nom, roy de Hierusalem, sans datte."

[6] Delaville Le Roulx, "Inventaire de pièces de Terre Sainte de l'Ordre de l'Hopital," 53, no. 62.

[7] Cart Hosp, 1:209.

[8] RRH Add, 21, no. 365[b]: "Josephus et Johannes, filii Sabae Georgiani, Hospitali casale arabice Hara dictum, quod in planitie sub monte S. Mosis arabice Jeham dicto situm est et patri ipsorum a Balduino II rege donatum fuerat, concedunt."

[9] Mayer, *Die Kreuzfahrerherrschaft Montréal*, 98.

[10] Ibid., 98–99.

[11] Mayer, *Urkunden*, 1:286–87.

[12] Mayer considers it feasible that Saba Georgii was Georgian, but leans towards the idea that he was an Orthodox Syrian Christian: Mayer, *Die Kreuzfahrerherrschaft Montréal*, 98. He believes that Saba Georgii is a misinterpretation and it should be replaced by *Saba, son of George*, in Arabic *Ṣabā ibn Ǧirǧīs*: Mayer, *Urkunden*, 1:286. Following Mayer, Pringle also refers to Saba, not as Georgian, but as Saba, son of George: Pringle, *Churches*, 2:377.

casale Ara and the church in the abovementioned Jeham and all their property on both banks of the river."[13]

As can be seen, the extensive Manosque entry differs significantly from the versions published by Delaville Le Roulx and Röhricht, and contains important additional information. Mayer pointed out that, due to a copyist's error, the Church of Moses was omitted from previous publications.[14] The document mentions a settlement located across the river (*ultra flumen*), which is referred to in different ways in different inventories: Arabic *Bara, Ara* or *Hara*. The village was located on the plain at the foot of St. Moses (*sub colle*), and the hill was called *Jeham, Leham, Seham* in Arabic.[15] Yet, the location of the settlement and the church remained unclear. Röhricht noted that nothing was known about Jeham.[16] Mayer detects the Arabic word for mosque, *ǧamī* in the word Jeham.[17] Mention of Mount Moses in the document became a starting point for scholars. Röhricht argued that it was not Mount Sinai, but Nebi Musa (south of Jericho, west of the Jordan River), which is considered to be Moses' burial place, or Mount Nebo (east of the Jordan), the place where Moses died.[18] Mayer rejects the identification of Mount Nebo with the shrine of Moses based on a number of arguments: in the Middle Ages, Nebo was not called Mount Moses; the former is a high mountain (*mons*) with two peaks and not a hill (*collis*). In addition, Nebo belonged to Transjordan, so the issuer of the document should have been its lord rather than the king. According to Mayer, the location could have been close to Wadi Musa (near Petra), although he added that this assumption was not geographically accurate, as Wadi Musa was not located across the river, but south of the Dead Sea.[19]

With some caution, noting the imperfection of existing inventories, this interpretation is also shared by Denys Pringle.[20] This settlement, which has not been identified yet, is also located next to Wadi Musa by Micaela Sinibaldi, who believes that one of the candidates may be the village of Khirbat al-Nawafla in the area of Wadi Musa, which was densely populated in the twelfth century and where the Spring of Moses was located.[21] At the same time, Sinibaldi also acknowledges

---

[13] Mayer, *Urkunden*, 1:286. Mayer maintains that Baldwin's title *Francorum rex* is a mistake, as such a title was not used and it should be *Latinorum*.

[14] Ibid.

[15] Mayer, *Die Kreuzfahrerherrschaft Montréal*, 98.

[16] *RRH Add*, 21.

[17] Mayer, *Urkunden*, 1:286–87.

[18] *RRH Add*, 21.

[19] Mayer, *Die Kreuzfahrerherrschaft Montréal*, 99; Mayer, *Urkunden*, 1:287. Despite his hypothesis, Mayer acknowledges that the question of the location of this settlement remains open: ibid.

[20] Pringle, *Churches*, 2:377.

[21] Micaela Sinibaldi, "Settlement in Crusader Transjordan (1100–1189): A Historical and Archaeological Study" (PhD Thesis, Cardiff University, 2014), 150, 152, 159; idem, "Settlement in the Petra Region during the Crusader Period: A Summary of the Historical and Archaeological Evidence," in *Crusader Landscapes in the Medieval Levant. The Archaeology and History of the Latin East*, ed. M. Sinibaldi, K. Lewis, B. Major, and J. Thompson (Cardiff, 2016), 88.

that the toponyms Hara (Bara, Ara) and Sehan (Seham, Jeham) are unknown and
that it is impossible to associate them with a more specific area of Wadi Musa.[22]

Georgian Sources

Clearly the document as it is known from the Western sources leaves several
questions unanswered.[23] Fortunately, the Georgian manuscripts produced in the
Holy Land allow us to establish the identities of the persons mentioned in the
Hospitaller records and the location of the church, or rather of the monastery.[24]

In 1975, Elene Metreveli published a study of the Georgian monastery of Shehan
and the identity of its founder.[25] Metreveli examined the Georgian manuscripts
of the Holy Land – Jer. 42 and Jer. 50 preserved in the Greek Patriarchate of
Jerusalem, and Géorgien 28, preserved in the Bibliothèque nationale de France
(BnF), Paris, which provides information about Gabriel Tpileli, bishop of Tbilisi
and founder of the Shehan Monastery, and his descendants. Manuscript Jer. 42
was copied in the Monastery of the Holy Cross in Jerusalem before 1061. The
manuscript is accompanied by a commemoration: "Christ have mercy on Father
Gabriel of Shehan" (164r). At that time Gabriel was called Shehan's father, which
means he had already founded Shehan Monastery and was its head.[26] From a
manuscript copied in Shehan (Jer. 50) in around 1065, we learn that there was
a Georgian scriptorium there. The colophon reads: "It was written in the Holy
Desert[27] of Shehan during the time of Father Gabriel Tpileli, who built the Desert
of Shehan" (67r).[28] The twelfth-century manuscript of the Monastery of the Cross
(Géorgien 28) contains a commemoration with a reference to the brothers Joseph
and John, which indicates that they were the grandchildren of Gabriel of Shehan,
and lived in the monastery that he had established: "God, protect and have mercy
on our brothers Joseph and John, the grandsons of Gabriel the builder of Shehan,
and make them worthy of our brotherhood of the Cross and Shehan" (246v).[29] The
brothers continued the tradition established by Gabriel of Shehan and were closely

---

[22]   Sinibaldi, "Settlement in Crusader Transjordan," 159.

[23]   Mayer, *Die Kreuzfahrerherrschaft Montréal*, 98.

[24]   See the Appendix below for the Testaments, Commemorations and *Agapes* from the Georgian
Manuscripts of the Holy Land.

[25]   Elene Metreveli, "Shehanis udabno – XI saukunis ucnobi kartuli skriptoriumi palestinashi" [The
Shehan Desert – An Unknown Eleventh-Century Georgian Scriptorium in Palestine], *Mravaltavi* 5
(1975): 22–44.

[26]   Ibid., 24–25. Based on the commemorations about Gabriel of Shehan found in the manuscripts of
the Monastery of the Cross, Metreveli believes that Gabriel must have been a member of a brotherhood
of the Cross, who maintained a connection with the Monastery of the Cross even after he had founded
Shehan: ibid., 23, 26.

[27]   *Desert* means monastery here.

[28]   Metreveli, "Shehanis udabno," 26–32.

[29]   Ibid., 23.

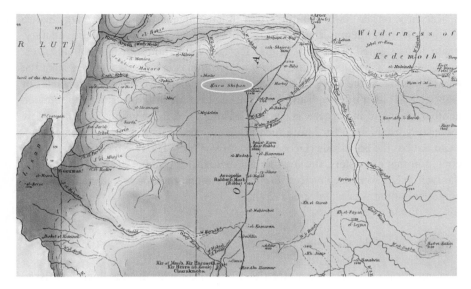

Fig. 1   Mount Shihan (Kara Shihan) in Jordan.
From *Atlas of the Historical Geography of the Holy Land,* by George Adam Smith and J. G. Bartholomew
(London, 1915), section VIII, 29–30.

associated with the Monastery of the Cross.[30] Metreveli believed that the Shehan
Monastery was built on Mount Shihan, near the River Arnon (see Figure 1).[31] In
addition to the resemblance of the toponyms, she also noted the fact that George-
Prokhore, founder of the Monastery of the Cross, had travelled to the Arnon Desert
at the end of his life, presumably, to his friend Gabriel in Shehan:[32] "He became
weak ... and after that he went to the Desert Arnon."[33]

---

[30] Ibid., 24.

[31] Ibid., 33–43. This location was first pointed out to Metreveli in the 1970s by Anzor Maisuradze,
an employee of the Soviet Committee for State Security, a historian by profession, who had worked in
Jordan. See Roin Metreveli, "Mogoneba" [Memoir], *The Criminologist* 1 (2016–17): 138–39. Shihan
Mountain "overlooks the Wadi al-Mujib (the Arnon) and the Dead Sea. Its summit is occupied by ruins
and caves": Fawzi Zayadine, "The Karak District in the Madaba Map," in *The Madaba Map Centenary,
1897–1997,* ed. M. Piccirillo and E. Alliata (Jerusalem, 1999), 229. On top of the hill the remains of a
large monastery complex are located, surrounded by a rectangular 60 × 40 m. wall (width 1.3 m.). Inside
are the ruins of a church, with a semicircular apse facing east, and a water cistern. On the opposite west
side is a small rectangular building, thought to be a tomb. Along the southern foot of the hill, a basalt
fence separates the area from a Muslim cemetery. Coordinates: 31° 22′ 46.99″ N; 35° 44′ 13.06″ E.
See Thomas M. Weber-Karyotakis and Ammar Khammash, *Islamic Heritage Sites in Jordan* (Amman,
2020), 423. The National Agency for Cultural Heritage Preservation of Georgia, in agreement with the
Kingdom of Jordan and with the participation of local specialists, is planning an expedition to explore
Mount Shihan and look for the monastery.

[32] Metreveli, "Shehanis udabno," 42–43.

[33] *Dzveli kartuli agiographiuli literaturis dzeglebi* [Monuments of Old Georgian Hagiographic
Literature], ed. Ilia Abuladze, 6 vols. (Tbilisi, 1963–89), 4:346.

Recently, on the basis of information on commemorative *agapes*[34] attached to another Georgian manuscript (H–886) copied in Jerusalem in the twelfth century, Temo Jojua studied the history of the Georgian noble house of the Sanivajisdzes. Saba-Sanivaji, a member of this family whose monastic name was *Saba*, spent the end of his life in the Holy Land. Saba-Sanivaji must have been a descendant of Gabriel, and father of Joseph and John. During his time in Jerusalem, Saba founded another Georgian monastery, so far unidentified, and the community of this new monastery established for him a funeral *agape* on the feast day of his namesake, Saint Sabbas the Sanctified (December 5) (56v–57r).[35] The H–886 Synaxarion was copied in this monastery, the founder and benefactor (*ktetor*) of which was Saba-Sanivaji.[36] His son Joseph served in the same monastery, on whose name another commemoration was established (73v).[37]

Comparison of the Georgian and Latin Sources

A comparison of the Georgian material offered here with the document discussed above may provide a definitive answer to the questions raised. According to the Georgian sources, Gabriel Tpileli, bishop of Tbilisi and later a member of the monastic community of the Cross in Jerusalem in the middle of the eleventh century, founded the Transjordanian Georgian monastery close to the Arnon River (Wadi al-Mujib). By 1061 Gabriel held the position of head of this monastic community. A scriptorium operated there, and in the first half of the twelfth century the grandchildren of Gabriel Tpileli – Joseph and John – worked in the monastery. The son of Gabriel was Saba-Sanivaji, who was the founder of another Georgian monastery in Jerusalem.[38]

We learn from the Latin document that King Baldwin II confirmed Saba-Sanivaji's (*Saba Georgii*) possessions in Jeham. These possessions consisted of: 1) the settlement named Hara located across the river, on the plain at the foot of Mount Moses; 2) St. Moses Church in Jeham; and 3) other assets on both banks of the river. Some time later, Joseph and John, the grandchildren of Gabriel Tpileli and

---

[34] A memorial feast for the deceased, intended for the monastic community.

[35] Temo Jojua, "Tsagvleli Basil Mjobaisdzisa da Eptvimes mier Mariam Mogelis dakvetit Ierusalimshi gadatserili XII saukunis svinaqsris (H–886) ucnobi anderdzebi, agapebi da minatserebi (teqstebis publikacia; kodikologiuri da istoriul-tskarotmcodneobiti gamokvleva)" [Unknown Testaments, Commemorative Agapes and Colophons from the Twelfth-Century Synaxarion (H–886) Copied by Basil Mjobaisdze from Tsagvli and Eptvime in Jerusalem on the Commision of Mariam Mogeli (Publication of Texts, Codicological, Historical and Source Study Research)], *The Proceedings of the Institute of History and Ethnology* 14–15 (2016–17): 198–202.

[36] Jojua, "Tsagvleli Basil Mjobaisdzisa da Eptvimes," 180.

[37] Ibid., 200–202.

[38] Metreveli, "Shehanis udabno," 23–43; Jojua, "Tsagvleli Basil Mjobaisdzisa da Eptvimes," 180, 198–202.

sons of Saba-Sanivaji, handed over to the Hospitallers the settlement of Hara and the Church of St. Moses located in Jeham.

Undoubtedly, Jeham or the St. Moses Church donated by the brothers Joseph and John, sons of *Saba Georgii* or Saba-Sanivaji, is the Georgian monastery of Shehan. The same document also clearly indicates that the Georgian monastery of Shehan was named after Moses and that the properties of Saba-Sanivaji and his children were not limited to the settlement of Hara and the monastery at Jeham, but that they also owned other assets on both banks of the River Arnon. It also appears that the Georgians handed over to the Hospital not only the settlement (Hara), but also the Shehan Monastery (Jeham).

As can be seen, the places mentioned in the document are not located in Wadi Musa. However, an interesting episode related to Wadi Musa sheds light on the relationship of the Franks and the Eastern Christians. Albert of Aachen mentions that Baldwin I learned from a certain Syrian, Theodore, that 3,000 Turks had moved from Damascus to the "ancient Valley of Moses" in order to establish a castle. On February 28, 1107, Baldwin set off with 500 soldiers to destroy the fortress. It took Baldwin eight days to cross the rivers of Sodom and Gomorrah and, exhausted, he reached the dwelling place of the Syrian Christians, where he was received with dignity. The local priest accompanied the king on a three-day journey and brought him safely to a place near the fort and the Turks. The same priest came to the Turkish camp at dawn and told them that King Baldwin was approaching with an enormous army to destroy them. The frightened Turks left their tents and fled. The local Arabs, on whose advice the Turks had come from Damascus, hid in caves. With fire and smoke, Baldwin forced the Arabs out of their shelter, killing some and capturing others.[39]

It is believed that in 1107 the aforementioned Eastern Christians and their priest, who guided and assisted Baldwin I, lived in Wadi Musa, identified as Jeham.[40] According to Albert, these Christians lived three days away from Wadi Musa, where the Muslim stronghold was located, which excludes their presence in the Valley of Moses.[41] Since it has been clarified that Jeham was located in Mount Shihan and not in Wadi Musa, the question arises as to whether this priest was from Shihan. This question has to be answered in the negative, because the location of Shihan does not coincide with the route of the Frankish expedition: to reach Wadi Musa, Baldwin I crossed the Dead Sea from the south,[42] and returned to Jerusalem taking the north road and crossing the Jordan. Therefore, the location of the settlement of

---

[39] AA, X.28–30, 744–47.

[40] See, for example, Pringle, *Churches*, 2:376–77.

[41] Even if Albert of Aachen was mistaken regarding the distance, it is still clear from the narrative that the Christian settlement was quite distant from Wadi Musa.

[42] The rivers of Sodom and Gomorrah mentioned by Albert should be sought south of the sea because the crusaders believed that Sodom and Gomorrah were situated to the south of the Dead Sea. See Claude R. Conder, *Tent Work in Palestine: A Record of Discovery and Adventure*, 2 vols. (London, 1878), 2:13; see also Frederick G. Clapp, "The Site of Sodom and Gomorrah: Diversity of Views," *American Journal of Archaeology* 40/3 (1936): 323–44, at 323.

the Eastern Christians referred to by Albert of Aachen remains unclear. At the same time, this episode may still be somewhat related to Shehan. Albert writes: "When these things were successfully done, the king, with all his army and the booty he had taken, assembled from places all over the region Syrian brothers and fellow Christians and he took some sixty of them with him on account of their fear of the Arabs, and returned as far as the River Jordan."[43] The gathering of Christians from all over the region means that the Georgian brothers of the Shehan Monastery may have been amongst them, especially since the Franks passed so close to Shihan on their way back. According to Sinibaldi, Albert in this passage distinguishes between two groups of Christians, the Syrians and the "fellow Christians," who, in her opinion, may have been in closer relationships to the Franks.[44] The Georgian monks could have been included in this category.

The Significance of Transjordan

The Shehan Monastery was located near the main caravan route, the King's Highway (*darb al-malik, darb al-sultan*) connecting Egypt and the Hijaz with Syria, upon which many merchants and Muslim pilgrims passed through. The annual Hajj caravan traffic would be interrupted only during the ongoing unrest and war in the region.[45] The kings of Jerusalem consistently pursued a policy of seizing and consolidating their rule in Transjordan. The Franks had begun a exploration across the Jordan very early.[46] In 1100, Baldwin I, with 150 knights and 500 infantry, invaded the Dead Sea area and Wadi Musa,[47] where he met with no resistance, meaning that at this time the Muslims did not hold garrisons in that region.[48] In 1107, Atabeg Toghtekin of Damascus sought to amend this situation and sent the Turkmen amir al-Ispahbad with his military detachment to the Valley of Moses.[49] With the help of a local Christian priest, Baldwin I drove them out of the region.[50] In 1112, Baldwin raided the Valley of Moses with 200 horsemen and 1,000 infantry and captured a rich caravan.[51] The first castle in Transjordan, from which the

---

[43]   AA, X.31, 746–47.

[44]   Sinibaldi, "Settlement in Crusader Transjordan," 191.

[45]   Robert Schick, "Southern Jordan in the Fatimid and Seljuq Periods," *Bulletin of the American Schools of Oriental Research* 305 (1997): 76–78; Marcus Milwright, *The Fortress of the Raven: Karak in the Middle Islamic Period (1100–1650)* (Leiden, 2008), 10–11.

[46]   For an overview of the early crusader period of the region, see Schick, "Southern Jordan in the Fatimid and Seljuq Periods," 78–81.

[47]   FC, pp. 370–84; AA, VII.38–42, 542–51.

[48]   Schick, "Southern Jordan in the Fatimid and Seljuq Periods," 79; Mohammed Al-Nasarat and Abd Alrzaq Al-Maani, "Petra During the Crusader Period from the Evidence of al-Wuayra Castle: A Review," *Mediterranean Archaeology and Archaeometry* 14/1 (2013): 223–24.

[49]   *The Damascus Chronicle of the Crusades*, extracted and translated from the Chronicle of Ibn Al-Qalānisī by H. A. R. Gibb (London, 1932), 81–82.

[50]   See above, AA, X.28–30, 744–47.

[51]   *The Damascus Chronicle of the Crusades*, pp. 130–31; AA, XII.8, 834–37.

Franks began to take control of the region, was Montreal, which Baldwin I had built and garrisoned at Shaubak in 1115.[52] In 1127, Baldwin II raided Wadi Musa and suppressed the local Muslims.[53] It seems that during this period (1127–31) the Franks built *Castellum Vallis Moysis* there, later referred to as al-Wuʿaira castle.[54] William of Tyre wrote that in 1144, after a revolt by the local population, the Turks captured the castle. The reaction of the Franks was immediate, and under the command of Baldwin III they regained the castle.[55] During the reign of Fulk of Anjou, in 1142, Pagan the Butler, lord of Transjordan, built the castle of Kerak[56] which for centuries remained the principal fortress of the region.[57]

Dating of Key Documents

The dating of two documents discussed above has to be ascertained. The first is the grant of Baldwin II to Saba-Sanivaji, the other is the donation of Joseph and John to the Hospitallers. I will start with the latter. As already mentioned, the document is only conditionally dated to 1160. This fact, considering the life expectancy of the three generations of the Georgian family, allows me to reconsider the dating: the patriarch of the family, Gabriel, was hegumen of Shehan already in 1061. Before that, he had sired his son (Saba) and served as Bishop of Tbilisi, which makes it likely that he was born in the first or second decade of the eleventh century. His son must have been born in the 1040s (at the latest) since by 1061 Gabriel would have had a son, become the bishop of Tbilisi, travelled to the Holy Land, and founded the Shehan Monastery.[58] Baldwin II could confirm the ownership of Saba only after 1118. Before this, Saba must have witnessed the birth of two of his children (probably in the 1070s), set out for Jerusalem, and become first the *ktetor* of the Georgian monastery, then the patron of Shehan. If the donation to the Hospitallers had been drawn up in 1160, Joseph and John would have been about 90 years of age, which seems unlikely. It is, therefore, highly probable that the donation of the property by the Georgian brothers to the Hospitallers took place in the 1150s or even in the 1140s.

The dating of the grant by Baldwin II to Saba-Sanivaji should also be revised. Based on the location at Wadi Musa, Mayer dated it to the last years of Baldwin II's reign (1127–31): according to Ibn al-Qalanisi, the area around Petra was in the

---

[52] FC, pp. 592–3; WT, p. 535.

[53] *The Damascus Chronicle of the Crusades*, 182.

[54] Probably on the site of the Muslim fortress which was conquered in 1107 by Baldwin I. Denys Pringle, *Secular Buildings in the Crusader Kingdom of Jerusalem: An Archaeological Gazetteer* (Cambridge, 1997), 105.

[55] WT, pp. 721–2.

[56] Ibid., pp. 703–4, 1056.

[57] For the history of the castle, see Milwright, *The Fortress of the Raven*, 29–52.

[58] It should be noted that high-ranking ecclesiastical or secular persons often travelled to the Holy Land in their old age to become monks and find their eternal resting place there.

hands of the Muslims in H. 521, in the month of Sha'ban (August 12 – September 9, 1127), which gives us the lower chronological limit, whereas the upper limit was the king's death in 1131.[59] In light of the discussion above, ascribing the document an earlier dating to the first years of Baldwin's reign seems more probable given Saba's age. It seems most likely that the document was issued right after Baldwin ascended the throne, on April 14, 1118, when "all the nobles of the kingdom were called together in the palace of King Solomon, and he granted each his fief, receiving fealty and an oath of allegiance from them, and sending each back home with honour."[60] It might have been at this time that Saba the Georgian received the charter under the royal seal concerning his property.[61]

Chronology of the Shehan Monastery

After the twelfth century the Shehan Monastery no longer appears in manuscripts from Jerusalem. The manuscript copied in Shehan (Jer. 50) was already in the Monastery of the Cross by the end of the thirteenth century, and in the fifteenth century the name of *Shehan* seems to be all but forgotten in the Monastery of the Cross and is misspelled *Shpnisa*. For this reason, Metreveli dated the existence of the Shehan Monastery between the eleventh and thirteenth centuries.[62] Gagoshidze suggests that Shehan was abandoned because of the Mongol campaigns.[63] Considering the charter to the Hospitallers, it can presently be concluded that the Shehan Monastery ceased to exist in the middle of the twelfth century, when it was handed over by the Georgian brothers to the Order of the Hospital.

Parish Church?

The notion that the St. Moses Church in the village of Hara served as the parish church cannot be sustained.[64] Mayer has argued that the Church of Moses was the only parish church known to us from the Crusader era on the Eastern bank of the Jordan.[65] Strictly speaking, St. Moses Church is mentioned as situated not in the village of Hara, but above it, on Mount Moses, in Jeham. In reality, Shehan was a monastery, and given the strict regulations of Orthodox monasteries restricting

---

[59] Mayer, *Die Kreuzfahrerherrschaft Montréal*, 99; Mayer, *Urkunden*, 1:287.

[60] AA, XII.30, 872–73.

[61] Though not a fief holder, Saba the Georgian might have sought an affirmation of his privileges and property from the new king, as it was the practice in feudal Georgia.

[62] Metreveli, "Shehanis udabno," 30.

[63] Iulon Gagoshidze, "Tsminda mitsaze kartuli sidzveleebis arqeologiuri gatkhrebis perspeqtivebi" [Perspectives of Archaeological Excavation of Georgian Antiquities in the Holy Land], *Academia* 5 (2003): 12.

[64] Mayer, *Die Kreuzfahrerherrschaft Montréal*, 98; Pringle, *Churches*, 2:377.

[65] Mayer, *Die Kreuzfahrerherrschaft Montréal*, 98.

the entry of foreigners, it is doubtful that the Georgian monastery functioned as a parish church.

Casale – a Village or a House?

What type of settlement is the *casal(l)e* mentioned in the document – a small house or a village? I lean more towards the village, as the name of the casale is clearly mentioned in the document, and this should mark a larger and more important settlement than only a detached house. In addition, it is known that Georgian monasteries owned villages in the Holy Land, which were one of their sources of income.[66] In this case, arguably, this toponym must have indicated a village-type settlement.

Pringle shares Mayer's view according to which the village east of the river was inhabited by Eastern Christians and ruled by Saba, who acted as steward to the king of Jerusalem.[67] The approval by Baldwin II of Saba as steward meant that the Franks' possessions extended to the Arnon Valley and the land of Moab from the beginning of their rule, and that these lands belonged to the royal domain. It is clear from Georgian sources that *Saba Georgii*, who was confirmed as steward of the Eastern Christian settlement in Shehan by Baldwin II, is in fact Saba the Georgian. Saba-Sanivaji was a member of a powerful noble family: son of the bishop of Tbilisi, and himself the founder (*ktetor*) of an unknown Georgian monastery in Jerusalem. By the time Baldwin II granted Shehan monastery to Saba, it was already a complex of settlements, with a monastery on the mountain, a village at its foot, and estates spread on both banks of the Arnon River. This property seems to have been, at least in part, a paternal inheritance, having been originally acquired by Gabriel of Shehan. Given Saba's activities in Jerusalem as a founder, it is quite probable that after his arrival in the Holy Land, he would add the new properties to the Shehan.

Toponyms

The toponym Shihan must be related to the biblical Sihon the Amorite, king of Heshbon. The Arabic equivalent of *Sihon* is *Shihan*.[68] In the nineteenth century, Henry Baker Tristram, a scholar and a canon, associated Sihon with Mount

---

[66] Gotcha Djaparidze, *Kartvelta savaneebi da samonastro temi tsminda mitsaze XI–XVIII saukuneebshi (arabuli naratiuli da dokumenturi tskaroebis mixedvit)* [The Georgian Monasteries and Monastic Community in the Holy Land in the 11th–18th Centuries (According to the Arabic Narratives and Documentary Sources)] (Tbilisi, 2018), 128–29.

[67] Mayer, *Die Kreuzfahrerherrschaft Montréal*, 99; Pringle, *Churches*, 2:377.

[68] *Cambridge Bible for Schools and Colleges: The Book of Deuteronomy*, revised with introduction and notes by George Adam Smith (Cambridge, 1918), 40, n. 26.

Shihan.[69] We learn from the Latin document that the Shehan monastery was located on St. Moses Mountain. Why was Shihan called Moses Mountain? In the thirteenth century, as mentioned by the Arab geographer Yaqut al-Hamawi (1179–1229), the tomb of Moses[70] was thought to have been located on a mountain near the village of Seihan in Moab. Metreveli maintained that Yaqut was mistaken in attributing the legends surrounding both Mount Nebo and the tomb of Moses to Mount Shihan.[71] However, the name of the mountain, confirmed in the document, shows that in the Middle Ages there was indeed a legend that linked the tomb of Moses to Mount Shihan and Yaqut apparently relied on it. This tradition is also narrated by the Persian traveler al-Harawi (d. 1215), who wrote that "there is in this country a village called Shihan famous for a tomb where light descends and is observed by the people. It is situated on a mountain, and people pretend it is the tomb of Moses son of ʿImran ...". This is also confirmed by al-Umari (1301–49).[72]

The name of the settlement at the foot of Mount Shihan – Ara (Hara) seems to be more problematic. The Onomasticon by Eusebius of Caesarea refers to the place in Moab as Aiē, and in Arnon as Ar.[73] The first must be the Areopolis in the Roman province of Arabia, which is associated with Ar Moab, the present-day Rabba (ancient Moab). On the sixth-century Madaba Mosaic Map the settlement in this area is marked as Aia.[74] Abulfeda, the scholar and geographer of the Mamluk era, mentions Rabba and Shihan Mountain as located side by side.[75] However, Rabba is not situated at the foot of Mount Shihan but is about twenty kilometres to the south. We would propose that the Aiē (Aia), and Ar gave birth to names transformed into Arabic as Ara (Hara).

The firmans of the Mamluk sultans concerning the Georgian monastic community in the Holy Land are kept in the Library of the Greek Orthodox Patriarchate of Jerusalem. The firmans issued by Qansuh al-Ashrafi on 9 September 1498, and by Tuman-Bay on 19 December 1500, forbade any persecution against the Monastery

---

[69] H. B. Tristram, *The Land of Moab: Travels and Discoveries on the East Side of the Dead Sea and the Jordan* (London, 1873), 122.

[70] N. A. Mednikov, "Palestina ot zavoevania ee arabami do krestovikh pokhodov po arabskim istochnikam" [Palestine from the Arab Conquest to the Crusades according to the Arabic Sources], *Orthodox Palestinian Collection* XVII/2 (3), no. 50 (1897), 1051; Zayadine, "The Karak District in the Madaba Map," 229–30.

[71] Metreveli, "Shehanis udabno," 41.

[72] Zayadine, "The Karak District in the Madaba Map," 229–30. Interestingly Zayadine notes that "a monastery on Jabal Shihan occupied by Russian/Georgian monks was mentioned in the last century by travelers" (ibid., 230). This indicates that in the nineteenth century there was still a functioning monastery on Mount Shihan. In 1872, H. B. Tristram's expedition found only ruins on the mountain: Tristram, *The Land of Moab*, 122–23.

[73] *The Onomasticon of Eusebius Pamphili: Compared with the Version of Jerome and Annotated*, trans. Carl Umhau Wolf (Washington, DC, 1971), 4.

[74] Ibid., 81–82.

[75] "There is a very high hill near Ar-Raba, which can be seen from afar, and its name is Sheihan": Mednikov, "Palestina ot zavoevania ee arabami do krestovikh pokhodov," 1149.

of the Cross and its monks.[76] The same firmans make clear that several villages, including Dayr Musa, belonged to the Monastery of the Cross. The location of Dayr Musa has not yet been identified. It can be cautiously argued that Dayr Musa, i.e. the settlement where the monastery of Moses was situated, might have been the village near Shehan Monastery, which, as we know, was named after Moses. Did the village become the property of the Monastery of the Cross under Muslim rule, as a formerly Georgian-held property that had been deserted? Contrary to this identification is the fact that the toponym Shehan was completely forgotten in the Monastery of the Cross in the fifteenth century and was misspelled as "Shpnisa," as noted above. This raises doubts regarding the presence of such a tradition of rural ownership and claims regarding Dayr Musa. However, if the village was renamed Dayr Musa whilst being in the hands of the Muslims after the Frankish occupation, this assumption would still remain valid.

Circumstances of the Transfer of Shehan to the Hospitallers

The transfer of Shehan to the Hospitallers might have been caused by a variety of reasons. A significant factor would have been that the two brothers who owned the monastery were quite old at that time and they had already retired from active life. They might not have had a worthy successor either from the monastery fraternity or from their own lineage. At the same time, they had another monastery, built by their father, in Jerusalem, which also required attention. It seems that the brothers must have made a choice in favor of the latter. The appearance of the commemoration for "weak Joseph"[77] in the Georgian monastery of Jerusalem, built under the patronage of Saba, must mean that the brothers had moved there from Shehan and Joseph ended his life in this monastery.

The deteriorating political situation could have also played a role in the process. From the middle of the twelfth century onwards, the strategic position of the Franks gradually deteriorated. In 1144, the Atabeg of Mosul, Imad al-Din Zengi, took Edessa. His successor Nur al-Din (1146–74) attacked the crusader states even more actively. In 1149, he defeated and killed the prince of Antioch, Raymond of Poitiers, and in 1154, he conquered Damascus. In 1161, Nur al-Din captured Raynald of Châtillon. In 1163, Nur al-Din was defeated near Tripoli, but the following year he defeated a Frankish, Byzantine, and Armenian coalition at Harim.[78] In such a tense situation, the protection of the border or internal territories required great

---

[76] Djaparidze, *Kartvelta savaneebi da samonastro temi tsminda mitsaze XI–XVIII saukuneebshi*, 128–29, 259.

[77] "On the same day [December 24] the prayers and agape on behalf of the weak Joseph" (73v): Jojua, "Tsagvleli Basil Mjobaisdzisa da Eptvimes," 171–72.

[78] Malcolm Barber, "The Career of Philip of Nablus in the Kingdom of Jerusalem," in *The Experience of Crusading vol. 2: Defining the Crusader Kingdom*, ed. Peter W. Edbury and Jonathan P. Phillips (Cambridge, 2003), 72; William of Tyre, *A History of Deeds Done Beyond the Sea*, trans. Emily A. Babcock and August C. Krey, 2 vols. (New York, 1943), 2:306.

effort, whereas the preparation and further maintenance of the fortresses needed considerable material resources and permanent garrison service. Therefore, border fortresses were given to the military orders to garrison and defend them. Thus in 1136, King Fulk handed over the castle of Bethgibelin to the Hospital to deter future Muslim invasions from Ascalon; in 1142–44, Count Raymond II of Tripoli presented a whole range of frontier fortifications, including Crac des Chevaliers, to the Hospital; and in the 1150s–60s, the Templars were given many fortresses (Tortosa, Arima, Chastel Blanc, Saphet, etc.).[79] The danger to Christians living east of the Jordan River would become especially acute after the capture of Damascus, when Nur al-Din's domain bordered Transjordan. The region was also attacked from the south. In 1158, the Egyptian army invaded the region and surrounded al-Wu'aira, but to no avail. Eight days later, they lifted the siege and pillaged the lands around Shaubak.[80] It is not accidental that donations to military orders took place in Transjordan in the 1150s. In 1152, Maurice, the lord of Transjordan, on the condition of aiding the defense of Kerak, handed over to the Hospitallers the lower bailey of Kerak castle, a house in Shaubak, two villages, and the right to sail on the Dead Sea.[81] One manifestation of this tendency must have been the fact that the Georgian brothers handed over their lands and monastery in Shihan to the Order of the Hospital.

Whatever the reason for the transfer of Shehan to the Hospitallers, it is difficult to overestimate the importance of this fact – the donation of an Eastern Christian monastery by Georgian monks to a Western Order – in the context of the interrelationship of different religions on the Holy Land.

Conclusions

The findings of this study are of consequence both for Georgian historians and for scholars of the Latin East. The research has revealed that:

1. *Saba Georgii* is Saba the Georgian and not Saba, son of George, and that from the middle of the eleventh century to the middle of the twefth century three (!) generations of one Georgian noble family lived and worked in the Holy Land. The family owned considerable property, bought lands and built at least two monasteries in this period.
2. The Shehan complex included St. Moses Monastery, the settlement Ara (Hara), and other estates on both banks of the Arnon River.
3. The village of Hara was located on the plain near Arnon, below Shihan Mountain.

---

[79] Adrian J. Boas, *Archaeology of the Military Orders: A Survey of the Urban Centres, Rural Settlement and Castles of the Military Orders in the Latin East (c. 1120–1291)* (Abingdon, 2006), 103.
[80] "Extraits d'Ibn Moyesser," in *RHC Or*, 3:472.
[81] Milwright, *The Fortress of the Raven*, 58–59.

4. There was no parish church in Jeham, but a Georgian monastery named after Moses was situated there.
5. Baldwin II appointed Saba the Georgian as his steward of the Eastern Christian settlement; this presumably happened in 1118.
6. This means that the crusader possessions in Transjordan, in the lands of Kerak and the valley of the Arnon were established in the early twelfth century.
7. The lands of Arnon, situated north of Kerak, belonged to the king and were not included in the lordship of Transjordan.
8. The donation to the Hospitallers must be dated to the 1140s or the 1150s.
9. Georgian monks handed over to the Order of the Hospital not only the village but also the Shehan Monastery.

According to Ellenblum, the Christian "political entities were led by the Frankish minority and by classes of local Christians (Armenians, Greeks, and, on rare occasions, also Syrians) which could be called the aristocracy."[82] Using the example of Shehan, we should also add Saba-Sanivaji, a Georgian lord, member of the Sanivajisdzes family, to the ruling class of the kingdom of Jerusalem.[83] The act of handing over Shehan to the Hospitallers shows the ease with which Orthodox Georgians could accomodate Western and crusader values.[84]

Mayer has attached great importance to the contents of the document for the study of the early expansion of the Franks to Transjordan, as well as to the fact that this region was controlled by the royal domain and not by the lordship of Transjordan.[85] The revision offered here allows an even broader perspective, presenting the process by which the kings of Jerusalem established relations with the local Christians and illuminates the impressive integration of the Eastern Christians not only with the royal power but also with the military orders. The voluntary transfer of the Orthodox monastery to the Catholic Order indicates a closer relationship between the representatives of these two confessions (at least, between the Franks and the Georgians) than has been assumed before. Considering the close contacts between the Georgian monastery of the Cross, the Franks and the Military Orders,[86] we see that this relationship was both deep and bilateral.

---

[82] Ronnie Ellenblum, *Frankish Rural Settlement in the Latin Kingdom of Jerusalem* (Cambridge, 1998), 37.

[83] In his feedback on an earlier draft of my paper, Professor Mayer pointed out that Saba was a lesser official, something like what is referred to in Latin charters from the crusader states as *dragoman* (estate manager). On the dragoman, see Jonathan Riley-Smith, "Some Lesser Officials in Latin Syria," *The English Historical Review* 87/342 (1972): 15–19.

[84] Interestingly, scholars consider a similar case which happened in the north of Acre in 1129, the transfer of a village to the Hospitallers by a local lord, as an example of borrowing cultural values of Western knights: E. A. Gurinov and M. V. Nechitailov, *Voiska i voini Latinskogo Vostoka: grafstvo Edesskoe* [Armies and Wariors of the Latin East: County of Edessa] (Moscow, 2017), 87; for the charter, see Mayer, *Urkunden*, 1:272.

[85] Mayer, *Die Kreuzfahrerherrschaft Montréal*, 99; Mayer, *Urkunden*, 1:287.

[86] See Mamuka Tsurtsumia, "Commemorations of Crusaders in the Manuscripts of the Monastery of the Holy Cross in Jerusalem," *Journal of Medieval History* 38/3 (2012): 318–34.

Appendix
Testaments, Commemorations and *Agapes*
from the Georgian Manuscripts of the Holy Land

Manuscript Jer. 42. Greek Patriarchate of Jerusalem. 11th c. (before 1061).

"Christ have mercy on Father Gabriel" (141v).
"Christ have mercy on Father Gabriel of Shehan" (164r).

Manuscript Jer. 50. Greek Patriarchate of Jerusalem. 11th c. (around 1065).

"It was written in the Holy Desert of Shehan during the time of Father Gabriel Tpileli, who built the Desert of Shehan. God forgive and give him what he deserves for his labour by the hand of most sinful Iovane. Forgive my hasty writing by God's grace" (67r).
"God, exalt Father Gabriel the builder of Shehan" (87v).
"Christ have mercy on Iovane, Gabriel" (163r).
"This book is from the Georgian monastery Shpnisa" (66v–67r).

Manuscript Géorgien 28. Bibliothèque nationale de France, Paris. 12th c.

"God, protect and have mercy on our brothers Joseph and John, the grandsons of Gabriel the builder of Shehan, and make them worthy of our brotherhood of the Cross and Shehan" (246v).

Manuscript H–886. Georgian National Centre of Manuscripts, Tbilisi. 12th c.

"On the same day [December 5] the agape on behalf of Saba-Sanivaji, the builder of the monastery. For it must be done each year with kind abundance, with many priests and the consolation of the poor" (56v–57r).
"On the same day [December 24] the prayers and agape on behalf of weak Joseph. Let it be as is established, as he was ordained as a monk on this day and made a vow to do so, and [let it be so] that God fulfils his desire" (73v).

The Sarcophagus of Templar Master Arnau de Torroja in Verona? Updated Results

Giampiero Bagni

University of Nottingham Trent/Università di Bologna
giampiero.bagni2@unibo.it

Abstract

In a previous article, in Crusades *17 (2018), I examined the recent discovery of a sarcophagus at the church of San Fermo Maggiore in Verona, which could potentially be identified with the tomb of Arnau of Torroja, Master of the Knights Templar (c. 1118–84). That article gave a brief outline of Arnau's career and explained why he came to Verona in 1184; it then followed the scientific trail linking him to the bones found in the tomb of San Fermo Maggiore. This article provides an update on the results of the analysis and research, which largely confirm this link.*

In *Crusades* 17 (2018), I wrote an article related to a 2016 discovery by parish priest Fr. Maurizio Viviani and volunteers from the Association of Catholic Templars in Italy. While repairing a wall in the churchyard of San Fermo Maggiore in Verona they found an imposing sarcophagus. Made of sandstone quarried in the nearby hills, the badly flaked tomb bears some illegible inscriptions. However, a well-preserved cross pattée with points inserted at both ends of the bottom arm (Figure 1), an image closely associated with Templar tombs, is also visible.[1] As argued below, there are powerful reasons to link this tomb to Arnau of Torroja, Master of the Knights Templar, who died in Verona in September 1184. My previous article gave a brief outline of Arnau's career and explained why he came to the city; it then followed the scientific trail linking him to the bones found in the tomb noted above. This article intends to update the results of the analysis and research which followed that publication, although Covid–19 restrictions considerably extended the timeline needed for this work.

This research required a multi-disciplinary approach, and so the help of the Bologna-based Scientific Committee for Research of Military-Religious Orders (Coordinamento Scientifico per le Ricerche sugli Ordini Religioso-Militari) was enlisted. The members of the investigating team were led by Committee Chair Mons. Fiorenzo Facchini, anthropologist and Professor Emeritus of Bologna University; Paola Porta, Professor of Christian and Medieval Archaeology at

---

[1] B. Capone, L. Imperio, E. Valentini, eds., *Guida all'Italia dei Templari* (Rome, 1996), 90–101; S. Sammarco, "La chiesa di Santa Maria di Norbello (Oristano): un probabile possedimento templare nel Giudicato di Arborea," in *Atti del XXXI Convegno di Ricerche Templari* (Tuscania, 2014), 171–99.

Fig. 1. The bones extracted from a sarcophagus discovered in Verona.
Photo taken by the author.

Bologna University; along with the author of this article, the Secretary of the
Scientific Committee.

    Initial inspection found that water had penetrated the sarcophagus, a circumstance
compatible with flooding, and that a hole would have enabled any objects, vestments
and valuables to be removed. The remains inside the tomb consisted of bones from
three skeletons: those of an elderly male at the bottom, of a woman in the middle

Fig. 2   The tomb of Guillem de Torroya (*bottom left*) in the cathedral of Tarragona.
Photo taken by the author.

and of a young male at the top; they were removed with the utmost care and respect for the deceased (Figure 1). C[14] analyses of bone fragments indicate the young male died around 1400 and the woman died in the early 1300s; the molar examined for the elderly male is datable to 1020–1220.[2]

With the support of Professor Carles Lalueza-Fox of the University of Barcelona, the team sent the femur of the elderly male to the Harvard Medical School in Boston for DNA sequencing and genome reconstruction for subsequent comparative testing.[3] The tests to verify whether the haplotype matches that of the Catalan population pointed to a positive correspondence. The extracted bone DNA needed another such sample for sequencing from a relative of Arnau to be sure of his identity. By considerable good fortune, further investigation found that Arnau's brothers, Pere and Guillem, are buried in their respective cathedrals in Zaragoza and Tarragona. While Pere's remains had been removed and reburied in a common reliquary containing the bones of other medieval bishops, Guillem's are still intact in his recently restored archbishop's tomb (Figure 2). Largely due to

---

[2] Centro di Datazione e Diagnostica – Unisalento (CEDAD), tests run on 7 December 2016 and commissioned by the Associazione dei Vincitori di Fossalta, Giampiero Bagni, president (Università del Salento, 2016).

[3] Carles Lalueza-Fox, Paleogenomic Lab, Istitut de Biologia Evolutiva, Universitat Pompeu Fabra, Barcelona.

Fig. 3   Piece of parchment from 1300 attesting that the bones of Guillem were moved
from another tomb.
Photo taken by the author.

the excellent work of, and collaboration with, genealogist Leticia Darna Galobart,
the team obtained permission from the current bishop of Tarragona to take a bone
sample from Guillem's remains.[4]

Guillem's tomb is in gothic style and thus from a period later than his death
in 1174. In fact, Guillem's remains were found in the cathedral, inside a stone
sarcophagus that was likely placed there in the fourteenth century, next to the high
altar, along with the sarcophagi of three other archbishops. On April 24, 2018, the
sarcophagus was opened and the body of Bishop Guillem was examined, and samples
of biological material taken. The very deteriorated bones found in the sarcophagus
had been collected in a linen bag from the fourteenth century and bore a fabric tag
where the words "Turre rubea" (Figures 3 and 4) are still legible. All this work was
supervised by Prof. Assumpció Malgosa Morera, a physical anthropologist at the
Universitat Autónoma de Barcelona. She immediately confirmed that "probably the
remains belonged to more individuals and the fact that the tomb was not the original
burial reduces the chances of finding the expected person. Unfortunately, a lot of
medieval tombs of important figures were desecrated in different periods ...."[5]

The sample was sent to the University of Rome for DNA comparison with
the sample of the person buried in Verona in order to verify if there were enough
common parts of the DNA to affirm that the two persons were brothers. This
analysis established that the sample from Verona was of good quality and 68
percent of the DNA was possible to map. The sample from Tarragona, however,

---

[4] L. Darna Galobart, "Descubrimientos después de una buena restauración en la Catedral de
Tarragona," in *Paratge: quaderns d'estudis de genealogia, heràldica, sigil·logràfica i nobiliària* 25–26
(2012–13): 361–68.
[5] E-mail information sent to the research group, dated 20 June 2018.

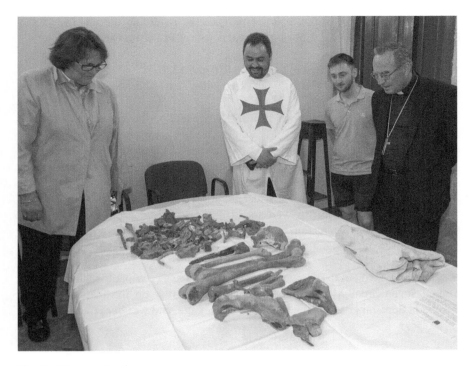

Fig. 4   The sample taken.
Photo taken by the author.

was of very low quality and it was only possible to sequence DNA from 22 percent of the sample.[6] Hence, it was impossible to determine the exact gender from the sample from Tarragona while the sample from Verona was certainly that of a male. From the limited part of the comparable DNA, it seems that the individuals did not have DNA in common, but this result is neither exhaustive nor decisive because of the poor quality of the Tarragona sample.

In the winter of 2019–20, another sample from Tarragona was requested, but the Covid-19 pandemic postponed the collection of this indefinitely. In the summer of 2019, another sample from the Verona tomb was sent to the University of Salzburg (Austria) to date the age of the skeleton buried and to study the deceased person's diet. The results revealed that the skeleton belonged to a person between 50 and 70 years old whose diet typically included fish.[7] This result is compatible with a Knight Templar living in the Holy Land.

---

[6] O. Rickards, "Analisi Preliminari effettutate sui repèerti attribuibili a Guillem de Torroja (T) e individuo rinvenuto a Verona (V)," formal e-mail communication (Università degli Studi di Roma "Tor Vergata," July 2019).

[7] D. Mattiangeli and J. Cemper-Kiesslich, "Wissenschaftlicher Vorbericht," formal e-mail communication, (University of Salzburg, July 2020).

Here is a summary of the information gathered regarding the remains of the elderly male buried in the imposing sarcophagus in San Fermo Church in Verona:

1. The skeleton can be dated to between 1020 and 1220.
2. The remains belonged to a male who died when he was between 50 and 70 years old.
3. The haplotypes tracked down in his DNA tended to be those typical of the Catalan population.
4. It was not possible to compare his DNA with that of his brother, Guillem, buried in the Tarragona cathedral, due to the deterioration of this second skeleton and the relocation of the original bones in the fourteenth century.
5. In the sarcophagus at Verona, under the most ancient skeleton of the elderly male, rich fragments of silk were found.
6. There is a strong connection between Templars and the medieval church of San Fermo (as explained in the first article).

In sum, the skeleton of the person buried in Verona seems compatible with the tomb of the Catalan Grand Master of the Templar Order, Arnau de Torroya, who died in Verona in September 1184, at around 70 years of age, and was buried in the city.

Papal Attitudes to Truces and Alliances between Christians and Muslims in the Iberian Peninsula in the Late Twelfth and Early Thirteenth Centuries

Alan Forey

University of Durham (Emeritus)
alan.forey@mybroadbandmail.com

Abstract

Pope Celestine III (1191–98) condemned both truces and alliances between Christian and Muslim rulers in the Iberian Peninsula, but Innocent III (1198–1216) was more ready to allow and even encourage truces. Papal action was influenced by various factors. The popes' interventions were dependent on the receipt of reports and petitions from the Peninsula, and Spanish rulers sought to manipulate the papacy in order to achieve their own ends. The two popes also had different crusading priorities. These matters do not, however, fully explain their differing approach. Innocent was more of a pragmatist than his predecessor, and was possibly also influenced by the views of decretists. Yet a more wide-ranging study, which takes account of varying circumstances, is needed before generalisations can be made about papal attitudes to truces and alliances with non-Christians.

It has long been recognised that truces and alliances were a common feature of relations between Christian and Muslim powers in the crusading period, and they have been discussed not only in general works on crusading in the Levant and the Iberian Peninsula but also in studies which focus specifically on this aspect of Christian-Muslim encounters.[1] The attitudes of popes to such truces and alliances between Westerners and non-Christians is a large topic which could be examined with reference to various frontier regions, including the Baltic as well as Iberia

---

[1] See, for example, Peter M. Holt, *Early Mamluk Diplomacy (1260–1290): Treaties of Baybars and Qalāwūn with Christian Rulers* (Leiden, 1995); Michael A. Köhler, *Alliances and Treaties between Frankish and Muslim Rulers in the Middle East: Cross-Cultural Diplomacy in the Period of the Crusades,* trans. Peter M. Holt (Leiden, 2013). Yvonne Friedman has written several articles on the subject, including "Peacemaking: Perceptions and Practices in the Medieval Latin East," in *The Crusades and the Near East*, ed. Conor Kostick (London, 2011), 229–57, and "Peacemaking in an Age of War: When Were Cross-Religious Alliances in the Latin East Considered Treason?" in *The Crusader World*, ed. Adrian Boas (Abingdon, 2016), 98–107. On the Iberian Peninsula, see María D. García Oliva, "The Treaties between the Kings of León and the Almohads within the Leonese Expansion Strategy, 1157–1230," *Journal of Medieval Military History* 15 (2017): 151–84. Robert I. Burns, "How to End a Crusade: Techniques for Making Peace in the Thirteenth-Century Kingdom of Valencia," *Military Affairs* 35 (1971): 142–48, discusses only surrender agreements.

and the Holy Land.[2] The present article will attempt to do no more than broach the subject by examining the papal stance regarding truces and alliances between Christian rulers in the Iberian Peninsula and the Almohads in the twenty-five years from 1191 until 1216. A survey of these years, which comprise the pontificates of Celestine III and Innocent III, reveals that, even in similar circumstances, not all popes adopted the same approach.

This was a period when the Almohads were the dominant power in Muslim Spain and North Africa, while Christian lands in the Peninsula were made up of five kingdoms. In the context of Christian-Muslim relations a truce signified merely a temporary cessation of hostilities between the Almohads and one or more Christian rulers,[3] and is to be distinguished from an alliance, which in the circumstances of the time implied a readiness on the part of a Christian ruler to fight alongside Muslims against another Christian kingdom; and this did commonly happen.

Celestine III was usually opposed to both truces and alliances with Muslim rulers. He sought to ensure that Christian kings did not make peace with the Almohads and that they always allied with each other against the infidel. In April 1191, less than a month after his election, he wrote to the archbishop and suffragans of Toledo, regretting that peace had not been made between Christian rulers in Spain, and that there was discord between them, while truces were being agreed with Muslims. He ruled that peace between Christians should be established for at least ten years and asserted that, while almost all Christendom wanted to avenge the loss of Jerusalem, Spaniards alone were allying with the infidel.[4] In a further letter to the archbishop in October of the following year, the pope threatened excommunication and interdict on those who did not agree to a peace for fifteen years between Christians and who did not fight against the Muslims; that truces with Muslims should not be made was implied, though not explicitly stated.[5]

In November 1193, when the Aragonese king was planning a campaign against the Muslims, the pope instructed Spanish prelates to order rulers who had

---

[2] Sophia Menache, "Pursuit of Peace in the Service of War: Papal Policy, 1198–1334," in *Religion and Peace: Historical Aspects*, ed. Yvonne Friedman (Abingdon, 2018), 115–28, focuses on peace within Western Christendom.

[3] In the Iberian Peninsula, as in the Holy Land, there could be no permanent peace with Muslim powers: cf. Jonathan Riley-Smith, "Peace Never Established: The Case of the Kingdom of Jerusalem," *Transactions of the Royal Historical Society*, 5th series, 28 (1978): 87–102.

[4] Juan F. Rivera Recio, *La iglesia de Toledo en el siglo XII (1086–1208)*, 2 vols. (Rome, 1966–76), 1:228–29; *Papsturkunden in Spanien. III. Kastilien*, ed. Daniel Berger, Klaus Herbers, and Thorsten Schlauwitz, Abhandlungen der Akademie der Wissenschaften zu Göttingen, Neue Folge 50 (Berlin, 2020), 488–89 doc. 265. In 1188, Clement III had already called for a ten-year peace between Christian rulers in the Peninsula: Rivera Recio, *La iglesia de Toledo*, 1:222–23; *Papsturkunden in Spanien. III*, 466–68 doc. 253.

[5] Rivera Recio, *La iglesia de Toledo*, 1:229–30; *Papsturkunden in Spanien. III*, 504–5 doc. 276. On Celestine's use of interdict, or the threat of interdict, in this context, see Carlos de Ayala Martínez, "El *Interdictum* eclesiástico en los reinos de León y Castilla hasta el IV Concilio de Letrán," in *Das Interdikt in der europäischen Vormoderne*, ed. Tobias Daniels, Christian Jaser, and Thomas Woelki, *Zeitschrift für Historische Forschung* 57 (Berlin, 2021), 375–411, here at 391–92, 395.

truces with Muslims to break them; if necessary, they were to be compelled by excommunication and interdict. He also decreed that, whatever kings did, their subjects, including the military orders, should continue to fight against the infidel; anyone seeking to prevent them was to be excommunicated.[6] When Gregory, cardinal deacon of Sant' Angelo and Celestine's legate in Spain, set out the terms for the peace between Alfonso VIII of Castile and Alfonso IX of Leon at Tordehumos in 1194, he warned against breaching these with the aid of Muslims.[7] These Iberian rulers swore to maintain peace between themselves and to fight against the Muslims for the following ten years, and in March 1195 Celestine sought to ensure that this undertaking was fulfilled.[8] On 10 July, only days before the Christian defeat at Alarcos, he further ordered Iberian rulers to observe the peace while Alfonso VIII was campaigning against the Almohads, complaining that "every time one of you plans to attack the pagans, others among you rise up in a hostile conspiracy against him" (*quotienscumque aliquis vestrum paganos infestare proponit, alii contra eum hostili conspiratione insurgunt*).[9] The accuracy of this statement was demonstrated in the succeeding years. In March 1196 the pope required Sancho VII of Navarre, who was then in alliance with the Almohads and who had been promised money by them on the condition that he would not assist other Christian rulers, to make peace with the latter and to fight against the Muslims.[10] In October of that year, he also ordered the excommunication of Alfonso IX of Leon who, instead of taking up arms against the infidel, had sided with the Muslims after the Castilian defeat at Alarcos and had attacked Castile, using Muslim troops. To those who took up arms against the Leonese king the pope offered the same remission of sins as was given to those

---

[6]   *Papsturkunden in Spanien. II. Navarra und Aragon*, ed. Paul Kehr, Abhandlungen der Gesellschaft der Wissenschaften zu Göttingen, Phil.-hist. Klasse, Neue Folge 22 (Berlin, 1928), 554–57 docs. 200, 201; see also *Gesta comitum Barcinonensium*, ed. L. Barrau Dihigo and J. Massó Torrents (Barcelona, 1925), 14, 48, 137.

[7]   Julio González, *El reino de Castilla en la época de Alfonso VIII*, 3 vols. (Madrid, 1960), 3:105–8 doc. 622; *Papsturkunden in Spanien. III*, 506–9 doc. 277. On Gregory's legations, see Kyle C. Lincoln, "'Holding the Place of the Lord Pope Celestine III': The Legations of Gregory, Cardinal-Deacon of Sant'Angelo (1192–4/1196–7)," *Anuario de historia de la iglesia* 23 (2014): 471–500.

[8]   Miguel Gómez and Kyle Lincoln, "'The Sins of the Sons of Men': A New Letter of Pope Celestine III concerning the 1195 Crusade of Alarcos," *Crusades* 16 (2017): 55–63, here at 62; *Papsturkunden in Spanien. III*, 510–12 doc. 279.

[9]   Piero Zerbi, *Papato, impero e "respublica Christiana" dal 1187 al 1198* (Milan, 1980), 179 doc. 1; Damian J. Smith, "The Iberian Legations of Cardinal Hyacinth Bobone," in *Pope Celestine III (1191–1198): Diplomat and Pastor*, ed. John Doran and Damian J. Smith (Farnham, 2008), 84–115, here at 109 doc. 1; *Papsturkunden in Spanien. III*, 514–15 doc. 282.

[10]   *Papsturkunden in Spanien. II*, 574–78 docs. 220, 221; Fidel Fita, "Bulas históricas del reino de Navarra en los postreros años del siglo XII," *Boletín de la Real Academia de la Historia* 26 (1895): 417–59, here at 418–20 doc. 1; idem, "Bulas inéditas. Sancho VIII, Duque y Rey de Navarra en 1196," *Boletín de la Real Academia de la Historia* 27 (1895): 223–34, here at 225–29 docs. 1, 2; *Archivo General de Navarra (1194–1236)*, ed. José M. Jimeno Jurío and Roldán Jimeno Araguren (Donostia, 1998), 14–15 doc. 9; *Colección diplomática medieval de la Rioja*, ed. Ildefonso Rodríguez de Lama, 4 vols. (Logroño, 1976–89), 3:148–49 doc. 368; Léon Cadier, "Bulles originales du XIIIᵉ siècle conservées dans les Archives de Navarre," *Mélanges d'archéologie et d'histoire* 7 (1887): 268–338, here at 293–95 docs. 4, 5.

fighting against the infidel. Celestine, in addition, threatened to release Alfonso's subjects from their obedience to their ruler.[11] In the following year the pope not only granted an indulgence to Sancho I of Portugal for taking up arms against Alfonso IX but also decreed that any Leonese territory which Sancho gained was to remain permanently under Portuguese control.[12] There is no evidence, however, to indicate that Celestine condemned the truce agreed by Alfonso VIII with the Almohads in 1197, and it has been suggested that the pope turned a blind eye to the Castilian king's action.[13]

Innocent III was less forthright in condemning truces with Muslims and even at times encouraged them, although on several occasions he expressed strong disapproval of alliances with the Almohads. In April 1198, he gave instructions that, if Celestine's legate Gregory had excommunicated Sancho of Navarre for breaching a peace with Castile, this sentence was to be publicized; and he added that if Navarre had allied with the Muslims, especially against Castile, the Navarrese king was to be censured and his kingdom placed under interdict.[14] He is not known, however, to have taken action in 1199–1201, when the Navarrese ruler, under attack from Castile, journeyed to Muslim territories to seek aid.[15] In February 1204, when Pedro II of Aragon was planning a campaign against the Muslims and requested the dispatch of a papal legate to bring peace between Christian rulers, the pope did not order other rulers to ally with the Aragonese king or to break any truces they had with the Almohads. He advised Pedro against launching an attack:

---

[11] Fita, "Bulas históricas," 423–24 doc. 3. On the situation after Alarcos, see Rodrigo Jiménez de Rada, *Historia de rebus Hispanie sive Historia Gothica*, 7.30, ed. Juan Fernández Valverde, CCCM 72 (Turnhout, 1987), 252; *Chronica Latina Regum Castellae*, ed. L. Charlo Brea, in *Chronica Hispana saeculi XIII*, CCCM 73 (Turnhout, 1997), 47–50; E. Lévi-Provençal, "Un recueil de lettres officielles almohades," *Hespéris* 28 (1941): 1–80, here at 66–67 doc. 35.

[12] *Papsturkunden in Portugal*, ed. Carl Erdmann, Abhandlungen der Gesellschaft der Wissenschaften zu Göttingen, Phil.-hist. Klasse, Neue Folge 20 (Berlin, 1927), 376–77 doc. 154; *Monumenta Henricina*, 15 vols. (Coimbra, 1960–74), 1:32–34 doc. 16; Smith, "Iberian Legations," 110 doc. 2. On early crusades against Christians, see Norman Housley, "Crusades against Christians: Their Origins and Early Development, c. 1000–1216," in *CS*, 17–36, although he does not allude to Celestine's decrees.

[13] Carlos de Ayala Martínez, "Holy War and Crusade during the Reign of Alfonso VIII," in *King Alfonso VIII of Castile: Government, Family and War*, ed. Miguel Gómez, Kyle C. Lincoln, and Damian Smith (New York, 2019), 118–42, here at 130.

[14] *La Documentación pontificia hasta Inocencio III (965–1216)*, ed. Demetrio Mansilla (Rome, 1955), 168–70 doc. 138; *Die Register Innocenz' III*, 1, ed. Othmar Hageneder and Anton Haidacher (Graz, 1964), 132–34 doc. 92; *Documentos pontificios referentes a la diócesis de León (siglos XI–XIII)*, ed. Santiago Domínguez Sánchez (Leon, 2003), 161–62 doc. 98; *Bulário Português: Inocêncio III (1198–1216)*, ed. Avelino Jesus da Costa and Maria Alegria F. Marques (Coimbra, 1989), 1–3 doc. 1.

[15] Rodrigo Jiménez de Rada, *Historia de rebus Hispanie*, 7.32, ed. Fernández Valverde, 254; *Chronica Latina Regum Castellae*, 50–51; Nevill Barbour, "The Relations of King Sancho VII of Navarre with the Almohads," *Revue de l'Occident musulman et de la Méditerranée* 4 (1967): 9–21; Jon A. Fernández de Larrea, "La conquista castellana de Alava, Guipúzcoa y el Duranguesado (1199–1200)," *Revista internacional de los estudios vascos* 45 (2000): 425–38; Anna Katarzyna Dulska, "Sancho el Fuerte y el Islam: las relaciones navarro-almohades a la luz de las fuentes cronísticas y documentales (s. XIII): mensaje ideológico y su lectura política," in *La Península Ibérica en tiempo de Las Navas de Tolosa*, ed. Carlos Estepa Díez and María A. Carmona Ruiz (Madrid, 2014), 425–39.

"we are not disposed to advise you to lead an army against the Saracens at the present time" (*tibi non duximus consulendum, ut hoc tempore contra Sarracenos exercitum duceres*). He was in favour of maintaining peace with the Muslims.[16] In the following year, as Castile had a truce with the Almohads, Innocent agreed that the orders of Santiago and Calatrava could fight on the Aragonese frontier. But when writing to these orders he added the words "if you consider it desirable" (*si ... videritis expedire*): he was not insisting on their doing so, and did not encourage them to break the truce. Nor did he make any adverse comment about the truce between Castile and the Muslims.[17] In a further letter sent at the same time to the archbishop of Compostela and the bishop of Tarazona, he expressed the need for peace between Christian rulers, as discord could endanger their kingdoms, but again he did not allude to truces with the Almohads.[18] Similarly, in 1206 Innocent did not condemn truces between Christians and Muslims in Spain when it was suggested that, because of these, the order of Calatrava should fight in the Holy Land; and again he did not advise the breach of truces.[19] In February 1210, when Castile still had a truce with the Almohads, Innocent did seek to persuade Alfonso VIII to follow Pedro II of Aragon's example in taking up arms against the Muslims, but he did not threaten censure if he failed to do so: he merely asked the Castilian king – if the latter was not prepared to fight – not to prevent his subjects from assisting the Aragonese ruler.[20] In December 1210, when the Infante Fernando of Castile was planning a campaign, Innocent did try to provide assistance against the Muslims, but only from those Spanish rulers "who are not committed to observing truces with them" (*qui non sunt cum illis ad treugas observandas astricti*). He was not insisting on the abrogating of agreements with the infidel.[21] Early in 1212, after

---

[16] *Documentación pontificia hasta Inocencio III*, 329–30 doc. 295; *Die Register Innocenz' III*, 6, ed. Othmar Hageneder, John C. Moore, and Andrea Sommerlechner (Vienna, 1995), 395–96 doc. 234. My interpretation of this document differs from that of Lucy K. Pick, *Conflict and Coexistence: Archbishop Rodrigo and the Muslims and Jews of Medieval Spain* (Ann Arbor, 2004), 37. Innocent advised Pedro merely to devote his life to God.

[17] *Documentación pontificia hasta Inocencio III*, 351 doc. 321; *Die Register Innocenz' III*, 8, ed. Othmar Hageneder and Andrea Sommerlechner (Vienna, 2001), 175–76 doc. 97; *Butllari de Catalunya: documents pontificis originals conservats als arxius de Catalunya (1198–1417)*, ed. Tilmann Schmidt and Roser Sabanés i Fernández, 3 vols. (Barcelona, 2016), 1:84–85 doc. 32. In a further bull, issued at the same time, Innocent alluded to Pedro II's plans to conquer Mallorca: *Die Register Innocenz' III*, 8:173–74 doc. 94; *Documentación pontificia hasta Inocencio III*, 349 doc. 318; *Butllari de Catalunya*, 1:84 doc. 31. In the Peninsula, military orders were expected to make both war and peace at the ruler's command: Hilda Grassotti, "El deber y el derecho de hacer guerra y paz en León y Castilla," in eadem, *Estudios medievales españoles* (Madrid, 1981), 43–132, here at 71–72; Alan Forey, "The Military Orders and the Spanish Reconquest in the Twelfth and Thirteenth Centuries," *Traditio* 40 (1984): 197–234, here at 220–21.

[18] Damian J. Smith, *Innocent III and the Crown of Aragon: The Limits of Papal Authority* (Aldershot, 2004), 270 doc. 8; *Butllari de Catalunya*, 1:86 doc. 34.

[19] *Documentación pontificia hasta Inocencio III*, 366–67 doc. 342.

[20] Ibid., 436 doc. 416; Javier Gorosterratzu, *Don Rodrigo Jiménez de Rada, gran estadista, escritor y prelado* (Pamplona, 1925), 411 doc. 1.

[21] *Documentación pontificia hasta Inocencio III*, 472–73 doc. 442; *Die Register Innocenz' III*, 13, ed. Andrea Sommerlechner and Herwig Weigl (Vienna, 2015), 272–73 doc. 181; Gorosterratzu,

the stronghold of Salvatierra, the headquarters of the order of Calatrava, had been lost and Alfonso VIII of Castile was organizing the campaign which culminated in the battle of Las Navas de Tolosa, the pope agreed to appeal for help in France and Provence, but also advised the Castilian king of the desirability of maintaining peace at that time with the Muslims in Spain: "we counsel and advise that if you can obtain a satisfactory truce, you should accept it, until there is a more opportune time when you can attack them with more confidence" (*consulimus et monemus, ut si competentes treugas inveneris, ipsas recipias, donec opportunius tempus adveniat, quo ipsos valeas securius expugnare*).[22] Two months later, however, in a letter to the archbishops of Toledo and Compostela the pope did order Spanish rulers to make peace with each other under pain of excommunication: they were to aid each other, and not ally with Muslims or give them counsel or aid. Alfonso IX of Leon was especially mentioned in this context.[23] Here the issue mainly concerned alliances of Christian and Muslim against Christian, but the letter was also implying that truces with the Almohads were to be eschewed.

When an explanation of the rulings of Celestine III and Innocent III is sought, it must first be remembered that popes were usually responding to reports coming from the Peninsula. They were dependent on incoming information and were, therefore, not always fully informed of all that was happening there. Thus Celestine III, who died in January 1198, may not have been apprised of Alfonso VIII's truce with the Almohads in 1197. The apparent lack of action by Innocent III against Sancho VII in the years 1199–1201 may also have been due to the absence of any communication about the Navarrese king from the Peninsula. If this interpretation is accepted, the actions of both popes become more consistent. As Innocent was taking measures against Sancho of Navarre in 1198, he would presumably also have acted in the following years if he had known of the Navarrese king's later links with the Almohads.

The source of reports is not always known: in some instances papal letters merely use words or clauses such as "we hear" (*audimus*) or "it has come to our attention" (*ad apostolatus nostri audientiam pervenit*), without stating who was the source of the information.[24] Reports were, however, frequently in the form of petitions, to which reference was made in papal replies. Papal rulings were inevitably influenced to a greater or lesser extent by the source and nature of a petition; and popes were in

---

Rodrigo Jiménez de Rada, 414–15 doc. 8; see also ibid., 415 doc. 9; *Documentación pontificia hasta Inocencio III*, 474–75 doc. 446; *Die Register Innocenz' III*, 14, ed. Andrea Sommerlechner et al. (Vienna, 2018), 6–7 doc. 3; *Bulário Português*, 293 doc. 152.

[22] *Documentación pontificia hasta Inocencio III*, 500–1 doc. 470; Gorosterratzu, *Rodrigo Jiménez de Rada*, 417 doc. 14; *Die Register Innocenz' III*, 14:240–41 doc. 154. For the preaching in France, see *Documentación pontificia hasta Inocencio III*, 497–98 doc. 468; Gorosterratzu, *Rodrigo Jiménez de Rada*, 417 doc. 15; *Die Register Innocenz' III*, 14:241–42 doc. 155.

[23] *Documentación pontificia hasta Inocencio III*, 501–2 doc. 471; Gorosterratzu, *Rodrigo Jiménez de Rada*, 416–17 doc. 13.

[24] *Papsturkunden in Spanien. III*, 488–89 doc. 265; Fita, "Bulas históricas," 423–24 doc. 3; *Documentación pontificia hasta Inocencio III*, 168–70 doc. 138.

these instances clearly not taking the initiative.[25] The request in 1206 that the Order of Calatrava should fight in the Holy Land was made by the abbot of the Cistercian monastery of Morimond, to which Calatrava was affiliated, and not by a Spanish ruler. It is therefore unlikely that on this occasion Innocent was asked to direct Iberian kings to break truces with the Almohads. When Celestine granted spiritual privileges and a right of conquest in Leon to Sancho I of Portugal in 1197, he was responding to a petition from the Portuguese ruler. Sancho was taking advantage of the papal stance about alliances with the infidel: the papal concession about conquered territories would otherwise probably not have been made.

Iberian kings were in fact at times seeking to manipulate the papacy by asking it to condemn truces and alliances between Christians and the Almohads when it was in their own interest, even though they themselves were ready on other occasions to enter into agreements with Muslims. Celestine's letters about Navarre and Leon in 1196 do not allude specifically to a petition from Castile, but it has been generally accepted that the pope had been approached on behalf of the Castilian king.[26] Yet, at the beginning of that decade Alfonso VIII had himself not only been ready to make a truce with the Almohads but had also been prepared to agree to fight alongside them against other Christian rulers.[27] At that time, as Leon was also at peace with the Almohads, Portugal had stood alone in bearing the brunt of Muslim attacks.[28] The Castilian king was also at peace with the Almohads from 1197 until 1210, and in the treaty of Calatayud in 1198 with Pedro II of Aragon the two kings agreed to act together in making truces with Muslims.[29] Pedro's father Alfonso II, on the other hand, had in 1193 sought to persuade Celestine to order Spanish rulers to break truces which they had with Muslims, and it was apparently at Pedro II's request that in February 1210 Innocent encouraged Alfonso VIII to follow the Aragonese king's example and fight against the Muslims.[30]

---

[25] In his discussion of Celestine's relations with Spain, Zerbi, *Papato, impero*, 149–67, does not attach sufficient weight to the importance of petitions and therefore tends to exaggerate the pope's role.

[26] González, *El reino de Castilla*, 1:720; José M. Lacarra, *Historia del reino de Navarra en la edad media* (Pamplona, 1975), 228; José Goñi Gaztambide, *Historia de la bula de la cruzada en España* (Vitoria, 1958), 100; Gonzalo Martínez Diez, *Alfonso VIII, rey de Castilla y Toledo* (Burgos, 1995), 75; Ayala Martínez, "Holy War and Crusade," 130. The pope's proposal in 1196 that Navarre should have a share of lands conquered from the Muslims was obviously not, however, part of Castilian plans.

[27] Lévi-Provençal, "Recueil de lettres," 64–65 doc. 34. This was before Celestine III became pope.

[28] On these campaigns, see Ambrosio Huici Miranda, "'Las campañas de Ya'Qub Al-Mansur en 1190 y 1191," *Anais*, 2nd series, 5 (1954): 53–74.

[29] Julio González, "Reclamaciones de Alfonso VIII a Sancho el Fuerte y tratado del reparto de Navarra en 1198," *Hispania* 3 (1943): 545–68, here at 562–68; idem, *El reino de Castilla*, 3:179–86 doc. 667.

[30] Cf. Damian J. Smith, "The Papacy, the Spanish Kingdoms and Las Navas de Tolosa," *Anuario de historia de la iglesia* 20 (2011): 157–78, here at 171. Pick, *Conflict and Coexistence*, 37–38, suggests that the papal letter in 1210 was sent on the initiative of the archbishop of Toledo, Rodrigo Jiménez de Rada; see also Peter Linehan, *Spain, 1157–1300. A Partible Inheritance* (Chichester, 2008), 46. The letter was addressed to the archbishop, and it would seem more likely that, if he had approached the pope, the latter would have written directly to the Castilian king.

Yet, as has been seen from Innocent III's letters, popes did not always accede to petitions, and papal actions were not influenced only by requests which were made to them. Celestine and Innocent had differing crusading priorities, which may help to explain their stance on the conflict with the infidel in Spain. Celestine III was elected during the Third Crusade, and the French and English kings were then still on their way out to the East. The early part of his pontificate was obviously not a favourable time for a major new initiative to recover Jerusalem; and although he later gave some support to the Emperor Henry VI's crusade in aid of the Holy Land, despite any misgivings he may have had about an imperial expedition, he did not seek help from the whole of Western Christendom.[31] It has been argued, in fact, that he favoured the Spanish Reconquest as a papally-backed rival to Henry's proposed crusade to the East,[32] although the emperor did not announce his plans until 1195, by which time Celestine's strong interest in the Iberian Peninsula had already become apparent. Yet, Celestine was certainly willing to allow men who had taken the cross for the Holy Land to fulfil their vows instead in the Peninsula.[33] Innocent, on the other hand, was in both the early and the later parts of his pontificate seeking to launch major expeditions to the East, and he described the liberation of the Holy Land as his "foremost concern" (*precipuum studium*).[34] It was for this reason that in 1213 he advised the archbishop of Narbonne to obtain truces in the conflict with the Albigensians,[35] and also sought to restrict recruitment for campaigns in Spain.[36] The war against heretics in the south of France itself influenced his attitude to the Spanish Reconquest, as is apparent from his request in 1209 that the Aragonese and Castilian kings should aid Simon de Montfort against the heretics, although the Holy Land remained his main priority: he informed Simon that he might have done

---

[31] Peter W. Edbury, "Celestine III, the Crusade and the Latin East," in *Pope Celestine III*, 129–35; Claudia Naumann, *Der Kreuzzug Kaiser Heinrichs VI* (Frankfurt, 1994), 79–83; Helmut Roscher, *Papst Innocenz III. und die Kreuzzüge* (Göttingen, 1969), 48–49.

[32] Zerbi, *Papato, impero*, 157; Francisco Ruiz Gómez, "La guerra y los pactos a propósito de la batalla de Alarcos," in *Alarcos 1195: Actas del Congreso Internacional conmemorativo del VIII centenario de la batalla de Alarcos*, ed. Ricardo Izquierdo Benito and Francisco Ruiz Gómez (Cuenca, 1996), 145–67, here at 152.

[33] Cadier, "Bulles originales," 292–93 doc. 3; *Papsturkunden in Spanien. II*, 572 doc. 217; *Colección diplomática medieval de la Rioja*, 3:147–48 doc. 367; *Archivo General de Navarra*, 13 doc. 8; see also Zerbi, *Papato, impero*, 180–82 docs. 2–3; *Papsturkunden in Spanien. III*, 518–21 docs. 285–86. The extent of Celestine's involvement in crusading in the Baltic is not altogether clear, but any papal action seems to have been in response to petitions; Celestine was not taking the initiative: Barbara Bombi, "Celestine III and the Conversion of the Heathen on the Baltic Frontier," in *Pope Celestine III*, 150–58.

[34] *Die Register Innocenz' III*, 1:661–62.

[35] PL 216:744–45; *The Cathars and the Albigensian Crusade: A Sourcebook*, ed. Catherine Léglu, Rebecca Rist, and Claire Taylor (Abingdon, 2014), 41–42.

[36] PL 216:817–22. Goñi Gaztambide, *Historia de la bula*, 132, exaggerates the long-term significance of this ruling. For a positive assessment of Innocent's contribution to the Spanish Reconquest, see Damian J. Smith, "'Soli Hispani'? Innocent III and Las Navas de Tolosa," *Hispania sacra* 51 (1999): 487–513.

more, had it not been for "the very pressing needs of the Holy Land" (*necessitatem urgentissimam terre sancte*).[37]

Some other possible factors also require consideration. In discussions of Innocent III's approach to crusading in Spain, it has been argued that he believed that the reform of the church and a society free from sin were prerequisites for the defeat of the Muslims.[38] In this context attention has been drawn to a letter which he sent in 1199 to the archbishop of Compostela and the bishops in the kingdom of Leon, when he was seeking to end the incestuous marriage of Alfonso IX and Berenguela, the daughter of Alfonso VIII. He argued that both in the East and in the West there had recently been incestuous marriages and that, "because of sins" (*peccatis exigentibus*), Muslims were in the ascendant. He mentioned that, following their marriages to Isabella, queen of Jerusalem, Conrad of Montferrat had been killed and Henry of Champagne had died. The letter clearly illustrates Innocent's view that defeat at the hands of the Muslims was occasioned by sin.[39] But in linking defeat with sin Innocent was obviously not expressing an isolated opinion: it was voiced after almost all crusading setbacks and disasters. In letters to the English clergy in 1193 and 1195, for example, Celestine III had himself discoursed at length about the reasons for losses in the Holy Land, mentioning those who had incurred "divine judgement against them for their wilful wrongdoing" (*divinum contra se suis perversitatibus judicium*) and asserting that Muslim conquests had been allowed "because in our time the evil of our contemporaries has grown so greatly" (*cum in diebus nostris in tantum excreverit malitia modernorum*), and similarly in letters relating to the Peninsula he stated that Christian success there had been hindered by sin.[40] It may be noted, however, that comments of this kind were normally expressed in the aftermath of disasters and that they did not usually inhibit the organising of new expeditions. The purpose of Celestine's letters in 1193 and 1195 was to seek assistance for the Holy Land, and Innocent III, despite setbacks, was quickly seeking to promote a new crusade to recover Jerusalem. A crusading expedition provided an opportunity for participants to redeem themselves. Innocent also – whatever the need for reform and whatever the lack of unity among Iberian kingdoms – gave support to some planned campaigns in the Peninsula, such as those of Pedro II in 1205 and 1210 and that of Fernando, also in 1210. It is further apparent that he did not always advise a particular Iberian ruler in the same way, as is clear from his letters to the Aragonese king; and he did not always advise truces. Innocent's letter in 1199 could, of course, be interpreted to imply that in the pope's

---

[37] *Documentación pontificia hasta Inocencio III*, 429–30 doc. 410; *Die Register Innocenz' III*, 12, ed. Andrea Sommerlechner and Othmar Hageneder (Vienna, 2012), 260–61 doc. 123.

[38] Smith, "'Soli Hispani'," 503–5; idem, "The Papacy, the Spanish Kingdoms," 162, 165.

[39] *Documentación pontificia hasta Inocencio III*, 209–15 doc. 196; *Die Register Innocenz' III*, 2, ed. Othmar Hageneder, Werner Maleczek, and Alfred A. Strnad (Rome, 1979), 2:126–34 doc. 72.

[40] Roger of Hoveden, *Chronica*, ed. William Stubbs, RS 51, 4 vols. (London, 1868–71), 3:200–2; Ralph of Diceto, *Historical Works*, ed. William Stubbs, RS 68, 2 vols. (London, 1872), 2:132–35; Gómez and Lincoln, "Sins of the Sons of Men," 62; *Papsturkunden in Spanien. III*, 510–12 doc. 279; *Papsturkunden in Spanien. II*, 574–76 doc. 200.

opinion the Leonese could achieve no victory against the Muslims while Alfonso IX was still married to Berenguela, but it was not linked to any proposed action – or inaction – against the Muslims in the Peninsula. It is to be seen primarily in the context of marital relations: Innocent was using suitable recent events to support his case for annulling the marriage.[41] In addition, it may be noted that early in his pontificate Innocent was planning a crusade to the Holy Land at a time when he was trying to persuade Philip II of France to take back his repudiated wife Ingeborg; and when the pope was beginning preparations for the Fifth Crusade, England was then still subject to the interdict which had been imposed in 1208. The extent of the difference between the two popes on these issues may be questioned, and it may be doubted whether their stance on moral issues helps to provide an explanation of their differing attitudes to truces.

Innocent's readiness to accept truces in the Iberian peninsula may, however, have been influenced in part by current legal opinion. The decretists, basing their arguments on the statement in the *Decretum* that faith promised to an enemy should be maintained, generally agreed that truces should be observed; and this notion was extended to relations between Christians and Muslims. Huguccio, who was teaching at Bologna when Innocent apparently studied there, argued that there could be faith between Christians and Muslims and that truces between them should be observed.[42] In this context it may be noted that, although he sought to initiate crusades in support of the Holy Land, Innocent was ready to accept the validity of truces between rulers of the crusader states and neighbouring Muslim powers. In a letter to the patriarch of Jerusalem and others in 1199, he alluded to a recent truce in the Holy Land with the Muslims, and stated that this had caused the enthusiasm of some in the West to wane. Yet, he did not express disapproval of it; he merely gave instructions about the distribution of supplies then being sent from the West.[43] It may further be pointed out that the date fixed by Innocent for the departure of the Fifth Crusade coincided with the end of a six-year truce made in 1211.[44] In the later years of his pontificate he was also seeking to use negotiation, as well as force, to recover the district of Jerusalem.[45] The attitude to truces in the Holy Land of Celestine III, who was a theologian rather than a lawyer, is not altogether clear: that made by Richard I in September 1192 is not mentioned in either of his letters to the

---

[41] When in 1266 Clement IV was seeking to castigate Jaime I of Aragon about his marital situation, he could not invoke recent military disasters, as Jaime had been instrumental in bringing Murcia back under Christian control; he alluded instead to the king's ultimate fate: *Documentos de Clemente IV (1265–1268) referentes a España*, ed. Santiago Domínguez Sánchez (Leon, 1996), 181–82 doc. 74.

[42] C. 23 q. 1 c. 3, in *Corpus Iuris Canonici*, ed. Emil Friedberg, 2 vols. (Leipzig, 1879–81), 1:892; Frederick H. Russell, *The Just War in the Middle Ages* (Cambridge, 1975), 105, 120. On Muslim views about truces with Christians, see Friedman, "Peacemaking: Perceptions and Practices," 229–31.

[43] PL 214:737–38; *Die Register Innocenz' III*, 2:345–46 doc. 180.

[44] Riley-Smith, "Peace Never Established," 100.

[45] Karl-Ernst Lupprian, *Die Beziehungen der Päpste zu islamischen und mongolischen Herrschern im 13. Jahrhundert anhand ihres Briefwechsels* (Vatican City, 1981), 110–15 docs. 3, 4; Roscher, *Papst Innocenz III. und die Kreuzzüge*, 147–48.

English clergy in 1193 and 1195.[46] He may have recognised that without assistance from the West in the early 1190s the crusader states could not easily pursue an aggressive policy. Yet, his letters indicate that he felt no qualms about breaking truces with Muslims in the Iberian Peninsula.

Breaches of truces could have practical consequences: they could, for example, lead to reprisals and might also encourage the abrogation of truces by the infidel. Innocent's letters about truces in the Peninsula certainly reveal that considerations of a practical nature, expressed in mundane terms, influenced his decisions. When writing to Pedro II in 1204, he advised the Aragonese king to keep the peace, since by attacking the Muslims "you would incite them to become even more hostile to Christians" (*eos contra christianos fortius excitares*). He also reminded the Aragonese king that the power of the Almohads was growing and mentioned their recent acquisition of Mallorca. He further referred to the lack of unity amongst Christian rulers in the Peninsula, and appears to have felt that the combination of growing Muslim strength and a lack of support among Christians would make success unlikely.[47] When advising Alfonso VIII to seek a truce with the Almohads in February 1212, he stated that "now almost the whole world is in tumult and beset by evil" (*nunc fere totus mondus turbatus est et positus in maligno*).[48] He was obviously not referring only to Spain, but did not elaborate further. As this comment was, however, made when he was agreeing to seek assistance in France and Provence, he may have been implying that, because of the war against the Albigensians, few would be recruited from these areas. He also alluded to the "misfortunes" (*infortuniis*) which Alfonso had recently suffered, and was probably alluding to the loss of Salvatierra as well as the death of Fernando in the previous year. He may also at that time already have been aware of the rumours which were circulating about the extent of Almohad ambitions. Certainly, two months later, in a letter to the archbishops of Toledo and Compostela, the pope wrote that the Almohads "not only seek the destruction of Spain but also threaten to unleash their savagery in other lands of the faithful and, if they can, which God forbid, extinguish the very name of Christ" (*non solum ad destructionem Hyspaniarum aspirant, verum etiam in aliis fidelium Christi terris comminantur suam seviciam exercere ac nomen, quod absit, si possint, opprimere christianum*).[49] Reports of these rumours

---

[46] Hoveden, *Chronica*, 3:200–2; Ralph of Diceto, *Historical Works*, 2:132–35.

[47] In 1211, when rejecting Alfonso VIII's request for a legate to be sent to the Peninsula, he alluded to "unpeaceful times" (*tempora impacata*), without fuller explanation, although on this occasion he did not seek to hinder Fernando's plans for a campaign: *Documentación pontificia hasta Inocencio III*, 475–76 doc. 447; Gorosterratzu, *Rodrigo Jiménez de Rada*, 415 doc. 10; *Die Register Innocenz' III*, 14:7–8 doc. 4. He made the same comment in a letter to the archbishop of Toledo and the bishops of Zamora and Coimbra sent at the same time: *Documentación pontificia hasta Inocencio III*, 474–75 doc. 446; Gorosterratzu, *Rodrigo Jiménez de Rada*, 415 doc. 9; *Die Register Innocenz' III*, 14:6–7 doc. 3.

[48] *Documentación pontificia hasta Inocencio III*, 500–1 doc. 470; *Die Register Innocenz' III*, 14:240–41 doc. 154.

[49] *Documentación pontificia hasta Inocencio III*, 501–2 doc. 471; Gorosterratzu, *Rodrigo Jiménez de Rada*, 416–17 doc. 13.

are found in numerous sources for the period,[50] and a version of an aggressive letter supposedly written by al-Nāṣir was copied into a Western chronicle.[51] Innocent may well have believed that not just the Iberian Peninsula was in danger. There were certainly other occasions when, after Christian setbacks there, popes alluded to the threat to those beyond the Pyrenees from Muslims in the Iberian Peninsula.[52]

By contrast, Celestine was not deterred by practical obstacles. He envisaged the possibility of success there. In 1195 he wrote that if it had not been for sin and the failure of Iberian rulers to maintain peace among themselves in the past "in the lands of Spain, on this side of the sea, there would be no corner left which was not under Christian rule" (*in cismarina terra Hispaniarum nec unus angulus remaneret, qui non esset Christianorum subditus potestati*).[53] He, therefore, sought to achieve his purpose by uniting Christian Spain against the infidel, and all necessary steps, including the breaking of truces, were to be taken for this end. It was, of course, common for Westerners, who were ignorant of the situation on the borders of Christendom and Islam, to wish to fight against, rather than treat with, the Muslims: the Templar master James of Molay, for example, said that when he and other young knights had first gone out to the East, they had wanted to engage in feats of arms and were dissatisfied with the master's readiness to observe a truce with the Mamluks; but in time they came to accept that a truce was necessary.[54] Celestine must, however, have been aware from the outset of the difficulties which he faced. Before he was elected pope, he had served as a diplomat and had experience of the situation in the Peninsula. He had been papal legate there in both the 1150s and the 1170s, and while in Spain he had been involved in matters relating to the Reconquest.[55] When he was encouraging Iberian rulers to take up arms against the Almohads early in his pontificate, he even felt it necessary to justify war against the Muslims: "Nor should anyone consider that this instruction which we have dispatched, about waging war against the Saracens and driving them out, is contrary to the catholic faith" (*Nec arbitretur aliquis hoc contra fidem catholicam esse mandatum, quod de persequendis et exterminandis Sarracenis emittimus*);[56] and the wording of his letter of 10 July 1195 shows his awareness

---

[50] On the rumours, see Martín Alvira Cabrer, "El 'desafío' de Miramamolín antes de la batalla de Las Navas de Tolosa (1212): Fuentes, datación y posibles orígenes," *Al-Qantara* 18 (1997): 463–90.

[51] *Annales Mellicenses: Continuatio Lambacensis*, ed. Wilhelm Wattenbach, MGH SS 9 (Hanover, 1851), 557–58.

[52] See, for example, *Documentos de Clemente IV*, 118–19 doc. 10; *Les registres de Clément IV*, ed. Edouard Jordan (Paris, 1893–1945), 7–8 doc. 19.

[53] Gómez and Lincoln, "Sins of the Sons of Men," 62; *Papsturkunden in Spanien. III*, 510–12 doc. 279.

[54] *Procès des Templiers*, ed. Jules Michelet, 2 vols. (Paris, 1841–51), 1:44–45; *Processus contra Templarios in Francia: Procès-verbaux de la procédure menée par la commission pontificale à Paris*, ed. Magdalena Satora, 2 vols. (Leiden, 2020), 1:98.

[55] Anne J. Duggan, "Hyacinth Bobone: Diplomat and Pope," in *Pope Celestine III*, 1–30, here at 5–6; Smith, "Iberian Legations," 81–111.

[56] Rivera Recio, *La iglesia de Toledo*, 1:229–30; *Papsturkunden in Spanien. III*, 504–5 doc. 276.

that unity was extremely difficult to achieve.[57] Yet, despite this knowledge, he still sought to achieve his aims.

The factors which have been discussed led Innocent to adopt a cautious and pragmatic approach to the Spanish Reconquest.[58] He adjusted his actions to the situation which existed within the Peninsula, rather than taking more positive steps to achieve unity amongst Christian kings: on two occasions – in 1204 and 1210 – he rejected requests for a legate to be sent to persuade them to act together against the infidel.[59] He regarded truces with the Almohads as legitimate and at times desirable: they were certainly not to be broken at will. He admittedly took stronger action in 1212, but this was only after Alfonso VIII had ignored his advice to seek a truce: in what was seen as a threatening situation, the pope had little choice but to give him as much support as he could. On the other hand, Celestine pursued a policy which was much more aggressive than that of his younger successor, and which included the prohibiting and breaking of truces with the Muslims. In contrast to Innocent's approach, it could be said to reflect a "triumph of hope over experience."

A wider study is obviously needed in order to judge how far the attitudes displayed by Celestine III and Innocent III were replicated at other times and in other areas. It is certainly not difficult to find echoes of both popes. In 1175, Alexander III had threatened with excommunication those Spanish rulers who did not terminate agreements with Muslims.[60] In 1225, Honorius III instructed the military orders to assist in the defence of the Castilian castle of Albocácer even if Spanish kings had truces with the Muslims. Six years later, however, Gregory IX told the military orders in the East not to break the truce which Frederick II had agreed with the sultan of Egypt.[61] Yet, the surviving evidence is not always as full as it is for the Iberian Peninsula during the two pontificates at the turn of the twelfth and thirteenth centuries. Nor were the issues always the same on all frontiers with non-Christians

---

[57]   See above, p. 53.

[58]   Giulio Cipollone, "Innocent III and the Saracens: Between Rejection and Collaboration," in *Pope Innocent III and his World*, ed. John Moore (Aldershot, 1999), 361–76, here at 367–68, refers to Innocent's flexibility in his dealings with Muslims; see also Roscher, *Papst Innocent III. und die Kreuzzüge*, 271–72, 288.

[59]   *Documentación pontificia hasta Inocencio III*, 329–30, 475–76 docs. 295, 447; *Die Register Innocenz' III*, 6:395–96 doc. 234; 14:7–8 doc. 4.

[60]   Fidel Fita, "Tres bulas inéditas de Alejandro III," *Boletín de la Real Academia de la Historia* 12 (1888): 164–68, here at 167–68; *Papsturkunden in Spanien. III*, 306–8 doc. 157. The wording "if any of you agree to a truce with the aforesaid Saracens, or aid them against Christians ..." (*si qui vero vestrum se predictis saracenis aliquo federe iunxerint, vel auxilium eis contra christianos prestiterint* ...) suggests that he was referring to truces as well as alliances. Alexander may have been advised at this time by the future Celestine III, who had recently returned from Spain. In 1147 both Eugenius III and St Bernard warned crusaders on the Wendish crusade against any agreement which allowed the pagans to retain their religion: Hans-Dietrich Kahl, "Crusade Eschatology as Seen by St Bernard in the Years 1146 to 1148," in *The Second Crusade and the Cistercians*, ed. Michael Gervers (New York, 1992), 35–47, here at 42–44.

[61]   *La Documentación pontificia de Honorio III (1216–1227)*, ed. Demetrio Mansilla (Rome, 1965), 421–22 doc. 569; *Epistolae saeculi XIII e regestis pontificum romanorum selectae*, ed. Carolus Rodenburg, 3 vols. (Berlin 1883–94), 1:345–46 doc. 427.

or at all times. In 1199, for example, Innocent III stated that force could be used in Livonia only if the pagans would not accept and observe peace agreements. But warfare in that region was commonly viewed by the papacy as having, at least in theory, a defensive purpose.[62] The situation was different from that in Spain, where the objective for the papacy was the recovery of lands which had earlier been Christian and the re-establishment of church organisation. A further factor was the situation in the neighbouring non-Christian world. At times when power in an adjacent non-Christian region was fragmented, alliances with non-Christian rulers could be beneficial in that they allowed Christians to play off one non-Christian ruler against another.[63] Differing circumstances would be expected to occasion differing responses, but the evidence concerning the Iberian Peninsula in the later twelfth and early thirteenth centuries reveals that even in the same situation not all popes acted in a similar way.

---

[62] Iben Fonnesberg-Schmidt, *The Popes and the Baltic Crusade, 1147–1254* (Leiden, 2007), 92.

[63] In the Holy Land, as in the Iberian peninsula, not all cross-religion alliances were of this kind: Friedman, "Peacemaking in an Age of War," 100–102.

The Reception of *Jihād* Literature in the Crusading Period

Benedikt Reier

Universität Hamburg
benedikt.reier@uni-hamburg.de

Abstract

This article re-examines two texts centred around the Islamic concept of jihād, *both written in the crusading period. Both of these texts, namely 'Alī b. Ṭāhir al-Sulamī's* Book of the Jihad *and Ibn 'Asākir's* The Forty Hadiths for Inciting Jihad, *are most often interpreted in light of a preconceived anti-crusader mindset of their authors and audiences without taking into consideration the broader context of their production and reception. This contribution aims at offering a reinterpretation of this view by discussing the specific production and usage contexts of these two books. It is argued that the two authors, their contemporaries, and scholars in subsequent centuries understood these books much more as part of the flourishing cultural practice of hadith transmission than as political or military "propaganda" endeavours. To this end, the two* jihād *texts are discussed in the broader context of their respective authors' biographies and their scholarly fields of activity. Second, the rather meagre audience of the two books is scrutinised based on the audition certificates on the two surviving manuscripts. The central claim of this article is that we have no positive evidence that the production and reception of the two* jihād *texts was linked to anti-crusader sentiments. Rather, the evidence points towards their embeddedness in the Damascus-centred hadith culture.*

The Reception of *Jihād* Literature in the Crusading Period

Writings related to the Islamic concept of *jihād* from the crusading period are frequently seen in light of endeavours to mobilise against the Franks in the Middle East. This endeavour, the "counter-crusade," is often construed as an orchestrated effort by political/military leaders who were eager to win over scholars for their ideological, political, and, ultimately, military ends. In practical terms, this encompassed the encouragement or patronage of scholars to write about, preach, and otherwise disseminate the idea of a militant *jihād* against the Franks. The idea of scholars furiously preaching *jihād* is tightly interwoven with the narrative of the crusading period as a "perennial holy war [...] punctuated by interludes of peace"[1] which is still prominent in research literature and popular perception. Especially

---

I am grateful to Konrad Hirschler, Laurenz Kern, and Ingrid Austveg Evans for reading and commenting on an earlier draft of this article.

[1] Yvonne Friedman, "Peacemaking in an Age of War: When Were Cross-Religious Alliances in the Latin East Considered Treason?", in *The Crusader World*, ed. Adrian J. Boas (London, 2016), 98.

in the popular historical consciousness, this narrative has not lost any momentum and is still used to argue for an all-out clash of two homogenous and irreconcilable blocs.[2] While some scholars have taken the wind – or, rather, thunder – out of this narrative's sails by showing that it was a period of calm punctuated by combats,[3] and that depictions of extraordinary violence were regularly deployed as *topoi* in chronicles rather than factual reports,[4] a militant notion of *jihād* is still often considered the spirit of the age.

The two most prominent scholars brought up in discussions about the fashioning of *jihād* in this period are ʿAlī b. Ṭāhir al-Sulamī (1039/40–1106) and Ibn ʿAsākir (1105–76), both authors of texts centred around *jihād*.[5] The former wrote a complex, multi-volume treatise, the latter compiled a short collection of hadith. Especially Ibn ʿAsākir's text is increasingly perceived of as directly linked to mobilisation efforts against the Franks. The interpretation of their impact rests mostly on a close reading of the texts themselves, disregarding (or misinterpreting) the broader context. Yet, research in the last few years has significantly enhanced our understanding of the literary and scholarly culture these books were born into. The aim of this article is to look at the social setting of these texts regarding the wider textual production of their period and their respective reception. The method of this paper is thus twofold: first, we will contextualise the books as related to the biographies of their authors and the scholarly environment which they were part of. Second, we will look at the reception of these two texts based on audition certificates attached to their manuscripts. I thus deliberately drop the anti-crusader lens to look at al-Sulamī's and Ibn ʿAsākir's books. Instead, the two most often quoted *jihād*-centred works from the crusading period will be scrutinised considering the scholarly interests and

---

[2]   Amy S. Kaufman and Paul B. Sturtevant, *The Devil's Historians: How Modern Extremists Abuse the Medieval Past* (Toronto, 2020), 53–79.

[3]   Most extensively: Michael A. Köhler, *Allianzen und Verträge zwischen fränkischen und islamischen Herrschern im Vorderen Orient: Eine Studie über das zwischenstaatliche Zusammenleben vom 12. bis ins 13. Jahrhundert* (Berlin, 1991). See also Suleiman Mourad, "A Critique of the Scholarly Outlook of the Crusades: The Case for Tolerance and Co-Existence," in *Syria in Crusader Times: Conflict and Co-Existence*, ed. Carole Hillenbrand (Edinburgh, 2020), 144–60. For the most recent overview of this strand of scholarship, see Scott Moynihan, "Peacemaking and Holy War: Christian–Muslim Diplomacy, c. 1095–1291, in Crusades Historiography," *History Compass* 18/2 (2020): 1–12.

[4]   Thomas Asbridge, "An Experiment in Extremity: The Portrayal of Violence in Robert the Monk's Narrative of the First Crusade," *History* 105, no. 368 (2020): 719–50; Konrad Hirschler, "The Jerusalem Conquest of 492/1099 in the Medieval Arabic Historiography of the Crusades: From Regional Plurality to Islamic Narrative," *Crusades* 13 (2014): 37–76.

[5]   For al-Sulamī, see for example Jonathan Riley-Smith, *The Crusades, Christianity, and Islam* (New York, 2008), 69–70; Nikita Elisséeff, "The Reaction of the Syrian Muslims after the Foundation of the First Latin Kingdom of Jerusalem," in *Crusaders and Muslims in Twelfth-Century Syria*, ed. Maya Shatzmiller (Leiden, 1993), 163–65; For Ibn ʿAsākir, see for example Suleiman A. Mourad and James E. Lindsay, *The Intensification and Reorientation of Sunni Jihad Ideology in the Crusader Period* (Leiden, 2013); Aḥmad ʿAbd al-Karīm Ḥalwānī, *Ibn ʿAsākir wa-dawruh fī al-jihād ḍidd al-ṣalībīyīn fī ʿahd al-dawlatayn al-nūriyya wa-l-ayyūbiyya* (Damascus, 1991); Muḥammad Muṭīʿ al-Ḥāfiẓ, *Al-Ḥāfiẓ Ibn ʿAsākir: Muḥaddith al-Shām wa-muʾarrikhuhā al-kabīr, 499–571 h.* (Damascus, 2003), 357–69.

fields of activity of their respective authors, their genre-specific fabric, and their attested audience.

There is a tendency to interpret any writ from a Muslim author in the crusading period against the backdrop of a preconceived anti-crusader zeitgeist. Semi-fictional topographies are interpreted as calls to arms; chronicles as well as prose and poetry are read as *jihād* propaganda.[6] This zeitgeist, current opinion has it, pervaded creative artists as much as scholars, the political and military elite, as well as "the people." But is that all? What happens if we jettison the crusades-focused perspective and take a fresh look? In two recent articles, Matthew Keegan abandoned the counter-crusades as the main framework for analysing the literature of the period. He shows that men of letters had many things on their mind, including licentious drinking parties, homoeroticism, and hunting, rather than solely ascetic fervour in fighting the Franks. Moreover, Keegan refutes the usefulness of "propaganda" as an apt analytical category of literary production by rightfully and convincingly noting that this term comes with a severely charged baggage of modernist and thus anachronistic assumptions. Most importantly, it diverts our attention from the audience of the written word: the peers of the respective author and the inner circles of the elite, not "the public."[7]

In a same vein, I argue that picking out the *jihād* literature from its larger context warps our perception: *jihād* appears as the prime concern for al-Sulamī and Ibn ʿAsākir while the big picture appears dwarfed. By looking at the scholarly context, we can straighten out this bias to show that *jihād* was but one of the many topics of interest. It will become clear that the books were much more embedded in a very specific set of cultural and social practices – the transmission of hadith (the words and deeds of the Prophet Muhammad) – rather than a demagogical propaganda machinery meant to mobilise the masses. This is not to deny that some scholars in the crusading period thought about a militant notion of *jihād*, wrote down their ideas, taught and preached them, genuinely believed in them, tried to convince

---

[6] Jelle Bruning, "A Call to Arms: An Account of Ayyubid or Early Mamluk Alexandria," *Al-ʿUṣūr al-Wusṭā* 28 (2020): 74–115; Luke B. Yarbrough, "Symbolic Conflict and Cooperation in the Neglected Chronicle of a Syrian Prince," in *Syria in Crusader Times: Conflict and Coexistence*, 125–43; Osman Latiff, *The Cutting Edge of the Poet's Sword: Muslim Poetic Responses to the Crusades* (Leiden, 2017); idem. "The Place of Faḍāʾil al-Quds (Merits of Jerusalem) Literature and Religious Poetry in the Muslim Effort to Recapture Jerusalem during the Crusades" (PhD Thesis, Royal Holloway University of London, 2011), 158–70; Devin Stewart, "The *Maqāmāt* of Aḥmad b. Abī Bakr b. Aḥmad al-Rāzī al-Ḥanafī and the Ideology of the Counter-Crusade in Twelfth-Century Syria," *Middle Eastern Literatures* 11 (2008): 211–32; Daphna Ephrat and Mustafa Daud Kabha, "Muslim Reactions to the Frankish Presence in Bilād Al-Shām: Intensifying Religious Fidelity within the Masses," *Al-Masāq* 15/1 (2003): 47–58.

[7] Matthew L. Keegan, "Rethinking Poetry as (Anti-Crusader) Propaganda: Licentiousness and Cross-Confessional Patronage in the *Ḫarīdat al-qaṣr*," in *Intellectual History of the Islamicate World* (forthcoming); idem, "*Adab* Without the Crusades: The Inebriated Solidarity of a Young Officer's Hunting Epistle," *Al-ʿUṣūr al-Wusṭā* 28 (2020): 272–96; For another *jihād*-related text from a different context, arguably written for an elite audience, see Meia Walravens, "Multiple Audiences of a History from Sixteenth-Century Malabar: Zayn al-Dīn al-Maʿbarī's *Gift of the Strugglers for Jihad*," *South Asian Studies* 35/2 (2019): 226–36.

others of them, and, at least as far as some of these scholars are concerned, even joined the fight. The point is more to caution about the use of the two hitherto mostly adduced sources which, I contend, do not live up to the expectations of them.

In order to gain a better understanding of the textual environment and reception of al-Sulamī's and Ibn ʿAsākir's works, it is necessary to scrutinise the broader literary and scholarly culture of which they were a part. We will thus first look at the recent progress in book history and the history of scholarship of the period and region under discussion, which allows for a much better (re)assessment of their works than that which had previously been possible. The two subsequent parts of this article will examine al-Sulamī's and Ibn ʿAsākir's biographies, contextualise their texts, and look at their reception.

Syrian Hadith Culture in the Crusading Period

When the crusaders reached the Levant, they encountered a society in which the book was a well-established and ubiquitous medium. With the adoption of paper from the ninth century onwards, their production and sale became an industry to be reckoned with. Scholars and men of letters wrote, copied, read, lent, borrowed, bought, sold, endowed, and transmitted books as a matter of course. Next to being the essential medium of scholarly dialogue, from the eleventh century onwards books also started to move beyond the elite circles and to gain the attention of a broader section of society. These changes are less visible in non-elite authorship but become much clearer when considering readership, broadly defined as visual and aural reception of the written word. Thanks to the exceptionally high number of notes on this period's manuscripts, we not only have substantial knowledge about reading at large, but we can also pin down the reception of many books with exact details such as the names of readers, locations, and dates. With an estimated (low) double-digit literacy rate for the urban population of Egyptian and Syrian cities, the book has to be regarded as an everyday object in the region mostly affected by the crusading activities.[8]

Books of all sorts were to be found in private or endowed libraries, many of which existed in the cities and towns of the Levant. Besides libraries of scholars and rulers, mosques and – increasingly from the eleventh century onwards – schools housed comparatively large collections of endowed books. The catalogue of the Ashrafiyya mausoleum library in Damascus, founded by the ruler of Damascus in the thirteenth century and the only Arabic crusading-period library for which a library catalogue has been identified so far, shows that even a minor library, which did not attract much attention in contemporary narrative sources, held more than

---

[8] Konrad Hirschler, *The Written Word in the Medieval Arabic Lands. A Social and Cultural History of Reading Practices* (Edinburgh, 2012), 29; Beatrice Gruendler, *The Rise of the Arabic Book* (Cambridge, 2020).

two thousand books of a broad variety of genres – and thus more than the total of all college libraries of Cambridge in the fifteenth century.[9]

The absence of further library catalogues from this period is remedied by an abundance of manuscript notes on the surviving codices. Especially from the Syrian lands there are tens of thousands of notes testifying to specific engagements with books. We can learn a great deal about book possession from countless endowment notes and private ownership notes. For reading practices in particular, private reading statements and audition certificates provide us with an abundance of names, dates, and exact locations of historically identifiable reading sessions. Taken together, these documentary notes give us an unmatched insight into the reception of texts.

When it comes to the production of books and the writing of manuscript notes, one particularly industrious strand of scholarship was centred around hadith – the textual world of al-Sulamī's and Ibn ʿAsākir's works. Put simply, hadith are the words and deeds of the Prophet Muhammad, and as such served as an exemplary code of conduct for Muslims. Hadith also formed the bulk of the raw material for Islamic law. To guarantee the sound transmission of the reports, a chain of transmitters (*isnād*) was to be prefixed to each substantive content (*matn*). By this means, scholars could trace back a hadith to the Prophet and gauge its veracity by critically evaluating each link in the chain. Through the centuries, the chain of transmitters grew due to continued oral/aural transmission from generation to generation. In the early centuries of hadith transmission, the chain of transmission was the means to guarantee the authenticity of a given hadith and to eradicate forged ones. When in the ninth century a large body of hadith was written down in collections which gradually started to be treated as the canon in the subsequent centuries, the chain of transmitters lost its original function. For many fields of Islamic scholarship, the formation and gradual acceptance of a hadith canon meant that the time-consuming oral/aural transmission sessions became obsolete. Now, a jurist could simply open the pages of a canonical collection, find and cite a hadith as evidence for his legislation without having to obtain a personal chain of transmission in an oral/aural transmission session first.[10]

But, for the hadith scholars of what is now called the post-canonical hadith period (in Damascus c. 1000–1400), oral/aural transmission continued to be of utmost importance. An unbroken chain remained indispensable, though its meaning shifted from a scholarly tool to a spiritual practice. The chain was now regarded essentially as a unique feature of the Islamic community and a direct connection to the Prophet. As a consequence, the oral/aural transmission of hadith did not cease but continued and eventually flourished. The appeal of short chains with their perceived close connection to the Prophet and ultimately God thrilled generations of scholars and

---

[9] Konrad Hirschler, *Medieval Damascus: Plurality and Diversity in an Arabic Library: The Ashrafīya Library Catalogue* (Edinburgh, 2016).

[10] Jonathan Brown, *The Canonization of Al-Bukhārī and Muslim: The Formation and Function of the Sunnī Ḥadīth Canon* (Leiden, 2007).

laypeople. To keep the chains as short as possible, especially old transmitters were sought after, and particularly those with a broad corpus of otherwise rare hadith. Parents often took their young children to transmission sessions, seeking blessing and hoping that, once their offspring reached a certain age, they themselves would become sought-after transmitters.[11] According to the current state of research, the post-canonical transmission activities had their epicentre in Damascus, the city al-Sulamī and Ibn ʿAsākir called home.

In the Damascene post-canonical hadith culture, the large canonical collections of hadith were only rarely transmitted. Much more common was the transmission of small collections, often cheaply produced booklets with various selection criteria, most famously collections of forty hadith. We do know quite a lot about the materiality of these works thanks to the efforts of the ninth/fifteenth-century scholar and avid book collector Ibn ʿAbd al-Hādī (d. 909/1503). In his various capacities, Ibn ʿAbd al-Hādī acquired hundreds of books, mostly short hadith booklets from the heyday of the post-canonical hadith transmission that had fallen out of fashion in his day. Some he even rescued from the flea market.[12] In a last-ditch effort to commemorate this specific culture, borne to a large extent by members of his very own family,[13] Ibn ʿAbd al-Hādī bound his booklets together with those he inherited from his father and endowed them to a local madrasa. His endeavour is of central importance for the present article, because among the many hadith booklets he preserved from destruction he saved the now famous works of al-Sulamī and Ibn ʿAsākir.

The second striking material feature of these booklets apart from their small size is the abundance of manuscript notes, most importantly the large number of audition certificates (samāʿāt). Once a transmission session of one of these booklets was over and the licence (ijāza) to transmit the text had been granted, the names of those present were noted down in audition certificates. The basic components of such a certificate are the name of the authorised transmitter (musmiʿ), often the author/compiler himself or, after his death, one of his authorised former auditors; the reader (qāriʾ), often the authorised transmitter (author or authorised former auditor) or a student in this session; and the audience members (sāmiʿūn). Frequently, the writer of the certificate (kātib al-asmāʾ) identified himself and provided further information about the location and time of the session.

These audition certificates are direct documentary witnesses of knowledge transmission, and as such provide an incomparably deep insight into many further questions concerning the history of books, reading practices, and reception history.

---

[11] Garrett A. Davidson, *Carrying on the Tradition: A Social and Intellectual History of Hadith Transmission Across a Thousand Years* (Leiden, 2020); Eerik Dickinson, "Ibn Al-Ṣalāḥ al-Shahrazūrī and the Isnād," *Journal of the American Oriental Society* 122/3 (2002): 481–505.

[12] Konrad Hirschler, *A Monument to Medieval Syrian Book Culture – The Library of Ibn ʿAbd al-Hādī* (Edinburgh, 2019), 68–74.

[13] Stefan Leder, "Charismatic Scripturalism: The Ḥanbalī Maqdisīs of Damascus," *Der Islam* 74 (1997): 279–304.

The number of these notes from the Syrian lands from roughly the twelfth to the fourteenth century is enormous and remains largely unprocessed. The largest edited corpus until today is a catalogue of around 1300 certificates from the years 1155 to 1349.[14] This Damascene Corpus of Certificates provides the names of 6,529 individuals who took part in hadith transmission. Only some of them are scholars who can be found in the rich biographical literature of the period. Most of them, however, are not recorded in other literary sources and appear only on these certificates. The Damascene Corpus of Certificates harks back to only 89 texts in merely 34 manuscripts of the National al-Asad Library in Damascus. In that library alone, not to mention further libraries around the globe, we find hundreds of manuscripts with thousands of certificates and tens of thousands of names waiting to be filed systematically.[15] In the following, I will use the Damascene Corpus of Certificates to contextualise the reading sessions of our two *jihād* texts within the wider culture of reading and transmitting the written world.

A Lost Cause: ʿAlī b. Ṭāhir al-Sulamī and the Reception of his *Book of the Jihad*

ʿAlī b. Ṭāhir al-Sulamī's (d. 500/1106) book about *jihād* has been a constant reference in studies on the reaction to the First Crusade ever since Emmanuel Sivan published extracts and a partial French translation in 1966. Suhayl Zakkār made available the first full edition of the Arabic text only in 2007. In 2015 these were followed by a revised edition and English translation by Niall Christie, who has worked most extensively on the text.[16] *The Book of the Jihad* is especially valuable for being the first surviving narrative source commenting on the Frankish presence in Syria, a period of relatively few Arabic sources. It is indeed a highly interesting text in that al-Sulamī puts the Frankish presence in Syria and Palestine in a broader context of earlier activities by Christians in Sicily and al-Andalus and designates the crusades a Christian *jihād*.[17] The book has been declared to provide a "razor-sharp image of the religious classes' perception of recent events,"[18] and to have "contributed

---

[14] Stefan Leder, Yāsīn M. al-Sawwās, and Maʾmūn al-Ṣāgharjī, *Muʿjam al-samāʿāt al-Dimashqiyya. Les certificats d'audition à Damas. 550–750/1155–1349*, 2 vols. (Damascus, 1996).

[15] A larger corpus, the Audition Certificate Database project by Said Aljoumani (Hamburg) and Konrad Hirschler (Hamburg), is in the works.

[16] Niall Christie, *The Book of the Jihad of ʿAli Ibn Tahir al-Sulami (d. 1106)* (Farnham, 2015). See also: idem. "Reflections on Editing *Kitāb al-Jihād* of ʿAlī ibn Ṭāhir al-Sulamī (d. 500/1106)," *Journal of Islamic Manuscripts* 12/2 (2021): 131–52; Suhayl Zakkār, *Arbaʿa kutub fī al-jihād min ʿaṣr al-ḥurūb al-ṣalībiyya* (Damascus, 2007); Emmanuel Sivan, "La génèse de la contre-croisade: une traité damasquin du début du XIIe siècle," *Journal asiatique* 254 (1966): 197–224.

[17] Paul E. Chevedden, "The View of the Crusades from Rome and Damascus: The Geo-Strategic and Historical Perspectives of Pope Urban II and Alī Ibn Ṭāhir al-Sulamī," *Oriens* 39/2 (2011): 257–329.

[18] Jonathan Phillips, *Holy Warriors: A Modern History of the Crusades* (London, 2010), 30–31.

to the popularization of *jihād* preaching and propaganda in Damascus,"[19] while al-Sulamī has been described as "an active Jihād propagandist."[20] Although some previous research has questioned the impact of the book,[21] this has not changed the role of *The Book of the Jihad* as one of the chief witnesses of the early days of an assumed *jihād* spirit of the age. It is thus time to assess in more detail the impact of al-Sulamī's book and the claim that he acted as a preacher.

In large parts of the scholarly literature, al-Sulamī is portrayed as preaching public sermons on *jihād*.[22] Is this assessment based on contemporary sources or rather a present-day assumption? If we turn to the narrative sources, it becomes evident that al-Sulamī was hardly remembered in the vast biographical literature of his time and the subsequent centuries – and he was definitely not remembered as a preacher or *jihād* campaigner of any kind. Though a member of an important scholarly family, only a few biographical dictionaries, Ibn ʿAsākir's *History of Damascus* being the earliest, mention him at all. Born in 431/1039–40, al-Sulamī is described as a trustworthy (*thiqa*) transmitter of hadith and, primarily, as a grammarian (*al-naḥwī*). He was running a teaching circle in "the mosque" (Umayyad Mosque) to whose library he endowed his books. Subsequent biographies rely exclusively on Ibn ʿAsākir and stress his expertise in grammar. In fact, most dictionaries that have an entry on him are confined to grammarians and even on the title page of his *Book of the Jihad* he is presented as a grammarian.[23] This overall insignificance of al-Sulamī, his profile as a grammarian and hadith transmitter, and the absence of any reference to his *Book of the Jihad* in the narrative sources has been either neglected or taken in modern scholarship as a conscious attempt by Ibn ʿAsākir to downplay

---

[19] Suleiman A. Mourad and James E. Lindsay, "Ibn ʿAsakir and the Intensification and Reorientation of Sunni Jihad Ideology in Crusader-Era Syria," in *Just Wars, Holy Wars, and Jihads: Christian, Jewish, and Muslim Encounters and Exchanges*, ed. Sohail H. Hashmi (Oxford, 2012), 112.

[20] Elisséeff, "The Reaction of the Syrian Muslims," 163.

[21] For example, Mourad, "A Critique," 145–47; Keegan, "Rethinking Poetry"; Swantje Bartschat, *Dschihad der Zunge, des Stifts und des Schwertes? Vierzig Dschihad Hadithe im Vergleich* (Baden-Baden, 2019), 30; Niall Christie, "Religious Campaign or War of Conquest? Muslim Views of the Motives of the First Crusade," in *Noble Ideas and Bloody Realities: Warfare in the Middle Ages*, ed. Niall Christie and Maya Yazigi (Leiden, 2006), 66; Carole Hillenbrand, *The Crusades: Islamic Perspectives* (Edinburgh, 1999), 108.

[22] For example, Hillenbrand, *The Crusades*, 109; Daniella Talmon-Heller, "Islamic Preaching in Syria during the Counter-Crusade (Twelfth–Thirteenth Centuries)," in *In Laudem Hierosolymitani: Studies in Crusades and Medieval Culture in Honour of Benjamin Z. Kedar*, ed. Iris Shagrir, Ronnie Ellenblum, and Jonathan Riley-Smith (Burlington, 2007), 65; Christie, *The Book of the Jihad*, passim.

[23] Abū Qāsim ʿAlī b. al-Ḥasan Ibn ʿAsākir, *Taʾrīkh madīnat Dimashq*, ed. ʿUmar b. Gharāma al-ʿAmrawī, 80 vols. (Beirut, 1995), 43:4; Abū Ṭāhir Aḥmad b. Muḥammad al-Silafī, *Muʿjam al-Safar*, ed. ʿAbd Allāh ʿUmar al-Bārūdī (Beirut, 1993), 133; Yāqūt al-Ḥamawī, *Muʿjam al-udabāʾ / Irshād al-arīb ilā maʿrifat al-adīb*, ed. Iḥsān ʿAbbās, 7 vols. (Beirut, 1993), 4:1774–75; Jamāl al-Dīn Abū al-Ḥasan ʿAlī al-Qifṭī, *Inbāh al-ruwāt ʿalā anbāh al-nuḥāt*, ed. Muḥammad Abū al-Faḍl Ibrāhīm, 4 vols. (Cairo, 1973), 2:283; Jalāl al-Dīn al-Suyūṭī, *Bughyat al-wuʿāt fī ṭabaqāt al-lughawīyīn wa-l-nuḥāt*, ed. Muḥammad Abu al-Faḍl Ibrāhīm, 2 vols. (Beirut, n.d.), 2:170; See also Khalīl b. Aybak al-Ṣafadī, *al-Wāfī bi-l-Wafayāt*, ed. Hellmut Ritter et al., 30 vols. (Beirut/Berlin, 1931), 21:154–55. For the note on the title page, see Damascus, National al-Asad Library, MS 4511 fol. 1a.

his predecessor's role in disseminating *jihād* ideas.[24] For instance, the fact that the topic of the exemplary hadith Ibn ʿAsākir quotes in al-Sulamī's biography is about almsgiving and not related to *jihād* has been described as "intriguing"[25] – as if al-Sulamī could not have done anything noteworthy but vigorously preach *jihād*.

However, this approach has no basis in the medieval sources and rests solely on a crusader-focused reading of the text which disregards the context. Besides the meagre information found in the biographical literature, the manuscript of *The Book of the Jihad* is the only witness to al-Sulamī's scholarly activity identified so far. Yet, even this sole work was hardly influential. There is no evidence that his book directly inspired subsequent treatises on *jihād*. Even more, the book survives only in fragments, which may be taken as a sign of its author's lack of reputation in following generations and of a lack of interest in the topic of *jihād* in general. The visual appearance of the manuscript indicates that it was not meant to impress anyone, and much less a member of the elite – as is often the case with splendid copies presented to rulers and other patrons. It is furthermore full of marginal additions, deletions, and blank passages. Its cataloguer thus even speculated that it was a draft by al-Sulamī himself.[26] Not dressed to impress, the surviving fragments look much like countless other Damascene manuscripts from this period.

Since al-Sulamī's text is hard to classify, it contains exhortations, and, based on a misunderstanding of the role of its audition certificates, the book is often described as a sermon and even compared to the preaching of Pope Urban II[27] – presuming a congregation with their eyes glued to his lips, ready to spring into action. But there is no evidence that this book was written as, or used for, a public address. Perceiving it as a sermon and picturing al-Sulamī ascending a pulpit is mere speculation.[28] Assuming that the non-extant parts had roughly the same length as the surviving parts, the book would have run up to more than 480 pages. A text of that length is anything but a sermon and can hardly be meant to incite a huge crowd of people.[29] In fact, this would be one of very few sermon texts surviving

---

[24] Mourad and Lindsay, *The Intensification*, 42–46; Al-Ḥāfiẓ's assumption of a tight relationship between Ibn ʿAsākir and al-Sulamī is based on a wrong identification of the al-Sulamī under discussion: *Al-Ḥāfiẓ, Ibn ʿAsākir*, 359–61.

[25] Christie, *The Book of the* Jihad, 5.

[26] Yāsīn M. al-Sawwās, *Fihris Majāmīʿ al-Madrasa al-ʿUmariyya fī Dār al-Kutub al-Ẓāhiriyya bi-Dimashq* (Kuwait, 1987), 300; Christie, more convincingly, deems it to be written by Aḥmad b. ʿAbd al-Bāqī b. al-Ḥusayn al-Qaysī, who also wrote most of the audition certificates: Christie, *The Book of the* Jihad, 7.

[27] Niall Christie and Deborah Gerish, "Parallel Preachings: Urban II and al-Sulamī," *Al-Masāq* 15/2 (2003): 139–48.

[28] For example, Christie, *The Book of the* Jihad, 33; Mourad and Lindsay, *The Intensification*, 33; Phillips, *Holy Warriors*, 31; Christopher Tyerman, *God's War: A New History of the Crusades* (London, 2006), 272; Hillenbrand, *The Crusades*, 108; Elisséeff, "The Reaction of the Syrian Muslims," 163.

[29] Niall Christie, "Motivating Listeners in the *Kitab al-Jihad* of ʿAli Ibn Tahir al-Sulami (d. 1106)," *Crusades* 6 (2007): 1–14; Christie notes that the text is "unsuitable for use as a conventional *khutba*, bearing closer resemblance to a work of *waʿz*": Christie, *The Book of the* Jihad *of ʿAlī Ibn Tahir al-Sulamī (d. 1106)*, 9.

from this period,[30] and the only one which received audition certificates, a practice so well-known and widespread in the transmission of hadith. Following this line of thought, it is more likely to picture al-Sulamī sitting in the corner of a mosque with a scholarly and devout audience eager to obtain a permission to transmit the hadith in the book through the chains al-Sulamī could supply.

Al-Sulamī wrote quite an idiosyncratic text which does not fall neatly into any genre. He is clearly referring to current events and calling for action. But his call is embedded in a lengthy anthology of sorts. Based on the surviving fragments, it was a comprehensive and complex treatise, a versatile text in which the author laid down his juristic understanding of the duty of *jihād*, its conduct and regulations, interspersed with philological explanations of Arabic and Persian words, blended with poetry, Quranic quotations, and descriptions of the merits of holy places in Syrian topography. The most innovative argument al-Sulamī puts forth is that in absence of a unifying leadership, *jihād* is incumbent upon any individual Muslim (*farḍ al-ʿayn*). In this, he was diverting from the previous understanding in which under the leadership of a caliph, *jihād* was only obligatory for a sufficient number of Muslims from amongst the entire community but not obligatory for every single Muslim (*farḍ al-kifāya*). Al-Sulamī was thus most likely trying to kick off an intellectual discussion, surely in view of the fragmented political landscape of his time to which the Frankish presence in Syria contributed, but mainly addressed to his scholarly peers, and as a second target group to the political elite who he blames for not uniting and organising the defence of Syria.[31] A broader target group is highly unlikely as it is rather difficult to imagine a scholar trying to incite a crowd with philological musings about rare words in obscure hadith in chapters with technical headings such as "Battle and Arrangement of the Cavalry, as they Join Ranks, and of the Infantry."[32]

Instead of interpreting *The Book of the Jihad* as a sermon, I argue that the book has to be understood within the hadith-minded milieu of its time and place. The audition certificates on its manuscript point to the fact that it was perceived by contemporaries to be part of the world of hadith. Even though it cannot simply be categorised into any of the popular hadith genres of its time, hadith loom large. More than Quranic passages, hadith are the references of choice for al-Sulamī's arguments. When citing hadith, al-Sulamī does not simply refer to the written canon but, following closely the post-canonical tradition of his day, he always provides his full chains back to the Prophet, at times even with additional detail

---

[30] Jonathan Berkey, *Popular Preaching and Religious Authority in the Medieval Islamic Near East* (Seattle, 2001), 17–19; Daniella Talmon-Heller, *Islamic Piety in Medieval Syria: Mosques, Cemeteries and Sermons under the Zangids and Ayyūbids (1146–1260)* (Leiden, 2007), 117.

[31] For the most recent and detailed analysis of the text, see Kenneth A. Goudie, *Reinventing Jihād: Jihād Ideology from the Conquest of Jerusalem to the End of the Ayyūbids (c. 492/1099–647/1249)* (Leiden, 2019), 63–118; idem. "Legitimate Authority in the *Kitab al-Jihad* of ʿAli b. Tahir al-Sulami," in *Syria in Crusader Times: Conflict and Co-Existence*, 21–33; For al-Sulamī's use of poetry, see Latiff, *The Cutting Edge*, 78–82.

[32] Christie, *The Book of the* Jihad, 282–307.

about the precise location where he heard a hadith.[33] The fact that *The Book of the Jihad* was part of the world of hadith explains the presence of audition certificates in the surviving manuscript. These certificates have played a crucial role in some previous scholarship in arguing for the wide reception of the text. However, if we compare these certificates with the Damascene Corpus of Certificates, we will see that they indicate a very different story.

The audition certificates on the surviving parts of *The Book of the Jihad* reveal two salient points about the dissemination of the book: first, comparatively low audience figures[34] and, second, a marginal place of these events in the lifetime of the author. Al-Sulamī himself presided over five distinct sessions, stretching over eight months in 499/1105 (for the different sessions and the audience, see Table 1, below). He transmitted part two twice, each session (1a and 1b) of which was attended by only three men. The sessions took place at an interval of two months and the second transmission (1b) was divided into different meetings (*majālis mutafarriqa*).[35] A new composition of audience members continued with the transmission of part eight (2). All six men from the previous two sessions (1a and 1b) took part. Session 2 started with an audience of six, and two further men joined later. With eight participants listening to the final portion of part eight, this was the biggest audience ever attested for a public reading of al-Sulamī's *Book of the Jihad*.[36] Part nine was read in the same month (3) to six men.[37] Two months later, al-Sulamī read part twelve (4) to an audience of five with one new audience member and two dropouts from the previous session.[38] This was the last attested reading session in al-Sulamī's lifetime. The only attested transmission session (5) after al-Sulamī's death started with three auditors, one of whom was the seven-year-old son (#10)[39] of the transmitter (#1). Some pages into the reading, another auditor joined but after only roughly a quarter of the sessions was completed, one listener left. If, or how often, this group reconvened to listen to other parts cannot be established due to the fragmentary survival. We know, however, that they did not reach part eight, the next surviving part, and thus the reading was most probably cut short and simply ceased for reasons unknown.

In sum, the audition certificates of *The Book of the Jihad* attest that al-Sulamī's public reading attracted only a handful of people. During al-Sulamī's lifetime, a total of nine individuals are attested in a constantly changing constitution of the group and only three men heard him reading all the four extant parts. Not one of the men who dropped out in the course of the reading returned for a later

---

[33] Christie, *The Book of the* Jihad, 31 n. 131, 32 n. 132; idem. "Reflections on Editing *Kitāb al-Jihād*," 140–41.

[34] In the following, audience is defined as listeners including the reader but excluding the presiding authority or authorities.

[35] Damascus, National al-Asad Library, MS 3796, fol. 173a, on the bottom of the page.

[36] Damascus, National al-Asad Library, MS 3796, fol. 192a.

[37] Damascus, National al-Asad Library, MS 4511, fol. 1a.

[38] Damascus, National al-Asad Library, MS 3796, fol. 213a.

[39] In the following, hashtag with a number refers to one of the twelve listeners, see Table 1.

Table 1 **Attendees of the six reading sessions of al-Sulamī's** *The Book of the Jihad*

#	Name	Session	Part
1	Abū Muḥmmad ʿAbd al-Raḥmān b. Aḥmad b. ʿAlī b. Ṣābir al-Sulamī[a]	1a, 2, 3, 4, 5	2, 8, 9, 12
2	Aḥmad b. ʿAbd al-Bāqī b. al-Ḥusayn al-Qaysī[b]	1a, 2, 3, 4	2, 8, 9, 12
3	Ḥassān b. Aḥmad b. ʿAlī al-Anṣārī	1a, 2	2, 8
4	[Abū al-Ḥusayn] Aḥmad b. Salāma [b. Yaḥyā] al-Abbār[c]	1b, 2, 3, 4	2, 8, 9, 12
5	[Abū Muḥammad] Al-Ḥasan b. Hibat Allāh [b. Ḥaydara Al-Anṣārī] al-Sarrāj	1b, 2 (p),[d] 3	2, 8, 9
6	[Abū ʿAlī] Al-Ḥasan b. al-Qāsim [b. Jāmiʿ al-ʿAdawī] al-ʿĀbir [li-l-ruʾiyā]	1b, 2, 3	2, 8, 9
7	Abū al-Ḥasan ʿAlī b. al-Ḥusayn al-Kattānī	2, 3, 4	8, 9, 12
8	Yaʿlā b. Ḥuffāẓ al-Sarrāj	2 (p)	8
9	Muẓaffar b. ʿAbd Allāh al-Muqriʾ[e]	4	12
10	ʿAbd Allāh Abū al-Maʿālī ʿAbd Allāh [al-Sulamī][f]	5	2
11	Hibat Allāh b. al-Ḥasan b. Hibat Allāh b. ʿAbd Allāh b. al-Ḥusayn[g]	5	2
12	Abū Manṣūr ʿAbd al-Bāqī b. Muḥammad b. ʿAbd al-Bāqī al-Tamīmī[h]	5 (p)	2
13	Al-Shaykh Abū al-Ḥusayn Aḥmad b. Rāshid b. Muḥammad al-Qurashī	5 (p)	2

Notes

  [a] Shams al-Dīn Muḥammad b. Aḥmad al-Dhahabī, *Taʾrīkh al-islām wa-wafayāt al-mashāhīr wa-l-aʿlām*, ed. ʿUmar ʿAbd al-Salām Tadmurī, 80 vols. (Beirut, 1987), 35:317.
  [b] Muḥammad b. Idrīs al-Shāfiʿī, *al-Risāla*, ed. Aḥmad Shākir (Beirut, n.d.), 42.
  [c] Ibid., 42.
  [d] A p in round brackets indicates partial attendance.
  [e] Ibn ʿAsākir, *Taʾrīkh madīnat Dimashq*, 58:379.
  [f] al-Dhahabī, *Taʾrīkh al-islām*, 40:214–15.
  [g] ʿImād al-Dīn al-Iṣfahānī, *Kharīdat al-qaṣr wa-jarīdat ahl al-ʿaṣr: Qism shuʿarāʾ al-Shām*, ed. Shukrī al-Fayṣal, 3 vols. (Damascus, 1955), 1:281.
  [h] Ibn ʿAsākir, *Taʾrīkh madīnat Dimashq*, 34:10–11.

session. The small size of the readings of al-Sulamī's work becomes apparent if we turn to the Damascene Corpus of Certificates. The average number of auditors in reading sessions of this corpus was 12.6[40] while al-Sulamī's book about *jihād* could only attract a much more modest average turnout of 4.8 listeners. Christie speculates that there were many others present in the readings who did not feel the need to get registered.[41] This is highly unlikely as audition certificates are such an

---

  [40] Stephanie Luescher, "Medieval Metadata: Samāʿāt as a Source for the Social History of Damascus (1150–1350)" (MA thesis, Freie Universität Berlin, 2019), 29. I am grateful to Stephanie Luescher (Princeton) for sharing her thesis and data with me.
  [41] Christie, *The Book of the Jihad*, 11; Christie, "Reflections on Editing *Kitāb al-Jihād*," 137.

exciting source precisely because they systematically included all non-scholarly participants. In the rare instances where this is not the case, mostly in later copies of audition certificates, their writers wrote "and others" to signal their intervention in the list (for example, see below, Table 2, #B, #J).[42] The low number of attendees also does not go well with the assumption that the book was overly captivating to its audience. Even when considering the fragmentary state of the manuscript and the likelihood of now lost audition certificates, based on the numbers we have, al-Sulamī's book was a flop, no matter how interesting it is for us nowadays.

The second noticeable point is the marginal location of the transmission in al-Sulamī's lifetime. Unfortunately, only the first certificate indicates the exact location, the mosque of Bayt Lihyā, a village in the eastern Ghouta, the rural hinterland of Damascus.[43] The peripheral location has led to different interpretations. Mourad and Lindsay surmise that it was either a highly important and consciously chosen site as the mosque of Bayt Lihyā was a converted church and local lore ascribes it as the place where Abraham had destroyed the idols his people worshipped – both stories a reminder of the victory of Islam over its enemies. Hosting the reading in the village may also have been the outcome of al-Sulamī's fear of ill treatment from the authorities to preach such a contested topic in the centre of the city.[44] Whether or not there really is some hidden significance in the choice of this location is anyone's guess. The fact of the matter is that the reading took place in a village outside the city and thus beyond the reach of a large audience. It is often assumed that al-Sulamī read the subsequent parts in the Umayyad Mosque of Damascus,[45] but there is no evidence in that regard. One may rather assume that a change of scenery to such a prominent and central location of Muslim worship and public life would have been noted down. It is only in the certificate for the transmission session after al-Sulamī's death (#5) where the Umayyad Mosque of Damascus is specified as the location of the transmission.

Who were the attested listeners of al-Sulamī's *jihād* treatise? The interpretation of al-Sulamī's audience in an anti-crusader reading rests on its sporadically exhortative tone, blended with the perception of a large congregation. But the evidence points towards a scholarly and chain-of-transmission-minded audience. Of the thirteen attested auditors, six can be found in biographical dictionaries, which puts them in the scholarly realm. We can find, for example, a Quran reciter (#9), an imam (#4), and a scholar working as a notary witness (#12). Five of these scholars are described either explicitly as engaged in hadith studies or depicted in the context of hadith transmission. Next to these six scholars, two further

---

[42] Said Aljoumani, "Wathīqa jadīda ʿan naql al-ʿilm fī al-taʾrīkh al-islāmiyya: Taḥqīq awrāq al-samāʿ li-Sunan al-Dāraquṭnī," *Majalla Kulliyat al-Sharīʿa wa-l-Dirāsāt al-Islāmiyya* 38/2 (2021): 23–24; Davidson, *Carrying on the Tradition*, 53.

[43] Damascus, National al-Asad Library, MS 3796, fol. 173a, under the title.

[44] Mourad and Lindsay, *The Intensification*, 33–34; Christie seconds the first interpretation. *The Book of the Jihad*, 21–23. Mourad and Lindsay wrongly assert that only Quran scholars and jurists were welcome to teach at the Umayyad Mosque.

[45] See, for example, Talmon-Heller, "Islamic Preaching," 65.

individuals (#2, #13) appear in other audition certificates of a book unrelated to al-Sulamī. This does not in and of itself make them scholars. However, the fact that one of them (#2) is the writer of four certificates (1, 2, 3, 4) for al-Sulamī's book and most likely its copyist, and that he appears in one unrelated reading session[46] in the company of two scholars who took part in the reading of al-Sulamī's book (#1, #12), makes it likely that he was indeed a scholar who remained unrecorded in the biographical literature. Similarly, a second individual (#13) appears in two unrelated audition certificates, one of which he wrote himself,[47] and is described as a "religious teacher" (*shaykh*) in the certificate for al-Sulamī's book. This puts him in the scholarly realm as well. On balance, seven of thirteen listeners of *The Book of the Jihad* were thus, at least to a certain extent, scholars with an interest in hadith. Assuming their motives for participating in the transmission session was the topic of *jihād* disregards the popular current of collecting short chains and reduces their most likely broader scholarly interest to one minor topic.

Who were the other listeners joining the transmission of *The Book of the Jihad*? Six of the thirteen attested listeners remain unidentified. Assuming their relational names (*nisba*s) reflect their occupation and were not part of their family names, we can pin down three craftsmen: two saddlers (#5, #8) and one linen weaver (#7). Another listener was a dream interpreter (#6). These men and the remaining two may very well have been laymen who participated for ritual reasons. If we put this observation into the wider world of hadith transmission in Damascus during this period, we see that this is in fact a very common phenomenon. In the Damascene Corpus of Certificates, 72.5 percent of all those recorded are only named once and cannot be considered scholars.[48] The bulk of these people remain unidentifiable in the biographical literature and are thus to be regarded as laymen. For the phenomenon of non-scholarly participation in reading sessions, Hirschler offers three explanatory approaches: participation as a ritual practice; an appreciation of the aesthetic aspect; and interest in the content.[49] Whatever made these individuals sit down and listen has to remain an open question, but there is no reason to assume that we are seeing here a distinctive *jihād*-related phenomenon.

The afterlife of the surviving parts of *The Book of the Jihad* is very much linked to two further hadith-minded scholars and one institution involved in hadith transmission. All surviving parts were owned by Yūsuf b. Muḥmmad b. Manṣūr al-Hilālī (d. 710/1310), a hadith scholar and avid book collector.[50] Although only the title page of part 9 carries a note showing that the manuscript was endowed to an institution concerned with the transmission and study of hadith, the Dār al-Ḥadīth al-Ḍiyā'iyya on Mount Qasyun, it is very likely that al-Hilālī had endowed the

---

[46]   al-Shāfiʿī, *al-Risāla*, 42.

[47]   al-Shāfiʿī, *al-Risāla*, 43, as writer in 44–45.

[48]   Luescher, "Medieval Metadata," 25.

[49]   Hirschler, *The Written Word*, 51–60.

[50]   Shams al-Dīn Muḥammad b. Aḥmad al-Dhahabī, *Muʿjam al-shuyūkh al-kabīr*, ed. ʿAlī Ḥabīb al-Hayla, 2 vols. (al-Ṭāʾif, 1988), 393–94; al-Ṣafadī, *al-Wāfī*, 29:336–37.

whole book, or all the parts he owned, to this institution, as he is one of the main endowers of this institution's library. The Dār al-Ḥadīth al-Ḍiyā'iyya was one of the epicentres of hadith transmission, founded in the beginning of the thirteenth century.[51] We do not know when the book became part of the Ḍiyā'iyya and how long it remained there. In the end of the fifteenth century, the abovementioned Ibn 'Abd al-Hādī came into possession of the parts. For a scholar such as Ibn 'Abd al-Hādī there was nothing *jihād*-specific about this book, but he bound parts 2, 8, and 12 together with other hadith texts on entirely different topics into one composite manuscript.[52] Part 9 was at that time already detached and we can find a note on its titlepage by Ibn 'Abd al-Hādī, claiming a licence to transmit (*ijāza*).[53]

Ibn 'Asākir: Propaganda or Business as Usual?

Next to al-Sulamī, the second chief witness to the importance of *jihād* has been a hadith collection of Ibn 'Asākir (d. 571/1176). Today, Ibn 'Asākir's fame rests on his monumental *History of Damascus*. With more than 10,000 biographies of men and women in 74 printed volumes, this is the most impressive testimony of his scholarly diligence.[54] In crusader studies, Ibn 'Asākir is predominantly mentioned in association with Nūr al-Dīn Maḥmūd b. Zankī's (d. 565/1174) efforts to bring *jihād* into prominence. In his own days, Ibn 'Asākir was mostly renowned as a scholar and transmitter of hadith, often labelled as *the* hadith scholar of Syria (*muḥaddith al-Shām*). Born in 499/1105, he started to collect hadith at the early age of six and heard from well over a thousand transmitters in the course of his life. This pursuit caused him to undertake extensive journeys, bringing him to Baghdad and as far east as Khorasan. Back in Damascus, Ibn 'Asākir is said to have lived a life removed from the daily political affairs of the times, declining various paid positions offered to him.[55] His seclusion from the day-to-day political life came to an end with the entry of Nūr al-Dīn into Damascus in 549/1154. Nūr al-Dīn not only appointed him to teach at a newly built school for the study of hadith, but also encouraged him to resume working on the *History of Damascus* and to compile a hadith collection on *jihād*.

---

[51] Muḥammad Muṭī' al-Ḥāfiẓ, *Dār al-Ḥadīth al-Ḍiyā'iyya wa Maktabuhā bi-Ṣāliḥiyya Dimashq* (Damascus, 2006). A note on part 12, MS Damascus, National al-Asad Library 3796/11, fol. 213a is not clearly readable but I assume it is al-Hilālī's endowment note due to similarities to his notes on the other parts.

[52] Damascus, National al-Asad Library, MS 3796/11, fols. 173a–236b.

[53] Damascus, National al-Asad Library, MS 4511. See entries 404e and 461j in Ibn 'Abd al-Hādī's *fihrist*; Hirschler, *A Monument*, 330, 380; Read Yūsuf, not Bursuq, Ibn 'Abd al-Hādī. Christie, *The Book of the Jihad*, 281.

[54] For the most recent introductory biography, see Suleiman A. Mourad, *Ibn 'Asakir of Damascus: Champion of Sunni Islam in the Time of the Crusades* (London, 2021).

[55] al-Ḥāfiẓ, *Al-Ḥāfiẓ Ibn 'Asākir*, 380.

Different catalogues of works by Ibn ʿAsākir list different titles referring to *jihād*.[56] It is an open question whether these refer to distinct works or all denote the same text. What has survived until today is a hadith collection titled *The Forty Hadiths for Inciting Jihad (al-Arbaʿūn ḥadīthan fī al-ḥathth ʿalā al-jihād)*. It is cast in the form of a forty-hadith collection, one of the most popular genres in the post-canonical hadith period. The popularity of the forty-hadith collections rests mostly on two reasons: first, it was a practical format, easily transportable and quickly transmitted; second, in a (mostly considered weak) hadith, the Prophet assured his intercession on the day of judgement to anyone who preserves forty hadith from amongst his community. In this form, over the centuries hundreds of scholars compiled a sample of forty hadith for which they had received a permission to transmit. These collections were based on a number of different criteria. This could be the topic of the hadith themselves, for example grey hair, ritual purification, or medical advice. Other criteria could be the shortness of the chains, the length of the substantive text, or the geographical scope of the collected hadith.[57] It is within this well-established genre of hadith collections that Ibn ʿAsākir placed his *Forty Hadiths for Inciting Jihad*.[58] Having composed (at least) five other titles in this specific genre, this was a go-to format for him to cast hadith collections. Next to the *jihād*-centred forty-hadith collection, he compiled, for example, one with forty hadith he received from forty transmitters in forty cities going back to forty companions of the Prophet; one in which he collected forty hadith for which he had chains as short as those of the five authors of the canonical hadith collections; and one confined to hadith with extremely long substantive content.[59]

Only one complete copy of Ibn ʿAsākir's *Forty Hadiths for Inciting Jihad* survives. Like al-Sulamī's book, it is part of a composite manuscript with mostly hadith-related material from the post-canonical period.[60] The copy was produced by Zakī al-Dīn Muḥammad b. Yūsuf al-Birzālī (d. 636/1238–39), a widely travelled scholar from Seville who ultimately settled in Damascus and became heavily involved in hadith transmission. Allusions in audition certificates and a copying statement on this single surviving manuscript show that more copies existed and one fragment of two folios can be found today in the National al-Asad library in Damascus.[61] After al-Birzālī finished his copy of the forty-hadith, he

---

[56] al-Ḥāfiẓ, *Al-Ḥāfiẓ Ibn ʿAsākir*, 388–89, 412; The Ashrafiyya library catalogue contains three, 229, 840, 842: Hirschler, *Medieval Damascus*, 175, (2x) 257.

[57] For the forty-hadith genre, see Swantje Bartschat, *"Wer meiner Gemeinde vierzig Hadithe bewahrt..."*: *Entstehung und Entwicklung eines Sammlungstyps* (Baden-Baden, 2019); and Davidson, *Carrying on the Tradition*, 204–18.

[58] For *jihād* specific forty-hadith collections, see Bartschat, *Dschihad der Zunge, des Stifts und des Schwertes?*

[59] Al-Ḥāfiẓ counts eight forty-hadith collections by Ibn ʿAsākir: *Al-Ḥāfiẓ Ibn ʿAsākir*, 386–91; Bartschat counts six: *"Wer meiner Gemeinde vierzig Hadithe bewahrt..."*, 250.

[60] Damascus, National al-Asad Library, MS 1592/3. For the composite manuscripts, see Yāsīn M. al-Sawwās, *Fihris Makhṭūṭāt Dār al-Kutub al-Ẓāhiriyya: al-Majāmīʿ* (Damascus, 1983), 423–25.

[61] Damascus, National al-Asad Library, MS 1205, fols. 46a–47b.

copied two audition certificates from the lifetime of Ibn ʿAsākir to activate his copy for subsequent transmission, that is to display how his teachers received their permission so that later generations can understand how he acquired his permission to transmit the collection. Nine further certificates show that the forty-hadith were transmitted at least until the year 1318.

The *Forty Hadiths for Inciting Jihad* was edited by Aḥmad Ḥalwānī in his study on Ibn ʿAsākir's role in the *jihād* in 1991.[62] It has been edited again, translated, and studied by Suleiman Mourad and James Lindsay, who have published widely on the text. In a dedicated monograph, they made extensive use of it and argued for its central role in an intensification and reorientation of *jihād* ideology in the crusading period, directed against external (Christian crusaders) and internal (non-Sunni Muslims) enemies of Islam. Their interpretation of the impact of Ibn ʿAsākir's *Forty Hadiths for Inciting Jihad* is largely based on the audition certificates, consistently mistranslated as "colophons."[63]

In contrast to al-Sulamī, Ibn ʿAsākir was a crowd-pleaser – not because of his extraordinary charisma or eloquence, but because he was *the* keeper of so many hadith with short (read: sought-after) chains. He began studiously collecting hadith in his early childhood and undertook two extensive journeys in this pursuit. A list of the male hadith transmitters he heard totals 1,621, and together with a now-lost list of 80 female transmitters, this may be taken as a yardstick to gauge his diligence in this regard.[64] Back in Damascus, he led a life fully devoted to the study and transmission of hadith and quickly became the paragon of hadith transmission. His fame grew throughout the Islamic world and he is even said to have transmitted to scholars older than him, indicating just how many hadith with short chains he was able to transmit.[65] Most often, Ibn ʿAsākir transmitted hadith in the Umayyad Mosque. Sometime after he entered Damascus in 549/1154, Nūr al-Dīn commissioned the building of a school solely devoted to the study of hadith, the Dār al-Sunna or Dār al-Ḥadīth al-Nūriyya. Ibn ʿAsākir became its first head teacher, and the earliest evidence of Ibn ʿAsākir's activities in the Dār al-Sunna date to 566/1171.[66] This school has been tied repeatedly to Nūr al-Dīn's endeavours to make use of *jihād* for his political and military goals and along these lines Ibn ʿAsākir is said to have "shaped the school into the intellectual epicentre of Nūr al-Dīn's jihad propaganda".[67] It might be more appropriate to see the construction in light of Nūr al-Dīn's large-scale building projects, including a hospital, a public

---

[62] Ḥalwānī, *Ibn ʿAsākir wa-dawruh fī al-jihād*.

[63] Mourad and Lindsay, *The Intensification*.

[64] Abū Qāsim ʿAlī b. al-Ḥasan Ibn ʿAsākir, *Muʿjam al-shuyūkh*, ed. Wafāʾ Taqī al-Dīn (Damascus, 2003). For more detail, see Shams al-Dīn Muḥammad b. Aḥmad al-Dhahabī, *Siyar aʿlām al-nubalāʾ*, ed. Shuʿayb al-Arnāʾūṭ and et al, 11th ed., 25 vols. (Beirut, 1992), 20:556.

[65] al-Ḥamawī, *Muʿjam al-udabāʾ* / *Irshād al-arīb ilā maʿrifat al-adīb*, 4:1698.

[66] Muḥammad Muṭīʿ al-Ḥāfiẓ, *Dūr al-ḥadīth al-sharīf bi-Dimashq* (Damascus, 2010), 10.

[67] Mourad and Lindsay, *The Intensification*, 50; Similarly, Suleiman A. Mourad and James E. Lindsay. "Rescuing Syria from the Infidels: The Contribution of Ibn ʿAsakir of Damascus to the Jihad Campaign of Sultan Nur al-Din," *Crusades* 6 (2007): 44, 48.

Table 2 Reading sessions of Ibn ʿAsākir's *Forty Hadiths for Inciting Jihad*

#	Date	Location	Participants	Al-Birzālī	Certificates[b]
A	7 Rajab 565/ 28 March 1170	Private Garden in Mizza	16 (1p)[a]	Copyist	79b
B	29 Ramaḍān 569/ 3 May 1174	Umayyad Mosque	31 and others	Copyist	79b–80a
C	25 Dhū al-Ḥijja 617/ 20 February 1221	Umayyad Mosque	3	Reader, Writer	79b
D	9 Rabīʿ I 624/ 26 February 1227	Khātūniyya School	6	Reader, Writer	80a
E	22 Rabīʿ I 624/ 12 March 1227	Umayyad Mosque	6	Reader	80a
F	26 Rabīʿ I 624/ 16 March 1227	Umayyad Mosque, Zāwiya Naṣr al-Maqdisi	4	Reader	80a
G	13 Ṣafar 626/ 12 January 1229	Umayyad Mosque	47	Reader	80b
H	8 Jumādā I 626/ 4 April 1229	Umayyad Mosque	30 (9p)		81a
I	2 Rabīʿ II 627/ 17 February 1230	Dār al-Sunna [Dār al-Ḥadīth al-Nūriyya]	28	Auditor	81b
J	21 Shawwāl 633/ 27 June 1236	Kallāsa School	9 and others	Reader	81b
K	8 Rabīʿ I 718/ 10 May 1318	Private home	3 and others		67a

Notes
[a] A p indicates partial attendance.
[b] MS Damascus, National al-Asad Library 1592.

bath, and dozens of other buildings in Damascus and other cities under his control.[68] Looking at the diverse topics around which Ibn ʿAsākir transmitted hadith, and keeping in mind that it was a modest building of "diminutive size,"[69] there is simply no evidence to support the idea that *jihād* was the scholarly flagship of this specific school. What audition certificates do reveal about Ibn ʿAsākir's class schedule at the Dār al-Sunna is a diverse range of topics: in the building he transmitted, for example, a hadith collection about the merits of fasting in the month of Rajab or his hadith collection titled *Tajrīd*.[70] His *Forty Hadiths for Inciting Jihad* was transmitted in this school only once (#I) and this took place more than half a century after Nūr

---

[68] Yasser al-Tabba, "The Architectual Patronage of Nur Al-Din (1146–1174)" (PhD dissertation, New York University, 1982).

[69] Ibid., 111.

[70] Damascus, National al-Asad Library, MS 3807, fol. 11a; Damascus, National al-Asad Library, MS 3747 fol. 27b.

al-Dīn's and Ibn ʿAsākir's deaths. This school was thus much more a centre of post-canonical transmission of hadith rather than a centre of *jihād* propaganda.

What do the audition certificates reveal about Ibn ʿAsākir's role in transmitting his booklet on *jihād*? The picture of Ibn ʿAsākir's as "minister of propaganda"[71] for Nūr al-Dīn is mitigated when looking at the first attested session (#A in Table 2, above). This session took place in the garden of his nephews in Mizza, a rural suburb of Damascus.[72] In and of itself, this is nothing remarkable in the context of hadith transmission in this period: a look at the Damascene Corpus of Certificates shows that quite a few sessions took place outdoors. What is important in our context is the exclusionary aspect of this location. A private garden outside the city was inaccessible for uninvited guests and thus renders it impossible to see this meeting as an event meant to incite a large group of people. This becomes even more clear when we look at who actually participated in this session. It was attended by sixteen men in total, fourteen of whom belonged to Ibn ʿAsākir's very own family. The odd non-family members were part of the larger Ibn ʿAsākir household: a slave of his maternal cousin and a farmer (*fallāḥ*), who heard the final part only. Previous research has shown that Ibn ʿAsākir strategically transmitted the hadith he collected to his family in order to let them accumulate his short chains as cultural capital.[73] This first session dovetails with this strategy, a move which turned out to be successful in the long run: Ibn ʿAsākir established a scholarly dynasty attested well into the fourteenth century. His offspring and extended family held for some six decades the professorships of the Dār al-Sunna/Dār al-Ḥadīth al-Nūriyya. In terms of audience and location, this first transmission session was thus a family affair and there are no grounds whatsoever on which one could impute broader political motives to Ibn ʿAsākir based on this reading.

The second and last attested transmission in Ibn ʿAsākir's lifetime took place on a Friday in late Ramaḍān 569/May 1174, four years after the first reading, and attracted more than 31 auditors.[74] Does this larger number point towards a propaganda-like nature of the event? The move to the Umayyad Mosque, the central place of public and religious life in Damascus, meant opening the transmission to the public. The larger turnout was enabled not only by the public location but also by the weekday, Friday, the preferred day for popular reading sessions in the Damascene Corpus of Certificates.[75] Besides these logistical details, Ibn ʿAsākir's

---

[71] Mourad and Lindsay, *The Intensification*, 54.

[72] Damascus, National al-Asad Library, MS 1592, fol. 70b. See also Mourad and Lindsay, *The Intensification*, 185.

[73] Konrad Hirschler, "Reading Certificates (*Samāʿāt*) as a Prosopographical Source: Cultural and Social Practices of an Elite Family in Zangid and Ayyubid Damascus," in *Manuscript Notes as Documentary Sources*, ed. Andreas Görke and Konrad Hirschler (Beirut/Würzburg, 2011), 82–87.

[74] Damascus, National al-Asad Library, MS 1592, fol. 70b–80a. A short note on the abovementioned fragment of the forty-hadith reveals that this copy was also present at this reading session: Damascus, National al-Asad Library, MS 1025, fol. 46a. For the first certificate, see also Mourad and Lindsay, *The Intensification*, 185–86.

[75] Hirschler, *The Written Word*, 40.

age might have played a role. He was approaching his seventies and his advanced age significantly increased his already great attraction as a hadith transmitter. His chains were becoming more and more valuable and indeed, he died two years later. At any rate, the numbers were not much higher than his average audience figures when he read hadith works entirely unrelated to *jihād*. In 566/1170, 60 people gathered to participate in his transmission of a hadith collection of Ibn Jurayj (d. 150/767), a work with no thematic profile, but centred around the figure of this early transmitter.[76] Some years earlier, in 559/1164, Ibn ʿAsākir read another such hadith collection centred around the person of an early transmitter in the Umayyad Mosque to an audience of 34 participants.[77] With these numbers in mind, this second attested transmission session of *The Forty Hadiths for Inciting Jihad* is a popular session of average attendance, but with no indication that the topic influenced the attendance figures.

With a total audience of more than 43 individuals during his lifetime and more than an additional 136 after his death (see Table 2, above), the number of auditors Ibn ʿAsākir's *The Forty Hadiths for Inciting Jihad* attracted is considerably larger than al-Sulamī's mere nine individuals during his life and four after his death. These attendance figures have led Mourad and Lindsay to conclude that it attained "tremendous attention"[78] among Damascene scholars, reflecting its "important role in promoting the ideology and mentality of jihad [...]."[79] This impression is the result of looking at the audience figures in isolation, without considering Ibn ʿAsākir's activities on a broader scale. When we add his other transmission sessions to the equation, we see that *The Forty Hadiths for Inciting Jihad* did not attract outstanding attention and his alleged role in intensifying the *jihād* spirit has to be reassessed. How, then, does the transmission of this book fare when compared to his activities overall? The everyday scholarly activities of Ibn ʿAsākir have not been studied in detail and this is not the place to give a comprehensive overview of the day-to-day schedule of one of the most industrious scholars in the Middle Period. Further research is needed to better understand the whirlwind of his teaching sessions and his massive audience figures, a task facilitated by the many extant manuscripts rife with notes witnessing his activities. In the following, I will adduce only a few examples which force us to rethink his role as a *jihād* "propagandist" based on audition certificates.

We can start with the reading sessions of Ibn ʿAsākir's *History of Damascus* that have attracted most scholarly attention so far. The work's transmission, during and after his life, attracted more than one thousand participants in total, with up to 80 participants per session. Ibn ʿAsākir himself transmitted this book in three different groups in the course of roughly 5–6 years to hundreds of people from all walks of life. The different readings can be divided into two groups: scholarly sessions and

---

[76]   Leder, al-Sawwās, and al-Ṣāgharjī, *Muʿjam al-samāʿāt*, 93.
[77]   Ibid., 78.
[78]   Mourad and Lindsay, *The Intensification*, 95.
[79]   Ibid., 82.

popular sessions. The former were mostly attended by a small number of scholars who returned regularly, and were often held in private locations. The latter were attended by a large number of people in a public space, the Umayyad Mosque, and only a small minority attended regularly. After Ibn ʿAsākir's death, his son al-Qāsim, his nephews ʿAbd al-Raḥmān and al-Ḥasan, and other scholars continued transmitting the *History of Damascus* and it took them up to ten years and hundreds of sessions to get through his tomes.[80]

However, it was not only his *History of Damascus* that attracted a large audience. In 533/1138–39, Ibn ʿAsākir started a series of numbered hadith transmission sessions (*majālis*), which according to his son reached 408.[81] In these sessions, he dictated hadith (*amālī*) revolving around a certain topic, either from memory or from notes. The sessions in this series started with a prayer for the Prophet before Ibn ʿAsākir transmitted hadith. The topics range from the merits of the month of Ramadan (*majlis* 405) to the merits of the month of Rajab (*majlis* 66), from the merits of fasting (*majlis* 405) to the merits of fasting in the month of Rajab (*majlis* 67), from repentance (*majlis* 32) to the attributes of God (*majlis* 139). At the end of each lecture, Ibn ʿAsākir would cite a poetic verse before audition certificates were prepared. Those in the audience with higher ambitions wrote down Ibn ʿAsākir's dictations, some of which are extant and bear witness to his enormous popularity and his activities in transmitting hadith.[82] To get an impression of the popularity Ibn ʿAsākir's transmission sessions enjoyed, we can take a glimpse at a small collection of hadith he collected linked to the village of Ḥurdān in the Ghouta.[83] In 1175, shortly before his death, he presided over a transmission in the mosque of the village itself. Even though the transmission took place in a village, it still attracted 23 individuals.[84] In the following years, no less than 21 transmission sessions were held in Damascus and its environs for this collection with many individuals participating. Therefore, Ibn ʿAsākir's popularity did not substantially change after his death as can be seen in the continuous transmission of his hadith oeuvre, of which his *jihād* booklet is but one example.

---

[80]   In more detail: Hirschler, *The Written Word*, 32–81; idem. "Reading Certificates (*Samāʿāt*) as a Prosopographical Source." More cursorily: Yehoshua Frenkel, "The Chain of Traditions, or Transmitting Knowledge in Medieval Damascus, based on *Samāʿāt* of Ibn al-ʿAsākir [sic]," in *Egypt and Syria in the Fatimid, Ayyubid and Mamluk Eras*, ed. U. Vermeulen and Jo Van Steenbergen, vol. 4 (Leuven, 2005), 165–84.

[81]   al-Ḥamawī, *Muʿjam al-udabāʾ / Irshād al-arīb ilā maʿrifat al-adīb*, 4:1701.

[82]   *Majlisān min majālis al-Ḥāfiẓ Ibn ʿAsākir fī Masjid Dimashq*, ed. Muḥammad Muṭīʿ al-Ḥāfiẓ (Damascus, 1979); *Thalātha Majālis li-Ibn ʿAsākir fī Saʿat raḥmat Allāh taʿālā wa nafī al-tashbīh wa ṣifāt Allāh taʿālā*, ed. ʿĀṣim al-Kayyālī (Dubai, 1996); *Dhamm al-Malāhī (al-Majlis al-thānī wa-l-khamsūn min amālī Abī al-Qāsim ʿAlī b. al-Ḥasan b. Hibat Allāh al-Shāfiʿī*, ed. al-ʿArbī al-Dāʾiz al-Fariyāṭī (Beirut, 2003). Al-Fariyāṭī provides an overview of 25 lectures in the introduction to his edition, ibid., pp. 13–18. On the *amālī* practice, see Marzoug Alsehail, "Ḥadīth-Amālī Sessions: Historical Study of a Forgotten Tradition in Classical Islam" (PhD thesis, University of Leeds, 2014).

[83]   Damascus, National al-Asad Library, MS 3771, fols. 184–93.

[84]   Damascus, National al-Asad Library, MS 3771, fol. 191a.

Everything we know about the transmission of *The Forty Hadiths for Inciting Jihad* after his death is closely linked to one single person, the copyist of the sole surviving manuscript, namely al-Birzālī. In six of the nine attested sessions after Ibn ʿAsākir's death, he acted as the reader of the book and in one other session he participated as listener (see the penultimate column in Table 2, above). If we allow ourselves to walk into the same trap again and look at this in isolation, it appears that al-Birzālī had a particular interest in this specific book or the topic of *jihād*. Again, the bigger picture offers a corrective. Al-Birzālī was one of the main transmitters in Syria of his day, and with 42 entries in the Damascene Corpus of Certificates, he is one of the most prominent names in the hadith-minded world of early thirteenth-century Syria.[85] His role in the transmission of the *The Forty Hadiths for Inciting Jihad* has thus to be seen in light of his larger activities in the field of hadith transmission and not singled out as a special devotion to the idea of *jihād*. That al-Birzālī was not specifically trying to revive Ibn ʿAsākir's *jihād* collection can be seen, for example, in his wider interest in Ibn Asākir's work. He is attested to have copied and read (at least parts of) the gigantic *History of Damascus*.[86] He did not stop there but also copied[87] and took part in the transmission of at least three hadith collections[88] by Ibn ʿAsākir. All this suggests a broad interest in Ibn ʿAsākir's oeuvre as a whole, and in his prestigious chains of transmission in particular. It is also in this regard that we should read the whole title al-Birzālī noted on his copy: *The Forty Hadiths for Inciting Jihad from the Prophet, God Bless Him and Grant Him Peace, with Contiguous Chains of Transmission* (*al-Arbaʿūn ḥadīthan fī al-ḥathth ʿalā al-jihād ʿan rasūl allāh ṣallā allāhu ʿalayhī wa-ṣallam muttaṣilatan al-isnād*). This exact wording of the title is not attested in other sources and thus clearly shows that what mattered for al-Birzālī at least as much as the content were the uninterrupted chains going back to the Prophet.

It took roughly 45 years after Ibn ʿAsākir's passing for the next four transmission sessions to take place, and in terms of audience figures they were modest. In his first session (#C), al-Birzālī collated his copy in 617/1221 whilst receiving a permission to transmit the text by a nephew of Ibn ʿAsākir, Zayn al-Umanāʾ Abū Barakāt al-Ḥasan. This nephew was one of the main transmitters of Ibn ʿAsākir's hadith oeuvre and himself received the permission to transmit the text in the first

---

[85]   al-Dhahabī, *Siyār*, 23:55–57.

[86]   For reading certificates in al-Birzālī's hand; see, for example, New York, Columbia University, MS X893.7 Ib66, fols. 22a, 42a, 63a, 84a, 105a, 126a, 147a, 167a. See also Hirschler, 'Reading Certificates (*Samāʿāt*) as a Prosopographical Source," 85–86.

[87]   Abū Qāsim ʿAlī b. al-Ḥasan Ibn ʿAsākir, *al-Arbaʿūn al-buldāniyya: Arbaʿūn ḥadīthan ʿan arbaʿīn shaykhan min arbaʿīn madinat li-arbaʿīn min al-ṣaḥāba*, ed. ʿAbdū al-Ḥājj Muḥammad al-Ḥarīrī (Beirut, 1993), 9. For al-Birzālī as copyist of particularly Ibn ʿAsākir's works, see also Umberto Bongianino, "Vehicles of Cultural Identity: Some Thoughts on Maghribi Scripts and Manuscripts in the Mashriq," in *The Maghrib in the Mashriq: Knowledge, Travel and Identity*, ed. Maribel Fierro and Mayte Penelas (Berlin, 2021), 469–71.

[88]   Damascus, National al-Asad Library, MS 3754, fol. 217a, Damascus, National al-Asad Library, MS 3744, fols. 15b, 55a. Damascus, National al-Asad Library, MS 3771, fols. 189b, 191b.

reading session (#A) for which he also wrote the original certificate which al-Birzālī copied into his manuscript. Although al-Birzālī's first reading session took place in the Umayyad Mosque with the potential of attracting a large audience, only two more men participated. The same tendency of low attendance figures holds true for the next three sessions, all taking place within a couple of weeks in February and March 624/1227. Al-Birzālī read the text to six men in the Khātūniyya school (#D), six in the Umayyad Mosque (#E), and four yet again in the Umayyad Mosque (#F), always dragging along his five-year-old son, Yūsuf.

Only in 1229, al-Birzālī's reading (#G) attracted a larger audience of 47 people. This session corresponds to the typical popular reading session by taking place on a Friday at the Umayyad Mosque. The next transmission (#H) stretched over two sessions with 21 participants in the first session and an additional 9 participants from hadith 21 onwards in a second and final session. Roughly ten months later, 28 participants, including two five-year-old children, heard the book in the Dār al-Sunna (Dār al-Ḥadīth al-Nūriyya) (#I). Another 9 "and others" came to a transmission session in a Damascene school in 1236 (#J). The last attested reading (#K) of *The Forty Hadiths for Inciting Jihad* took place in 1318 in a private home. Only three men are named, but others took part too. As the reading took place 27 years after the last Franks had left the region, it appears that the hadith collection's currency cannot be reduced to the crusading period but was valued even after they had left the Levant.

With 11 attested instances, the number of transmission sessions for Ibn ʿAsākir's *jihād* booklet may seem quite large. However, this is the case only when we look at it in isolation. Compared to 14 transmission sessions for his hadith collection on the merits of the month of Ramadan and at least 22 for his hadith collection revolving around the village of Ḥurdān, the reception of *The Forty Hadiths for Inciting Jihad* is rather meagre or at least below average. Similarly, the turnout of more than 184 auditors in total was not limited to Ibn ʿAsākir's booklet but can be seen in sessions unrelated to him. A look at the Damascene Corpus of Certificates shows that, for example, a copy of the *Kitāb al-Arbaʿīn* by Ḥasan b. Sufyān al-Shaybān al-Fasawī (or al-Nasawī) (d. 303/916) with forty hadith about different topics in Islamic law carries 34 audition certificates attesting to a total audience of 124 individuals. The manuscript of the *Arbaʿūn Ḥadīth* by ʿAbd al-Khāliq b. Zāhir b. Ṭāhir al-Shaḥāmī (d. 549/1154–55) carries 25 audition certificates with 138 attested auditors. The *Majlis al-baṭāqa min amālī Ḥamza al-Kinānī* carries 83 audition certificates with 533 attested auditors and the *Sitta Majālis min Amālī* of Abū Yaʿlā al-Farrāʾ (d. 458/1066) attracted a total audience of 292 individuals in 16 sessions, one of which counted 124 auditors.[89] On balance, therefore, the impact of Ibn ʿAsākir's *jihād* booklet was not exceedingly high and there is no evidence that

---

[89] Leder, al-Sawwās, and al-Ṣagharjī, *Muʿjam al-samāʿāt*, 64–67 for al-Fasawī, 25–27 for al-Shaḥāmī, 30–39 for al-Kinānī, 138–39 for al-Farrāʾ.

the audience for this book was attracted by the topic rather than the valuable chains through which he was able to transmit the hadith.

Jihād Literature beyond al-Sulamī and Ibn ʿAsākir

Al-Sulamī and Ibn ʿAsākir have so far been the most prominent names linked to the dissemination of *jihād* ideology in the crusading period. While I have argued above that the two texts and their reception cannot be considered evidence for a particular interest in *jihād*, one might object that they were not the only authors writing about the topic. The catalogue of the abovementioned Ashrafiyya library from the thirteenth century, for example, contains twelve *jihād*-related books, eight written in the period under discussion, and Bartschat lists five forty-hadith collections with a thematical focus on *jihād* from between the years 1098 and 1291.[90] In the cases where these books have survived, they should receive dedicated studies along the methodological lines of this article to take their audiences into account. A detailed examination lies outside the scope of this article.

However, I will briefly mention two further examples which seem to corroborate the argument that *jihād* literature and its reception are much more firmly embedded in the cultural practice of hadith transmission than in a context of preaching with the aim to mobilise people to fight. The two examples are both written by members of the famous Maqdisī family which fled the crusaders from the Nablus region to eventually settle to the north of Damascus. Due to their migration history, the Maqdisīs have been described as "stand[ing] out for their active participation in the *jihad* propaganda of the time."[91] Naturally, their *jihād* texts would fit neatly into this assumed role, but this remains to be analysed in detail. For Mourad and Lindsay, these two books confirm "that the intensified and reoriented jihad had become normative among the Sunni religious establishment."[92] But without a more careful look at these two texts, this is a snap judgment, while evidence for their role in the assumed *jihād* zeitgeist remains to be found. What research by now has shown is the outstanding role of the Maqdisī family in hadith transmission in Syria during the crusading period and beyond: they are by far the most prominent family in the Damascene Corpus of Certificates.

The first exemplary text is by ʿAbd al-Ghanī b. ʿAbd al-Wāḥid al-Maqdisī (d. 600/1203). A list of his writings reveals one *jihād*-related title, *The Seeker's Delight on Jihād and Jihād Fighters* (*Tuḥfat al-ṭālibīn fī al-jihād wa-l-mujāhidīn*).[93] The National al-Asad Library in Damascus holds a unique manuscript by him

---

[90]   Hirschler, *Medieval Damascus*, 35; Bartschat, *Dschihad der Zunge, des Stifts und des Schwertes?*, 33.

[91]   Yehoshua Frenkel, "Muslim Responses to the Frankish Dominion in the Near East," in *The Crusades and The Near East*, ed. Conor Kostick (London, 2011), 34.

[92]   Mourad and Lindsay, *The Intensification*, 62.

[93]   al-Dhahabī, *Taʾrīkh al-islām*, 42:446.

with the title *The Merit of Jihād (Faḍl al-jihād)*,[94], but we do not know if this is one and the same text.[95] Regardless, we must see this title again in light of his broader scholarly activities. ʿAbd al-Ghanī al-Maqdisī was another prime example of the chain-collecting hype of the post-canonical hadith transmission period, travelling from Alexandria in the west to Isfahan in the east to collect hadith. He wrote "beyond description, he composed useful compositions, and he continued hearing hadith and being heard from, to write, and compile until he passed away,"[96] a bibliography which ran up to around one thousand booklets.[97] Similar to the case of Ibn ʿAsākir, we should not single out one title from this large oeuvre and attach undue importance to it. When we look at the broader context we see that, next to *The Merit of Jihad*, he wrote similar books with titles such as *The Merits of Mecca (Faḍāʾil al-Makka)*, *The Merits of the Pilgrimage (Faḍāʾil al-Ḥajj)*, *The Merits of the 10th of [the Muslim Month] Dhū al-Ḥijjā (Faḍāʾil ʿashar Dhī al-Ḥijja)* amongst others.[98] *Jihād*, it appears, was one of many topics around which he framed a hadith collection. And not a successful one at that. There is not a single manuscript note on his autograph that would allow any speculation about any reception whatsoever. The same holds true for the second example from the Maqdisī family, a *jihad* collection by Aḥmad b. ʿAbd al-Wāḥid al-Maqdisī al-Bukhārī (d. 623/1226).[99] Al-Bukhārī started travelling in pursuit of hadith in his early teens and reached as far east as Bukhara. He left a booklet with the title *The Merit of the Jihad and Jihad Fighters (Faḍl al-jihād wa-l-mujāhidīn)*;[100] its sole surviving manuscript carries only one note, stating it was copied by and transmitted to a single family member.[101]

The increasingly pressing question is whether *jihād*-related texts from the crusading period are best understood in the interpretive framework of anti-crusader endeavours. Were they used to preach resistance against the Franks? A close look at the two scholars mostly seen in this light, al-Sulamī and Ibn ʿAsākir, suggests otherwise. Al-Sulamī barely made it into the history books. In the few biographical dictionaries in which he is mentioned, he is portrayed as a grammarian and a hadith transmitter, not as a preacher or a proponent of *jihād*. His *jihād* treatise, surviving only in a unique and fragmentary copy, is not mentioned anywhere, and remained uncited in the rich literary tradition of its time. In contrast to al-Sulamī, Ibn ʿAsākir was a widely celebrated scholar. His fame rested on his knowledge of hadith, the discipline in which he published most extensively. *Jihād* was but one of the topics around which he produced a collection of hadith, and this did not even happen on

---

[94]   Damascus, National al-Asad Library, MS 3831, fols. 17a–23a.

[95]   Mourad and Lindsay do not provide shelf numbers for their manuscript evidence. The online catalogue of the National al-Asad library, however, does not provide any results for *Tuḥfat al-ṭālibīn fī al-jihād wa-l-mujāhidīn*.

[96]   al-Dhahabī, *Taʾrīkh al-islām*, 42:444.

[97]   al-Dhahabī, *Siyar*, 21:445.

[98]   al-Dhahabī, *Siyar*, 21:446–48; al-Dhahabī, *Taʾrīkh al-islām*, 42:446.

[99]   al-Dhahabī, *Taʾrīkh al-islām*, 45:143–44.

[100]   Damascus, National al-Asad Library, MS 3744, fols. 112b–123a.

[101]   Damascus, National al-Asad Library, MS 3744, fol. 123a.

his own initiative. It took the request of Nūr al-Dīn for him to do so. Immediate threats by the Franks, like the siege of Damascus in 1148, did not trigger such an idea in his head.

The analysis of the reception of these two books has shown that they dovetail with hundreds of contemporary sessions centred around the transmission of hadith and the fascination with short chains. The *Book of the Jihad* by al-Sulamī had a remarkably unsuccessful reception history. Based on the surviving evidence, the author transmitted it only to a handful of people in a suburb of Damascus. The transmission of his book after his passing was even less of a success – we have evidence for only one reading session. This was certainly different in the case of Ibn ʿAsākir's much shorter booklet, which he himself transmitted twice, once to family members and once to a larger public audience. In this single public transmission session, Ibn ʿAsākir drew a crowd of more than 30 people, while his forty-hadith collection was transmitted in nine sessions as long as 150 years after his death. But there are no clues which would justify setting apart the transmission of the two texts from the thousands of other transmission sessions in Damascus in this period. On the contrary, their general conditions correspond to what we can see in the comparative Damascene Corpus of Certificates.

The recontextualisation of two *jihād* texts urges us to stay attentive when dealing with Islamic sources from the crusading period before drawing (or, indeed, leaping to) hasty conclusions.[102] Taking the context of textual production and reception into consideration (an opportunity we have relatively often for Arabic sources of that period) may offer a corrective to a ready-made interpretative framework. In this framework, Muslim scholarship and literary production are depicted largely as a reaction to Frankish action. Furthermore, the purported reaction is often wrapped in ahistorical terminology to accord with modern perceptions. Adhering to this framework runs the risk of distorting authorial intentions and cultural practices beyond recognition. It is when we zoom out and include the big picture in our interpretations that a more grounded appreciation can be achieved.

---

[102] For a comparable case, see Antonia Bosanquet, "From Obscurity to Authority: The Changing Reception of Ibn Qayyim al-Jawziyya's *Aḥkām Ahl al-Dhimma* from the Eighth/Fourteenth to the Fifteenth/Twenty-First Century," *Islam and Christian–Muslim Relations* 32/3 (2021): 237–59.

The Duchy of Philippopolis (1204–c. 1236/37): A Latin Border Principality in a Byzantine (Greek/Bulgarian) Milieu

Filip Van Tricht

Independent scholar, Melle
filip.van.tricht@telenet.be

Abstract

The duchy of Philippopolis was created after the crusader conquest of Constantinople in 1204. Ruled by members of the Trith and Estreux families, local lords from the county of Hainaut in the Low Countries, this little-studied principality lasted for several decades, possibly until the mid-1230s. Bordering the Bulgarian kingdom/empire, the region suffered the consequences of successive military campaigns during the early years of its existence. Following Emperor Henry's victory at Philippopolis in 1208 against Tsar Boril and the concomitant Latin-Bulgarian peace and alliance in 1213, a more tranquil and harmonious period ensued. While a lack of sources prevents a detailed analysis, a number of hypotheses can be formulated regarding various aspects, such as the secular and ecclesiastical organization of the principality, the cohabitation of Latins and local Greeks and Bulgarians, and the relationship with other major players in Latin Romania including the Latin Emperor, the city of Venice, and the neighbouring lord of the Rhodope region, despot Alexios Sthlabos.

The Duchy of Philippopolis was one of the feudal principalities created after the Latin conquest of Constantinople in April 1204 in the wake of the Fourth Crusade. Until now no attempt at an encompassing study addressing the main aspects of its history has been undertaken. Benjamin Hendrickx touched upon it briefly in his article on the various "duchies" in Latin Romania and Kalin Yordanov has recently drawn attention to Bulgarian folklore, art historical and literary relicts illuminating some aspects of the duchy's history.[1] In this article I intend to sketch a picture of Philippopolis during the Latin period. The source situation, as we will see, is far from ideal and outright meagre as time progresses, inevitably leading to a somewhat speculative approach as to filling in the missing pieces of the puzzle.

---

[1] Benjamin Hendrickx, "Les duchés de l'empire latin de Constantinople après 1204: origine, structures et statuts," *Revue belge de philologie et d'histoire* 93 (2015): 305–314; Kalin Yordanov, "One Reflection of the Fourth Crusade on the Boyana Church Frescoes (1258/9)," *Annuaire de l'Université de Sofia "St. Kliment Ohridski"/Centre de Recherches Slavo-Byzantines "Ivan Dujčev"* 100 (2019): 48–67; idem, "Bulgarian Folklore Relicts from the Time of the Fourth Crusade and the Frankokratia in North-Western Thrace," *Proceedings of the National Museum of History (Sofia)* 32 (2020): 368–70. See also: Filip Van Tricht, *The Latin Renovatio of Byzantium. The Empire of Constantinople (1204–1228)*, The Medieval Mediterranean 90 (Leiden, 2011), 170–71.

Nevertheless various elements of its political as well as its ecclesiastical and socio-cultural history can be traced. The following topics will be examined in order: the establishment and initial period of the principality under Renier of Trith (until 1208); the second phase of its history under the Estreux family; the ducal status of the principality within the empire; the local governmental structures along with the cohabitation of Latins, Greeks and Bulgarians; and, finally, the end of Latin rule in the region.

Renier of Trith and the Establishment of the Duchy

At the end of the twelfth century Philippopolis was the administrative centre of the Byzantine *thema* (or *theme*) of Philippopolis, Beroe, Morra and Achridos, comprising northern Thrace and the eastern part of the Rhodope mountains (see Fig. 1).[2] As such Philippopolis served as an important base for military campaigns in the region. Chronicler and imperial marshal Geoffrey of Villehardouin considered it to be one of the empire's three greatest cities, no doubt after the capital Constantinople and Thessaloniki. Emperor Henry of Flanders/Hainaut (1205/6–1216) in an August 1206 letter characterized it as a *civitas maxima and munitissima*.[3] The city and the surrounding region (just like, for example, Thessaloniki) are nevertheless absent from the *Partitio terrarum imperii Romaniae*. This 1204 document lists the territories attributed to the Latin emperor, the non-Venetian crusaders, and the city of Venice respectively, but has only been preserved in an unfinished version. The said chronicler, however, informs us that emperor Baldwin I of Flanders/Hainaut (1204–5) granted the "duchy of Philippopolis" (*duchee de Phinepople*) to Renier II of Trith(-St-Léger). The latter was an important baron from Hainault – one of the six peers of the county of Valenciennes – and had been one of Baldwin's most trusted advisers for years.[4]

In November 1204, Renier arrived in Philippopolis with a large garrison of 120 knights. If we apply the standard equation of 1 knight = 2 sergeants on horseback

[2] Catherine Asdracha, *La région des Rhodopes aux XIIIe et XIVe siècles. Etude de géographie historique*, Texte und Forschungen zur byzantinisch-neugriechischen Philologie 49 (Athens, 1976), 154–62; Peter Soustal, *Thrakien (Thrake, Rodope und Haimimontos)*, Tabula Imperii Byzantini [hereafter TIB] 6 (Vienna, 2004), 399–404.

[3] Geoffroy de Villehardouin, *La conquête de Constantinople*, ed. Edmond Faral (Paris, 1961), §401. Michel J. Brial, ed., *De varia Latinorum in imperio fortuna*, RHGF 18:528.

[4] Villehardouin, *La conquête de Constantinople*, §304. On Renier II, lord of Trith-St-Léger, and his lineage: Jean Longnon, *Les compagnons de Villehardouin* (Geneva, 1978), 151–52; Edouard Grar, "Famille des seigneurs de Trith, pairs de Valenciennes, du XIIe au XIVe s.," *Mémoires historiques sur l'arrondissement de Valenciennes* 2 (1868): 57–84. For the *Partitio* see: Antonio Carile, "Partitio terrarum imperii Romanie," *Studi Veneziani* 7 (1965): 125–305; Nikolaos Oikonomides, "La décomposition de l'empire byzantin à la veille de 1204 et les origines de l'empire de Nicée: à propos de la 'Partitio Romaniae'," in *XVe Congrès international d'études byzantines. Rapports et co-rapports. I. Histoire. 1. Forces centrifuges et centripètes dans le monde byzantin entre 1071 et 1261* (Athens, 1976), 1–28; Van Tricht, *The Latin Renovatio of Byzantium*, 47–53.

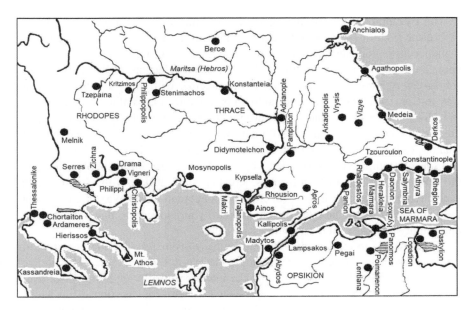

Fig. 1   Map of Philippopolis and the wider region.
Created by the author.

= 4 foot soldiers, Renier's troops may have totalled about 840 men. According to Villehardouin, Renier was well received by the local population, who are said to have accepted him as their new lord. The chronicler explains that the city had been under constant threat from the Bulgarian tsar Kalojan (1197–1207). With the new Latin military aid they were now able to withstand this threat and to reassume control over the surrounding region that before had partly been conquered by the Bulgarians.[5] The reception given to Renier rather contrasts with the way emperor Alexios III Angelos (1195–1203) and his entourage were refused entry after he had abandoned his capital in July 1203.[6] In early 1205, however, discontented Byzantine magnates connected to the former emperor Alexios III – who meanwhile had been captured in Thessaly by Marquis Boniface I of Montferrat, lord of Thessaloniki (1204–7) – found fertile ground in the region of Adrianople and Didymoteichon to start a revolt against Latin rule with the aid of the Bulgarian tsar.[7]

---

[5] Villehardouin, *La conquête de Constantinople*, §311.

[6] Georgios Akropolites, *Historia*, ed. August Heisenberg, *Georgii Acropolitae Opera* 1 (Leipzig, 1903), §5.

[7] On this short-lived Byzantine-Bulgarian collaboration: Theodoros Vlachos, "Kalojan plündert Thrakien und Makedonien," *Byzantina* 2 (1970): 271–83; Günter Prinzing, *Die Bedeutung Bulgariens und Serbiens in den Jahren 1204–1219 im Zusammenhang mit der Entstehung und Entwicklung der byzantinischen Teilstaaten nach der Einnahme Konstantinopels infolge des 4. Kreuzzuges*, Miscellanea Byzantina Monacensia 12 (Munich, 1972), 1–63; G. Cankova-Petkova, "A propos des rapports bulgarofrancs au commencement du XIIIe siècle," *Bulgarian Historical Review* 4 (1976): 51–61; Jean-

The Byzantine elite of Philippopolis did not turn to Tsar Kalojan and join in, as is clear from the tsar's subsequent treatment of the city. However, the crisis in the adjacent region caused some of the Latin knights to lose their nerve. Renier's eponymous son Renier, his brother Gilles, his nephew Jacques of Bondues and his son-in-law Achard of Verly abandoned him together with thirty knights. On their way to Constantinople they were captured by rebellious Byzantines and delivered to Kalojan who executed them. This upsetting news caused eighty more knights to quit Philippopolis, who, using a different route, safely reached the coastal town of Rhaidestos in southern Thrace.[8] Renier was now left with only about fifteen knights and some accompanying troops that were divided between Philippopolis itself and the town and fortress of Stenimachos, situated about 20 km to the southeast. In such circumstances part of the local elite and population must have started to doubt the Latins' ability to guarantee the city's security any longer or may have seen an opportunity to further their own interests.

Villehardouin informs us that the Paulicians (*Popelican*) – having been told of Emperor Baldwin I's defeat at Adrianople (14 April 1205) – turned to Kalojan, whose army was only days away, with the intention of offering him control over their city.[9] These Paulicians, who represented a significant portion of the city's population, can be identified as the adherents of the dualist Paulician heresy (and possibly also those adhering to Bogomilism), a heterogenous group comprising mostly members of the local Armenian and Bulgarian communities.[10] The fact that they turned to Kalojan may indicate that Renier himself in late 1204 had primarily opted for cooperation with the Greek or Orthodox component of the local elite, possibly frustrating other groups. The Paulicians' opposition to his authority caused Renier to ultimately abandon the city in order to concentrate the remnant of his troops in the castle of Stenimachos, situated 2 km south of the eponymous town. This fortress was evidently easier to defend with a small force than a large and

---

Claude Cheynet, *Pouvoir et contestations à Byzance (963–1210)*, Byzantina Sorbonensia 9 (Paris, 1990), 470–71; Van Tricht, *The Latin Renovatio of Byzantium*, 388–89; idem, "The Byzantino-Latin Principality of Adrianople and the Challenge of Feudalism (1204/6–ca. 1227/28). Empire, Venice, and Local Autonomy," *Dumbarton Oaks Papers* 68 (2015): 227–29; Alexandru Madgearu, *The Asanids. The Political and Military History of the Second Bulgarian Empire (1185–1280)*, Eastern Europe in the Middle Ages 41 (Leiden, 2017), 144–65.

[8] Villehardouin, *La conquête de Constantinople*, §345–436.

[9] Villehardouin, *La conquête de Constantinople*, §399–402.

[10] On the Paulicians of Philippopolis: Asdracha, *La région des Rhodopes*, 61–62, 72–74. On the ethnic composition of the population of Philippopolis, see also: Dimitri Obolensky, *The Bogomils. A Study in Balkan Neo-Manichaeism* (Cambridge, 1948), 232–33; Borislav Primov, "Bulgari, gurci i latinci v Plovdiv prez 1204–1205 g. Roljata na bogomilite" [Bulgarians, Greeks and Latins in the history of Philippopolis at the beginning of the 13th century. The role of the Bogomils], *Izvestija na Bulgarskoto Istoricesko Druzestvo* 22–23 (1948): 156–58; Krassimira Gagova, "La Thrace du Nord dès la fin du XIIe jusqu'à la fin du XIVe siècle (La Bulgarie au Sud de Hemus)," *Byzantinobulgarica* 8 (1986): 193–94; Benjamin Hendrickx, "Les Arméniens d'Asie Mineure et de Thrace au début de l'Empire latin de Constantinople," *Revue des études arméniennes* 22 (1990–91): 217–23. Janet Hamilton and Bernard Hamilton, *Christian Dualist Heresies in the Byzantine World, c.650–c.1450* (Manchester and New York, 1998), 23–24, 41–44, 114, 164–71, 259–60.

internally divided city. On their departure Renier and his companions burnt down a suburb where many Paulicians lived, dealing a clear blow to their opponents, and thus possibly – intentionally or not – strengthening the position of the Greek population.

The fact that Renier did not withdraw to Constantinople indicates that he was not planning to give up on his principality and had every intention of regaining it once the Bulgarian threat had subsided. Left to their own devices the Greek elite of Philippopolis, however, elected one of their members, Alexios Aspietes, to be their leader and new emperor even, a move that may well be taken as reflecting a rather strong sense of local autonomy or regional patriotism. Aspietes belonged to a Byzantinized/Grecisized family with Armenian roots, had been governor of the region around Serres in Macedonia in 1195 and had spent some time in Bulgarian captivity.[11] It is probably this move that led emperor Henry of Flanders/Hainaut in his abovementioned letter of August 1206 to his brother Godfrey, provost of St Amé in Douai, to indiscriminately accuse – quite unlike Villehardouin's report – the entire city of rebelling against Renier, without considering the internal divisions among local elite and population.[12] Tsar Kalojan likewise, as the move was rather aimed against him than the Latins (who for the time being seemed a spent force), did not appreciate Aspietes' proclamation as emperor and attacked the city. Not being in a position to withstand a prolonged siege, the defenders surrendered on the condition that no harm would come to themselves or their city. Kalojan, however, broke his promise and executed Aspietes and many members of the elite in gruesome ways, and inflicted extensive damage to the city and its defences.[13]

While Henry may have been critical of Aspietes and his supporters, Kalojan's unrestrained aggression would prove to be the stepping stone for renewed Latin-Byzantine cooperation. Some members of the elite of Philippopolis managed to flee to Adrianople and Didymoteichon, where they convinced the local Byzantine archons that the Bulgarian tsar was not a trustworthy ally and that they should compromise with the Latins.[14] This suggests that, from a Byzantine perspective, earlier relations with the Latins in Philippopolis were evaluated as acceptable and presumably had only broken down as a consequence of a series of ill-advised actions by members of both groups in a time of acute crisis. Some aristocrats of Philippopolis, however, did choose to seek refuge with Emperor Theodore I Laskaris (1206/08–1221) in

---

[11] Niketas Choniates, *Historia*, ed. Jean-Louis Van Dieten, Corpus Fontium Historiae Bizantinae. Series Berolinensis 11 (Berlin, 1975), 2: 465, 627; Alexis G. Savvides, "Notes on the Armeno-Byzantine family of Aspietes, late 11th–early 13th centuries," *Byzantinoslavica* 52 (1991): 70–79.

[12] Brial, RHGF 18:528. The discrepancy between Villehardouin's and Henry's reports may be explained by a difference in purpose: the letter was a propagandist piece written in the moment, while the chronicle was written several years later allowing for a more nuanced and possibly better informed approach.

[13] Villehardouin, *La conquête de Constantinople*, §401. Choniates, *Historia*, 627. Brial, RHGF 18:528.

[14] On this see Van Tricht, "The Byzantino-Latin Principality of Adrianople," 329–30.

Nicaea instead of staying within the Latin space of influence.[15] One element that may point to good relations is that Renier had quite possibly allowed the local Byzantine metropolitan to remain in office. This would seem to follow from the fact that no Latin incumbent is attested and that the metropolitan was still present in the city at the time of its capture by Kalojan, who had him executed.[16] If Renier had deposed or exiled him, one would expect the metropolitan to have found refuge elsewhere as did a number of his colleagues, not in the city or the surrounding area (although it cannot be excluded that he might have remained in hiding in the vicinity and regained Philippopolis after the Latins' departure).[17] Additionally, we might perhaps hypothesize that Renier had confirmed or appointed Aspietes as head of the local Byzantine administration, just as one George Phrangopoulos is attested as *doux* in Latin Thessaloniki around 1213. This could help explain his leadership after the Latins had left.[18]

Renier and his companions managed to maintain themselves at the fortress of Stenimachos for thirteen months. Part of that time they were besieged from the nearby eponymous town. At the same time, however, they seem to have remained in contact with the broader region. In July 1206 imperial regent Henry of Flanders/Hainaut – in the context of yet another campaign to relieve the region of Adrianople from Kalojan's continued attacks – mounted a rescue expedition to deliver Renier from his isolated position. The latter was able to confirm to Henry and the Constantinopolitan barons that Emperor Baldwin had in fact died in Bulgarian captivity.[19] Evidently credible reports of the emperor's death had managed to reach him in the preceding weeks or months in spite of the presence of enemy forces. Renier then returned to Adrianople with Henry, with Stenimachos (and Philippopolis) abandoned for the time being. The baron from Hainaut next fades from view for almost two years. We have no way of knowing whether Renier

---

[15] Choniates, *Historia*, 627.

[16] Villehardouin, La conquête de Constantinople, §401; John V. A. Fine, *The Late Medieval Balkans: A Critical Survey from the Late Twelfth Century to the Ottoman Conquest* (Ann Arbor, 1994), 84–85; Johannes Preiser-Kapeller, *Der Episkopat im späten Byzanz. Ein Verzeichnis der Metropoliten und Bischöfe des Patriarchats von Konstantinopel in der Zeit von 1204 bis 1453* (Saarbrücken 2008), 362.

[17] Patriarch John X Kamateros in 1204 had sought refuge in Didymoteichon, some 250 km from the capital (Peter Wirth, "Zur Frage eines politischen Engagements Patriarch Joannes X. Kamateros nach dem vierten Kreuzzug," *Byzantinische Forschungen* 4 (1972): 239–52). Metropolitan Constantine Mesopotamites of Thessaloniki fled to Epiros: Alicia Simpson, *Niketas Choniates. A Historiographical Study* (Oxford, 2013), 32–34. Metropolitan Niketas Choniates of Athens at first tried to stay in Latin-occupied Euboia, but was soon forced to relocate to the desolate and at the time still unoccupied island of Kea: Michael Choniates, *Epistulae*, ed. Foteini Kolovou, Corpus Fontium Historiae Byzantinae. Series Berolinensis 41 (Berlin, 2001), 6*–7*.

[18] On George Phrangopoulos and the partial continuation of the Byzantine administration: Van Tricht, *The Latin Renovatio of Byzantium*, 122–44, 245–46 (with further references).

[19] Villehardouin, *La conquête de Constantinople*, §439–441. Brial, RHGF 18:529. Approaching Stenimachos the army also camped at the fortresses of Ephraïm and Mneiakos (Moniac), which were surrendered to Henry. Villehardouin does not make explicit mention of permanent garrisons having been stationed there at this time.

played any role in the counter-campaigns Henry undertook in the region shortly after his coronation (20 August 1206), leading him to plunder and/or destroy Beroe (Stara Zagora), Therma and Anchialos, or whether he was part of the successive Latin garrisons that were stationed in Adrianople.[20]

A lacuna in our source material – Villehardouin's chronicle breaking off in early September 1207 and Henry of Valenciennes' work, in effect a continuation of Villehardouin's history and one of our few narrative sources for the period, only starting in July 1208 – makes it hard to evaluate what became of Philippopolis in the meantime. John Fine advanced the hypothesis that local Greek aristocrats may have retaken control, but this seems unlikely as the city's fortifications had probably not yet been restored and it was thus still in an undefendable state.[21] A close reading of Valenciennes suggests a different hypothesis. The chronicler from Hainaut, as he informs us, started writing his work in order to tell his readership of Emperor Henry's recent victory over the new Bulgarian tsar Boril (1207–18), which took place near Philippopolis on 31 July 1208. Valenciennes starts his report with the news of an invasion of the empire's territories by Boril reaching the imperial court in Constantinople, but the exact place or region of the attack is not stated. Emperor Henry decided to take immediate action and assembled his army at Selymbria, situated about two days from the capital. Next he moved to Adrianople, where he encamped with his army apparently reinforced by local units made up of Greeks. There a battle plan was decided upon: they would march towards Bulgaria (*vers Blaquie*) to obtain the aid of Alexios Sthlabos (*Esclas*) to attack Boril. Sthlabos is identified as a *haut hom* and Boril's cousin with whom he was at war. The Bulgarian tsar is said to have taken (part of) his land, but conversely Sthlabos had captured several of Boril's castles.[22]

Next we find the army at Beroe where they stayed the night. The next morning Boril attacked them and an indecisive skirmish followed. Henry then decided to leave the Bulgarians for the time being and moved to Philippopolis (*laissommes les Blas à tant et tornons viers Phinepople*). Valenciennes' report here may be interpreted in the sense that the Bulgarians had been driven back to their own territory and Henry now wished to regain imperial lands. The chronicler says nothing explicitly about the political situation at Philippopolis, but the imperial army is depicted as setting up camp just outside the city, swiftly and without difficulty. Obviously there was no immediate Bulgarian threat and Henry did not have to fear hostile action from the inhabitants of Philippopolis either. Valenciennes' account in fact reads

---

[20] In fact the available sources mention hardly any baron by name in the context of these events: Villehardouin, *La conquête de Constantinople*, §441–452. Brial, RHGF 18:529; Van Tricht, "The Byzantino-Latin Principality of Adrianople," 331–32.

[21] See Fine, *The Late Medieval Balkans*, 93.

[22] Henri de Valenciennes, *Histoire de l'empereur Henri de Constantinople*, ed. Jean Longnon, Documents relatifs à l'histoire des croisades 2 (Paris, 1948), §504–505, §545; on the Greek units: §543, §549. On the battle of Philippopolis see Filip Van Tricht, "A Comparison of the Battles of Adrianople (1205) and Philippopolis (1208). Event, Impact and Resonance," in *Studies on Edirne from Prehistory to Republic*, ed. Ergün Karaca (Edirne, 2021), 69–95.

much the same as the army's earlier stops at Selymbria and Adrianople. Both these towns indubitably were firmly under Latin imperial control, the former belonging to the imperial domain itself and the latter being ruled by imperial vassal and *kaisar* Theodore Branas. Valenciennes, however, does not care to mention that such an important city as Adrianople was not under direct imperial control and had been given in fief, probably in an effort not to diminish his imperial hero's authority and prestige in the eyes of his audience. This could mean that Philippopolis at this time simply also acknowledged Latin imperial authority and was under the control of a local vassal.

If so, this did not change the fact that local circumstances were still unsettled. Valenciennes notes that victuals were hard to come by in the region they had just crossed (*en douse grans jornées ne croissoit ne blés, ne orges, ne vins, ne avaine*). He also has the army's chaplain Philip state, just before the start of the Battle of Philippopolis, that the army found itself in a foreign land and on unfamiliar terrain, without any safe haven being available (*vous ki chi estes assamblé en estrange contrée, ne n'i avés castiel ne recet ù vos aiiés esperanche de garant avoir*).[23] These statements indicate that agricultural production in Thrace had suffered greatly from the ongoing war and that the city's fortifications had not yet been adequately restored, in the sense that it could not function as a secure fall-back position in case of defeat. For most participants the region of Philippopolis was also unfamiliar terrain and in any case far from their Western homelands. This was, however, not the case for everyone. Quite strikingly it is precisely at Philippopolis that we again meet Renier of Trith. Valenciennes tells us that he – together with Peter of Douai, Anselm of Cayeux and some other unnamed knights – was responsible for guarding the foragers who went out, in the neighbourhood of Philippopolis, to gather provisions for the army.[24] In my opinion Renier did not merely execute this task because he was familiar with the local geography and conditions: he may very well have been present here as the local feudal lord. Valenciennes does not say so explicitly – just as he does not mention *kaisar* Theodore Branas in the context of Adrianople – but at least part of his audience in Hainaut and Flanders would have known from earlier reports that Philippopolis was or had been Renier's city.[25]

That the region of Philippopolis was quite possibly again under Latin imperial and Renier's control would also seem to be borne out by the comparison of two other passages. After his victory against Boril, Henry marched to Kritzimos (*Crucemont*), about 25 km southwest of Philippopolis. Valenciennes explicitly states that the imperial troops "took the town and castle" (*asseurerent le ville et le castiel*). This phrase indicates that the town and fortress had not yet been under Latin control. It is here that envoys sent by Alexios Sthlabos, who was based at

---

[23] Valenciennes, *Histoire de l'empereur Henri de Constantinople*, §514, §523.

[24] Ibid., §515–518.

[25] See Henry's 1206 letter to his brother Geoffrey, which must have circulated in his homeland (see reference in note 3).

Tzepaina (Tsepina, some 50 km west of Kritzimos), first made contact with the imperial army. Sthlabos subsequently came in person and recognized Henry as his suzerain, with a marriage between him and the emperor's (illegitimate) daughter being arranged.[26] Clearly Kritzimos around this time had not been under Sthlabos' control either. The emperor then marched to Stenimachos (20 km southeast of Philippopolis). In doing so he must have passed through Philippopolis once more, as there was no direct road from Kritzimos to Stenimachos. Valenciennes describes the army's arrival there as follows: "our people turned back to a castle called Stenimachos" (*nostre gent s'en revinrent à un castel ke on apiele Estanemach*).[27] Apparently there was no need to secure the castle (or the nearby eponymous town for that matter), in spite of the fact that it was an imposing fortress and that the imperial army had not yet passed through there. This would seem to imply that the castle had been under Latin control again for some time, probably then with Renier of Trith as local lord. It may well have been Renier's main residence for the time being, awaiting the restoration of Philippopolis' fortifications. Here Sthlabos came to meet the emperor a second time and the details of the planned marriage were worked out. Before departing the emperor gave him two contingents of troops – one Latin, one Greek from Adrianople – under the command of his own half-brother, Eustace of Hainaut.

It is not clear what became of Renier after Emperor Henry's resounding victory at Philippopolis. He may, for example, have cooperated with Eustace and his troops in further securing or expanding his principality. Some of Eustace's Greek troops from Adrianople could have been refugees from Philippopolis (following Kalojan's conquest) and may eventually have returned home. We simply do not know. In a 1209 charter, one Baudry of Hargnies (near Maubeuge), confirms a donation by his father to the abbey of Hautmont in the county of Hainaut. The seal of his suzerain Renier of Trith is used to corroborate the act.[28] It is, however, not clear where this charter was produced. It may have been enacted in either Hainaut or Latin Romania. It was not unusual for lords/knights settled in Latin Romania to undertake from abroad property transactions with respect to ecclesiastical institutions in their homeland. There was a quite constant coming and going of relatives, messengers, clerics and others between Latin Romania and the home regions of the participants in the Fourth Crusade.[29]

---

[26] Valenciennes, *Histoire de l'empereur Henri de Constantinople*, §545–548.

[27] Ibid., §549.

[28] Léopold Devillers, *Description analytique de cartulaires et chartriers accompagnés du texte de documents utiles à l'histoire du Hainaut*, vol. 3 (Mons, 1867), 181, n° 95.

[29] See the example of the extended Villehardouin family: Jean Longnon, *Recherches sur la vie de Geoffroy de Villehardouin* (Paris, 1939), passim. See also, for instance, Robert of Eperlecques who in February 1205, while still in Constantinople, transferred a fief in Flanders to Walter of Courtrai, with the assent of Emperor Baldwin I: DiBe ID 25192, in Walter Prevenier, ed., *Diplomata Belgica. Les sources diplomatiques des Pays-Bas méridionaux au Moyen Âge* (Brussels, since 2015), URL: www.diplomata-belgica.be.

Another possible mention of Renier concerns the fourteenth-century text entitled *S'ensieult dont vient la saincte vraie croix à Douchy*. This brief account narrates how one Jacques of *Puvinaige* (Puvinage near Flobecq) – identified as the younger brother of the (unnamed) lord of Trith and as having a *grant seignourie* in Douchy(-les-Mines) and Noyelles(-sur-Selle) – participated in the Fourth Crusade. After Count Baldwin had become emperor, Jacques sent home a relic of the True Cross to be delivered to the town of Douchy. The relic was subsequently taken away by Jacques' elder brother, who apparently had stayed home. The lord of Trith then fell sick and ultimately agreed to return the relic.[30] The text's editor, Louis Cellier, suggested that the mentioned lord of Trith should be identified as Renier. However, this presents several problems. First, according to the account the lord of Trith did not participate in the crusade, while Renier obviously did. Secondly, to my knowledge no Jacques of Puvinage is mentioned in any other medieval source. Cellier's suggestion that Puvinage should be identified with Jacques of Bondues – Renier's nephew mentioned by Villehardouin – does not help much. Bondues was not Renier's brother and there is no link between the Bondues family (or a hypothetical *Puvinaige* family) and Douchy or Noyelles in this period. All this quite rightly led Edouard Grar to question the veracity of the translation story and relegate it to the realm of legend.[31] The account in any case cannot serve as a sound basis for arguing that Renier ever returned to his homeland.

A final piece of information with regard to Renier of Trith concerns the abbey of St. John the Baptist in Valenciennes. Louis Le Merchier's seventeenth-century history of this abbey mentions a list of relics that were preserved there until the great fire of 1520 that destroyed the complex. One of these relics was a piece of the True Cross said to have been "brought from the overseas lands" (*rapporté des pays outre marins*) by Renier of Trith, identified as a nobleman from Valenciennes (*gentilhomme Vallencenois*), who had donated it to the abbey.[32] In the absence of any original or contemporary sources with regard to this relic, it is hard to evaluate the veracity of this account. Again we have no sound basis for arguing that Renier ever returned home. Ultimately, the question is not that relevant. Many barons or knights at some point revisited their region of origin and then returned to their often much more extensive domains in their new homelands.

The Subsequent Fate of the Duchy: Estreux or Alexios Sthlabos?

After Renier's fading from view, Philippopolis is next mentioned in a December 1219 status report by the Venetian podestà Jacopo Tiepolo addressed to doge Pietro Ziani.

---

[30] Louis Cellier, "La sainte vraie croix de Douchy," *Revue agricole, industrielle, littéraire et artistique de la société impériale de Valenciennes* 15 (1863): 235–36, 238–39.

[31] Grar, "Famille des seigneurs de Trith," 77–79.

[32] Louis Le Merchier, *Abbregé de la naissance et progrez de la maison et abbaye de S. Jan en Vallencienne* (Douai, 1635), 145.

In this letter, written shortly after empress Yolande of Flanders/Hainaut had died, Tiepolo informs Ziani that, at a parliament held in Selymbria in October to discuss the affairs of the empire, he had requested from the newly appointed regent Conon I of Béthune that Venice would be granted her share in the *terra Phillipopolis*.[33] This, however, should not be taken as an indication that Philippopolis had only recently come under Latin imperial control again. Presumably it was a longstanding issue, since in the letter Tiepolo mentions an identical request with respect to the *terra regni Saloniki*, which had been in Latin hands continuously since 1204. Similarly, in 1225 emperor Robert of Courtenay would grant the Serenissima certain property rights in Constantinople itself that until then had been denied Venice since 1204.[34] Previously Alexios III Angelos' 1198 chrysobul for the city of Venice had listed the *Provincia Phylipupleos, Veroys, Moras et Archridij* – along with many others – as one of the territories where Venetian merchants were granted various trade privileges.[35] Venetians may thus have been present there before 1204, possibly continuing their commercial activities after the conquest.[36]

Next, the 1229 pact between the Constantinopolitan barons and the new emperor-elect John of Brienne mentions the *ducatus Phinepople* as belonging to *baro imperii* Gerard of Estreux (*Girardus de Stroim*) and states that he and *sui antecessores* had held it *de jure*.[37] Estreux himself is first attested in Romania with certainty as first witness (*Girardus de Ostrerie*) in Emperor Robert's 1221 confirmation of the constitutional treaties of 1204–5.[38] By 1223/4 Gerard (*Girardus de Streu*) was willing to recognize the suzerainty of the Venetian doge for the land that he held, no doubt the part of the duchy of Philippopolis that was claimed by the Serenissima.[39] The plural *antecessores* in the 1229 pact indicates that Philippopolis had been held by more than one – no doubt Latin – lord before Gerard. In this context a passage in a version of the Old French continuation of William of Tyre's chronicle attributed to Ernoul and Bernard le Trésorier (written c. 1230) is interesting. The fragment relates how Emperor Baldwin after his coronation had granted *le ducée de Sinepople* to *Jerarz de Struen*, who had conquered the duchy with his brothers

[33] Gottlieb L. Tafel and Georg M. Thomas (eds.), *Urkunden zur älteren Handels- und Staatsgeschichte der Republik Venedig*, Fontes Rerum Austriacarum. Diplomataria et Acta, 3 vols. (Vienna, 1856–57), 2:219, n° 257.

[34] Filip Van Tricht, "Robert of Courtenay (1221–1227): An Idiot on the Throne of Constantinople?", *Speculum* 88 (2013): 996–1034, at 1030–31.

[35] Tafel and Thomas, *Urkunden*, 1:269, n° 85.

[36] On the growth of the economy of Philippopolis by the late twelfth century: Angeliki E. Laiou, "Regional Networks in the Balkans in the Middle and Late Byzantine Period," in *Trade and Markets in Byzantium*, ed. Cécile Morrison (Washington, DC, 2012), 125–46.

[37] Tafel and Thomas, *Urkunden*, 2:269, n° 273.

[38] Tafel and Thomas, *Urkunden*, 2:230, n° 260.

[39] Roberto Cessi, *Deliberazioni del Maggior Consiglio di Venezia*, 3 vols. (Bologna, 1930–34), 1:66, n° 69: "de Girardo de Streu qui hominem esse cupit domini ducis ex terra quam habet de quo capitulo interrogabitis dominum Marinum Storlato."

(*si frere*).[40] The chronicler obviously is mistaken in considering Gerard as the first Latin lord of Philippopolis, but the passage does indicate that for an observer writing around 1230 it seemed as if Gerard and the Estreux family had been in possession of Philippopolis for over two decades.

To explain the plural *antecessores* in the 1229 pact, we might hypothesize that one of Gerard's brothers had in fact held the duchy before him (or perhaps together with him). One of the Estreux brothers could simply have inherited Philippopolis from Renier of Trith. Estreux is situated close to Trith and the two families were acquainted with one another, with members of both families acting as witnesses in the same comital charters and with members of the Estreux family acting as witnesses in charters of the Trith family.[41] Perhaps one of the Estreux brothers, who may have participated in the Fourth Crusade in Renier's retinue, had married a daughter or other relative of Renier and in this way became heir to Philippopolis. Renier's sons in the West, Gilles and Adam, do not appear to have been interested in their father's Byzantine principality as they are continually attested in their homeland.[42] Another possibility is that Renier died without an heir apparent or left the empire for good at some point, with the emperor granting Philippopolis to a member of the Estreux family, that, hailing from the same geographical area in Hainaut, may have risen to prominence under Renier.

Kalin Yordanov has proposed that the already mentioned Alexios Sthlabos, ruler of the Rhodope region, in addition would have ruled Philippopolis between 1209 and 1217. The author does so on the basis of a papal letter of August 1217 mentioning a *S. princeps Philippensis* who is said to have murdered the Latin archbishop of Philippi, William of Rouen. Following Pierre-Vincent Claverie, Yordanov identifies this S. as Sthlabos, but – realizing that the latter's dominion over the Thessalonikan fief of Philippi would be hard to explain – at the same time proposes that *Philippensis* in relation to S. refers not to Philippi but to Philippopolis, assuming that the papal chancery mixed up the two similar sounding toponyms. Sthlabos then would have acquired Philippopolis in 1208 in the wake of Emperor Henry's victory there, while losing it again around 1217/18 as a consequence of action taken against him after the murder.[43] The problem with Yordanov's thesis, however, is that there is no need to posit that a mistake was made at the papal court in the first place. The murder case can indeed be explained adequately without

---

[40] Louis de Mas Latrie, ed., *Chronique d'Ernoul et de Bernard le trésorier* (Paris, 1871), 376 (manuscript O).

[41] Alufus of Estreux together with Renier of Trith in 1200: Charles Duvivier, *Actes et documents anciens intéressant la Belgique (nouvelle série)*, vol. 2 (Brussels, 1903), 274–75, n° 141. Godfrey of Estreux in a charter by Gilles, lord of Trith: http://www.cn-telma.fr/chartae-galliae/charte211687/.

[42] Gilles and Adam of Trith in the years 1211–19 are attested in several charters produced in their homeland: DiBe ID 33074, 33387, 33388, 33494, 33503, 33912, in Prevenier, *Diplomata Belgica*.

[43] Pierre-Vincent Claverie, *Honorius III et l'Orient (1216–1227)* (Leiden, 2013), 164; Kalin Yordanov, "The Case of 'S., Princeps Philippensis': Two Recently Edited Letters by Pope Honorius III from 1217 and 1218 as Sources for the Relations between Alexis Slav and the Latins," *Bulgaria Mediaevalis* 8 (2017): 173–218.

having recourse to Sthlabos.[44] There are also other arguments against him having ever controlled Philippopolis.

First of all, the chronology I have just outlined – with Renier and the Estreux family – leaves little space for Yordanov's hypothesis. Secondly, Yordanov's interpretation of a key passage in Valenciennes's chronicle – where it is said that Emperor Henry granted Sthlabos all recent conquests in return for the recognition of imperial suzerainty (*toute le conqueste ke nous avons faite ichi, par tel manière ke vous en serés mes hom et m'en siervirés*) – is debatable.[45] The grant took place in the context of Sthlabos' prospected marriage with Henry's daughter and can be considered as her dowry. Just before Henry had recognized Sthlabos as his vassal for the lands he already controlled. Yordanov now is of the opinion that *tout le conqueste* includes Philippopolis. However, Philippopolis was not a new conquest that Henry could dispose of without negating his brother Baldwin's earlier grant and Renier's *droit de conquête*. Also, although the region temporarily had been lost in 1205–6, by 1208 it may well, together with Stenimachos, have been re-occupied by Renier as I have argued.

The *tout le conqueste* phrase can be explained in a different way. As we have seen, Henry during the Philippopolis campaign had to secure the fortress of Kritzimos, that at the time was not yet under Sthlabos' control. It follows that the entire southeastern Rhodope Mountains cannot have been under his authority at this point. No source informs us of Latin imperial rule having been established there either. Probably Tsar Boril held sway in this region until 1208. In my view *tout le conqueste* should then be identified with the southeastern Rhodope region to the west of Philippopolis, Stenimachos, Adrianople and Didymoteichon.[46] That the phrase did not refer to Philippopolis also finds some support in the whereabouts of Henry's brother, Eustace of Hainaut, around this time. We have seen that after the meeting at Stenimachos Eustace had accompanied Sthlabos back to his domains. The next time we meet Eustace is at Drama in Macedonia in late December. There he paid a visit to his brother Henry, who was on his way to address the so-called Lombard rebellion in Thessaloniki.[47] This indicates that Eustace's – and thus probably also Sthlabos' – field of operations was not northern Thrace (with Philippopolis), but rather the western Rhodope in the direction of Melnik.

---

[44] Filip Van Tricht, "Who Murdered Archbishop William of Rouen? The Valley of Philippi under Latin Rule (1204–circa 1224/25)," *Jahrbuch der Österreichischen Byzantinistik* 70 (2020): 305–34, at 328–31.

[45] Valenciennes, *Histoire de l'empereur Henri de Constantinople*, §548.

[46] In his 1208 letter to Pope Innocent III informing him of his victory at Philippopolis, Emperor Henry writes that *quindecim dietas terrae imperio nostro de suo [= Boril] acquisitas habemus*: RHGF, 19:514. This probably means the entire Rhodope Mountains – both the part controlled by Sthlabos (who goes unmentioned in the letter) and the part controlled by Tsar Boril – together with an enlarged principality around Philippopolis, possibly in the direction of the Black Sea coast.

[47] Valenciennes, *Histoire de l'empereur Henri de Constantinople*, §571. On the Lombard rebellion: Van Tricht, *The Latin Renovatio of Byzantium*, 212–13.

Yordanov also argues that Sthlabos' presumed loss of Philippopolis in 1217 is the factor explaining his relocation to Melnik. The author accepts the historiographical consensus that Sthlabos already captured Melnik c. 1211 (and possibly earlier, c. 1209), but at the same time proposes that he only made it his capital after the murder episode. However, this is not borne out by the available sources, especially the May 1216 testament of the then metropolitan of Melnik, Paul Klaudiopolites, and the January 1220 *sigillion* by Alexios Sthlabos himself for the *Theotokos Spelaiotissa* monastery in that same town. In the latter document Sthlabos explicitly states that he had moved from his earlier residence Tzepaina to Melnik, where he founded and built the *Speleaiotissa* monastery. He entrusted it to the monk and archimandrite Klaudiopolites, who, as Sthlabos mentions, by the time the *sigillion* was composed had become the local metropolitan.[48] Now, in his May 1216 testament, Klaudiopolites already acted as metropolitan bishop, having been appointed through an election by many other bishops.[49] This implies that Sthlabos had moved to Melnik and made it his capital well before May 1216, as the planning and building of a monastery inevitably would have taken a considerable period of time. Consequently Sthlabos' move to Melnik and the 1217 murder are unconnected.

Perhaps more importantly: if Sthlabos ever possessed Philippopolis then why does he mention Tzepaina as his former residence in his *sigillion* of 1220? The renown of the city of Philippopolis was much greater, so why did he not refer to it? In the document Sthlabos could easily have bypassed the supposed unpleasant reason that had brought him to relocate to Melnik. An additional element may be that in the *sigillion* Sthlabos refers to himself with the title of *despotes* that had been granted to him by Emperor Henry.[50] This unambiguous association with Latin imperial authority suggests that at this time he was still loyal to Latin Constantinople.[51] This would be curious if he had lost Philippopolis by countermeasures from the Constantinopolitan court in the context of Archbishop William's murder. Had he fallen out with the Latins, Sthlabos, as a member of the Bulgarian royal dynasty, would seem to have had more appropriate means to bolster his prestige or underscore the legitimacy of his rule than merely retaining the title given to him by Henry. Akropolites' description of Sthlabos' territories points in the same direction: the

---

[48] Jacques Bompaire, Jacques Lefort, Vassiliki Kravari and Christophe Giros, eds., *Actes de Vatopédi*, Actes de l'Athos 21 (Leuven, 2001), vol. 1, n° 13. An English translation in: Kiril Petkov, *The Voices of Medieval Bulgaria. Seventh–Fifteenth Century. Records of a Bygone Culture*, East Central and Eastern Europe in the Middle Ages, 450–1450 5 (Leiden, 2008), 478–81.

[49] Bompaire, *Actes de Vatopédi*, n° 12. See also: Elena Kostova, "Zaveshtanieto na melnishkiya mitropolit Pavel Klavdiopolit" [The testament of Paul Klaudiopolites, metropolitan of Melnik], *Istorichesko bŭdeshte* 2016 (1–2): 197–205.

[50] On Sthlabos' acquisition of the *despotes* title: Akropolites, *Historia*, §24. See also: Van Tricht, *The Latin Renovatio of Byzantium*, 177. Elena Kostova, *Medieval Melnik from the Late 12th to the Late 14th Centuries: Historical Vicissitudes of a Small Balkan Town* (Sofia, 2013), 40–41 (with references to older historiography).

[51] Sthlabos was an altogether remarkably Latinophile ruler, open to influence and innovation also in the religious sphere. See Van Tricht, "Who Murdered Archbishop William of Rouen?", 317–18.

Rhodope Mountains – also called Achridos, the historian adds – with the towns in that region plus Melnik.[52] No mention is made of Philippopolis. Ultimately there seems to be no sound ground for proposing that Alexios Sthlabos ever controlled Philippopolis.

Philippopolis as a "duchy" and the Title of "*baro imperii*"

Apart from the elements already mentioned, precious little information is available on the duchy of Philippopolis under the Trith and Estreux families. One notable aspect is that in the – exclusively Western – contemporary sources the principality is always referred to as a "duchy" (*ducatus* or *duché*). This term here should not be seen as the exact equivalent of a Western duchy, but rather be understood in its more general meaning of "province."[53] In the context of Latin Romania it was probably derived from the Byzantine nomenclature for a provincial governor or *doux*, who was the top official of a Byzantine province or *thema* in the preceding period. Neither Renier nor his successors are ever designated in any source with the most prestigious title, from a Western perspective, of duke (*duc*, *dux* or *doux*), and neither were there any of the other Latin barons or authorities in Romania who had been awarded or administered a territory designated as *duchée* or *ducatus*, at least not before 1261. For example, Angelo Sanudo (1227–62) – who inherited from his father, Marco I, the *ducatus* of Naxos and Andros, also called *ducatus Agyepelagi*, clearly after the former twelfth-century *thema tou Aigaiou Pelagous* – styled himself *dominator* and not *dux* in various charters from 1239, 1245 and 1251. No "duke" is attested for the duchy of Nikomedia (*ducatus Nicomedie*), situated in the imperial quarter, either.[54] Otho I of La Roche, lord of Athens (1204–before 1234), in a sense is an exception to the rule. He styled himself *dominus Athenarum* in his own charters (from 1217 and 1221) and is designated as such in most other documents (e.g. in a series of papal letters by Innocent III and Honorius III, in the Ravennika pact from May 1210 concerning the ecclesiastical rights and possessions in the region from Thessaloniki to Corinth, and in Valenciennes's chronicle). However, in some other (mostly posthumous) sources – a single 1208 papal letter, a 1234 charter by his son Otho II and the chronicle by Alberic of Trois-Fontaines (written c. 1240) – he is, apparently unofficially or even mistakenly (in the case of the

---

[52] Akropolites, *Historia*, §24. On the Rhodopes region and Achridos: Soustal, *Thrakien*, TIB 6, 160–61, 427.

[53] Charles Du Fresne Du Cange, *Glossarium Mediae et Infimae Latinitatis* (Paris, 1842), 2:946–47.

[54] Van Tricht, *The Latin Renovatio of Byzantium*, 108, 122, 208–9, 234–35. See also: Carile, "Partitio," 226–27. Jean-Claude Cheynet, "Du stratège de thème au duc: Chronologie de l'évolution au cours du XIe siècle", *Travaux et Mémoires* 9 (1985): 181–94. Hendrickx, "Les duchés de l'empire latin de Constantinople après 1204," 305–14. Angelo Sanudo: ASV, Procc. di S. Marco (de Citra), Misti, Misc. Pergg., B. 2 (1239) and S. Stefano, B. 1 pergg. (Arch. Fam. Venier dei SS. Apostoli) (1251); Raimondo Morozzo della Rocca and Antonino Lombardo, eds., *Documenti del commercio veneziano nei secoli XI–XIII*, Regesta Chartarum Italiae 28–29 (Rome and Turin, 1940), n° 774 (1245).

1208 papal letter), called duke.[55] Somewhat similarly with regard to Venetian Crete – again a former Byzantine *thema* – the local governor was styled *duca* in official Venetian documents (no doubt after the Byzantine *doux*), but not *dux*. The difference is subtle, but the message is clear: the latter title remained exclusively reserved for the Venetian doge (*dux Venecie*). This being said, locally the *duca* was nevertheless known as the *dux*: in his 1224 agreement with the local Byzantine magnates Theodore and Michael Melissenos, Paolo Quirini styles himself *duca Crete*, but the Melissenoi brothers themselves in their oath inserted in the document call him *dux Crete*.[56]

Renier and his contemporary colleagues surely were important hereditary feudal barons (or prominent officials, in the case of Crete) enjoying a large measure of governmental autonomy, but officially they were not dukes, a fact which Hendrickx appears to have missed in his otherwise interesting analysis of duchies in Latin Romania. The explanation may well be that the adoption by local lords or Latin imperial functionaries of the title of *dux*, with its Western connotations of far-reaching autonomy and virtual independence, was not acceptable to either the Latin emperor or to the Latin barons whose fiefs were not based on former Byzantine *themata*.[57] This being said, Kalin Yordanov recently has drawn attention to the "Duko of Latina" (*Дуко от Латина*) character in the late medieval Bulgarian Krali Marko epic cycle. The author argues convincingly that this character derives from the Latin lords of Philippopolis.[58] We may then assume that the population of the city and its region transferred out of habit the title of the former Byzantine *doux* to Renier and Gerard (and his brother(s)). The latter may well have been pleased with this local use of the prestigious (in Western eyes) title, although from a Byzantine perspective it was simply the appellation for the provincial governor who was nothing more than an imperial official. The same sort of process may well have occurred in Athens. Otho I of La Roche gradually managed to extend his lordship around Athens in Attica so as to include Thebes in Boeotia. As Athens and Thebes were the chief cities of the former *thema* of Hellas (with Thebes being its capital), this may have induced the local population to call Otho I of La Roche "duke" after the former Byzantine *doux*. While the rulers of Philippopolis and Athens/Thebes during these first decades of the thirteenth century do not appear to have adopted the ducal title officially, at the same time they would have seen

---

[55] Innocent III, *Die Register*, ed. Othmar Hageneder (Vienna, 1964–2018), 11: n° 116 (121); Jean Longnon, "Les premiers ducs d'Athènes et leur famille," *Journal des Savants* (1973): 61–80; Andreas Kiesewetter, "Ricerche costituzionali e documenti per la signoria ed il ducato di Atene sotto i de la Roche e Gualteri V di Brienne (1204–1311)," in *Bisanzio, Venezia e il mondo franco-greco (XIII–XV secolo)*, ed. C. A. Maltezou and P. Schreiner, Istituto Ellenico di Studi Bizantini e Post-bizantini di Venezia / Centro Tedesco di Studi Veneziani, Convegni 5 (Venice, 2002), 310–19. Otho I's son and successor in Athens Guy I (c. 1234 – after 1262) likewise styled himself or was called "lord of Athens" and not "duke," e.g. in charters of 1240, 1251 and 1260.

[56] Tafel and Thomas, *Urkunden*, 2:251–53, n° 266.

[57] See Van Tricht, *The Latin Renovatio of Byzantium*, 108, 122, 208–9, 235.

[58] Yordanov, "Bulgarian Folklore Relicts," 368–70.

no reason to discourage the local elite and population from using it in daily life. Andreas Kiesewetter has demonstrated that in Athens the ducal title was only used officially from 1280, long after Latin Constantinople had fallen and Latin imperial suzerainty had ceased to exist.[59]

A title that the lords of Philippopolis did officially possess was that of "imperial baron" or *baro imperii*. We have seen that Gerard of Estreux is designated as such in the context of the 1229 pact with emperor-elect John of Brienne. In two charters from September and December 1238 Gerard is again mentioned as one of the *barones imperii* and moreover as one of the *consiliarii* that enacted the mortgage of the Crown of Thorns to Venetian merchants, alongside Anselm I of Cayeux (imperial regent in September), Narjot of Toucy (imperial regent in December), imperial constable Geoffrey of Merry, imperial marshal Vilain of Aulnay, and Milo Tirel.[60] It is hard to establish how well defined this group of "imperial barons" was or its exact status, but it is clear that it must have included the holders of a number of important principalities and lordships in Romania. While Philippopolis may rank as a regional principality comparable to the lordship of Athens or perhaps even the principality of Achaia, from a 1266 charter by Emperor Baldwin II we know that smaller fiefs like Ainos, Makri and Madytos also had the status of baronies directly and exclusively held from the emperor, making the *barones imperii* a somewhat heterogenous collective.[61] As prominent barons, in the context of the feudal duty of *auxilium* the lords of Philippopolis no doubt participated or provided troops in the various military confrontations with the rulers of Bulgaria, Epiros, and Nicaea. From the abovementioned status report of December 1219 by podestà Jacopo Tiepolo, we know that, following the death of Empress Yolande, the *barones Francigenae* met in October at successive parliaments at Rhaidestos and Selymbria, to decide *inter alia* the imperial succession, on this occasion choosing her son Philip of Courtenay, count of Namur, as their new emperor.[62] Gerard of Estreux may well have been present at one or both of these, especially since, as we have seen, at Selymbria Tiepolo raised the subject of the Venetian share in Philippopolis. If so, we may perhaps assume that Gerard actively supported the choice of Philip, as the continuation of an imperial lineage stemming from his home region probably best furthered his own interests.

---

[59] Kiesewetter, "Ricerche costituzionali," 319–25.

[60] Alexandre Teulet, ed., *Layettes du Trésor des Chartes*, vol. 2 (Paris, 1866), n° 2744 and n° 2753.

[61] J. A. C. Buchon, *Recherches et matériaux pour servir à une histoire de la domination française aux XIIIe, XIVe, XVe siècles dans les provinces démembrées de l'Empire grec à la suite de la Quatrième Croisade*, vol. 1 (Paris, 1811), 28–29. The group of "imperial barons" seems to derive from the *barones Francigenae* mentioned in the October 1205 pact between the then imperial regent Henry of Flanders/Hainaut and Venetian podestà Marino Zeno. These barons together with the podestà and his councillors were to form a "mixed council" with as its main competencies the defence of the empire and arbitrating conflicts between the emperor and his vassals. After 1207, however, this "mixed council" appears to have led a mostly dormant existence (except during interregna), leaving virtually all aspects of imperial policy to the emperor and his council. See extensively Van Tricht, *The Latin Renovatio of Byzantium*, 54–58, 251–54.

[62] Tafel and Thomas, *Urkunden*, 2:217–20, n° 257.

It is difficult to say how often the lords of Philippopolis (some 400 km from Constantinople) were present in the metropolitan area, and as imperial barons participated in the imperial council there. For example, imperial marshal Geoffrey of Villehardouin, lord of Makri, Trajanopolis and Mosynopolis (the latter in the kingdom of Thessaloniki) – all situated about 300 km from the capital, habitually or at least frequently resided in the capital and was a key figure in the imperial government.[63] This, however, may have been less feasible for the lord of a border principality, at least in times of Latin-Bulgarian war or tension (1204–13 and after 1230). In any case, as we have seen, in March 1221 Gerard of Estreux was present in Constantinople to witness the coronation of Emperor Robert of Courtenay, who succeeded after his elder brother Philip had declined the imperial crown. Since Robert's journey from the West went overland through Germany, Hungary and Bulgaria, at Philippopolis Gerard may well have been the first imperial baron to welcome Robert to his empire. It stands to reason that Gerard would have accompanied Robert and his entourage, which included the Hungarian crown prince Bela (IV), to the capital, allowing him the time and opportunity to build a personal relationship with the new ruler and also with the political elite of neighbouring countries. The special mention of Philippopolis in the 1229 pact with John of Brienne and Gerard's place among the top Constantinopolitan barons in the 1238 charters concerning the Crown of Thorns, in any case, confirm that the lords of Philippopolis carried considerable political weight in the capital.

Geographical Limits, Administration and Society

Philippopolis appears to have suffered no irreparable damage after Kalojan's destructive conquest in 1205 and, as the duchy's chief city, was presumably quickly restored. Despite also demographic losses, Philippopolis regained its position as the major urban centre of northern Thrace. After the Nicaean capture of the city in the mid-thirteenth century, its metropolitan bishop at some point acquired the exalted title of "exarch of all Europe and Dragobintia," which gives a clear indication of its importance. In the early fourteenth century, John VI Kantakouzenos characterized Philippopolis in his *Historia* as marvellous and great, noting its impressive fortifications.[64] Other towns that had suffered from the Bulgarian invasion of Thrace and Macedonia in 1205/6 were likewise quickly refortified by the new Latin rulers, for example Pamphilon by Emperor Henry and Serres by Boniface

---

[63] Longnon, *Recherches sur la vie de Geoffroy de Villehardouin*, 84–104.

[64] Asdracha, *La région des Rhodopes*, 154–62; Alexander Kazhdan, "Philippopolis," in *Oxford Dictionary of Byzantium*, ed. Alexander Kazhdan, 3 vols. (Oxford, 1991), 3:1654–55. Kalojan had enslaved and displaced part of the population. Some inhabitants ended up in Melnik, either as refugees or forcefully displaced; among them, members of the Manglabites family: Akropolites, *Historia*, §44; see also: George Akropolites, *The History. Translated with an Introduction and Commentary*, trans. Ruth Macrides (Oxford, 2007), 232–33.

of Monferrat.[65] The duchy's territorial extent remains unclear. Deriving from the earlier Byzantine *thema* of Philippopolis it probably no longer included Achridos and Morra in the southeastern Rhodope Mountains, which now presumably fell under Alexios Sthlabos. Towns that may have belonged to the duchy are: to the east, Konstanteia (near Simeonovgrad) and perhaps Therma (on the Black Sea coast); to the north, Beroe (Stara Zagora); and to the south, (Hy)perperiakon (near Gorna Krepost).[66]

Archaeological finds in the region indicate a Latin presence at some point in the fortresses and towns of Dyadovo (near Beroe, possibly to be identified with Blisnos, Villehardouin's *Blisme*), Stenimachos (near Philippopolis), Ephraïm (Efrem), Okopa (near Madjarovo in the Rhodope region), Mneiakos (Moniak) and Mezek in the Rhodope mountains, Sozopolis, Lakoto Kale and Therma near the Black Sea coast. It is, however, difficult to connect these finds with this or that principality or lordship (Philippopolis, Adrianople-Didymoteichon, Alexios Sthlabos' principality in the Rhodope mountains, possibly others) within the Latin Empire. The items in question mostly include pieces of weaponry and armature of Western origin. Trendafilov attempts to connect various finds with specific campaigns described by Villehardouin and Valenciennes in the years 1206–8 in the Rhodope mountains and the Bulgarian border region. It seems, however, more prudent – especially in view of the only very patchy state of archaeological research of the medieval sites in the region – to associate them in general with the Latin presence in the area over a longer period of time, including the passage of the Third Crusade in 1189/90, to which the author himself also refers.[67] The fact that the Fourth Crusade led to a Western presence lasting several decades, in any case, makes it more likely that most of these finds should be associated with the partial Latin take-over of Byzantium, rather than with the transitory passage of the Third Crusade army. Indeed, while Trendafilov chooses to see them as the result of direct and momentary military confrontations between Latin and Bulgarian troops, they should perhaps rather be interpreted as evidence for the more permanent stationing of Latin lords and/or garrisons in the places in question.

The Latin presence in Philippopolis must have been accompanied by the introduction of Western feudal institutions. The region became a feudal principality within the empire and its rulers must in turn have distributed fiefs to people in their personal entourage and to knights and sergeants with whom they took possession of it, as was the case in the other regions of Latin Romania. The new military order of St. Samson, founded with the enthusiastic support of Emperor Henry,

---

[65] Valenciennes, *Histoire de l'empereur Henri de Constantinople*, §550–551, §554. Villehardouin, *La conquête de Constantinople*, §456.

[66] On these localities, see: Soustal, *Thrakien*, TIB 6, 116, 203–5, 395–96, 477–78.

[67] See the interesting overview in Angel Dimitrov Trendafilov, "Crusaders Against the Cross. The Fourth Crusade Depicted in Orthodox-Slavic Written Sources and Archaeological Evidence" (PhD thesis, University of Canterbury, 2018), 191–247. See also Soustal, *Thrakien*, TIB 6, 210, 261, 361, 365, 454–55, 460–61,

may have acquired Konstanteia, if the *locum Constantiae* in Innocent IV's 1244 enumeration of their possessions is indeed to be identified with this town.[68] If so, it was possibly a grant from either Renier or Gerard, who in this way would have shown their support for this imperially favoured and Constantinopolitan-based order, although it cannot be excluded that it may have been a direct imperial grant.[69] None of the other military orders – or Western religious orders in general – seem to have gained possessions in the region, or at least none are attested, which might be due to the scarcity of the sources.[70] The fate under Latin rule of, for example, the important Byzantine-Georgian *Theotokos Petritzonitissa* monastery (8 km southwest of Stenimachos) is unknown. There is no indication that it was ever Latinized, but it may well have lost part of its extensive possessions, especially in those places situated outside the duchy (among others in or around Thessaloniki, Serres and Mosynopolis).[71] In the absence of relevant sources the extent of the region's feudalization – its scale and its depth – can likewise not be assessed. Nor do we know whether members of the local Byzantine elite were incorporated in this feudal system, as was the case in other regions of Latin Romania (e.g. in northwestern Asia Minor, in the kingdom of Thessaloniki, in southern Thessaly, and in the principality of Achaia), though in widely varying degrees.[72] Ancestral lands may have been reconfirmed to their owners as fiefs or new possessions may have been awarded in the same way. Kalojan's destructive invasion and deportation of part of the local elite and population must, in any case, have created opportunities for a partial redistribution of land to both Latin and Byzantines. As elsewhere, the new Latin rulers must have continued at the local level the existing Byzantine administrative and fiscal system and they must have relied at least in part on local

---

[68] Theodosius T. Haluscynskyj and Meletius M. Wojnar, eds., *Acta Innocentii Papae IV (1243–1254)*, Pontificia commissio ad redigendum codicem iuris canonici Orientalis. Fontes. Series 3, vol. 4/1 (Rome, 1966), 27, n° 15. For Konstanteria, see Soustal, *Thrakien*, TIB 6, 314.

[69] Emperor Henry in 1210, for example, had granted the Order of St Samson the castle and settlement of Garella (*castellum quod Garelis vulgariter appellatum cum pertinentiis suis*) in eastern Thrace, which according to the 1204 *Partitio* was not part of the imperial quarter, but had been awarded to the non-Venetian crusaders. See: Innocent III, *Die Register*, 13: n° 17. On Garella: Andreas Külzer, *Ostthrakien (Europe)*, TIB 12 (Vienna, 2008), 877–78.

[70] See Marie-Anna Chevalier, "Ordres religieux-militaires, seigneurs croisés et nouvelles élites laïques de Romanie et de Morée. Premières alliances et rivalités (1204–1212)," in *Élites chrétiennes et formes du pouvoir (XIIIe–Xve siècle)*, ed. Marie-Anna Chevalier and Isabelle Ortega (Paris, 2017), 139–76.

[71] Soustal, *Thrakien*, TIB 6, 475–476. On the initial largescale secularization of ecclesiastical possessions in Latin Romania: Robert L. Wolff, "Politics in the Latin Patriarchate of Constantinople," *Dumbarton Oaks Papers* 8 (1954): 255–74; Van Tricht, *The Latin Renovatio of Byzantium*, 196–205.

[72] See, for example, David Jacoby, *La féodalité en Grèce médiévale. Les "assises de Romanie": sources, application et diffusion* (Paris/La Haye, 1971), 33–36, 55, 70, 90, 188, 249, 284; idem, "Les archontes grecs et la féodalité en Morée franque," *Travaux et Mémoires* 2 (1967) 422–45; Van Tricht, *The Latin Renovatio of Byzantium*, 234–48; idem, "Being Byzantine in the post-1204 Empire of Constantinople," *Istorijski časopis* 71 (2022) (forthcoming).

Byzantines for its operation.[73] That Byzantines were probably not only employed at the lower echelons of government may be deduced from the consideration that quite likely a Byzantine metropolitan bishop remained in place.

To substantiate this hypothesis we have to rely on an *argumentum ex silentio*. The available sources – in particular the *Provincialia Romana* (catalogues of all archbishoprics subject to Rome with their suffragan sees) from 1210 and 1228 and the papal registers – never mention a Latin archbishop of Philippopolis or a Latin bishop occupying one of Philippopolis' suffragan sees.[74] The same is true for the autocephalous archbishopric of Beroe and the diocese of Sozopolis (a suffragan of Adrianople), two localities that may have belonged to the duchy. I have argued elsewhere that such an absence in these sources is a strong indication that some or most of the diocese(s) in question were probably never Latinized.[75] In the case of Philippopolis this is all the more so since an entire ecclesiastical province goes completely unmentioned. The situation was probably similar to that in the neighbouring feudal principality of Adrianople, that was ruled by the Byzantine/ Greek lord Theodore Branas, who was married to ex-empress Agnes, daughter of King Louis VII of France, and later by his presumed son-in-law Conon II of Béthune. For Adrianople we know from the correspondence of John Apokaukos, metropolitan of Naupaktos in Epiros, that a Byzantine/Greek metropolitan was still in place around 1222. Like Philippopolis, Adrianople is never mentioned in the papal registers, although it is listed in the abovementioned *provincialia* as an archbishopric but without any suffragan bishoprics. From Apokaukos' letter it is, however, clear that the Greek metropolitan of Adrianople did elect and ordain suffragan bishops.[76] The obviously incorrect information in the *provincialia* with regard to Adrianople, in combination with the total absence of the province in papal correspondence, which also applies to Philippopolis, illustrates how little actual influence the Latin church authorities – the Latin patriarch of Constantinople and the papacy – must have had in the region.

If a Byzantine – no doubt Greek – metropolitan and Byzantine suffragans did indeed remain in place in Philippopolis and its dependent dioceses, they probably continued to play a prominent role. Metropolitans and bishops in this period

---

[73] See for the early period of Latin Romania for instance the unique fiscal survey in Latin of the Venetian-held town of Lampsakos (1219), clearly based on a Byzantine *praktikon*: David Jacoby, "The Venetian Presence in the Latin Empire of Constantinople (1204–1261): The Challenge of Feudalism and the Byzantine Inheritance," *Jahrbuch der Österreichischen Byzantinistik* 43 (1993): 146, 150–51 and 160. See in general Van Tricht, *The Latin Renovatio of Byzantium*, 113–44.

[74] In the twelfth century Philippopolis counted ten suffragan bishoprics (Agathonikeia, Lititza, Skutarion, Leukè, Bleptos, Dramitza, Ioannitza, Konstanteia, Belikeia, Bukuba). In the fourteenth century only two suffragans are attested (Ioannitza and (Hy)perperiakon). See Asdracha, *La région des Rhodopes*, 155–56; Preiser-Kapeller, *Der Episkopat im späten Byzanz*, 362–65.

[75] In general: Van Tricht, *The Latin Renovayio of Byzantium*, 321–32. For the archdiocese of Philippi, idem, "Who Murdered Archbishop William of Rouen?", 312–17.

[76] Van Tricht, "The Byzantino-Latin Principality of Adrianople," 334, 337–38. The case of Adrianople indicates that a mention in the *provincialia* does not make it certain that a bishopric had been Latinized.

occupied a central place within their city or town and region. Benjamin Moulet has characterized the Byzantine bishop as "the religious, political, and juridical heart of his city, replacing the civil and military authorities when they are absent, or sharing power with them."[77] This is also the image that emerges for instance from the correspondence of Michael Choniates, the metropolitan of Athens before 1204.[78] In 1213, in Latin Thessaloniki under the young King Demetrios, six Byzantine suffragan bishops together with *doux* George Phrangopoulos still headed a local tribunal, passing sentence on local civil cases.[79] A similar situation may well have existed in Philippopolis with the metropolitan together with the local archontal families sharing power with Renier of Trith, Gerard of Estreux and their knights. Part of the elite and population of Philippopolis that had fled to Adrianople during Kalojan's invasion may have returned. Emperor Henry's successive campaigns in the region in 1206–8 may also have allowed a number of inhabitants of Philippopolis who had been taken captive by the Bulgarian tsar to regain their homes.[80] Some, however, had left the city for good, for instance the Manglabites and a number of unnamed other families attested in Melnik in the 1250s.[81]

The suggested collaboration between Latins and Byzantine Greeks in Philippopolis would have probably begun as a marriage of convenience, but the Latin feudalization of the Byzantine empire also entailed tangible benefits for the local elite and population. The feudal restructuring offered a large measure of regional autonomy. The province was no longer governed from a Constantinopolitan perspective, but for its own sake. This must at least have held some attraction for the local aristocracy. It could have provided an answer to the regionalist and even separatist tendencies that had started to build in the provinces prior to 1204 and that were in part based on regional feelings of being neglected and disdained by the central government and aristocracy in the capital (the empire's so-called "Constantinopolization"), a sentiment that, as we have seen, may have been present in Philippopolis itself as well before 1204.[82]

---

[77] Benjamin Moulet, *Evêques, pouvoir et société à Byzance (VIIIe–XIe siècle). Territoires, communautés et individus dans la société provinciale byzantine* (Paris, 2011), 421: "le cœur religieux, politique et juridique de sa cité, remplaçant les fonctionnaires et les militaires quand ceux-ci sont absents, ou partageant avec eux l'autorité."

[78] Kenneth M. Setton, "Athens in the Later Twelfth Century," *Speculum* 19 (1944): 187–207; idem, "A Note on Michael Choniates, Archbishop of Athens (1182–1204)," *Speculum* 21 (1946): 234–36; Teresa Shawcross, "Golden Athens: Episcopal Wealth and Power in Greece at the Time of the Crusades," in *Contact and Conflict in Frankish Greece and the Aegean, 1204–1453*, ed. Nikolaos G. Chrissis and Mike Carr, Crusades – Subsidia 5 (Ashgate, 2014), 65–96.

[79] Demetrios Chomatenos, *Ponemata Diaphora*, ed. Günther Prinzing, Corpus Fontium Historiae Byzantinae. Series Berolinensis 38 (Berlin, 2002), n° 106; Dieter Simon, "Witwe Sachlikina gegen Witwe Horaia," in *Fontes Minores* 6, ed. Dieter Simon, Forschungen zur Byzantinischen Rechtsgeschichte 11 (Frankfurt am Main, 1984), 335; Van Tricht, *The Latin Renovatio of Byzantium*, 245–46.

[80] See for example with regard to Didymoteichon: Villehardouin, *La conquête de Constantinople*, §442–449.

[81] Akropolites, *Historia*, §44 (see also note 64).

[82] Jurgen Hoffman, *Rudimente von Territorialstaaten im byzantinischen Reich (1071–1210). Untersuchungen über Unabhägigkeitsbestrebungen und ihr Verhältnis zu Kaiser und Reich*, Miscellanea

There also seems to have been an openness to Latin influence in other spheres. The bell-tower of the *Theotokos* church at the fortress of Stenimachos may well be an example of this. Bell-ringing and bell-towers were distinctly Western features of church life and unheard of in the region, where traditionally Byzantine wooden *semantra* were used (either portable or hanging from some structure like an arch). Although scholars disagree on the construction date, assigning it to either the twelfth or thirteenth century, a connection with the Latin occupation seems hard to dismiss.[83] Indeed, the only other known bell-tower from this period in the broad surrounding region is found at the episcopal church of St. Nicholas in Melnik, capital of Emperor Henry's son-in-law Alexios Sthlabos' feudal principality in the Rhodope Mountains, and it was the latter, in fact, who had the bell cast and was no doubt also involved in the construction of the bell-tower itself. Sthlabos in various ways appears to have been something of a latinophile.[84]

An art-historical element suggests that up to a point a process of acculturation may have started to develop during the decades of Latin rule. In one of the 1258/9 Byzantine-style frescoes in the Boyana Church (Sofia), namely "The Miracle at Sea" in the St. Nicholas cycle in the narthex, on the stern of the saint's ship is clearly depicted a triangular shield decorated with the Trith coat of arms as we know it from early thirteenth-century seals and later sources, i.e. a red crescent on white or silver background (argent, a crescent gules).[85] This may result from the Latin lords of Philippopolis using the coat of arms in their self-representation with the emblem subsequently being adopted and disseminated locally, ultimately ending up as a decorative element in the Boyana fresco in Bulgarian Sofia. Taken together with other elements – including the Latinism as described by André Grabar

Byzantina Monacensi 17 (Munich, 1974), 77–140; Judith Herrin, "Realities of Byzantine Provincial Government: Hellas and Peloponnesos, 1180–1205," *Dumbarton Oaks Papers* 29 (1975): 252–84. Cheynet, *Pouvoir et contestations à Byzance*, 427–30; Ralph-Johannes Lilie, "Die Zentralbürokratie und die Provinzen zwischen dem 10. und dem 12. Jahrhundert. Anspruch und Realität," *Byzantinische Forschungen* 19 (1993): 65–75; Michael Angold, "The Road to 1204: the Byzantine Background to the Fourth Crusade," *Journal of Medieval History* 25 (1999): 275–76; Alicia Simpson, "Perceptions and Interpretations of the Late Twelfth Century in Modern Historiography," in *Byzantium, 1180–1204: "The Sad Quarter of the Century"?*, ed. Alicia Simpson (Athens, 2015), 13–34; Ilias Anagnostakis, "'From Tempe to Sparta': Power and Contestation prior to the Latin Conquest of 1204," in ibid., 135–57.

[83] Alex Rodriguez Suarez, "When Did the Serbs and the Bulgarians Adopt Bell Ringing?," *CAS Sofia Working Paper Series* 10 (2018): 24–25 (with further references).

[84] See Van Tricht, "Who Murdered Archbishop William of Rouen?", 317–18.

[85] Yordanov, "One reflection of the Fourth Crusade on the Boyana Church frescoes (1258/9)," 48–67. For the Trith coat of arms: DiBe ID 33494, in: Prevenier, *Diplomata Belgica* (1211 charter by Gilles of Trith); Aimé N. Leroy and Arthur Dinaux, "Les blasons et cris d'armes des chevaliers des comtés de Flandre, Hainaut, Artois et Cambrésis," *Archives historiques et littéraires du Nord de la France* 4 (1842): 7. Grar, "Famille des seigneurs de Trith," 72. On the Boyana Church: Zarko Zhdrakov, "Za podpisite na boyanskiya maĭstor Dimitŭr" [On the Signatures of the Boyana Church Master Demeter], *Paleobulgarica* 1 (2008): 47–68; Nina Gagova, "The Life of St. Nicholas in Boyana and the Hagiographical Narratives about the Saint in the South Slavic Manuscript Tradition in the 13th Century," in *The Boyana Church between the East and the West in the Art of the Christian Europe*, ed. Biserka Penkova (Sofia, 2011), 100–125.

in the portrayal (posture, position of the hand) of Desislava (wife of *ktetor* and *sebastokrator* Kalojan), the presence in the just mentioned nautical scene of a Western-style ship with travellers/pilgrims wearing Franco-Venetian hats and being protected by St. Nicholas (venerated by sailors, merchants and crusaders alike), the use of the Latin word *cortina* in the depiction of a church curtain in the St. Panteleimon chapel – this perhaps points to some measure of latinophilia (or the absence of latinophobia) and, in any case, of Latin-Bulgarian interaction.[86] It has also been observed that the Boyana frescoes reflect Constantinopolitan Byzantine models. The artists and workshop responsible for the frescoes may then have personally acquainted themselves with the art and monuments of the Byzantine capital. They may also have encountered the Franco-Byzantine style that was being developed there during the Latin period.[87] In these artistic interactions Latin Philippopolis possibly played some role as conduit.

That an Orthodox metropolitan was quite possibly allowed to remain in place would have favoured a relatively good working relationship between Latins and Byzantine Greeks, but with regard to the Paulician section of the population – mainly Armenians and Bulgarians – things may have been different in view of their 1205 contacts with Kalojan. More generally the Latins appear to have adopted from the Greeks a feeling of cultural superiority vis-à-vis the Bulgarians in particular. In the context of the battle of Philippopolis, the chronicler Valenciennes depicts the Bulgarian enemy army as not believing in God (with the imperial army shouting the crusader battle cry *Saint Sepulcre*), while Emperor Henry himself, in a letter of August 1208 to Pope Innocent III, brands Tsar Boril as a persecutor of the Christian Church. Apart from questioning and casting doubt on the Christianity of the Bulgarian enemy, a friendly Bulgarian vassal like Alexios Sthlabos was also viewed from a somewhat condescending perspective. Valenciennes has Emperor Henry portraying Sthlabos as "somewhat barbaric/uncivilized" (*auques sauvages*) while addressing his daughter about to be married to the Bulgarian ruler, apparently mimicking the Byzantine view of the Bulgarians as *barbaroi*.[88]

One local element perhaps points to an effectively strained relationship with the Bulgarian rural population, which might in part – and on top of the class divide – have originated from this patronizing view. Yordanov has recently drawn attention

---

[86] André Grabar, "Un reflet du monde latin dans une peinture balkanique du 13e siècle," *Byzantion* 1 (1924): 229–43. See also note 85.

[87] On the development of a Franco-Byzantine style in Constantinople: Jaroslav Folda, *Crusader Art in the Holy Land, from the Third Crusade to the Fall of Acre, 1187–1291* (Cambridge, 2005), 299–310; Filip Van Tricht, *The Horoscope of Emperor Baldwin II. Political and Sociocultural Dynamics in Latin-Byzantine Constantinople*, The Medieval Mediterranean 114 (Leiden, 2019), 199–202.

[88] Valenciennes, *Histoire de l'empereur Henri de Constantinople*, §538–539, §558; Brial, RHGF, 19:514. On Byzantine-Bulgarian relations in the late twelfth century: Robert L. Wolff, "The 'Second Bulgarian Empire': Its Origin and History to 1204," *Speculum* 24 (1949): 167–206; Madgearu, *The Asanids*. For the de-Christianizing and Holy-War rhetoric against the Bulgarians at this point; see also Nikolaos G. Chrissis, *Crusading in Frankish Greece: A Study of Byzantine-Western Relations and Attitudes 1204–1282* (Turnhout, 2012), 36–41.

to a piece of oral history that was first recorded in the 1950s by Nikolay Haytov in the village of Yavorovo (near Stenimachos/Asenovgrad), the legend of the *frántsalie*. These were small equestrian bands of horsemen, clad in iron and riding large horses. During assaults of the *frántsalie* the population hid in neighbouring areas. At other times the village people were obliged to meet them with meals positioned on round wooden slabs, so that they could spear the offered food with their huge knives while still mounted. Yordanov convincingly argues that this tale refers to the Latin – or Frankish – occupation of the region after 1204.[89] The mentioned assaults in my opinion more specifically refer to the period of the Latin-Bulgarian war in 1205–8, while the obligation to meet the *frántsalie* with food can no doubt be interpreted as referring to a *droit de gîte*. In Western Europe vassals and subjects were obliged to show their lords hospitality by offering them food and lodgings. Similarly the Byzantine fiscal system allowed the government to requisition food (*epereia*) and lodgings (*mitaton*) for officials and soldiers, while dependent peasants (*paroikoi*) were obliged to periodically give their lords food (*kaniskion*). This piece of oral lore then, for what it's worth, would appear to confirm that in the rural area around Philippopolis the local Latin elite, as elsewhere in Latin Romania, feudalized Byzantine fiscal charges and assimilated them to the feudal customs from their homelands. The *droit de gîte* is, for example, also attested in the principality of Achaia, where it was exercised by both Latin and Byzantine lords.[90]

For what it is worth, the *frántsalie* legend suggests that there generally was little love lost between the Bulgarian rural population and the Latin newcomers. This can be seen as a continuation of the pre-1204 relations between the Bulgarians and the Greeks, on whom the Latins in this region seem to have primarily relied in terms of collaboration and power-sharing. The comparatively prolonged period of relative peace in Thrace that ensued after the battle of Philippopolis (1208), especially after the Latin-Bulgarian alliance concluded in 1213 with Emperor Henry marrying a Bulgarian princess, may have further reconciled the local elite with the new Latin rulers.[91] Such a period of relative peace and calm must have

---

[89] Yordanov, "Bulgarian Folklore Relicts," 357–64.

[90] On the feudal *droit de gîte*: Carlrichard Brühl, *Fodrum, gistum, servitium regis. Studien zu den wirtschaftlichen Grundlagen des Königtums im Frankenreich und in den fränkischen Nachfolgestaaten Deutschland, Frankreich und Italien vom 6. bis zur Mitte des 14. Jahrhunderts*, Kölner historische Abhandlungen 14/1–2 (Cologne, 1968). On the *droit de gîte* in Achaia: David Jacoby, "Un régime de coseigneurie gréco-franque en Morée: Les 'casaux de parçon'," *Mélanges d'archéologie et d'histoire* 75 (1963): 112–13 and 124. There is no need to connect – as does Yordanov – this passage in the *frántsalie* with Giselbert of Mons' quite different description of specific rights that the count of Hainaut held in the towns of Valenciennes and Mons; cf. Gislebert de Mons, *La chronique*, ed. Léon Vanderkindere (Brussels, 1904), §66.

[91] The lord of Philippopolis may well have aided in repelling Boril's abortive invasion of Thrace in 1212, which ended with the Bulgarian tsar retreating to his own territories and avoiding the confrontation with the Latin imperial army: Günter Prinzing, "Der Brief Kaiser Heinrichs von Konstantinopel vom 13. Januar 1212. Überlieferungsgeschichte, Neuedition und Kommentar," *Byzantion* 43 (1973): 413–14; for the date, see Filip Van Tricht, "La politique étrangère de l'empire de Constantinople, de 1210 à 1216: Sa position en Méditerrannée orientale. Problèmes de chronologie et d'interprétation (première partie),"

been most welcome. Since the late 1180s the region had witnessed frequent and quite continuous upheavals in the context of first the Third Crusade and next the rebellion of the Asen brothers, that led to a large-scale Byzantine-Bulgarian war and the establishment of an independent Bulgarian state, with Philippopolis being situated in the frontline.[92]

Gerard of Estreux's 1223/4 recognition of being a vassal of Venice for part of his lands may well have introduced or reinforced a more permanent Venetian presence in Philippopolis, but no confirmation can be found in the sources.[93] As we have seen, Venetian merchants may already have been operating in the area in the late twelfth century. The fact that podestà Tiepolo deemed the matter important enough to raise at the parliament of October 1219 in Rhaidestos may indicate that there was real Venetian interest in developing or expanding commercial activities there, although it may also have been a matter of principle. Regent Conon of Béthune had referred the matter to be discussed at a later date in Constantinople, but the Venetian request seems to have fallen flat at this point, presumably in consultation with Gerard who then must have taken a dismissive stand.[94] That Gerard changed his mind two or three years later and recognized the Venetian rights to part of his territory might be explained by the fact that by this time, with the ongoing successful Epirote offensive by Theodore Doukas against the kingdom of Thessaloniki, the need for allies was growing stronger. In these changing geopolitical circumstances access to Venetian support and also credit may have seemed well worth a more or less symbolic sacrifice after all. Gerard may well have been assured by the fact that the recognition of Venetian feudal rights in the neighbouring principality of Adrianople (already since 1206) had not led to any significant political influence of the Serenissima there.[95] Another aspect may have been that Gerard realized that stronger Venetian involvement could help further develop Philippopolis' economy, which in turn could be beneficial to his own treasury. As we have seen, by the later twelfth century Philippopolis had already grown into a regional economic centre of importance, with ties to both the trading networks orientated towards Constantinople and Thrace and those orientated towards Macedonia.

Le moyen âge 107 (2001): 221–27, with the addition that the date of Theodore I Laskaris' victory over the sultan of Konya, Ghiateddin Kaikosrau I, at Antioch on the Maeander should of course be dated 25 March 1212 (*kyrion pascha*).

[92] Wolff, "The 'Second Bulgarian Empire'," *Speculum* 24 (1949): 167–206; Alicia J. Simpson, "Byzantium's Retreating Balkan Frontiers during the Reign of the Angeloi (1185–1203): A Reconsideration," in *The Balkans and the Byzantine World before and after the Captures of Constantinople, 1204 and 1453*, ed. Vlada Stankovic (Lanham, 2016), 3–22; Madgearu, *The Asanids*, 35–114.

[93] Cessi, *Deliberazioni del Maggior Consiglio di Venezia*, 1:66, n° 69.

[94] Tafel and Thomas, *Urkunden*, 2:219, n° 257.

[95] Van Tricht, "The Byzantino-Latin Principality of Adrianople," 335–36.

The End of Latin Rule in Philippopolis

Exactly when Latin rule in Philippopolis ended is open for debate. It is generally assumed that the city must have been lost in the wake of the major Latin imperial defeats against John III Vatatzes at Poimanenon and against Theodore Doukas near Serres and in Thessaloniki (1224). Both the Nicaean and the Epirote rulers followed up their victories with a series of conquests in northwestern Asia Minor and Macedonia/Thrace.[96] The neighbouring principality of Adrianople was thus captured successively by Vatatzes and Doukas probably around 1227/8, but Philippopolis goes unmentioned in the sources.[97] Ivan Asen II's resounding victory in 1230 over Doukas at Klokotinitza, situated 70 km southeast of Philippopolis on the main road to Adrianople, with its accompanying conquests is usually considered as the ultimate *terminus ante quem*.[98]

Asen's famed contemporary inscription in the Holy Forty Martyrs church in Veliko Tarnovo, however, does not list Philippopolis among his acquisitions, whereas Adrianople, the other important city in the region, is mentioned explicitly and the Bulgarian tsar also boasts that the Latins in and around Constantinople were de facto subjugated to his empire as they had no emperor of their own, a clear reference to the interregnum at the time (after emperor Robert of Courtenay's death in 1227 and awaiting John of Brienne's coronation in 1231). One might propose that Asen captured Philippopolis sometime before 1230 (or even before 1227/8), but there is one element contradicting this. Philippe Mouskes in his *Chronique rimée* explicitly states that in late 1236/early 1237 – after the Nicaean-Bulgarian siege of Constantinople in 1235–6 and around the time of Emperor John of Brienne's death in March 1237 – "the Vlachs [Bulgarians] acquired Philippopolis and regained the land" (*li Blac quièrent Finepople / et la tière ont regaégnie*).[99] Mouskes was a Western chronicler from the town of Tournai – situated in the border region between France, Flanders and Hainaut – who generally is rather well informed about Latin Romania. Admittedly his narrative is not free from errors, but in this particular case there seems to be no reason to simply dismiss his account.

Alexandru Madgearu on the basis of this passage has hypothesized that the Latins must have reconquered the city after Asen had taken it in 1230, but it is difficult to see how this would have happened. Philippe Mouskes, Alberic of Trois-Fontaines, and George Akropolites all agree that Emperor John of Brienne after arriving in Constantinople in 1231 did not achieve any largescale reconquests,

---

[96]   Van Tricht, "Robert of Courtenay," 1024–28.

[97]   Van Tricht, "The Byzantino-Latin Principality of Adrianople," 340–41.

[98]   Asdracha, *La region des Rhodopes*, 242; Madgearu, *The Asanids*, 219; Yordanov, "The Case of 'S., Princeps Philippensis'," 214.

[99]   Philippe Mouskes, *Chronique rimée*, ed. Frédéric de Reiffenberg, 2 vols. (Brussels, 1836–38), 2: vv. 29506–35. For an overview of Ivan Asen II's fluctuating alliances with Nicaea and the papacy/Latin Constantinople in these years: Chrissis, *Crusading in Frankish Greece*, 94–95, 107–8, 114–15, 119–20.

apart from a limited successful campaign around Pegai in northern Asia Minor.[100] The logical conclusion then would be that until 1236/7 Philippopolis had always remained in Latin hands. Worth mentioning here is Ivan Asen's privilege for the merchants of Ragusa (Dubrovnik) issued shortly after 1230. Philippopolis is conspicuously absent from this charter, while neighbouring regions or towns are mentioned, among others Adrianople, Didymoteichon, and Beroe (which by this time in any case was no longer part of the duchy).[101] This can hardly have been the result of Ragusan disinterest, judging by the interest of the other commercial and maritime power, i.e. Venice, in the city.

The clauses related to Philippopolis in the 1229 pact between the then emperor-elect, John of Brienne, and the Constantinopolitan barons likewise indicate that Philippopolis was probably still in Latin hands at the time. The document states that Gerard of Estreux is to hold the land, which has already been held by himself and his predecessors before him, from either the new emperor-elect or his heirs. It does not, in any case, contradict Latin rule there at this point.[102] The survival of such an enclave amidst Bulgarian and Greek (Nicaean or Epirote) possessions may seem surprising, but it should be recalled that in the later twelfth and early thirteenth century this type of autonomous regional political entity was in fact not uncommon within the Byzantine sphere, though most often also quite short-lived.[103] Also, as seen above, Renier of Trith had already managed once to hold the isolated castle of Stenimachos for thirteen months. If so, it would tend to confirm that a mutually viable Latin-Byzantine collaboration was established in the region, since otherwise the principality could hardly have subsisted. This said, a 1231 inscription shows that at that point the fortress of Stenimachos was under Ivan Asen's control at least temporarily, again indicating that part of the duchy – including also Beroe and Konstanteia in the neighbourhood of Klokotinitza – had anyway already slipped from Latin control and that its continued existence had become precarious.[104]

---

[100] Albericus Trium Fontium, *Chronica*, ed. Paul Scheffer-Boichorst, MGH SS 23 (Hanover, 1874), 933; Philippe Mouskes, *Chronique rimée*, v. 29026–29038; Georgios Akropolites, *Historia*, §30.

[101] Madgearu, *The Asanids*, 204–205.

[102] In the original pact negotiated between the emperor-elect and the Constantinopolitan envoys it is stated that the new emperor will choose lands for his own heirs to inherit, with Philippopolis being mentioned as one of the options (as part of an ensemble of other territories): "et totum Ducatum de Finepople, quisquis eum tenet." In an additional clause added at the request of the Constantinopolitan barons this is clarified: "scilicet de Ducatu Phinepople, ut illud, quod de jure tenuit dilectus et fidelis consors eorum et Baro imperii, dominus Girardus de Stroim et antecessores sui, libere teneat per debitum servitium ab eo, in cujus partem predictus Ducatus cesserit, scilicet Imperatoris vel heredum suorum" (Tafel and Thomas, *Urkunden*, 2:269, n° 273).

[103] Hoffman, *Rudimente von Territorialstaaten im byzantinischen Reich*, 77–140. Cheynet, *Pouvoir et contestations à Byzance*, 427–30.

[104] The inscription mentions as date the 6739th year of the Byzantine era, 4th indiction. It is unclear whether the town of Stenimachos, having its own set of fortifications, 2 km to the north, likewise had come already under Asen's control. See Vasil Zlatarski, "Asenevijat nadpis pri *Stanimaka*," *Izvestija na balgarskoto istorichesko druzhestvo* 2 (1911): 231–47; Phaedon Malingoudis, *Die mittelalterlichen kyrillischen Inschriften der Hämus-Halbinsel. 1. Die bulgarischen Inschriften* (Thessalonica, 1979),

As mentioned earlier, in September and December 1238 the former lord of Philippopolis, Gerard of Estreux, was one of the *consiliarii et barones imperii* that enacted the mortgage of the Crown of Thorns to Venetian merchants.[105] This being the last certain mention we have of him, his presence in these charters among the highest metropolitan aristocracy confirms that in the preceding years he had not lost touch with the imperial court in Constantinople. There is no information available as to if or how Estreux was compensated for the loss of his duchy, probably with a much more modest fief – a single local town or castle, or possibly even a money fief – in the region around Constantinople, in the remaining parts of either Thrace or Optimaton across the Bosphoros. Two documents from the St Nicholas abbey of Arrouaise – from c. 1252 and 1265/7 respectively – mention a *Gerars et Sainte d'Estruens* and *Gerart de Struen* with lands held from the abbey in Gimbermont (36 km south of Estreux) in Cambrésis in the border region between Flanders and Hainaut.[106] While it was not uncommon for lords and knights who had been exiled from their Eastern lands to return to their Western homeland, it is, however, in this particular case and at this stage impossible to confirm whether or not this person should be identified with the former lord of Philippopolis or one of his descendents or relatives.

Conclusion

The scant evidence does not allow us to draw a full picture of the duchy of Philippopolis. We would wish to know more about which Latin families settled there and how they interacted with the local Greek and Bulgarian population. We would like to know how the local Byzantine elite viewed the Latin newcomers and the Latin emperor in Constantinople. It would be interesting to learn more about the conditions of coexistence in the religious and ecclesiastical sphere. Nevertheless it would seem that, as in various other parts of Latin Romania, some viable equilibrium – with areas of mutual interest on the one hand and tension on the other – was established that allowed the duchy to subsist for several decades. The border principality's fall in the 1230s indeed appears to have been due rather to the external pressures of the geopolitical dynamics in the wider area – with the ongoing and ever evolving confrontations between Constantinople, Nicaea, Epiros and Bulgaria, all claimants to the same imperial legacy – than to local factors or divisions. In the decades following Asen's conquest, Philippopolis and its region would change hands regularly between the Nicaeans/Byzantines and the Bulgarians, possibly fostering a sense of local/regional identity that, as we have seen, had its

60–62, n° XIII. In English translation: Petkov, *The Voices of Medieval Bulgaria*, 426, n° 156. See also Madgearu, *The Asanids*, 1.

[105] Teulet, *Layettes du Trésor des Chartes*, 2: n° 2744 and n° 2753.

[106] Benoît-Michel Tock and Ludo Milis, eds., *Monumenta Arroasiensia*, CCCM 175 (Turnhout, 2000), n° 646 and n° 649.

origins even before 1204 and may well have grown stronger during the period of Latin rule, when it was for a longer period of time governed as an autonomous principality, albeit with solid ties with and continuing loyalty vis-à-vis the imperial government in Constantinople. In the principality of Achaia, where the source situation is markedly better and where Latins and Byzantines also shared power, Teresa Shawcross has tentatively identified the gradual development over time of a mixed local identity and of sentiments of "proto-nationalism."[107]

---

[107] Teresa Shawcross, *The Chronicle of Morea. Historiography in Crusader Greece*, Oxford Studies in Byzantium (Oxford, 2009), 216, 219, 236, 255.

Manuele Zaccaria's Report on the Fleet in Outremer after the Fall of Acre (1292–1293): Jacques de Molay, the War of Curzola, and Genoese-Cypriot Conflict

Antonio Musarra
(Sapienza Università di Roma; antonio.musarra@uniroma1.it)
Christopher D. Schabel
(University of Cyprus; schabel@ucy.ac.cy)
Philippe Josserand
(Nantes Université; ph.josserand@wanadoo.fr)

Abstract

After the fall of Acre in 1291 the Christian West was unable to recover the Holy Land and the Muslim East could not continue its advance and conquer quickly the kingdoms of Armenia and Cyprus. This does not mean that great efforts were not made on both sides to reverse the tide of, or capitalize on, recent events. A brief document now bound among miscellaneous materials at the end of Reg. Aven. 54 illustrates the measures that the papacy took to protect Cilician Armenia and Cyprus and to lay the foundations for a future reconquest in Syria. The document, discovered by Jean Richard and published here, is the report that the Genoese Manuele Zaccaria drew up for the Roman Curia concerning his maintenance of the papal fleet in Outremer in 1292–93. In addition to providing details about the number of ships and men, their points of origin, and their terms of service, the report sheds new light on the movements of the last Templar master, Jacques de Molay, contextualizes the decline of Cypro-Genoese relations within the conflict between Venice and Genoa, and fills in some gaps in the narrative of the naval arms race with the Mamluk sultanate. Most important, the impression resulting from the report is in contrast with much modern historiography, for, relying on hindsight and falling into teleology, too many specialists on the Middle Ages and even on the crusades continue to assert repeatedly that after the fall of Acre the Holy Land was definitively forgotten and abandoned by the West.

In memory of Jean Richard (1921–2021)

No doubt while examining the papal registers of Benedict XII (1334–42) for letters concerning Cyprus to be calendared in the *Bullarium Cyprium*,[1] the late Jean Richard discovered among the miscellaneous documents at the end of Reg. Aven. 54 a brief and undated report of Manuele Zaccaria concerning his maintenance of a fleet in Outremer. Professor Richard ran into thousands of such items, too many to

---

[1] Charles Perrat and Jean Richard, with Chris Schabel, *Bullarium Cyprium*, vol. III: *Lettres papales relatives à Chypre 1316–1378* (Nicosia, 2012).

exploit fully, and as far as we know the only use to which he put the document was in a famous article on Cyprus and the embargo on trade with Egypt, published in 1984, where the information is buried in a footnote.[2] Philippe Josserand published an edition of the short document in 2019 in the context of his study of Jacques de Molay[3] and, independently, Chris Schabel ran into the document in the same way as had Richard, in the process of turning the calendared papal letters into a full edition and scouring the papal registers exhaustively for more bulls concerning Cyprus. Because there is more to say about the text, when *le Doyen* passed away a couple of weeks shy of his 100th birthday, we decided, along with Antonio Musarra, who had already published a document pertinent to the subject,[4] to re-examine the report for what it tells us about the defense of Outremer after the fall of Acre and about relations between Genoa, Cyprus, and the Templars.

Few individuals are mentioned in the report, but they are among the most famous and/or influential figures in the history of the crusades and the Latin East, especially Jean de Villiers and Jacques de Molay, grand masters of the Hospital and the Temple;[5] Benedetto and Manuele Zaccaria, Genoese leaders in eastern trade and naval warfare, and members of a family that was instrumental in Latin expansion in the Eastern Aegean;[6] and Philippe d'Ibelin, uncle of King Henry II of Cyprus and future seneschal, a key figure in the fateful anti-Genoese direction that Cyprus would soon follow.

The Context

On 18 May 1291, after a siege, the walls of Acre collapsed under the blows of a young and ambitious Mamluk sultan, followed, ten days later, by the Templar castle, the fulcrum of the city's inner defenses. After almost two centuries, the Latin presence in the Holy Land ceased.[7] The news caused a stir among contemporaries,

---

[2]   Jean Richard, "Le royaume de Chypre et l'embargo sur le commerce avec l'Égypte (fin XIIIe–début XIVe siècle)," *Comptes rendus des séances de l'Académie des Inscriptions et Belles-Lettres* 128 (1984): 120–34, at 123 n. 16. Some later studies rely on Richard's note.

[3]   Philippe Josserand, *Jacques de Molay. Le dernier grand-maître des Templiers* (Paris, 2019), no. 4 (edition 453–56, French translation 456–58); see also idem, "La fabrique d'un diplomate: Jacques de Molay, grand-maître de l'ordre du Temple, et ses voyages en Occident (1292–1296)," *Revue historique* 696 (2020): 3–21.

[4]   Antonio Musarra, *In partibus Ultramaris. I Genovesi, la crociata e la Terrasanta (secc. XII–XIII)* (Rome, 2017), Appendix C, 600–604.

[5]   The common expression "grand master," frequent in the historiography, is actually attested in the late Templar documentation, especially under Jacques de Molay: see Xavier Hélary, *Les Templiers. Leur faux trésor, leur vraie puissance* (Paris, 2018), 152–53; and Josserand, *Jacques de Molay*, 207–8.

[6]   For the Zaccaria family, see Michel Balard, *La Romanie génoise (XIIe–début du XVe siècle)*, 2 vols. (Rome, 1978); Enrico Basso, "Gli Zaccaria," in *Dibattito su famiglie nobili del mondo coloniale genovese nel Levante*, ed. Geo Pistarino (Genoa, 1994), 46–55; and Mike Carr, *Merchant Crusaders in the Aegean: 1291–1352* (Woodbridge, 2015).

[7]   For a recent review, see Antonio Musarra, *Acri 1291. La caduta degli stati crociati* (Bologna, 2017). See also Reinhold Röhricht, "Die Eroberung Akkas durch die Muslimen," *Forschungen zur deutschen*

most of whom did not perceive the situation as entirely irreversible. European Christianity reacted with great shouting and many recriminations without actively recovering what was lost. The search for the culprits began almost immediately. The weakness of the Jerusalem monarchy, the impotence of the papacy, the inactivity of the European rulers, the bitter rivalry between the military religious orders, the fratricidal struggles between the merchants of the Italian maritime cities: these were considered the leading causes of the disaster.[8] Pope Nicholas IV was informed at the beginning of August, about two months after the end of the siege, while he was in Orvieto. From a letter dated 28 July 1291, we learn, in fact, that he was aware of the death of the master of the Temple, William of Beaujeu, who had fallen on 18 May,[9] but not yet of the election of his successor, Thibaud Gaudin, which took place after the fall of Acre, probably at Sidon, since the pope addressed the procurator of the house of the Temple in Jerusalem, André Mathie, as his principal interlocutor.[10] Again on 1 August, in issuing a general call for a crusade, aimed at organizing a general *passagium* – an expedition in grand style, in which the prominent European rulers were to participate, with a departure date set for 24 June of 1293 – Nicholas did not mention the conclusion of the siege, showing, instead, that he wanted to follow up on a series of agreements on plans for a crusade previously made with the king of England, Edward I.[11] The first news relating to the Acre catastrophe appeared in the bull promulgated on 13 August, *Dire amaritudinis calicem*, with

---

Geschichte 20 (1880): 93–126; idem, "Der Untergang des Königreichs Jerusalem," *Mittheilungen des Instituts für Österreichische Geschichtsforschung* 15 (1894): 1–59; Gustave L. Schlumberger, "Prise de Saint-Jean-d'Acre en l'an 1291 par l'armée du Soudan d'Égypte; fin de la domination franque en Syrie," in idem, *Byzance et Croisades: Pages Médiévales* (Paris, 1927), 207–79; Erwin Stickel, *Der Fall von Akkon. Untersuchungen zum Abklingen des Kreuzzugsgedankens am Ende des 13. Jahrhunderts* (Bern, 1975); Donald P. Little, "The Fall of 'Akkā in 690/1291: The Muslim Version," in *Studies in Islamic History and Civilization in Honour of Professor David Ayalon*, ed. Moshe Sharon (Leiden, 1986), 159–82; Andreas D'Souza, "The Conquest of 'Akkā (690/1291). A Comparative Analysis of Christian and Muslim Sources," *The Muslim World* 80 (1990): 234–49.

[8] Sylvia Schein, *Fideles crucis: The Papacy, the West and the Recovery of the Holy Land* (Oxford, 1991). For an analysis of the Latin reactions, see now Antonio Musarra, *Il crepuscolo della crociata. L'Occidente e la perdita della Terrasanta* (Bologna, 2018), and Matthieu Rajohnson, *L'Occident au regret de Jérusalem (1187–fin du XIVe siècle)* (Paris, 2021), 555–622.

[9] Louis de Vasselot de Régné, *Le dernier Templier de Terre sainte. Vie et mort de Guillaume de Beaujeu* (Paris, 2021), 115–18.

[10] *Les Registres de Nicolas IV [1288–1292]. Recueil des bulles de ce pape publiées ou analysées d'après les manuscrits originaux des Archives du Vatican*, ed. Ernest Langlois (Paris, 1886–93), no. 5763.

[11] *Les Registres de Nicolas IV*, nos. 6800–6805. The date of departure, together with the relative spiritual privileges, had been promulgated on the previous 29 March: *Universis Christi fidelibus*: ibid., nos. 6683–6692. In the months preceding the fall of Acre, an intense correspondence had developed between Edward and Nicholas: Edward had agreed to take command of the *passagium* (of course, in exchange for large tithes). The exchange of letters would continue until the pope's death on 4 April 1292, which, however, hindered the implementation of all effective help: ibid., nos. 5739, 5740, 6664–6682, 6836, 6837, 6857, 6858; regarding the collection of tithes, see ibid., nos. 6693–6701. The situation is well outlined in Bartholomaeus de Cotton, Monachus Norwicensis, *Historia anglicana (AD 449–1298)*, ed. Henry Richards Luard (London, 1859), 176–78.

which the pope announced the tragic epilogue to Christianity: "O abominable madness of the pagans! O monstrous savagery! O accursed and deadly cruelty!" (*O nefanda rabies paganorum! O immanis feritas! O execrabilis et funesta sevitia!*).[12]

As Sylvia Schein has pointed out, the writing had unusual tones: Nicholas offered no theological explanation for the disaster – there is no trace, for example, of the classic motif of *nostris peccatis exigentibus* – merely emphasizing the ardor and devotion of those who had participated in the defense of the city, reduced to a heap of rubble, and appealing to all believers to mobilize for a general crusade "for the speedy recovery of said land" (*ad recuperationem celerem dictae terrae*). Only in this way, the offense done to Christ and the Church would be avenged.[13] The pope, therefore, called on Christianity to rally, ordering immediate relief for Cyprus and the Armenian kingdom of Cilicia. He added the need to impose a strict naval blockade on Egypt to weaken its economic and military power. Not surprisingly, on the same day, the encyclical was sent to the Genoese and the Venetians, the only ones who could accomplish this, ordering them to put an end to their ongoing conflicts via a peace treaty or, at least, a truce for a "lengthy time" (*longo tempore*), so as not to divide their forces. Pope Nicholas also stipulated the convocation of provincial councils, composed of members of both the secular and regular clergies, requiring them to formulate, before the next feast of the Purification (2 February 1292), in written form an analysis of the situation and suggestions for possible remedies.[14] The same request was received and confirmed in *Dura nimis et amara*, promulgated on 18 August, sent to the kings of France and England, to the master of the Hospital, commanders of the Temple, and some bishops. Nicholas – who did not fail to underline the heavy burdens incurred by the papacy to organize fleets and military units – also suggested that the possible merger of the military orders be included among the topics of discussion, since the loss of the Holy Land was accompanied by the elimination of their role in defending pilgrimage routes: both the Church and the *vox communis*, he affirmed, would welcome the measure.[15] This was a request with consequences.

Modern historiography has paid little attention to the effects of the fall of Acre on the reformulation of the idea of the crusade. Sylvia Schein herself dedicated an important book to it, arguing for a sort of continuity in the development of the crusader ideal between the Council of Lyon in 1274 and that of Vienne in 1311–12. In reality, it was a substantial break, capable of impressing itself on consciences.[16] Rightly, she questioned why the pope did not convene a new general council.[17] The gravity of the situation seemed to demand quick action. But it is also

---

[12]   *Les Registres de Nicolas IV*, no. 5763.
[13]   *Les Registres de Nicolas IV*, no. 5763.
[14]   *Les Registres de Nicolas IV*, no. 7625. For copies sent to Italian seaside towns see nos. 6782–6783. A further copy was sent, on 18 August, to the archbishop of Milan: nos. 6791–6792.
[15]   *Les Registres de Nicolas IV*, nos. 6793–6799, 7626, 7628.
[16]   Josserand, *Jacques de Molay*, 158 and 367.
[17]   Schein, *Fideles crucis*, 100.

possible that Nicholas intended to await the work of the provincial councils. On 23 August, following previous agreements which proved unsuccessful, the pope wrote – through the Dominican Gerardo Picalotti bishop of Spoleto – to the king of France, Philip IV, asking him to follow the example of his forefathers – and, therefore, of Louis IX – and send an army to the East. If the king refused, the messenger was to insist that the tithe assigned to his father, Philip III, be given to the French crusaders. Predictably, Philip refused, requesting instead permission to use another levy for the next six years to finance his ongoing war against the kingdom of Aragon; this infuriated the pope, who resolved to seek help elsewhere.[18] In February 1292, Nicholas allegedly complained to the English ruler that nothing had come "into the hands of the Church" (*ad manus Ecclesie*) of the tithes collected in the kingdom of France or from the lands subject to the king of Castile, who had been authorized since the time of Gregory X to use these funds to fight the Moors in Spain. Similarly, only a tiny portion of the tithes was collected in the lands of the Empire, and no news had come from Scotland and Ireland. In any case, Nicholas reaffirmed his will, ensuring the appointment of a papal legate for the imminent *passagium* of 1293. If the leading European rulers' behavior was deplorable, this did not entail abandoning the Holy Land to its fate.[19]

The picture one sees in the papal sources is somewhat confusing. Pope Nicholas IV seemed to perceive the gravity of the situation, taking steps that might have led to a great expedition. In any case, the relative lack of interest of the prominent European rulers in recovering what was lost – or, at least, in quickly doing so – is evident, so it fell to the pope to take any serious initiative. Undoubtedly, he also had in mind the fate of Cyprus and the Armenian kingdom of Cilicia, on which the Mamluks might have been setting their sights. The pope moved quickly to ensure the defense of these final bastions of Christianity in the East, requesting financial support from the military orders and arranging for a fleet of 20 galleys, 10 of which – according to documents dated 17 and 23 January 1292 – were under the command of Vitale Torzevalle and Ruggero de Thodinis, which was to be sent to the Levant as soon as possible. The combatants would be guaranteed the same indulgences as in a *passagium generale* to the Holy Land.[20] According to the Genoese chronicler Iacopo Doria, who was very attentive to the maritime events of the time, the papal fleet had the purpose of defending the last Christian territories of the East as well as the aim of proceeding against anyone who illegally traveled to the sultan's lands in contempt of the embargo (*devetum*) that Nicholas had issued against trade with the Muslims on 21 October 1290, which was

---

[18] *Les Registres de Nicolas IV*, nos. 6778–6781, 6849. Relations with the French king, which had begun long before, resulted, in December 1290, in detailed negotiations relating to the forfeiture of tithes: ibid., nos. 4409–4414.

[19] *Les Registres de Nicolas IV*, no. 6857.

[20] *Les Registres de Nicolas IV*, nos. 6432, 6850–6856 (6850: *indulgentias, privilegia et gratias concedimus que transfretantibus in Terre Sancte subsidium sunt concesse*).

reaffirmed after the fall of Acre.[21] Soon afterwards, al-Ashraf, the Mamluk sultan, turned against the Cilician kingdom. Since 1285, there had been a truce between the two sides, probably renewed in 1289, when, during the siege of Tripoli, Armenian ambassadors went to the Mamluk camp begging for the sultan's benevolence.[22] Now faced with the resurgent threat, Het'um II of Armenia asked the West for help, sending a legation led by the Franciscan Tommaso of Tolentino to the pope and the kings of France and England. He carried letters with him, three of which were quoted by the English chronicler Bartholomew Cotton. In addition to a request for assistance from the king of Armenia, the embassy handed Edward I of England two letters from al-Ashraf drawn up during the siege of Acre, announcing his goal.[23]

From the Mamluk point of view, the action was nothing more than the natural continuation of what had taken place in Syria-Palestine in 1291. Complete domination over the region would only be possible through the eradication of the weak Armenian and Christian presence from the northern borders of Syria, to come into direct contact with the Seljuk domains and at the same time eliminate an annoying ally of the Il-khanate. On 23 January 1292, with the bull *Pia mater Ecclesia*, Nicholas IV ordered the preachers of the crusade to encourage the defense of the Armenian kingdom, and, as mentioned above, offered the combatants the same indulgences as for a crusade to the Holy Land.[24] On the same day, he wrote to the masters of the Temple and the Hospital, Thibaud Gaudin and Jean de Villiers, asking them to bring relief to the region, extending the request to the commander of the papal fleet, Ruggero de Thodinis.[25] But the death of the pope on 4 April 1292 – which would be followed by more than two years of vacancy on the papal throne – hampered further efforts to transform the planned expedition into the vanguard of the *passagium* designed for the following year. It fell to the college of cardinals to deal with the matter. They managed to gather the necessary galleys thanks to the solicitude of two private Genoese citizens: Tedisio Doria and Manuele Zaccaria, the latter appointed admiral of the fleet (it is not certain that he replaced the captains personally selected by Nicholas IV). These are well-known figures:

---

[21] *Les Registres de Nicolas IV*, no. 4403; Iacobus Aurie, *Annales Ianuenses ann. MCCLXXX–MCCLXXXXIII*, in *Annali genovesi di Caffaro e de' suoi continuatori*, ed. Luigi T. Belgrano and Cesare Imperiale di Sant'Angelo, 5 vols. (Genoa and Rome, 1890–1929), 5:143–44.

[22] Peter M. Holt, *Early Mamluk Diplomacy (1260–1290). Treaties of Baybars & Qalāwūn with Christian Rulers* (Leiden, 1995), 92–105. See also Angus D. Stewart, *The Armenian Kingdom and the Mamluks. War and Diplomacy during the Reigns of Het'um II (1289–1307)* (Leiden, 2001), 55–61, 72, and Marie-Anna Chevalier, *Les ordres religieux-militaires en Arménie cilicienne. Templiers, hospitaliers, teutoniques et Arméniens à l'époque des croisades* (Paris, 2009), 543 and 548–49.

[23] Bartholomaeus de Cotton, *Historia*, 215–23. The Templar of Tyre recalls the sending of further letters to the Templar master: *Cronaca del Templare di Tiro (1243–1314). La caduta degli Stati Crociati nel racconto di un testimone oculare*, ed. Laura Minervini (Naples, 2000), 204.

[24] *Les Registres de Nicolas IV*, nos. 6850–6856; cf. note 20 above.

[25] *Les Registres de Nicolas IV*, nos. 6855–6856. There is no news about the arrival of the papal fleet in the region.

Tedisio was the uncle of the main Genoese annalist of the time, Iacopo Doria;[26] Manuele was the brother of the famous Benedetto, admiral and merchant, who, in 1289, had tried to place himself at the head of the municipality of Tripoli.[27] It is no coincidence that it is Iacopo who provides the best account of the story. According to him, Manuele promised to supply twelve galleys to the college of cardinals; Tedisio, on the other hand, was to provide eight to him. It seems, however, that the Genoese government expressed reservations regarding the action, probably due to their fear of breaking the commercial treaty arranged with the Egyptian sultanate in 1290.[28] But the arguments of the cardinals were more compelling. On the other hand, it is likely that the military orders, or at least the Hospital, were behind the action. A deed kept in the notarial fonds of the Genoese State Archives shows, in fact, how Tedisio Doria promised, on 1 April 1292, to arm three galleys to be sent to the Levant – three of the eight provided for by a previous deed, drawn up by the notary Lanfranco of Acre on the previous 25 January, of which, however, no trace remains – to fight "against perifidious Hagarenes and malevolent Christians" (*contra perfidos Agarenos et malivolos Christianos*) on behalf of the brothers Benedetto and Manuele Zaccaria and the Hospitaller Bonifacio di Calamandrana, who, after long experience in overseas affairs, then held the role of grand commander of the West (*in partibus cismarinis*).[29] On 13 December 1291, Nicholas IV had expressly commissioned him to organize the expedition.[30]

The Report of Manuele Zaccaria

The brief document that Jean Richard first described in 1984 and that Philippe Josserand first edited in 2019, which we re-edit below with a few minor corrections, is a report (*ratio*) that Manuele Zaccaria sent to the cardinals concerning the galleys "that he maintained and is maintaining in areas of Outremer and for the service of

---

[26] Antonio Musarra, "Unpublished Notarial Acts on Tedisio Doria's Voyage to Cyprus and Lesser Armenia, 1294–1295," *Crusades* 11 (2012): 175–99.

[27] Musarra, *Acri 1291*, 143–56; idem, "Benedetto Zaccaria e la caduta di Tripoli (1289): la difesa d'Outremer tra ragioni ideali e opportunismo," in *Gli Italiani e la Terrasanta. Atti del Seminario di Studio (Firenze, Istituto Italiano di Scienze Umane, 22 febbraio 2013)*, ed. Antonio Musarra (Florence, 2014), 219–37.

[28] Iacobus Aurie, *Annales*, 144. For the treaty of 1290, see Musarra, *Acri 1291*, 161–63.

[29] This act is published in Antonio Musarra, *In partibus Ultramaris*, Appendix C, 600–604. See also Anthony Luttrell, "The Hospitallers in Cyprus after 1291," in *Πρακτικά του πρώτου διεθνούς κυπρολογικού συνεδρίου. Τόμος Β΄, Μεσαιωνικόν Τμήμα*, ed. Athanasios Papageorgiou (Nicosia, 1972), 161–71, at 162, reprinted in Anthony Luttrell, *The Hospitallers in Cyprus, Rhodes, Greece and the West, 1291–1440* (London, 1978), study II; Jochen Burgtorf, "A Mediterranean Career in the Late Thirteenth Century: The Hospitaller Grand Commander Boniface of Calamandrana," in *The Hospitallers, the Mediterranean and Europe. Festschrift for Anthony Luttrell*, ed. Karl Borchardt, Nikolas Jaspert, and Helen J. Nicholson (Aldershot, 2007), 73–85.

[30] *Cart Hosp*, 3: no. 4177.

the Holy Land."[31] Richard dated the document to the fall of 1292,[32] but it must postdate the month of December 1292, since it explicitly mentions the return to Italy of Guglielmo di Santo Stefano, "prior of the Hospital in Lombardy," future commander of Cyprus and official historian of the order, who "came to parts on this side of the sea December last" [§2]. The *terminus post quem non* seems to be 30 April 1293, because of mentions of what happened "on 1 May last" [§§4 and 6], meaning 1 May 1292.[33] Further precision might also come from the meaning of the last phrase: "a full report concerning these will be made at the end of the year" [§16], but probably this merely means the end of the year-long service of the galleys in question. If it refers to the calendar year, we nevertheless assume that it was either Christmas, as in most Genoese documents, or 1 January, usually employed by the papacy. At any rate, on internal grounds all we can say is that the report was most likely composed in February, March, or April 1293.

The report concerns two separate groups of galleys, one that Manuele "maintained" and the other that he is still "maintaining." The text first discusses the obligation to maintain eight galleys at sea for six months, as agreed between Manuele and the Hospitaller Bonifacio di Calamandrana, who paid for the service. Of these eight galleys, we are told that a portion had entered service in March 1292, another in April, another departed on 1 May, and another left "after said deadline." We are not told what the original deadline was, but because of the staggered and delayed start, in Rome at some later point it was agreed that they would count the six-month service from 1 May 1292, "since they were obliged to begin earlier, according to said agreement that had been made." The term for these galleys was to end just five months later, on 1 October 1292, but the phrase "insofar as service in areas of Outremer is concerned" suggests that this was the date they could return to the West, allowing for the travel time and for avoiding winter weather. In the end, however, Manuele maintained these galleys and armaments around ten days beyond the deadline, so the ships did not start their return trip until 10 October or so [§1]. The practice of arranging the time of service in advance was normal, as shown by the plan that Benedetto Zaccaria, brother of Manuele, drew up for Philip IV the Fair in 1294 concerning raids on the English coastal areas: on that occasion, the minimum time of expected engagement was four months.[34] In addition to defining the time limits of the operation, the purpose was purely economic, since it was necessary to establish the crews' pay and related advances. In fact, Manuele did not maintain eight separate galleys, but rather the men and armaments enough to equip eight galleys were maintained on only seven actual ships [§1]. If we posit a

---

[31]   See Appendix, below.

[32]   Richard, "Le royaume de Chypre et l'embargo," 123.

[33]   Josserand, *Jacques de Molay*, 114, and idem, "La fabrique d'un diplomate," 7, proposing a date of March or April 1293.

[34]   Antonio Musarra, "Un progetto italiano di razzia del suolo inglese redatto per Filippo IV il Bello (1294 ca.)," *Francigena. Rivista sul franco-italiano e sulle scritture francesi nel Medioevo d'Italia* 2 (2016): 249–73.

complement of 120 men per galley, this comes to 960 men, although distributed over only seven galleys, so almost 140 per galley. It is possible, however, that Manuele's galleys, as well as those of his brother Benedetto, already adopted the "reef" system, the third man per counter, in which case we would be faced with about 1440 men, employed in service for six months on seven galleys, which counted as eight.[35]

Next, the text discusses a second group of galleys that was added to this initial force, since Manuele also "promised to maintain ten galleys for one year in the service of the Church" [§3], although here again Manuele chose to distribute men and arms for ten galleys on just nine actual ships [§9]. The provenance of these galleys is described in detail: two from Rome, in service since 14 May 1292 [§4]; one from Ancona, which left around 1 June [§5]; two from the Naples area, which departed on 31 May [§6]; two from Genoa, owned by Tedisio Doria, departing around 1 June [§7]; and one from Foggia – called the "Divitia" – that carried arms for two galleys and was thus counted for two, which also set out around 1 June [§8]. The report goes on to number the above as nine galleys counting for ten [§9], but the document as we have it lists only eight with a complement for nine. It is probable that the ninth galley of this group was omitted by a scribal error, perhaps an omission *per homoeoteleuton*, since the copy in Reg. Aven. 54 is not the original. Of the eight galleys whose departure dates are specified, six left on or around 31 May or 1 June while the other two had left on 14 May. Judging from what occurred for the first group of ships, the one-year service of the second squadron was probably calculated to begin on 1 June 1292, when most of the galleys actually set off, and thus the end of the service should be set at 31 May 1293.

In total, therefore, the report declares that up until 10 October 1292 Manuele always maintained 16 galleys with men and arms for 18, plus a yacht (*pamphylum*) and a bolt (*sayecteam*), with the documents to prove it. In addition, at any given time there were 100 to 200 men in excess of the normal crews, although the report does not tell us what the original numbers agreed for the fleet were [§9]. The document does inform us how, in areas of Outremer, Manuele had asked the masters of the Temple and the Hospital to send the necessary men and arms sufficient to equip all the above galleys [§10]. At the conclusion of the service of the first squadron, Manuele asked the master of the Hospital for a receipt or quittance, and the master replied that he was content and satisfied. Since the arrangement had been made with the Hospitaller Bonifacio di Calamandrana, Manuele also asked him for a quittance. For this purpose Manuele requested that the master of the Hospital should compose a letter declaring that Manuele had carried out his promises, which

---

[35]   For the evolution of warships in the Mediterranean, see in general John H. Pryor, *Geography, Technology and War. Studies in the Maritime History of the Mediterranean, 649–1571* (Cambridge, 1992), 57–86.

letter Guglielmo di Santo Stefano brought to the West on his return from Outremer in December 1292 [§2].[36]

The second part of the document contains fascinating background information. Gathering a fleet from different places was quite a logistical challenge. In order to ensure that he could fulfill the substantial promises that he had made, Manuele "sent to many parts of the world" to request the arming of extra galleys to make up for any shortcomings and to meet his deadline, "so that if there were not enough from one place, they would be supplied from another." As it turned out, no galleys were missing of those that he met en route after Rhodes and elsewhere, so as a result five additional galleys and armed vessels reached him, which cost him dearly and in vain [§11]. The final clauses are somewhat cryptic. Manuele asked the cardinals to send a nuncio to the "emperor of the Greeks" at Manuele's expense, "concerning the deed about which he spoke to you" [§12]. The report adds that his brother Benedetto sent a letter to the cardinals and Benedetto's nuncio had already been at the curia for a long time awaiting an answer, so the report asks for the response so that the nuncio can return with the answer [§13]. It is not clear what the report is referring to or if these two items are connected, but it could be argued that the Apostolic See was then trying to make agreements with Andronikos Palaiologos for the reunification of the churches, a policy that had been pursued by his father, Michael VIII. In the lead-up to the Second Council of Lyon of 1274, Pope Gregory X decided to take advantage of the fact that Girolamo Masci, the future Pope Nicholas IV, was Franciscan provincial minister of Sclavonia – a region including present-day Dalmatia and part of the Balkans – and in 1272 invested him with a delicate mission to Michael VIII to discuss the possibility of ecclesiastical union.[37] On the other hand, these items may instead concern sea-borne trade and naval warfare, since the report goes on to remind the cardinals of Manuele's intention to send galleys against Alexandria, about which he had spoken to the cardinals, and a great fleet was preparing for the expedition [§14].

Finally, Manuele informs the cardinals that when he left Cyprus, presumably after 10 October, he arranged for ten armed galleys to complete the service of one year as promised. He adds that one of these ten galleys took the master of the Temple to Brindisi before returning quickly to Cyprus, while another transported Philippe d'Ibelin, the uncle of King Henry II of Cyprus, to Ancona, and at the time the report was drawn up it was due to return as soon as the cardinals gave their response, certainly meaning the response to the report and not the one that Benedetto Zaccaria's nuncio was waiting for [§15]. Since the last clause relates that "eight of these galleys remained for the protection of Cyprus," one assumes that this was while the two ships took the Templar master and Philippe d'Ibelin to the West. Thus when the report ends "And a full report concerning these [galleys] will be made at the end of the year," we interpret this as meaning that this report would

---

[36] On Guglielmo di Santo Stefano, see Jochen Burgtorf, *The Central Convent of Hospitallers and Templars. History, Organization, and Personnel (1099/1120–1310)* (Leiden, 2008), 140–41 and 160–61.

[37] Musarra, *Il crepuscolo della crociata*, 33.

cover all ten galleys at the end of the year of service that began around 1 June 1292 (although the first two ships had left port on 14 May) and thus would end around 31 May 1293 [§16].

The Movements of Jacques de Molay

The Templar master whom the Genoese galley took to Brindisi was Jacques de Molay, who had succeeded Thibaud Gaudin before 20 April 1292. Unfortunately, Professor Richard made a minor palaeographical error in his note, reading "*qui*" instead of "*que*," which error led to a more significant interpretative mistake, since the text as Richard has it indicates that Jacques de Molay himself returned to Cyprus, whereas the correct reading means that it was the galley that returned to Cyprus. In the *editio princeps*, Josserand maintained Richard's reading and therefore concluded that the Templar master made two trips to the West one right after the other, the first in the winter of 1292–93 and the second beginning in the spring of 1293.[38] Once the necessary palaeographical correction is made, however, the theory of a separate, first voyage by Jacques de Molay is called into question. The passage merits translation, because much of what follows below will hinge upon it:

> *Item*, the same Manuele informs [the cardinals] that upon his withdrawal from Cyprus he arranged for ten armed galleys to complete the year's service. The master of the Temple came as far as Brindisi on one of them, which returned to Cyprus, and lord Philippe d'Ibelin came to Ancona on another, which is supposed to return as soon as your holiness's response is obtained. And eight of these galleys remained for the protection of Cyprus, and a full report concerning these will be made at the end of the year [§§15–16].

Aside from the fact that the manuscript reads "*que*" for "*galea*" rather than "*qui*" for "*magister*," there are other reasons to interpret the text as referring to the galley and not the man. First, the entire report concerns the galleys, and the only reason these personal voyages of Jacques de Molay and Philippe d'Ibelin are mentioned is that, for a period, instead of ten galleys (or the equipment and men for ten galleys) only eight remained to protect Cyprus, since two went on journeys to the West, and the final note in fact mentions that eight galleys remained in Outremer to protect the Lusignan kingdom [§16]. Second, there is a linguistic parallel in the description of these two galleys: "*in una quarum... que rediit... et in una alia... que debet redire...*" At the time the report was composed, one galley had already returned and the other was obliged to do so. Third, as we shall see, Philippe d'Ibelin did not return on the galley that brought him to Ancona, but instead he later took a Venetian galley back to Cyprus.

---

[38]   Josserand, *Jacques de Molay*, 117–18 and 319–22; idem, "La fabrique d'un diplomate," 7–9.

Going west, the routes of the two galleys would normally have been the same until they reached the Adriatic, at which point the galley heading to Ancona would probably have gone up along the Balkan coast before crossing. The galley that took Molay to Brindisi was the first to return to Cyprus, but this does not necessarily mean that it had departed first from the island, because the voyage to Ancona covered an additional 500 kilometers and took anywhere from four to ten more days, depending on various factors, and then the galley had to remain in Ancona until it received the cardinals' response. In any case, the report states that the two galleys were both away from Cyprus at the same time for at least a certain period: when he left Cyprus, Manuele arranged for ten galleys to finish the service of one year; at some later point two galleys sailed west, leaving eight to guard the Lusignan kingdom while the two galleys were away [§§15–16].

Philippe d'Ibelin did not begin his return journey until June or July 1293, after Jacques de Molay had arrived in Provence. Philippe's return thus tells us nothing about the master's movements after he arrived in Brindisi, whether he went west or back east. In order to determine this and when he most likely left Cyprus and arrived in Apulia, it is necessary to work backwards from his presence in Provence. Lacking papal letters because of the vacancy on the papal throne, it is very difficult to establish Molay's itinerary until the summer of 1293, at which point his movements are well known until his return to Cyprus three years later in the autumn of 1296.[39] The first surviving and dated letter of the master in the West was sent from Montpellier on 10 August 1293 on the occasion of the Chapter General of the Templars, which he had convoked earlier.[40] For the previous months of 1293 there are significant doubts. Nevertheless, we know that, in response to an undated letter from Molay originating in Provence,[41] on 18 June 1293 King Edward I allowed Guy de Forest, the Templar provincial commander of England, to attend the Chapter General in Montpellier.[42] Since it probably would have taken at least 18 days for Molay's letter to travel from Provence to London, ca. 1,200 kilometers, and for the royal court to deliberate and compose the letter, it has been assumed that Molay arrived in Provence in May.[43] He could have arrived earlier, of course, but it had to have been before the end of May to accommodate the letter to London.

---

[39] Josserand, *Jacques de Molay*, 118–23 and 320–28; idem, "La fabrique d'un diplomate," 9–12.

[40] Archives départementales de la Haute-Garonne, Toulouse, H Malte, Sainte-Eulalie 4, n° 130, published in Josserand, *Jacques de Molay*, 458–59, no. 5.

[41] National Archives, Public Record Office, A.C. SC 1/21, f° 4. This somewhat damaged document was published by Joseph Kervyn de Lettenhove, "Deux lettres inédites de Jacques de Molay," *Bulletin de l'Académie royale des sciences, des lettres et des beaux-arts de Belgique* 38 (1874): 234–35. As the Belgian editor noted, the letter was written "lorsque le grand-maître venait de quitter l'Orient et était déjà arrivé en Provence," but in 1293 and not in 1306, as he claimed. The date was corrected by Marie Luise Bulst-Thiele, *Sacrae Domus Militiae Templi Hierosolymitani Magistri. Untersuchungen zur Geschichte des Templerordens (1118/19–1314)* (Göttingen, 1974), 305 and n. 49.

[42] *Calendar of Patent Rolls, Edward I*, vol. III: *1292–1301*, ed. H. C. Maxwell Lyte (London, 1895), 22.

[43] Bulst-Thiele, *Sacrae Domus Militiae Templi Hierosolymitani Magistri*, 356.

Molay could have arrived in Provence before the end of May via Brindisi – more or less directly, perhaps making a stop in Naples, Gaeta, Civitavecchia, Genoa, or elsewhere – because Manuele Zaccaria's report, written between February and April 1293, does not say that the master returned to Cyprus, but that the galley that had brought him to Apulia did go back and was once again able to contribute to the defense of the island. The theory that Molay, in the winter of 1292–93, made a brief, first trip to Brindisi, then returned to Cyprus, before departing again in the early spring on another voyage to the West is, therefore, substantially weakened. One could still justify the hypothesis on the basis of the urgency of the situation in Outremer and the need for the newly elected master to assure the Templar connections in Apulia at the heart of the Mediterranean,[44] but once the correction from "*qui*" to "*que*" is made the report can no longer be employed to prove that a first winter voyage occurred.[45]

While Manuele Zaccaria's report specifies that the recently elected Templar master went to the West and arrived in Brindisi, the contents of the report itself do not allow us to fix a precise date for this. Taking into consideration Molay's close connection with the knight Othon de Grandson, one of the last defenders of Acre, whom in anticipation of his coming King Charles II of Naples provided a safe-conduct dated December, but without the year, Josserand dated the safe-conduct to 1292 and suggested that Molay and Grandson may have travelled together from Cyprus to Brindisi.[46] This is only a hypothesis, however, and the Angevin safe-conduct has been dated two years later, to December 1294, according to the old chronology proposed by George Digard, in order to accommodate the Templar of Tyre's description of Grandson's activities in the East down to 1294.[47]

Regardless, Molay's voyage to the West, lasting more than three and a half years, must have begun before historians from Marie Luise Bulst-Thiele to Alain Demurger have thought,[48] in order to accommodate a stopover in Brindisi, and perhaps a passage through the kingdom of Naples, as in the case of the later voyage the master made at the end of the year 1306.[49] Contrary to a frequent view among historians, Manuele Zaccaria's report itself makes plain that in cases of necessity galleys could be kept at sea at all times of the year, and both Jean-Claude Hocquet and Michel Balard have shown that the winter hiatus in sailing was never total

---

[44] Josserand, *Jacques de Molay*, 116–17 and 318–20.

[45] *Contra* Josserand, *Jacques de Molay*, 118, and idem, "La fabrique d'un diplomate," 8–9.

[46] Josserand, *Jacques de Molay*, 117.

[47] *Cronaca del Templare di Tiro*, 208–10, 218–20, 262; Georges Digard, *Philippe le Bel et le Saint-Siège*, 2 vols. (Paris, 1936), 1:206, n. 2; David Jacoby, "Cypriot Gold Thread in Late Medieval Silk Weaving and Embroidery," in *Deeds Done Beyond the Sea. Essays on William of Tyre, Cyprus and the Military Orders Presented to Peter Edbury*, ed. Susan B. Edgington and Helen J. Nicholson (Farnham, 2014), 101–14, at 106–07; Alan Forey, "Otto of Grandson and the Holy Land, Cyprus and Armenia," *Crusades* 16 (2017): 79–93, at 87.

[48] Bulst-Thiele, *Sacrae Domus Militiae Templi Hierosolymitani Magistri*, 305 and 356; Alain Demurger, *Jacques de Molay. Le crépuscule des Templiers* (Paris, 2014), 121.

[49] Josserand, *Jacques de Molay*, 133–34 and 342–43.

and that in the thirteenth century it was even less comprehensive than before.[50] Nevertheless, in order to avoid the worst winter weather, Molay could have departed Cyprus as late as mid-March.

In any case, even with a single trip and a late departure, the historian of the Templars is driven to wonder why Molay, only a year or so after his election, chose to embark on a long journey, completely unprecedented, setting off on a galley that did not belong to his order and lasting weeks or even months, during which he left no surviving trace in the West, before calling a Chapter General that was at that moment a high priority.

The Outbreak of the Second Venetian-Genoese War and the Start of Genoese-Cypriot Conflict

Although uncertainties thus remain to be cleared up, the voyage of Philippe d'Ibelin, fortunately, turns out to be easier to trace than Molay's and provides even more valuable information. Given that the ship that carried Philippe was still in Ancona while the report was written, it is likely that he arrived in Ancona not long before, i.e., between 1 January and 30 April 1293. Chronicles from the perspectives of Genoa and Outremer describe an incident in which Philippe d'Ibelin was sailing east with some Venetian galleys when they encountered a Genoese fleet returning from Romania.[51] In the Outremer chronicles known as that of the Templar of Tyre and of Amadi, the incident is vaguely dated to 1292, and it is said that four Venetian galleys accompanied by two Templar galleys met seven Genoese galleys. According to the Genoese chronicler Iacopo Doria, however, the event took place in July 1293, and Philippe d'Ibelin was with four Venetian galleys commissioned by the Temple to transport the crews of two other galleys to Cyprus. Near Coron, according to Iacopo, the fleet blocked the way of seven Genoese market galleys returning from Romania, under the command of a certain Giovannino Malocello ("Joannin Melosel" in Amadi), trusting in the fact that they had onboard a surplus of soldiers, equal to the men of two other galleys. Neither of the two fleets saw fit to give way, although custom required that the smaller fleet wait for the larger one to pass. Whereas the Templar of Tyre claims that he had his information from Philippe d'Ibelin himself, this report must have come to him much later, so the incident, which seems to have started the new conflict between Genoa and Venice, must indeed have taken place in July 1293 and not 1292.[52]

---

[50] Jean-Claude Hocquet, *Voiliers et commerce en Méditerranée, 1200–1650* (Lille, 1979), 172–75; Michel Balard, *La Méditerranée médiévale. Espaces, itinéraires, comptoirs* (Paris, 2006), 57–58. According to Jacques de Vitry, the Genoese were traveling in the winter on occasion as early as 1216: Antonio Musarra, *Medioevo marinaro. Prendere il mare nell'Italia medievale* (Bologna, 2021), 141.

[51] Antonio Musarra, *Il Grifo e il Leone. Genova, Venezia in lotta per il Mediterraneo* (Rome-Bari, 2020), 166–67.

[52] *Cronaca del Templare di Tiro*, 234–36; *Chronique d'Amadi*, ed. René de Mas-Latrie (Paris, 1891), 230–31; Iacobus Aurie, *Annales*, 167.

We can only speculate, but it does not seem far-fetched to link – even politically – the voyages of Jacques de Molay and Philippe d'Ibelin to the West noted in Manuele Zaccaria's report. Philippe was the maternal uncle of King Henry II of Cyprus (1285–1324). After the death of his brother, Balian d'Ibelin, in 1302, Philippe succeeded him as seneschal of Cyprus, and by the time of the coup against Henry by his brother Amaury de Lusignan, lord of Tyre, in 1306, Henry's enemies accused Philippe of being almost the king's sole advisor, contrary to custom. Eventually imprisoned in Armenia, Philippe resumed his role with even more power and wealth after Amaury's assassination in 1310, Henry's restoration, and Philippe's release, before dying on 25 September 1318.[53]

Manuele Zaccaria's report suggests that Philippe d'Ibelin was already one of Henry II's closest associates just after the fall of Acre. Based on Philippe's family connections, Rudt de Collenberg estimated that he was born around 1250/55, so he was already quite seasoned in 1291. After a first marriage to an Armenian and perhaps an early stay in Armenia, when his wife died Philippe requested a dispensation to wed the daughter of the Genoese Guy de Gibelet, Maria, to whom he was related in the fourth degree of consanguinity and affinity. Explicitly addressing Philippe as King Henry's uncle, Pope Boniface VIII granted the dispensation on 1 September 1295, in part "out of consideration for our most dear son in Christ H. the illustrious king of Cyprus and our beloved son the nobleman A. lord of Tyre," i.e., both Henry and Amaury, in both of whose graces Philippe must still have been.[54] Philippe's journey to the West in 1293 must have been on royal business. In hindsight, the Templar of Tyre enigmatically wrote concerning 1285 that King John of Cyprus died and "crowned after him [king] of Cyprus was his brother, Henry, who destroyed the Genoese" (*fu courouné aprés luy dou royaume de Chipre Henry, son frere, quy destrust les jenevés*),[55] although it was in the 1290s that relations between Cyprus and Genoa first became strained, leading eventually to the Genoese invasion of 1373 and occupation of Famagusta and its environs for 90 years.[56] That

---

[53] *Chronique d'Amadi*, 241–399, passim; Charles Perrat, "Un diplomate gascon au XIV⁰ siècle. Raymond de Piis, nonce de Clément V, en Orient," *Mélanges d'Archéologie et d'Histoire de l'École française de Rome* 44 (1927): 35–90, at 69 no. 1, 81–82 no. 2, 88–90 no. 3; Jesús Ernesto Martínez Ferrando, *Jaime II de Aragón, su vida familiar*, 2 vols. (Barcelona, 1948), 2:142–43 no. 206, 161–62 no. 226; Wipertus H. Rudt de Collenberg, "Les Ibelin aux XIIIᵉ et XIVᵉ siècles. Généalogie compilée principalement selon les registres du Vatican," Επετηρίδα του Κέντρου Επιστημονικών Ερευνών 9 (1977–79): 117–265, at 190–91; Peter W. Edbury, *The Kingdom of Cyprus and the Crusades, 1191–1374* (Cambridge, 1991), 114–15, 138–39, 184; Chris Schabel, "Who's in Charge Here? The Administration of Nicosia Cathedral 1299–1319," *Crusades* 11 (2012): 199–208, at 206.

[54] Rudt de Collenberg, "Les Ibelin aux XIIIᵉ et XIVᵉ siècles," 190–91; Chris Schabel, *Bullarium Cyprium*, vol. II: *Papal Letters Involving Cyprus 1261–1314* (Nicosia, 2010), no. o–18.

[55] *Cronaca del Templare di Tiro*, 168.

[56] Peter W. Edbury, "Cyprus and Genoa: The Origins of the War of 1373–1374," in Πρακτικά του Β΄ διεθνούς κυπρολογικού συνεδρίου. Τόμος Β΄, Μεσαιωνικόν Τμήμα, ed. T. Papadopoullos and B. Englezakis (Nicosia, 1986), 109–26, reprinted in idem, *Kingdoms of the Crusaders* (Aldershot 1999), study XIV; Jean Richard, "Le 'compromis' de 1330 entre Gênes et Chypre et la guerre de course dans les eaux chypriotes," *Atti della Società Ligure di Storia Patria* NS 53 (2013): 17–36. A number of previously unknown papal letters pertinent to the story are calendared in *Bullarium Cyprium* III, and

the strife originated in the context of one of the wars between Genoa and Venice can only have exacerbated the problem, which grew so serious that King Henry's (and hence Philippe's) failure to deal with Genoese hostility and threats of war in late 1305 topped one list of grievances that Amaury and his supporters sent to Pope Clement V to justify the coup of April 1306.[57]

Yet the Zaccaria brothers, Benedetto and Manuele, played an odd role in this decline of relations. While in charge of Tripoli before the fall of the last Western outposts on the crusader states' mainland, Admiral Benedetto went to Cyprus and reached an agreement with Henry II, put in writing on 21 September 1288. The government in Genoa, however, did not accept the document and eventually rejected it officially on 17 May 1292, leading George Hill to remark that, "As a result of that repudiation the King became hostile to the Genoese."[58] Despite this decision, from his report of early 1293 we learn that Manuele continued to honor his promises regarding the defense of Cyprus, making sure that galleys remained there until mid-1293 and allowing one galley to take Philippe d'Ibelin to Ancona. In July 1293, after the fleet's term was over, Philippe was aboard a Venetian galley when the encounter with the Genoese occurred off Coron: the Genoese seized the Venetian galleys and killed hundreds of the Venetian men in addition to the Templar turcopolier Guillaume de La Tor, but otherwise the Genoese were careful to ensure that Philippe was reimbursed for what he lost and the surviving Venetians were treated well.[59] Nevertheless, the following spring, when the Venetians sailed to Cyprus with 25 galleys, in the midst of their attacks on the property of the Genoese in Limassol and elsewhere, they met with King Henry and Philippe d'Ibelin, who do not seem to have made much effort to fulfill their obligations to protect Genoese interests.[60]

Under the circumstances, one has to wonder whether Philippe d'Ibelin's mission was to secure another fleet to replace the Genoese galleys, whose term was to end around the end of May 1293. The fact that the four Venetian galleys also carried crews for two Templar ships still in Cyprus, probably in Limassol, is perhaps not a coincidence. Did Henry II and Jacques de Molay agree to seeking Venetian assistance in the face of the king's growing hostility toward the Genoese? Was Philippe taken

---

Schabel has found and edited still others since then in Peter W. Edbury, "A Threat to Invade Cyprus: Pope John XXII, Walter of Brienne Duke of Athens, and the Latin East in 1331," *Frankokratia* 2 (2021): 179–95 (appendix by Schabel). A new survey of the history of Genoese-Cypriot relations is thus required.

[57] Chris Schabel and Laura Minervini, "The French and Latin Dossier on the Institution of the Government of Amaury of Lusignan, Lord of Tyre, Brother of King Henry II of Cyprus," *Επετηρίδα του Κέντρου Επιστημονικών Ερευνών* 34 (2008): 75–119, at 92b and 112; cf. 94a.

[58] George Hill, *A History of Cyprus*, vol. II: *The Frankish Period, 1192–1432* (Cambridge, 1948), 183. See also Musarra, "Benedetto Zaccaria e la caduta di Tripoli (1289)," which reconstructs the facts, and Musarra, *In partibus Ultramaris*, Appendix B, 599–600, in which is published an act drawn up in Tripoli by Benedetto on 22 January 1289.

[59] *Cronaca del Templare di Tiro*, 234–36; Hill, *A History of Cyprus*, vol. II, 207–08; Musarra, *Il Grifo e il Leone*, 166–67.

[60] *Cronaca del Templare di Tiro*, 259; *Chronique d'Amadi*, 231; Hill, *A History of Cyprus*, vol. II, 208; Musarra, *Il Grifo e il Leone*, 169–71.

to Ancona because it was a safe port that was not too far distant from Venice, just 225 kilometers by sea, so that Philippe could travel to the Serenissima and negotiate on behalf of both parties? Did the Zaccaria brothers know or care about this?

Conclusion

Manuele Zaccaria's report ends by providing information about the activities still to be carried out, as mentioned in the beginning. The final note in fact mentions that eight galleys remained in Outremer to protect Cyprus [§16]. The development of this story is narrated by the Templar of Tyre:

> And all these galleys went together to a castle of the Turks called Candeloro, and they took the tower located on the sea. They thought of taking the other one, but they were unable to take it because the Turks had been informed of their coming and were on guard, and they were well equipped for defense. And had it not been for this large army, they would not have taken that tower that was taken. But as there was nothing else they could do, they abandoned the tower and went and arrived at Alexandria, and they stayed a few days in front of it, and then they went back to Cyprus.[61]

The reasons for the diversion of the fleet towards the Anatolian coast are not explicit. It is possible, however, to connect the episode to the need to defend the Armenian kingdom of Cilicia, which, as has been said, was attacked during 1292. The attempt to blockade Alexandria represented, in any case, a provocation. According to Muslim sources, al-Ashraf responded by ordering the construction of a large number of galleys (about sixty) with the aim of assaulting Cyprus:[62]

> And when it was the year of the incarnation of Our Lord Jesus Christ 1291, the Sultan of Babylon, who had thus destroyed the Christianity of Syria, saw that the galleys had come to besiege his port of Alexandria, as I have told you. He was very irritated by it, and he was afraid and thought that Cyprus could harm him very much. Therefore he gathered his emirs and told them that he certainly wanted to take Cyprus. Consequently, he established a hundred emirs who were supposed to furnish him with a hundred galleys, each emir according to his ability, and the emirs agreed, since they feared him very much. As you have heard, he wanted to destroy all Christianity and the poor people who had taken refuge in Cyprus, but God, who is full of mercy, made things happen differently.[63]

All efforts – on both sides – were in vain.

---

[61] *Cronaca del Templare di Tiro*, 235. Marino Sanudo mentions a total of 25 galleys: Marinus Sanutus, *Liber secretorum fidelium crucis*, in *Gesta Dei per Francos sive Orientalium expeditionum et Regni Francorum Hierosolimitani historia a variis sed illius aevi scriptoribus litteris commendata*, ed. Jacques Bongars, 2 vols. (Hanau, 1611), 2:233.

[62] Albrecht Fuess, "Rotting Ships and Razed Harbors: The Naval Policy of the Mamluks," in *Māmluk Studies Review* 5 (2001): 45–71, at 51, 62–63.

[63] *Cronaca del Templare di Tiro*, 235.

The efforts of historians are also frequently in vain, but we hope that our own contribution advances in a small way the state of our knowledge and provokes new questions about the initial Latin reaction to the fall of Acre. Relying on hindsight and falling into teleology, too many specialists on the Middle Ages, and even on the crusades, continue to assert repeatedly that after the fall of Acre the Holy Land was definitively forgotten and abandoned by the West.[64] Even without pursuing the paths of inquiry that Manuele Zaccaria's report opens, this fascinating text declares emphatically that nothing could be further from the truth.

---

[64] Martin Aurell, *Des chrétiens contre les croisades (XIIᵉ–XIIIᵉ siècles)* (Paris, 2013), 349.

Appendix
Manuele Zaccaria's Report on the Galleys Maintained in Outremer

Manuscript: Archivio Apostolico Vaticano, Reg. Aven. 54, ff. 467va–468ra (= A)

In nomine Domini, amen.

Hec est ratio quam sanctis patribus dominis cardinalibus facit Manuel Zacharias de galeis quas tenuit et tenet in partibus transmarinis et servitio Terre Sancte.

[1] Primo debebat tenere galeas VIII, pro quibus fuit sibi solutum pro sex mensibus a fratre Bonifatio de Calamandrana. De quibus galeis pars incepit servire de mense Marcii, et pars de mense Aprilis, et pars in kalendis Mai, et pars ultra dictum terminum. Et facta ratione in Urbe cum dicto fratre Bonifatio, placuit eidem fratri Bonifatio quod idem terminus omnium ipsarum galearum inciperet currere[1] in kalendis Mai proxime preteriti, cum ante deberent incipere iuxta factam dictam rationem, et servitium ipsarum quantum ad partes transmarinas debebat finiri in kalendis Octubris proxime preteriti. Qui Manuel dictas galeas habuit et tenuit seu armamentum ipsarum deputatum in VII galeis. Quas galeas et armamentum tenuit in dicto servitio per dictum terminum et ultra per dies X vel circa.

[2] Et in fine dicti termini dictus Manuel petiit instrumentum quietationis a magistro Hospitalis, qui respondit quod multum se tenebat bene contentum et sibi satisfactum esse. Set quia dictus Manuel obligatus erat fratri Bonifacio de Calamandrana, volebat pro honore dicti[2] fratris Bonifatii quod ipse frater B[3] faceret instrumentum dicte quietationis, et quod ipse magister mitteret per suas litteras per fratrem Guillelmum de Sancto [*A 467vb*] Stephano, priorem Hospitalis in Lombardia, quod dictus Manuel bene et fideliter satisfecerat et compleverat quod promiserat. Qui frater Guillelmus venit ad cismarinas partes in mense Decembris proxime preterito.

[3] Item, ex decem galeis quas ipse Manuel promisit tenere per annum in servitio Ecclesie iuxta formam pactorum habuit et extraxit dictas galeas de diversis locis per tempora inferius denotata:

[4] Primo galeas duas de Urbe, quarum terminus incepit die XIIII mensis Mai proxime preteriti.

[5] Item, galeam unam que recessit de Ancona circa[4] kalendas mensis Junii proxime preteriti.

[6] Item, de versus Neapolim galeas duas, que recesserunt die ultima Mai.

[7] Item, de Janua per Tedisium Aurie galeas duas, que recesserunt circa kalendas Junii.

[8] Item, de Fogia galeam vocatam "Divitiam" cum armamento duarum galearum et computata pro duabus galeis, que recessit de Fogia circa kalendas mensis Junii proxime preteriti.[5]

[9] Et sic sunt in suma dicte galee VIIII, in quibus erat armamentum hominum pro galeis decem. Et sic habuit ipse Manuel semper usque kalendas Octubris galeas XVI cum armamento hominum galearum decem et octo in forma supradicta. Et habuit ultra quam promiserat semper homines a C usque in CC. Similiter, habuit ultra dictas galeas unum

---

[1] currere *coni.*] cureret *A*
[2] dicti *coni.*] dictis *A*
[3] *Scilicet* Bonifatius
[4] circa] circha *a.c. A*
[5] preteriti] preterite *a.c. A*

pamphylum et unam sayecteam. Et de predictis galeis et recessu[6] ipsarum de dictis locis sunt publice scripture et instrumenta. [*A* **468ra**]

[10] Preterea, notificat idem Manuel quod requisivit in partibus transmarinis a magistris Templi et Hospitalis quod mitterent ad exquirendum armamentum galearum[7] omnium predictarum, tam hominum quam armorum et aliorum necessariorum, pro dictis galeis.

[11] Item, notificat quod, cum ipse Manuel, habens semper puram voluntatem complendi et attendendi quod promiserat, ex superhabundanti misisset ad multas partes mundi pro galeis habendis, ut si de uno loco difficerent, de alio supplerentur, et nullus posset esse deffectus in tempore debito, cum nulle requisite deffecissent inter illas que obviaverunt sibi in via ultra Rodum et alias, pervenerunt sibi ultra predictas quinque inter galeas et ligna armata, in quibus et de quibus frustra substinuit sumptis maximos et iacturam.

[12] Item, suplicat dictus Manuel quatenus dignetur vestra sanctitas mittere unum nuntium[8] Imperatori Grecorum ad expensas dicti Manuelis super facto de quo vestre sanctitati locutus fuit.

[13] Item, cum frater suus dominus Benedictus miserit suas litteras sanctitati vestre et nuntius eius diu expectaverit responsionem, suplicat ut dicta responsio fiat, ita quod nuntius possit cum ipsa responsione recedere.

[14] Item, reducit ad memoriam vestre sanctitati de facto galearum euntium Alexandriam, de quibus locutus[9] fuit[10] vobiscum, que in magna quantitate se preparant ad eundum. [*A* **468rb**]

[15] Item, notificat idem Manuel quod in recessu suo de Cipro ordinavit galeas decem armatas pro complendo servitio anni. In una quarum venit magister Templi usque Brundusium, que rediit in Ciprum, et in una alia venit[11] dominus Phylipus de Ybelino Anconam, que debet redire in continenti habita responsione sanctitatis vestre.

[16] Et octo ex dictis galeis remanserunt ad custodiam insule Cipri. Et in fine anni fiet de ipsis plena ratio.

---

6   recessu] recessia *a.c. A*
7   galearum] *s.l. A*
8   nuntium *coni.*] nutium *A*
9   locutus] locuti *a.c. A*
10   fuit *coni.*] fui *A*
11   venit] dominus *add. sed del. A*

Almost Tancred: Tasso's Sources, Rinaldo, and the Estensi as Crusaders

Francesca Petrizzo

University of Leeds
f.petrizzo@leeds.ac.uk

Abstract

Torquato Tasso's Gerusalemme liberata *(1581) has proven one of the most enduringly influential depictions of the First Crusade. This article aims to analyse it as a propaganda poem written in the service of the House of Este, Tasso's patrons, which celebrates their role in the fight against the Ottoman Empire, and projects a concept of Italian national identity consonant with the crusading movement. By examining the role played by Rinaldo in this poem, this article highlights how Tasso's sophisticated use of historical and literary references underpins a complex and sometimes contradictory ideological agenda in* Liberata. *The article demonstrates how Rinaldo was explicitly written as a stand-in for the Estense dynasty, and how the description of his fight against the Muslims was intended to idealise the House of Ferrara's hoped-for role as defeaters of the Turks. Furthermore, it is shown how Rinaldo was based on the historical Tancred as depicted by William of Tyre and Albert of Aachen, something which anchored the fictional character to historical "truth" in accordance with the ideals of the Counter-Reformation, and strengthened his propagandistic appeal. It is then demonstrated how the focus on "Italian crusaders," achieved by centring much of the poem's action on Rinaldo and Tancredi (a fictionalisation of Tancred), inspired a trend of unpopular but historically significant poems on "Italian" crusaders across the peninsula. The article concludes by showing the contextual and ephemeral nature of this achievement, and how Tasso's revision of* Liberata *in the later (and quite unpopular)* Gerusalemme conquistata *completely left behind both Rinaldo and the ideological and political agenda of the original version.*

Among myriad memorialisations of the crusading movement, Torquato Tasso's 1581 *Gerusalemme liberata* remains a landmark. An Italian vernacular poem in twenty *canti* which fictionalises the siege and conquest of Jerusalem during the First Crusade, *Liberata* was a runaway success that strongly influenced perceptions of the events it depicted.[1] *Liberata* found an instant audience across Europe, with translations, adaptations for music and theatre, and depictions in painting,

I would like to acknowledge the fundamental contribution of the Leverhulme Trust, as this article was written out of the research accomplished as Leverhulme Study Abroad Scholar at the Università di Roma Tor Vergata, Rome (2018–19). I wish to thank Anna Carocci for her vital feedback on the first draft, and for our ever-helpful discussions as I developed the idea for this article, and Tancredi Artico for generously sharing his work on Sempronio. I also wish to thank the anonymous reviewers for their suggestions on how to improve the article.

sculpture, and the decorative arts making it a powerful cultural force from Poland to Britain.[2] This article focuses on a specific aspect of *Liberata* and its depiction of the First Crusade: the attempted bestowal upon the House of Este, the author's patrons, of the prestige of a fictitious crusader identity. It will demonstrate how the character of Rinaldo, one of the poem's heroes, was constructed out of a sophisticated intersection of historical sources, literary influences, and references to Tasso's contemporary history in order to glorify the Estensi. The poem aimed to present them as heirs to the crusading enterprise, while reflecting the concerns of the contemporary Italian political and intellectual debate.

The article proceeds as follows. First, I examine how Rinaldo's name and presentation link him to the history and intellectual patronage of the Estensi. Then I argue that Rinaldo was modelled on the historical Tancred, prince of Antioch, and his cousin Roger of Salerno. The link to the crusading enterprise adds lustre to the Italian national identity, and satisfies the demands of the literary debate surrounding a new kind of epic poetry rooted in *il vero*, "the truth." This will allow me to engage with a number of issues surrounding *Liberata*'s beginning, from the transition of Italy's hotly discussed poetic production into the Baroque period, to the development of Italian responses to the Turkish military threat in the Mediterranean. Finally, I will explore how Tasso's successive poetic evolution, and the transformation of *Liberata* in the unpopular and little-known *Gerusalemme conquistata*, highlight the specificity of Rinaldo, a character closely tied to a particular moment in the intellectual and political debate surrounding the currency and memorialisation of the crusading era in early modern Italy.[3]

Between Ferrara, Rome, and the Ottoman Sea: A Complex Beginning

Notably, the text of *Liberata* as it has come down to us was neither prepared nor approved by the author. It was the product of a long and torturous effort that extended from c. 1567 to its publication in 1581.[4] Tasso's writing was closely

---

[1]   The edition used here is Torquato Tasso, *Gerusalemme liberata*, ed. Lanfranco Caretti (Turin, 1971). All translations from Italian and Latin are mine. The most recent English translation is Torquato Tasso, *The Liberation of Jerusalem*, trans. Max Wickert (Oxford, 2009).

[2]   See for example *Torquato Tasso. Comitato per le celebrazioni di Torquato Tasso, Ferrara 1954* (Milan, 1957) [hereafter cited as: *Torquato Tasso* (1957)]; Elizabeth Siberry, "Tasso and the Crusades: History of a Legacy," *Journal of Medieval History* 19 (1993): 163–69; Alessandra Coppo, *All'ombra di Malinconia. Il Tasso lungo la sua fama* (Turin, 1997); *Tasso e l'Europa. Atti del Convegno Internazionale (IV Centenario della morte del Poeta), Università di Bergamo, 24–25–26 Maggio 1995*, ed. Daniele Rota (Viareggio and Lucca, 1996); Chandler B. Beall, *La fortune du Tasse en France* (Eugene, 1942); Jason Lawrence, *Tasso's Art and Afterlives: The* Gerusalemme liberata *in England* (Manchester, 2017).

[3]   Torquato Tasso, *Gerusalemme conquistata*, ed. Luigi Bonfigli (Bari, 1934). It is to be noted that this edition is controversial: see Anthony Oldcorn, "A Recensio of the Sources of the *Gerusalemme conquistata*: Notes for a New Edition," *Forum Italicum* 9/1 (1975): 15–36.

[4]   See Claudio Gigante, *Tasso* (Rome, 2007), 148–68; Emilio Russo, *Guida alla lettura della "Gerusalemme liberata" di Tasso* (Bari, 2014), 26–44; Lanfranco Caretti, "Ancora sul testo della

bound up with his own reflections on the art of poetics, on which he would write *Discorsi dell'arte poetica* (*Discourses on Poetic Art*, written mid-1560s, published 1587) and *Discorsi del poema eroico* (*Discourses on the Heroic Poem*, 1594).[5] The poet's time was animated by the intellectual battle for a new form of Italian poetics. After the phenomenal success of Lodovico Ariosto's *Orlando Furioso* (1532), a debate sprang up among the closely linked Italian intellectual centres as to how Italian poetics should evolve.[6] The Counter-Reformation placed further pressure on Italian intellectuals to produce poetry that would reflect the values of a renewed Church. While Ariosto's work was universally praised for the quality of its poetry, his fondness for racy and fantastical plots was criticised as incompatible with these new ideals.[7] Tasso was heavily invested in the debate, and aimed to create the first popular Italian epic poem, one that would live up to Ariosto's quality but also reflect the renewed values. Accordingly, Tasso engaged in the revision of his poem by committee, sending drafts of his *canti* to five intellectuals (one of them, Silvio Antoniano, a Roman cardinal closely involved with the Counter-Reformation process) throughout the 1570s, making the text of the *Liberata* a work-in-progress.[8]

As we shall see, Tasso chafed against the programme he had set himself even as he sought to advance it. In a letter to Scipione Gonzaga, he wrote that he had "removed the wonder following rather the judgment of others, than my own pleasure," attesting to the difficulty he felt in sticking to his own plan.[9] A close look at the correspondence that the poet conducted with the editors shows that he bargained for every criticised element, all the while steadily losing ground.[10] But the crucial influence on the final edition was the author's own complex personal life. In 1579 Tasso was interned, due to a bout of mental illness, in the hospital of Sant'Anna in Ferrara, where he would remain for the following seven

---

Liberata," in *Torquato Tasso* (1957), 343–364.

[5]   Edited in Torquato Tasso, *Scritti sull'arte poetica*, ed. Ettore Mazzali (Milan, 1959).

[6]   On Ariosto and his success see Daniel Javitch, *Proclaiming a Classic: The Canonization of Orlando Furioso* (Princeton, 1991).

[7]   The fundamental work on this complex debate remains Francesco Sberlati, *Il genere e la disputa. La poetica tra Ariosto e Tasso* (Rome, 2001). See also Mario Sansone, "Le polemiche antitassesche della Crusca," in *Torquato Tasso* (1957), 525–74; Guido Baldassarri, *Il sonno di Zeus: Sperimentazione narrativa del poema rinascimentale e tradizione omerica* (Rome, 1982); Emilio Russo, *L'ordine, la fantasia e l'arte. Ricerche per un quinquennio tassiano (1588–1592)* (Rome, 1992); Amedeo Quondam, "'Stanotte mi sono svegliato con questo verso in bocca': Tasso, Controriforma e classicismo," in *Torquato Tasso e la cultura estense*, ed. Gianni Venturi, 2 vols. (Florence, 1999), 2:535–94; Marco Corradini, "Torquato Tasso e il dibattito di metà Cinquecento sul poema epico," *Testo, Studi di Teoria e Storia della Letteratura e della Critica* 40 (2000): 159–69; Stefano Jossa, *La fondazione di un genere: Il poema eroico tra Ariosto e Tasso* (Rome, 2002); and Guido Sacchi, *Fra Ariosto e Tasso: vicende del poema narrativo* (Pisa, 2007).

[8]   On Tasso's correspondence with his editors see Torquato Tasso, *Lettere poetiche*, ed. Carla Molinari (Parma, 1995).

[9]   Tasso, *Lettere poetiche*, Letter 35.

[10]   Gigante, *Tasso*, 148-68, for a detailed account.

years.[11] Interest in the well-publicised *Liberata*, however, was high, and after the unauthorised publication of the first fourteen *canti* in 1580 the editors thought it necessary to provide a version of the poem to the public. In 1581 *Liberata* was published to instant success, with the "official version" endorsed by the dukes of Ferrara and assembled by the printer Febo Bonnà.[12] Indeed, the title *Gerusalemme liberata* itself derived from a previous, wholly unauthorised version, published in Parma, with a title clearly inspired by Gian Giorgio Trissino's work *L'Italia liberata dai Goti* (1547–8).[13] The poet did not acknowledge the printed version of the poem (referring to it as a "bastard child"), but it was nonetheless assembled out of his manuscripts, and it preserves *Liberata* at a stage of its revision, if not the final one.[14] With an awareness that its poetic choices were not final, the text is treated here as the surviving expression of one stage of Tasso's thinking on the poetics of the crusading era.

Of the three main heroes of the poem (Rinaldo, Goffredo, based on Godfrey of Bouillon, and Tancredi, based on Tancred), Rinaldo is the only explicitly fictional one.[15] His name, which had been used twice among the medieval Estensi, takes us immediately to the House of Este. Moreover, Rinaldo was the name of the dashing young knight, cousin to the paladin Orlando, who was one of the heroes of Ariosto's poem.[16] As the fictional ancestor of the House of Este, it tied Ariosto's work to his patrons.[17] Tasso had already shown his fondness for the character of Rinaldo during his teenage years, when he had written a short chivalric poem about the knight's further adventures after the end of the *Furioso*.[18] The reprisal of the character, therefore, established a line of descent from the earlier work, evoked the Estensi, and opened the way for a scene in *canto* 10 in which the greatness of the dynasty is prophesied to the crusader Rinaldo.[19] Tasso's knight is told by the sorcerer of Ascalona that from him will spring forth a line of heroes, culminating with Alfonso II, Tasso's contemporary and patron, to whom the poem is dedicated,

---

[11] Despite the intervening century and a quarter, no other biography has equalled the philological precision and methodological value of Angelo Solerti's monumental *Vita di Torquato Tasso*, 3 vols. (Turin and Rome, 1895). For a summary, see Gigante, *Tasso*, 13-51.

[12] *Gierusalemme Liberata, Poema Heroico del Signor Torquato Tasso* (Ferrara, 1581).

[13] *La Gierusalemme Liberata Overo il Goffredo del Sig. Torquato Tasso* (Parma, 1581).

[14] Quondam, "Stanotte," 592.

[15] In this article I refer to the historical figures of Tancred and Godfrey by the English form of their names, and to Tasso's characters modelled on them by their Italian ones (Tancredi, Goffredo).

[16] There were two Rinaldo d'Este between the thirteenth and fourteenth centuries. For Ariosto's dynastic strategies, see Eleonora Stoppino, *Genealogies of Fiction: Women Warriors and the Dynastic Imagination in the* "Orlando Furioso" (New York, 2011).

[17] For an analysis of Rinaldo as a chivalrous character, see Mario Santoro, *"Rinaldo* ebbe il consenso universale," in *Letture ariostesche* (Naples, 1973), 81–133; Peter DeSa Wiggins, *Figures in Ariosto's Tapestry: Character and Design in the* "Orlando Furioso" (Baltimore, 1986); Michael Sherberg, *Rinaldo: Character and Intertext in Ariosto and Tasso* (Saratoga, 1993); Rinaldo L. Martinez, "Two Odysseys: Rinaldo's Po Journey and the Poet's Homecoming in *Orlando furioso,*" in *Renaissance Transactions: Ariosto and Tasso*, ed. Valeria Finucci (Durham, NC, 1999), 17–55.

[18] Torquato Tasso, *Rinaldo*, ed. Matteo Navone (Alessandria, 2012).

[19] *Liberata*, 10.74–77.

and who is presented as the defender of Italy from the Turks.[20] Tasso was thus following well-established models in order to praise his patrons, and his work confirmed Ferrara as the seat of the most sophisticated chivalric poetry in Italy.[21]

Tasso's work in this sense followed what had been a sensitive and targeted activity as a court poet, highly adapted to his patrons' tastes and wants. It was for the Estensi court, and their summer garden parties, that in 1573 Tasso had produced *Aminta*, a pastoral fable narrating the love between the shepherd Aminta and the nymph Silvia.[22] The fable encountered immediate and widespread success, setting the stage for the anticipation that would force *Liberata* to be published early.[23] Much has been written about the possible identification of the various characters in *Aminta* with contemporary figures in the Estensi court, and in contemporary Italy at large.[24] Indeed, Elisabetta Graziosi has argued that *Aminta* was written to promote the marriage of the young Alfonsino d'Este, son of the duke, to his illegitimate cousin Marfisa, further contextualising the fable in the specific environment of the court.[25] For Tasso, the sophisticated weaving of the context of his time into the poetic works he produced was a habitual, and highly successful, process. His careful insertion of his epic poem into the larger context of the court would have been expected of him, but it would also have dovetailed with his larger poetic practice. Indeed, the fact that *Liberata* was read out to the dukes several times as it was being written confirms their investment in the project, as well as Tasso's wish to keep them apprised of his progress and gauge their reactions as the work took shape.[26]

Far from being an idle gesture of homage, then, the insertion of Rinaldo into the poem is the key to an in-depth analysis of Tasso's concerns, engagement with the crusader sources, and political projects. For Tasso, heroic poetry was a highly contextualised enterprise. Notably, in his *Discorsi del poema eroico* he praised Virgil for his awareness of the needs of Augustus' political programme, and for his engagement with the state in suiting the *Aeneid* to the environment in which it was conceived.[27] In his own work, the name Rinaldo serves as much more than a signifier of the poet's gratitude to the dukes; it constitutes the link between the

[20]   *Liberata*, Dedication, 1.4–5.

[21]   For the context in which Tasso worked, see Marina Beer, "Poemi cavallereschi, poemi epici e poemi eroici negli anni di elaborazione della *Gerusalemme liberata* (1559–1581). Gli orizzonti della scrittura," in *Torquato Tasso e la cultura estense*, 1:55–66; Dennis Looney and Deanna Shemek, eds., *Phaethon's Children: The Este Court and Its Culture in Early Modern Ferrara* (Binghamton, NY, 2005).

[22]   Torquato Tasso, *Aminta*, ed. Marco Corradini (Milan, 2015).

[23]   An essential introduction to *Aminta* is Giosuè Carducci, *L'Ariosto e il Tasso* (Bologna, 1954), 137–275; see also Riccardo Bruscagli, "L''*Aminta*' di Tasso e le pastorali ferraresi del '500'," in *Studi di filologia e critica offerti dagli allievi a L. Caretti* (Rome, 1985), 278–318; Arnaldo Di Benedetto, "L''*Aminta*' e la pastorale cinquecentesca in Italia," in *Torquato Tasso e la cultura estense*, 3:1121–49.

[24]   Angelo Solerti, *L'Aminta annotata* (Turin, 1908); Sergio Zatti, "Natura e potere nell'*Aminta*'," in *T. Tasso quattrocento anni dopo*, ed. A. Daniele and F.W. Lupi (Soveria Mannelli, 1997), 11–24.

[25]   Elisabetta Graziosi, Aminta *1573–1580. Amore e matrimonio in casa d'Este* (Lucca, 2001).

[26]   Gigante, *Tasso*, 127–28.

[27]   Tasso, *Discorsi del poema eroico*, in *Scritti* (1959), Libro sesto.

crusading enterprise and the wider political aims Tasso sought to endorse. In this perspective, in the poet's vision the unity of the Christian faith triumphed over the Muslim forces, and a renewed Italian identity was validated by the crusading movement, considered a historically relevant precedent to the contemporary military conflict with the Ottoman Empire.

The orthodoxy of *Liberata*, and its potential to reaffirm Christian primacy, was of paramount importance to both Tasso and his editors. Tasso had offered the Estensi several choices for the topic of his poem: one celebrating the Byzantine liberation of Italy from the Goths, reprising the theme which Gian Giorgio Trissino had reworked in his ambitious but widely disliked poem; one narrating Charlemagne's campaigns against the pagan Saxons, inscribing himself in the popular cycle of the Carolingian chansons; or, a poem about the First Crusade.[28] Tasso's proposal of this final theme, and the Estensi's preference, should come as no surprise. The conflict with the Ottoman Empire animated the political debate of Tasso's day. The latest edition of poems about the struggle between Christians and Turks in the Mediterranean produced in Italy in the sixteenth century assembles nearly one hundred works aimed at a popular audience.[29] As charted by Giovanni Ricci and Marina Formica, the "Turkish threat" captured contemporary imaginations and political preoccupations, making it an omnipresent topic in the time and place in which Tasso's poetry flourished.[30] The confluence of a rich, if not necessarily high-quality, poetic production with the urgency of the political situation made antecedents of Christian-Muslim strife a particularly attractive topic for the intellectual circles of Tasso's day. In his youth in the 1560s, Tasso began to compose, but abandoned, a crusader poem (*Gierusalemme*); it survives in a fragment, whose form closely resembles the opening of *Liberata* itself, revealing his ambition to translate his absorption in the current political situation into a celebration of a past in which the Christians had been victorious.[31]

Nor was he alone in this ambition. While Pietro Angelio Barga's Latin poem *Syrias*, about the crusaders conquering Antioch, followed *Liberata* by several years (1591), the poet claimed he himself had given the idea for the theme to the

---

[28] *Le Lettere di Torquato Tasso*, ed. C. Guasti, 5 vols. (Florence, 1852–55), 5:214, no. 1551. The poor fortunes of Trissino's poem mean that the fundamental edition remains the *princeps*, which was published in three instalments in two different cities: Gian Giorgio Trissino, *La Italia liberata da'Gotthi (canti I–IX)*, (Rome, 1547); *La Italia liberata da' Gotthi (canti X–XVIII)*, (Venice, October 1548); *La Italia liberata da' Gotthi (canti XIX–XXVII)*, (Venice, November 1548).

[29] *Guerre in ottava rima*, 4 vols. Vol. *IV. Guerre contro i Turchi (1453–1570)*, ed. Marina Beer and Cristina Ivaldi (Ferrara/Modena, 1989). The topic is more amply discussed in Chiara Natoli, "La guerra d'oriente e la minaccia turca nella lirica di metà Cinquecento," *Italique* 12 (2019): 211–33.

[30] Giovanni Ricci, *Ossessione turca: in una retrovia cristiana dell'Europa moderna* (Bologna, 2002); Marina Formica, *Lo specchio turco. Immagini dell'altro e riflessi del sé nella cultura italiana d'età moderna* (Rome, 2012). These depictions, in turn, built on centuries of complex representations of Muslim alterity in Europe. See Suzanne Conklin Akbari, *Idols in the East: European Representations of Islam and the Orient, 1100–1450* (Ithaca, NY, 2009). See also Giovanni Ricci, *I turchi alle porte* (Bologna, 2008), which engages concretely with the history of Turkish incursions into Italy.

[31] Torquato Tasso, *Il Gierusalemme*, ed. by Guido Baldassarri (Rome, 2013).

young Tasso.[32] Contemporary Venetian intellectual Giovanni Maria Verdizzotti, to whom we will return below, would claim the same.[33] The multiplication of possible inspirations strengthens the impression that the need for a crusader poem was rather felt in the already febrile intellectual environment in which Tasso worked. The relevance of a poem of *Liberata*'s theme to the Ottoman-Christian struggle is also attested by its epigons. Many of Tasso's imitators adopted his style and structure to celebrate the victory of Lepanto, and applied the associations of the crusader poem to the more contemporary conflict.[34] By explicitly evoking the connection between the crusade and the Ottoman conflict, and placing Rinaldo at the heart of it, Tasso tied the relevance of the Estensi on the frontlines of the strife against the Turks to the crusading heritage.

Making Rinaldo: Tasso's Sources and the Character They Built

If, on the one hand Tasso was channelling some of the most heartfelt preoccupations of his time, on the other he was dealing with the most delicate process of Counter-Reformation poetics: the production of a poetic style that would be both engaging and deeply rooted in Catholic orthodoxy. Rinaldo embodies the crux of the problem: although a conventional chivalric hero, he also aspires to solve the conflict between attractive but morally dubious poetic conventions, and orthodox but potentially staid ideals. Trissino's perceived failure in making his programmatically impeccable but nearly universally disdained *Italia liberata* readable seemed to haunt Tasso, who asked for copies of Trissino's work late in his life, seemingly both as inspiration and warning.[35] Tasso wrote at length of his preoccupation with developing what he called "*il meraviglioso cristiano*," a sparkling but orthodox idea of "Christian wonder," which would join the charming nature of chivalric storylines and content to the theological demands of the Counter-Reformation.[36]

---

[32] *Petri Angelii Bargaei Syrias* (Florence, 1591); Antonio Belloni, *Gli epigoni della Gerusalemme liberata. Con un'appendice bibliografica* (Padua, 1893), 1–28; Claudio Gigante, "Dal Tasso a Bargeo, dal Bargeo a Tasso. Per un'interpretazione del ventesimo libro della *Gerusalemme conquistata*," *Esperienze Letterarie* 26 (2001): 61–72 and "Poetica del Bargeo," in *Esperienze di filologia cinquecentesca: Salviati, Mazzoni, Trissino, Costo, Il Bargeo, Tasso* (Rome, 2003), 104–17.

[33] Daniela Foltran, *Per un ciclo tassiano. Imitazione, invenzione e "correzione" in quattro proposte epiche fra Cinque e Seicento* (Alessandria, 2005), 94–96.

[34] For a painstaking catalogue, see Belloni, *Gli epigoni* (1893), 481–531, and for an analysis *La fortuna del Tasso eroico tra Sei e Settecento. Modelli interpretativi e pratiche di riscrittura*, ed. Tancredi Artico and Enrico Zucchi (Alessandria, 2017). On Lepanto in poetry, see Alberto Casadei, "Panegirici per la vittoria," in *Atlante della letteratura italiana*, ed. S. Luzzatto and G. Pedullà (Turin, 2010–12): vol. 2, *Dalla Controriforma alla Restaurazione*, ed. E. Irace (Turin, 2011), 224–31.

[35] Sergio Zatti, "L'imperialismo epico del Trissino," in *L'ombra del Tasso. Epica e romanzo nel Cinquecento* (Milan, 1996), 59–110, and "Tasso lettore del Trissino," in *Torquato Tasso e la cultura estense*, 2:597–612; Federico Di Santo, *Il poema epico rinascimentale e l'"Iliade": Da Trissino a Tasso* (Florence, 2018).

[36] Gigante, *Tasso*, 169–204, for a summary of the discussion; and Sergio Zatti, *L'uniforme cristiano e il multiforme pagano. Saggio sulla "Gerusalemme Liberata"* (Milan, 1983), for an analysis

An analysis of Rinaldo immediately reveals the difficulty of such an endeavour. Rinaldo's storyline and characterisation do not substantially differ from those of his Ariostean namesake. Rinaldo is the youngest, strongest, and most handsome of the crusaders. He is somewhat of a hot-head, and highly passionate, something represented by his break with the Christian army and his subsequent relationship with the Muslim sorceress Armida.[37] Rinaldo disobeys Goffredo, his commander, and, when he is reprimanded for his behaviour, storms out of the Christian camp.[38] Besotted with Armida's beauty, he follows her to her enchanted garden, where he lingers in earthly delight while, in his absence, the crusading enterprise is threatened.[39] When the crusaders Carlo and Ubaldo go to recover him, Rinaldo is shamed into returning to the Christian camp, but his callous abandonment of Armida is itself framed as morally dubious.[40] While he eventually rejoins the crusade, becoming instrumental to the conquest of Jerusalem, Rinaldo's final meeting with Armida seems to confirm the endurance of his passion for a Muslim woman: he prevents her suicide and embraces her.[41]

Nor is Rinaldo alone in his vivacious amorous adventures. Tancredi, the other young hero of the poem, and his commitment to crusading are constantly hobbled by his complex love life. Tancredi's obsessive love for the Muslim warrior Clorinda often impairs his ability to fight; and while Clorinda's baptism at the point of death absorbs her into Christian orthodoxy, the ending of the poem leaves Tancredi entangled with Erminia, the unconverted princess of Antioch, who has long loved him for his beauty and chivalry.[42] As Antoniano sternly pointed out in his letters to Tasso, his heroes' disorderly erotic life rather belied the ideals of renewed Catholic morality enshrined in the Counter-Reformation project, to which the poet had theoretically committed himself.[43] The problem was possibly unsolvable; Gigante has persuasively argued that Tasso may well have been in the process of wholly complying with Antoniano's requests, by progressively removing these romantic plotlines. Tasso's internment, however, froze the text of *Liberata* mid-revision, preserving his more "chivalric" storylines, and offering us a glimpse of the

---

of its applications in the poem. More briefly available in English as "Christian Uniformity, Pagan Multiplicity," in Sergio Zatti, *The Quest for Epic: From Ariosto to Tasso*, ed. Dennis Looney and Sally Hill (Toronto, 2006), 135–59.

[37] *Liberata*, I.10, 45, 58–60; III.37.

[38] *Liberata*, V.50–60.

[39] Goffredo dreams of the necessity of bringing back Rinaldo after nine *canti* of mayhem in *Liberata*, XIV.12–15.

[40] *Liberata*, XV describes the delights of Armida's garden, and Carlo and Ubaldo's mission to rescue Rinaldo; *Liberata*, XVI lingers on the knight and the sorceress's bitter goodbye.

[41] *Liberata*, XX.123–36.

[42] *Liberata*, XII.66–68; XIX.90–119; on the ending of *Liberata* Giorgio Petrocchi, "I fantasmi di Tancredi," in *I fantasmi di Tancredi. Saggi sul Tasso e sul Rinascimento* (Caltanissetta and Rome, 1972), 65–83, cf. 79–81, and Beatrice Corrigan, "Erminia and Tancredi: The Happy Ending," *Italica* 40/4 (1963): 325–33.

[43] Tasso, *Lettere poetiche*, Letter 43, "A Luca Scalabrino," has the poet lamenting Antoniano's persistence in his own opinions despite the poet's justifications.

relationship of his characters to the sources, and, in particular, whence the historical inspiration for Rinaldo came. Ironically, these romantic themes have proven the poem's most enduringly popular.[44]

Tasso's chief defence was simple: everything he wrote, he claimed, he took from the chronicles.[45] The poet could not be blamed for the breaches with Christian orthodoxy which had taken place in history itself, and the poem, he assured his editors, was deeply rooted *nel vero*, in historical truth. Yet, this declaration is more problematic than meets the eye. Tasso openly admitted to using five sources: Robert the Monk, William of Tyre, Paolo Emilio, the *Chronicon Uspergense* and Rocoldo di Prochese (or Procoldo di Rochese, depending on when he is mentioned).[46] The suspiciously alternating names present an immediate problem, and as Murrin tersely notes, "if Procoldo exists, no one has yet been able to find him."[47] The suspicion is heightened by the fact that the poet invokes Procoldo as the source for the most controversial aspects of the characterisation and writing. Tasso also declares that he received the book in a rare copy personally given him by the duke of Ferrara.[48] Whether or not Procoldo existed, and whether he was in fact a minor chivalric reteller of the crusade Tasso conveniently chose to take at face value, he is hardly a guarantee of historical accuracy.[49] Moreover, as Vivaldi has shown, there was another source Tasso seems to have used: Albert of Aachen, whose *History of the Journey to Jerusalem*'s rare manuscripts he could have encountered during his travels in France, or through his unfettered access to the rich libraries of Ferrara and Rome. Several of the extant manuscripts of Albert's *History* are preserved in Paris or in Rome itself, and we know of at least two lost manuscripts, so more copies may have been available in Tasso's time.[50] Given how little is known of the provenance of many of them, it is reasonable to suppose that at least one or two may have been available to Tasso in the libraries he frequented. Overall, while not all of his sources are "historical," Tasso still seems to have engaged extensively with some of the most relevant crusader chronicles.

---

[44] Gigante, *Tasso*, 155–68.

[45] Tasso, *Lettere poetiche*, Letter 38, "A Silvio Antoniano." In this he is not alone, as the reference to past *auctoritates* was somewhat traditional in chivalric poems; but, as Luigi Pulci shows by joyously making fun of this trope in his poem *Morgante*, this had never been quite so serious as it was now for Tasso: Luigi Pulci, *Morgante*, 2 vols., ed. Davide Puccini (Milan, 1989), 1:I.3–8.

[46] On the sources of Tasso, Vincenzo Vivaldi's monumental work *Sulle fonti della* Gerusalemme liberata (Catanzaro, 1893); *Prolegomeni ad uno studio completo sulle fonti della* Gerusalemme liberata (Trani, 1904); *La Gerusalemme liberate studiata nelle sue fonti (episodi)* (Trani, 1907) remains impressive for its thoroughness and accuracy. Salvatore Multineddu's *Le fonti della* Gerusalemme liberata (Turin, 1895) makes a valuable contribution to the field. See also Franco Cardini, "Torquato Tasso e la crociata," in *Torquato Tasso e la cultura estense*, 2:615–24, though not engaging closely with Tasso's relationship with the crusading movement.

[47] Michael Murrin, *History and Warfare in Renaissance Epic* (Chicago, 1994), 294 n. 32.

[48] *Le Lettere di Torquato Tasso*, 1:61-66, no. 25. Notably, here "Procoldo di Rochese" becomes "Rocoldo di Prochese."

[49] I am grateful to Alan Murray for suggesting this elegant solution to the problem.

[50] Vivaldi, *Prolegomeni*, 25, 45, 108–9, 121–22, 283. As catalogued in AA, xxxvii–xlvii. *Conquistata*, XXIII.107–9.

The product of this effort to stitch chivalric models into the fabric of history is visible in the historical figure that can be seen in filigree through Rinaldo, and which clearly identifies Tancred as Tasso's model. Grandson of Robert Guiscard and nephew of Bohemond of Taranto, Tancred was the youngest among the leaders of the First Crusade; probably in his late teens when he took the cross.[51] Tancred immediately distinguished himself for his military ability, conquering cities in Cilicia on the way to Jerusalem, and taking part in the successful storming of the city with Godfrey of Bouillon, whom he served after Bohemond chose to remain in Antioch. Tancred is also, of course, explicitly fictionalised in *Liberata*, in the shape of Tancredi. But a closer look, I would argue, shows that Tancredi and Rinaldo share a historical inspiration. Throughout the poem, the two appear to shadow each other, exhibiting remarkably similar characteristics that betray their common origin. In particular, Tancredi seems to be the "almost-but-not-quite" Rinaldo. He is the youngest of the crusaders, but for Rinaldo; the strongest and most beautiful, but for Rinaldo.[52] Rinaldo first breaks the defences of Jerusalem and allows Goffredo to plant his banner on the walls of Jerusalem; Tancredi goes over the wall "almost in that same instant."[53] Rinaldo is overcome by anger; Tancredi, older and a little wiser, attempts to calm him down, while still being reprimanded by Goffredo for his youthful impudence.[54] The two share intemperate, inappropriate feelings for enemy women, and it is only with their redemption, and their return to the Christian fold, that Jerusalem can be conquered. While the primacy of Rinaldo is restated throughout the poem, his likeness to Tancredi is obvious. While the Ariostean Rinaldo was developed in opposition to his cousin Orlando (a more reliable, "adult" kind of hero), Tasso's Rinaldo is an "alter Tancredi," the slightly more brilliant model of a solidly historical "anchor" character who would give the poem legitimacy.

The differences between Tancredi and Rinaldo, moreover, are easily traceable to different aspects of Tancred's historical characterisation. Tancredi is portrayed as a model of chivalry, a pious knight who declares that he "always wore iron for Christ, and was his champion," a model of virtue in his dealings with his peers, his superiors, his enemies, and women such as Erminia.[55] In this, he closely mirrors William of Tyre's Tancred. Modern commentators have noted how William spares his usually critical pen when it comes to Tancred, constructing him as an emblematic hero of the First Crusade.[56] But William of Tyre's idea of Tancred was far from universally accepted: most notably, by one of his own sources, Albert of Aachen, which, as we have seen, others have suggested Tasso used. And indeed, at no point does the poet

---

[51]   On Tancred's age, Francesca Petrizzo, "The Ancestry and Kinship of Tancred, Prince Regent of Antioch," *Medieval Prosopography* 34 (2019): 41–85, at 46–48.

[52]   *Liberata*, 1.45, 58.

[53]   *Liberata*, XIX.18.99–101, "quasi in quello istante."

[54]   *Liberata*, 40–51.

[55]   *Liberata*, VII.34; VI.54–60.

[56]   William of Tyre, *A History of Deeds Done Beyond the Sea*, trans. Emily A. Babcock and August C. Krey, 2 vols. (New York, NY, 1943), 1:186 n. 24.

claim he provided an exhaustive list of his sources. The case for Tasso's knowledge of Albert of Aachen seems conclusively established by the similarities between the young crusaders in his poem, and Albert's depiction of Tancred.

The similarities between the episode in which Rinaldo fights with Goffredo before abandoning the crusader camp and Book I of the *Iliad* have already been noted. Like Achilles, Rinaldo abandons his army after a disagreement with his commander, precipitating a crisis and nearly losing the war.[57] But Goffredo, unlike Homer's Agamemnon, is in the right in the poem: the crusading leader is shown upbraiding the younger knight for disobeying his rules and fighting with a fellow Christian.[58] When Tancredi attempts to defend Rinaldo, guilty, according to him, of understandable pride given his status and virtue, Goffredo scolds him too: the Christian cause takes precedence over individual crusaders.[59] This episode closely echoes one in Albert of Aachen's *History*. When Tancred unleashes his anger because fellow crusaders have killed the prisoners whom he had attempted to save by giving them his banner on the roof of the Temple, Godfrey of Bouillon cuts him down to size, chastising him for his hastiness and for putting his "sloth, avarice or mercy" ahead of the crusader army.[60] The two episodes are clearly similar in dynamics and moral, with youth and hot-headedness disciplined by age and wisdom in pursuit of Christian warrior models. The effect of the episode is doubled in Tasso by Goffredo scolding two young knights rather than one, reaffirming the primacy of a veteran ruler like himself over a younger, flashier, and less temperate knight.

What is more, Tasso's knowledge of the episode is confirmed by his adaptation of it in his work. Thus, in *Gerusalemme conquistata*, Tancredi hangs his banner over a house of enemy women during the sack of Jerusalem in order to save their lives.[61] The episode is a poetic modification of Tancred's attempt to save civilians during the looting of the Temple, an episode not reported by William of Tyre or Robert the Monk, but which Albert of Aachen, as we have seen, dwelt upon. But while of course *Conquistata* was a much later product of Tasso's imagination, the episode, and a suggestion of the historical Tancred's association with enemy women, is well-rooted in *Liberata* itself. Tasso claimed Tancred was "madly enamoured of the embraces of Saracen women" in one of his revision letters, alluding to an episode, whose source has remained undiscovered, but which clearly had been on his mind from the start.[62] His substitution of women specifically for generic civilians in

---

[57] Gigante, *Tasso*, 169-204.

[58] For the dispute between Achilles and Agamemnon: Homer, *Iliade*, ed. Thomas W. Allen and Rosa Calzecchi Onesti (Turin, 2014), book 1, lines 148–492.

[59] *Liberata*, V.35–38.

[60] Albert of Aachen, *History*, vi.28–29, 438–40.

[61] *Conquistata*, XXIII.107–9.

[62] Tasso, *Lettere poetiche*, Letter 38, "A Silvio Antoniano"; Multineddu (*Le fonti*, 204–5) attempted to identify this passage, but his reference to William of Tyre is wrong. Fulcher of Chartres has it that God punished the crusaders at the siege of Antioch also because *cum feminis exlegibus commiscuerunt se*, that is, they had unlawfully mixed themselves up with women: FC, I.xix.3, 243. I am grateful to Andrew Buck for bringing this to my attention. This might suggest, either that Tasso knew Fulcher, or

Conquistata allows us to infer where he might have picked up the idea. Had it been directed at women, Tancred's gesture of mercy would have become, according to Tasso's norms, one of chivalry. And Tancredi's chivalry towards enemy women is already present in *Liberata* where by showing the princess Erminia courtesy, setting her free with the crown jewels of Antioch, Tancredi causes her to fall in love with him.[63]

But if Albert of Aachen offers a model of the "chivalrous" Tancred, a crusader willing and able to bridge the gap with the non-Christian inhabitants of the Holy Land, William of Tyre instead shows a model of the lustful crusader, bringing us back to Rinaldo's erotic exploits. If, for William, Tancred is a model of virtue, his cousin Roger of Salerno, heir to Antioch, is a very different character. William condemns Roger for being a lascivious adulterer with no respect for marriage, who is redeemed, even so, at the point of death. According to the *Chronicon*, Roger was taken by remorse for his sins on the eve of battle, and asked for forgiveness before going into the fight where he would lose his life.[64] Roger died fighting Il-ghazi, *atabeg* of Mosul. While he failed to hold him back, he did pursue the conflict against the Muslims of Syria to the end.[65] Rinaldo undertakes a similar journey, through the transformative power of poetry: his relationship with Armida distracted him from the war, and his return to battle redeemed him. Tasso had said that it was Tancred who was "mad for the embraces of women," but it is easy to see how he might either have misattributed the *adulterium* mentioned by William (who paints Tancred in a positive light in the same passage) or, in the heat of intellectual debate, sought to streamline the argument.

Rinaldo's character arc, virtues and vices, therefore, can indeed be traced back to solidly historical models, tied, moreover, to the southern Norman contingent of the First Crusade. Rinaldo, whose hot-headedness, youth and martial prowess shadow Tancred's, both in the poem and in history, also seems to bear the imprint of Roger of Salerno's sinfulness and redemption. Tasso's choice brings us back to *Liberata*'s propagandistic programme, namely one of glorifying the Estensi by creating a fictional crusader ancestor, believably rooted in history, but also placing them at the forefront of the Italian national scene.

---

that the idea of the sexual licentiousness of the crusaders spread into further sources. In addition, Marion Wells, in *The Secret Wound: Love Melancholy and Early Modern Romance* (Palo Alto, 2007), discusses Tancredi as a perfect example of baroque melancholy hero, showing how deeply the character is woven into the conventions of its time.

[63] *Liberata*, XIX.92–98.

[64] WT, 12.10.

[65] See Thomas Asbridge, "The Significance and Causes of the Battle of the Field of Blood," in *Medieval Warfare 1000–1300*, ed. John France (Aldershot, 2006), 395–410; and Nicholas Morton, *The Field of Blood: The Battle for Aleppo and the Remaking of the Medieval Middle East* (New York, 2018).

Tancredi the Italian: National Identity in Sixteenth- and Seventeenth-Century Epic Literature

Liberata's original title was *Gottifredo*, a nod to Tasso's determination to find a unity of intent in the poem by focusing on one protagonist, but also to pay tribute to the hero depicted in post-crusades lore as the most virtuous of the holy warriors.[66] *Liberata* ends, significantly, with Goffredo's adoration of the Holy Sepulchre and fulfilment of his crusade vow, which reaffirms the primacy of the holy war wished for by Tasso's editors.[67] In the hallowed shadow of Goffredo, however, the poem's other leads are united by a fundamental characteristic: they are both "Italian."

As a Norman of Italy, Tancred was not simply a leader whose striking youth could easily be dressed in chivalric sparkle, but also and most importantly "one of our own," in the words of Verdizzotti about Bohemond, namely, a crusader from Italy itself.[68] The absence of Italian crusaders has long puzzled historians; thus, for Tasso, celebrating the conquest of Jerusalem offered both a challenge and an opportunity.[69] Overwhelmingly, *Liberata* hinges on the adventures of Tancredi, Rinaldo, and the women they love and who love them. While Goffredo's virtue also ties the poem together, the rest of the protagonists of the crusade are substantially cut down to size in their role. By focusing on two "Italian" crusaders, Tasso rewrote the conquest of Jerusalem as a "national" enterprise, dominated, on the one hand, by a historic figure who could lend his narrative historical truth, and on the other, by the avatar of the Estensi, reframed as Italy's saviours both from the Turks and from its long history of infighting. Tasso garnishes the rank and file of the crusaders in *Liberata* with an additional Italian fighter, Camillo, an imaginary ancestor of the Orsini family of Rome, further contextualising Rinaldo and Tancredi within a strong and highly motivated force from the peninsula.[70] Tancred's choice as a

---

[66] Tasso, *Discorsi dell'arte poetica*, "Discorso secondo" on the need for unity. Simon John, *Godfrey of Bouillon: Duke of Lower Lotharingia, Ruler of Latin Jerusalem, c.1060–1100* (London, 2018), 227–53.

[67] *Liberata*, 20.144, "e qui l'arme sospende, e qui devoto/il gran Sepolcro adora e scioglie il voto."

[68] Foltran, *Per un ciclo tassiano*, 98–100.

[69] On the lack of interest of the southern Normans in crusading after the First Crusade see Luigi Russo, "Bad Crusaders? The Normans of Southern Italy and the Crusading Movement in the Twelfth Century," *Anglo–Norman Studies* 38 (2016): 169–81, and idem, "I normanni e il movimento crociato: una revisione," in *Il papato e i Normanni. Temporale e spirituale in età normanna. Atti del Convegno di studi da CNR (Consiglio Nazionale delle Ricerche), CESN (Centro Europeo di Studi Normanni), SISMEL (Società Internazionale per lo Studio del Medioevo Latino), Ariano Irpino, 6–7 dicembre 2007*, ed. Edoardo D'Angelo and Claudio Leonardi (Florence, 2011), 163–74; Graham A. Loud, "Norman Italy and the Holy Land," in *Horns*, 49–62; Ewan Johnson and Andrew Jotischky, "Les Normands de l'Italie méridionale et les états croisés au XIIe siècle," in *911–2011: Penser les mondes normands médiévaux. Actes du colloque international de Caen et Cerisy (29 septembre–2 octobre 2011)*, ed. David Bates and Pierre Bauduin (Caen, 2016), 163–76; Paula Z. Hailstone, *Recalcitrant Crusaders? The Relationship Between Southern Italy and Sicily, Crusading and the Crusader States, c. 1060–1198* (London, 2020); Francesca Petrizzo, "Wars of Our Fathers: Hauteville Kin Networks and the Making of Norman Antioch," *Journal of Medieval History* 48/1(2022): 1–31.

[70] *Liberata*, I.64.

model for Rinaldo, therefore, becomes programmatic for the entirety of the work: Robert Guiscard's grandson becomes the thin end of a wedge that allows Tasso to claim the crusading enterprise, not just for the Estensi but for Italian identity at large. That this project resonated deeply with his contemporaries can be discerned by its reception.

Tasso's celebration of Tancred immediately raised a cry for an additional, historical, "Italian" crusader to be celebrated: Bohemond. Tancred's uncle is lauded *in absentia* in *Liberata*. Tasso praises him, but also places him firmly in Antioch, away from the main scene.[71] The reason is clear: Bohemond, a mature hero, of much-celebrated brilliance, would most likely have overwhelmed the scene, having to vie for primacy with Goffredo (the foremost and irreplaceable crusader model) and inevitably overshadowing any stand-in for the Estensi.[72] By focusing on Tancredi instead, Tasso was able to develop a companion for Rinaldo, a foil who would guarantee the fictional hero's believability and path, but who would also not overshadow him, given his junior status and similar, flawed Christian virtue. By retaining Goffredo and Tancredi as the two main "historical" heroes, Tasso was clinging to well-established tropes by placing at the forefront examples of mature virtue versus passionate chivalric youth. Still, he left enough space to develop Rinaldo, as an additional "Italian" hero who could, at one and the same time, be the standard-bearer for the Estensi and the representative of a "national" reclamation of the crusading enterprise.

Where Tasso, however, had chosen to cast Bohemond aside, many of his imitators placed him front and centre. Verdizzotti only wrote one *canto* of his projected poem *Boemondo*, but Pietro Angelio da Barga's *Syrias*, with its focus on the conquest of Antioch, and the large part played by Bohemond in it, further cements the case for a hankering after "national" crusader heroes in the tightly knit, closely interconnected Italian intellectual community.[73] Tommaso Balli's *Palermo liberato* (1612) sought to connect the crusading enterprise to Italy's own struggle against the Muslims. Thus Balli anachronistically credits a young Bohemond with the conquest of Palermo from the Muslims, doubling down on Tasso's premise, despite the evidence that the Norman conquest of Sicily was not perceived as holy war in its own time.[74] Giovan Leone Sempronio's *Boemondo, ovvero Antiochia difesa* ("Bohemond, or Antioch defended," 1651) is a carefully curated prequel to *Liberata*, which writes itself painstakingly into the plot.[75] Sempronio respects

---

[71] *Liberata*, I.9, III.63, V.49.

[72] For a problematised reading of the figure of Goffredo, see Andrea Moudarres, "A Less Perfect Captain: Reconsidering Goffredo in the *Gerusalemme Liberata*," *Forum Italicum* 55/1 (2021): 3–20.

[73] Giovan Maria Verdizzotti, *Boemondo ovvero l'acquisto di Antiochia* (Venice, 1607); Belloni, *Gli epigoni della* Gerusalemme liberata (1893), 77–80.

[74] Tommaso Balli, *Palermo liberato* (Palermo, 1612). See Francesca Petrizzo, "'Conquest in Their Blood:' Hauteville Ambition, Authorial Spin and and Interpretative Challenges in the Narrative Sources," in *Warfare in the Norman Mediterranean*, ed. Georgios Theotokis (Woodbridge, 2020), 35–54, at 49–50.

[75] Giovan Leone Sempronio, *Boemondo, ovvero Antiochia difesa* (Bologna, 1651).

the place of Tancredi in Tasso's vision, preserving his character and creating episodes such as Erminia's falling in love with him, and the first meeting of Clorinda and Tancredi by a spring, which the original poem had only mentioned in flashbacks.[76] But Tancredi's role in Sempronio's poem is altogether minor. He is a dashing knight, but his station is subordinate to that of his glorious uncle, who is depicted as the perfect example of chivalry and crusading virtue.[77] By focusing on Bohemond, Sempronio discusses a model of leadership alongside one of glory. The poem aims to make Bohemond both an example of leadership and of martial valour, if with mixed results, which reflect the complexity of baroque narrative codes.[78] These qualities were separate in *Liberata*, where Goffredo, albeit reluctantly, does not join the battle but remains behind to preserve his life.[79]

The desire to show Italian crusaders not just as young and impetuous, but also as models for rulership is even more evident in the one among *Liberata*'s epic sequels to focus on Tancredi: Ascanio Grandi's *Tancredi* (1632).[80] Grandi follows Tancredi on his way back from the crusade. His hero is older and still dashing (handsome enough to make Empress Matilde fall in love with him on sight), but he is also wise, modelled on the heroic pattern of Aeneas which Tasso had followed for Goffredo.[81] Heroic antics and exciting amours are instead reserved for Idro, Tancredi's son by an enchanting water nymph.[82] Profoundly rooted in the southern Italian reality (he was a native of Lecce, and it is in his home region that he earned his success), Grandi weaves into his poem descriptions of the southern coastline, contextualises memories of southern Norman domination, and paints historically inaccurate but evocative links to the Norman kingdom of Sicily.[83] His work restates at once the value of Tancred as a "local" hero, and the deeply felt need to elevate him above chivalric glamour, into the stuff mature heroes, along the enduringly popular outline of Goffredo, are made of. Like Tasso, Grandi attempted to connect his poem to a larger vision for an Italian nation, by dedicating it to Duke Charles Emmanuel I of Savoia, whose exploits in northern Italy deeply excited Italian intellectuals. As the duke, however, appears to have ignored the homage, the second edition of the poem

---

[76] Sempronio, *Boemondo*, IV, 1–26, 80–86; XIX, 19–46, 500–506.

[77] For a discussion of Sempronio's literary influence and role in the epic of his time, see Luisella Giachino, *Giovan Leone Sempronio tra "lusus" amoroso e armi cristiane* (Florence, 2002).

[78] Tancredi Artico, "Un imperfetto capitano nell'epica barocca: il *Boemondo* di G. L. Sempronio come antitesi di Goffredo," *Acta Iassyensia Comparationis* 15 (2015): 31–40.

[79] *Liberata*, VII.61–62.

[80] Ascanio Grandi, *Il Tancredi poema heroico* (Lecce, 1630). I have used the faithful reprint published in Lecce in 1868 in three volumes, rather than the recent edition (Ascanio Grandi, *Il Tancredi e la Vergine Desponsata*, ed. Antonio Mangione [Galatina, 1997]), whose introduction presents numerous inaccuracies, including the date of publication of the poem, which Mangione places at 1582. For an analysis of Grandi see Foltran, *Per un ciclo tassiano*, 129–85.

[81] Grandi, *Tancredi*, 4.lxxxvii ff.

[82] Grandi, *Tancredi*, 1.lxvi–lxvi, 2.cvii.

[83] Grandi, *Tancredi*, 3.xxii, cxlviii–cxlix.

was more modestly (and somewhat bitterly) dedicated instead to a local notable, Marchese, whose family was intent on tracing their descent to Tancred.[84]

While none of Tasso's imitators attained even a fraction of his success, their attempts further confirm the value of Tasso's vision for an "Italian" crusade, and his ability to give voice to aspirations which were clearly felt from Venice to Sicily.[85] Tasso's work on Tancredi allowed him to make space for Rinaldo: it was by capitalising on the one "Italian" crusader at the fall of Jerusalem that the poet could harness the crusade to the cause of Italian identity. At the same time, the specificity of his solution, and its unsatisfactory implications for anyone who did not belong to the House of Este, were denounced by his imitators. The only afterlife of Rinaldo beyond *Liberata* places him squarely back into the love life of which Antoniani disapproved, entirely subordinate to the glamour of his lover Armida.[86] While Tasso made Rinaldo something more than Tancredi, it was the value of Tancredi as a "national" crusader that his imitators leveraged, disregarding the character crafted specifically for the dukes of Ferrara.

Rinaldo, nonetheless, functions as the gateway into intersecting layers of concern for both Tasso and his readers. Far from idly evoking the strong literary and chivalric heritage of the Estensi, he actively links the historical baseline of Tancred, and his successful wars against the Muslims, with the contemporary preoccupation for Ottoman expansion. Moreover, Rinaldo builds on the idea of "reclaiming" the crusade for the Italian national identity, while at the same time placing the House of Este centre-stage. The character embodies the likely unsolvable dilemma of Tasso's poetics: he is at once a flawed young knight, beholden to the charms of a Muslim sorceress (albeit one who agrees to convert by the end of the poem), and the Christian hero who allows Goffredo to place his standard on the walls of Jerusalem. That the Rinaldo of *Liberata* was tailored to a specific audience, political moment, and ideological concern, is clearly shown by his complete transformation in *Conquistata*.

Rinaldo Vanishes: Tasso after *Liberata*

The degree to which the fully revised *Liberata* might have resembled the finished *Conquistata* is moot. As Gigante notes, even when writing his *Giudicio sovra la Gerusalemme Riformata* (1595), with which he defended his unpopular revised

---

[84] Girolamo Cigalá in the dedication of the second edition of *Tancredi* (Lecce, 1636). For the Marchese and their possible relationship to Tancredi: Ferrante della Marra, *Discorsi delle famiglie estinte, forastiere o non comprese ne' Seggi di Napoli, imparentate colla Casa della Marra* (Naples, 1641), 224–30; and Petrizzo, "The Ancestry and Kinship," 74–75.

[85] See also Michele Catalano, *La venuta dei Normanni in Sicilia nella poesia e nella leggenda* (Catania, 1903), 44–58.

[86] For a thorough catalogue of the fortune of Armida and Rinaldo's romance in music, see Ilaria Gallinaro, *La non vera Clorinda. Tradizione teatrale e musicale della Liberata nei secoli XVII–XIX* (Milan, 1994).

poem, Tasso was still editing it, demonstrating that his demanding vision of poetics was perpetually in flux.[87] *Conquistata* has not matched the favour of *Liberata*. As mentioned, the enduring popularity of *Liberata* has overwhelmingly been tied to its romantic and chivalric storylines, which are almost wholly excised from *Conquistata*.[88] Tancredi is returned to a more historical dimension. In the new poem he is much less prominent, presented simply as one of many, equal heroes from the sources. Tancredi is now depicted as a far less dashing character who, if he still enjoys a tragically truncated love for Clorinda, no longer completes his character arc in the arms of Erminia. As we have seen above, *Conquistata*'s Tancredi follows more closely the trajectory of his historical counterpart, attempting to defend civilians during the taking of Jerusalem, and he is last seen on the beach at Ascalon, taking part in the attack on the town.[89]

Rinaldo disappears, and he is renamed Riccardo in *Conquistata*. The new name mimics the rhythm and metre of the original, but it evokes entirely new associations. Gone at a stroke are all memories of Ariosto, gone is the model of rebellious chivalry. Evoking Richard Lionheart, the name Riccardo has impeccable crusader associations, but no literary ones. This carries through into the characterisation. Far from being an immature but valiant hero, Riccardo is a hero on a journey, a journey which, as Girardi persuasively argues, has much in common with that of traditional religious fables.[90] While Armida still attempts to distance him from the crusading enterprise – and, for a time, succeeds in doing so – her defeat is absolute. In *Conquistata*, Armida is last seen, chained, in the ruins of her enchanted castle, while Riccardo, now free, rejoins the crusade without a backward glance.[91] If the fundamental conflict of Rinaldo in *Liberata* was the fight against the passions of his own heart, Riccardo's progress is far more sombre, characterised by grief for his lost friend Ruperto and the remorseful abandonment of his affair.[92] In *Conquistata* Tancredi shrinks to a more manageable, more historical dimension, save his doomed love for Clorinda, whose lack of consummation and final conversion made it more ideologically acceptable. But Riccardo has been wholly transfigured, evolving from a vessel for the glory of the Estensi into the now fully realised ideal

---

[87] Claudio Gigante, *Esperienze di filologia cinquecentesca. Salviati, Mazzoni, Trissino, Costo, il Bargeo, Tasso* (Rome, 2003), 199–201. In the same volume, see also "Tradizione e critica del Giudicio sovra la 'Gerusalemme' riformata," 228–54. For Gigante's in-depth study of *Conquistata*, see Claudio Gigante, *"Vincer pariemi più sé stessa antica." La* Gerusalemme conquistata *nel mondo poetico di Torquato Tasso* (Naples, 1996).

[88] With dramatic consequences for the female characters. For an in-depth study, see Giuliana Picco, *"Or s'indora ed or verdeggia". Il ritratto femminile dalla "Liberata" alla "Conquistata"* (Florence, 1996).

[89] *Conquistata*, XXIV.116.

[90] Maria Teresa Girardi, "La parabola di Riccardo," in *Tasso e la nuova Gerusalemme. Studio sulla Conquistata e sul Giudicio* (Naples, 2002), 21–84; and Matteo Residori, *L'idea del poema. Studio sulla* Gerusalemme conquistata *di Torquato Tasso* (Pisa, 2004), 201–34.

[91] *Conquistata*, XIII.70–75.

[92] *Conquistata*, XXI.25–27, 56–74.

of the Counter-Reformation.[93] If Rinaldo embodied the tension between chivalric glamour and spiritual renewal, Riccardo successfully snaps it, tilting the scale in favour of the latter and revealing Rinaldo as a highly contextual creation, and thus one with a short shelf life in the grander perspective of Tasso's poetic ideal.

The character of Rinaldo, then, represents a definite stage of Tasso's evolution: the poet as celebrator of a particular court, as the interpreter of a political and ideological debate pinpointed in time, and as a man enmeshed in the tension between the chivalric ideals and forms of his early poems and the more religious aspirations of his later years. The moment can be precisely triangulated thanks to a thorough analysis of the intertextual web underpinning Rinaldo, and it would have been fleeting, had Tasso pursued the revision he had been committed to from the start. But the poet's dramatic personal life interrupted *Liberata*'s revision, and preserved Rinaldo, and his rich possibilities as a character, at an artificial albeit highly successful station on his journey. Rinaldo is at once a crusading hero crafted for the Estensi, the embodiment of a wish for Italian unity in the face of Ottoman expansion, and the utopic last heir of chivalric glamour. At the same time, he functions as the standard-bearer of renewed poetics in service of the ideals of the Counter-Reformation which Tasso controversially sought to the end of his life.

---

[93] Clorinda, the daughter of Ethiopian Christian parents, was born "miraculously" white (*Liberata*, XII.20–40). This plotline is possibly based on the *Aethiopica*, a fifth-century Greek novel by Heliodorus of Emesa. For a discussion of Tasso's use of the text, and the racial politics of Clorinda's character, see: David Quint, *Epic and Empire: Poetics and Generic Form from Virgil to Milton* (Princeton, 1993), 234–47; David Quint, "Perché Clorinda è un 'Etiope'," in *La rappresentazione dell'altro nei testi del Rinascimento*, ed. Sergio Zatti (Lucca, 1998), 133–45; Sergio Zatti, "Dalla parte di Satana: sull'imperialismo cristiano nella *Gerusalemme liberata*," ibid., 146–62; Valeria Finucci, "Performing Maternity: Female Imagination, Paternal Erasure, and Monstrous Birth in Tasso's *Gerusalemme liberata*," in *The Manly Masquerade: Masculinity, Paternity, and Castration in the Italian Renaissance* (Durham, NC, 2003), 119–58; Michael Paschalis, "Did Torquato Tasso Classify the Aethiopica as Epic Poetry?," in *Fictional Traces: Receptions of the Ancient Novel*, vol. 1, ed. Marília P. Futre Pinheiro and Stephen J. Harrison (Eelde, 2011), 151–82; Corrado Confalonieri, "Tasso, the Aethiopica, and the Debate on Literary Genres between Renaissance and Baroque," in *Re-Wiring the Ancient Novel*, 2 vols., Volume 1: *Greek Novels*, ed. Edmund Cueva, Stephen Harrison, Hugh Mason, William Owens, and Saundra Schwartz (Eelde, 2018), 263–78.

Review Article:
Historiographical Trends and Crusader Narratives

Jessalynn Bird

Saint Mary's College, Notre Dame, IN

Marcus Bull, *Eyewitness and Crusade Narrative: Perception and Narration in Accounts of the Second, Third, and Fourth Crusades*. Woodbridge: Boydell and Brewer, 2018. Pp. x, 396. ISBN 978 1 78327 335 5.

Beth C. Spacey, *The Miraculous and the Writing of Crusade Narrative*. Woodbridge: Boydell and Brewer, 2020. Pp. xvi, 198. ISBN 978 1 78327 518 2.

In recent years, many new historiographical trends have revolutionized the ways in which historians read crusade narratives. These trends include the study of the relationships between crusading and devotional, social, political, and economic developments in Europe (and in the East); the construction and readership of eyewitness, composite, local, and vernacular narratives; depictions of emotion, gender, and the natural and supernatural worlds in narrative; and the various narrative and literary traditions available to medieval writers (such as chronicles, hagiography and miracle collections, biblical exegesis, sermons, poems or songs, liturgy, apocalypses, and prophecies, all potentially drawn from Greco-Roman, European, Islamic, and/or eastern Christian literary traditions). The volumes reviewed here engage with these developments and encourage scholars to re-evaluate historians' traditional privileging of accounts consciously constructed by their authors as "eyewitness" as those primary sources best enabling scholars and students to examine the creation and evolution of crusading identity and ideology. The volumes' authors also re-examine the usefulness of entire narratives (or portions of them) once considered potentially tainted or suspect because of their hybrid nature, partly because this very hybridity reveals the ways in which individual authors or regional traditions adopted and adapted crusading concepts and rhetoric to appeal to varied audiences.

Neither Marcus Bull nor Beth Spacey succumbs to relativism or Foucauldian assumptions that authorial intention and original audiences are ultimately irrelevant; both acknowledge that medieval authors drew on concepts of truth from the classical and biblical traditions even while consciously constructing texts to convey that verity. If history were a form of observation of – and inquiry into – events, eyewitness accounts must be evaluated and measured against written texts and authorial experiences. Medieval historians were aware that when writing world histories, time and distance made it impossible for the author and other witnesses to have experienced every event in person; authors were forced to utilize oral histories and testimonies, as well as written texts. In particular, as Katherine Allen Smith has also recently noted, monastic chroniclers of the First Crusade felt the need to balance potentially untrustworthy eyewitness accounts of the first crusaders against the more venerable and less error-prone sources of spiritual truth and insight into human nature privileged in the religious tradition: liturgy, sermons, confession, exegesis.[1] In order to escape falling into the trap of rating historical narratives as more or less empirically true based on the amount of "eyewitness" or "biographical" material incorporated into them, Marcus Bull suggests turning to narratological analysis, which views historical works as cultural artifacts, as loci for discourses between history and alternative means of perceiving and representing reality, relating stories, and constructing meaning and group memory, such as theology, hagiography, prophecy, and poetry.

Bull convincingly argues that historians therefore must apply literary analysis to historical texts and analyze the authors' various roles as constructed in the text: as author, character, narrator, and historical actor. To what degree does the authorial narrator maintain access to his own storyworld (as an all-knowing or elided guide, as a highly visible or largely invisible curator)? Readers' experience of this constructed historical storyworld hinged on writers' selecting and fashioning settings and events; authors sometimes implanted their own (or others') eyewitness memories into third-party characters, who then functioned as surrogate narrators for conveying meaning. This proved particularly true for shared and prolonged sequences of events, such as lengthy crusade expeditions that tested and re-forged both communal and individual identities. As part of the process of authorial curation and creation, both the visual framing of the narrative (by means of headings, rubrications, marginalia, illuminations) and the associated texts with which the narrative was copied or bound might influence viewers to accept the narrative as authentic and assist medieval readers in interpreting the texts' meaning and function. Manuscript studies and variants, therefore, become equally or more important than critical editions, which often represent an artificial amalgamation of variant textual traditions, or privilege a certain textual transmission as more authentic than another. As William Purkis and Matthew Gabriele have aptly demonstrated, the incorporation of the Pseudo-Turpin legend into the *Codex Calixtanus* meant that that particular text assumed, by association with other texts, a distinctively different meaning for Iberian audiences engaged in pilgrimage to Compostela and warfare with local Muslim rulers, compared to that of tales of Charlemagne for other audiences in other regions. The Charlemagne legend was therefore both widespread and cross-cultural and yet also mediated and interpreted in different ways for various audiences.[2]

---

[1] Katherine Allen Smith, *The Bible and Crusade Narrative in the Twelfth Century* (Woodbridge, 2020).

[2] William J. Purkis, *Crusading Spirituality in the Holy Land and Iberia, c.1095–c.1187* (Woodbridge, 2008); Matthew Gabriele, *Empire of Memory: The Legend of Charlemagne, the Franks,*

In the best interdisciplinary sense, Marcus Bull also borrows from psychology, forensics, and the law to elucidate the process of memory making and to query the nature, limits, and function of individual and collective eyewitness perception and recall, as well as their contribution to personal and communal construction of memory. These queries directly challenge modern audiences' tendency to assume that texts which position themselves as "eyewitness" accounts are therefore more truthful and better sources for empirical data. As Bull notes, even eyewitness authors would have processed their sensory impressions through cultural filters and templates (of language, emotion, literary registers) and would have rehearsed and edited their memories with fellow participants. These consensus-censored individual memories would have been embedded within a collective and coherent authorial narrative shaped by cultural conventions (for example, epic poetry or biblical history). Twenty-first-century individuals still do this; the author of this review became only too aware of this multi-layered process and her own participation in it when asked to share her memories of 9/11 with audiences too young to have experienced that event. Her responses were edited by the student newspaper to conform with the other interviewees' accounts, local history and agendas, and established cultural memory – all references to President Bush's disastrous invocation of the word "crusade" and of crusade historians' attempt to set the record straight at the time were deleted.[3]

Similarly, medieval authors did not write in isolation, but fashioned their texts in dialogue with other textual and oral traditions and living communities. As part of this process, they had to select how they would position themselves as narrators within their own texts. Moreover, as new texts were read and copied (or orally performed), they joined the process of collective memory formation and influenced the language and templates available for the creation of long-term collective memory and literary genres. These templates ranged from travel or pilgrim literature to hagiography and sermons to lyrical poetry and liturgy, including hybrid genres such as vernacular histories, historical *chansons de geste*, or romances. Some of these genres required both detachment from and appealing to authorial eyewitness status, an effect which could be achieved through vivid descriptions and references to documents (letters) and material artifacts (relics, holy places).

Both Marcus Bull and Beth Spacey therefore point towards new possibilities for the study of crusade narratives which diverge sharply from the traditional empirical assessment of them as sources of verifiable data, a tension which points to history's attempts to encompass both the methodologies of the social sciences and the humanities. For example, was the crusade historian's tendency to subsume the narratorial voice to the collective "we" true only for high-stakes communal

---

and Jerusalem before the First Crusade (Oxford, 2011); William J. Purkis and Matthew Gabriele, eds., *The Charlemagne Legend in Medieval Latin Texts* (Woodbridge, 2016).

[3] Genevieve Coleman and Dagny Brand, "9/11: The significance of the tragedy, 20 years later," *The Observer*, September 10, 2021, https://ndsmcobserver.com/2021/09/9-11-the-significance-of-a-tragedy-20-years-later/.

experiences such as crusading or did it extend to other contexts and genres? If memories were forged as part of community consensus-making, did the process occur between communities potentially ambivalent or hostile to one another? For example, did Arabic narratives of the Third Crusade and Greek narratives of the Fourth Crusade dialogue with and shape Latin narratives? Did these traditions possess distinct conventions or exchange conventions for how to fashion an account which felt "true"? Similarly, cross-cultural conceptions of witnessing or bearing witness in sacred, liturgical, legal, hagiographical, confessional, and medical texts might also be fruitfully applied to narrative texts. Amnon Linder, M. Cecilia Gaposchkin, and many others have begun this work for crusading liturgy and memory, while Elizabeth Lapina and Beth Spacey have recently investigated the function of the miraculous in Latin crusade narratives.[4] After all, as anyone familiar with collections of miracle stories, visions, canonization inquests, hagiography, and the narrative tradition can attest, the verification and interpretation of the miraculous had to be carefully constructed for audiences to accept that an actual supernatural event had occurred and to reach consensus on what that event then meant for its immediate audiences and for the readership of the text recording it.

Similarly, Beth Spacey argues that, because crusades were often challenged, medieval authors consciously deployed the miraculous as a narrative strategy to depict divine approval or punishment. To determine what was viewed as miraculous required distinguishing between natural and supernatural, between visions, dreams, and prophecies, between heavenly signs and astrology/astronomy, pagan augury, and divination. For example, the well-known case of Kerbogha's mother illustrates how narrators employed prognostication to define non-Christian religions as "superstition," to convey the urgency of and divine pre-ordering of impending events, and to sanctify particular individuals or groups. Miraculous signs or happenings such as (from the crusader perspective) the capture of Jerusalem (1099) or Constantinople (1204) were legitimized as divine intervention in the natural order and in history – modelled in many cases after similar incidents in the Old Testament. However, as new theories of causation of the marvelous emerged, chroniclers employed "sceptical narrative intervention" to carefully rate their sources' reliability.[5]

The miraculous is arguably most commonly associated with hagiography, so it is perhaps unsurprising that chroniclers and hagiographers depicting Bernard of Clairvaux's organization of the failed Second Crusade presented Bernard as divinely inspired. Spacey notes, in contrast, the relative lack of the miraculous in descriptions of preparations for the Third Crusade, which she attributes to the many recruiters

---

[4] Amnon Linder, *Raising Arms: Liturgy in the Struggle to Liberate Jerusalem in the Late Middle Ages* (Turnhout, 2003); M. Cecilia Gaposchkin, *Invisible Weapons: Liturgy and the Making of Crusade Ideology* (Ithaca, NY, 2017); Elizabeth Lapina, *Warfare and the Miraculous in the Chronicles of the First Crusade* (University Park, PA, 2015); Beth C. Spacey, *The Miraculous and the Writing of Crusade Narrative* (Woodbridge, 2020).

[5] Spacey, *The Miraculous in Crusader Narrative*, 22–23.

at work, lengthy preparations, and the crusade's failure to recover Jerusalem. An alternative explanation may lie in contemporary propaganda's description of the loss of both Jerusalem and the True Cross to Saladin as indicative of divine ire and the necessity for repentance to re-win divine favor.[6] In fact, Spacey notes that those miracles which were reported for crusades immediately post-Hattin were used largely to exculpate particular recruiters, and either hinged on the repentant state of the recipient or punished recalcitrant sinners. However, most miracles were employed to indicate divine approval and intervention in battles. Heavenly armies or champions were reported to align crusaders' activities with the righteous warfare championed in the books of the Maccabees and/or apocalyptic literature.

It is perhaps at this point that Spacey's book might have benefitted from the work done on exegesis and the crusades.[7] While Spacey notes that divine chastisement for sins is a recurring leitmotif in crusader narrative, for medieval authors and readers alike, the Old Testament's cyclical presentation of history in terms of God's covenant with a chosen people (or individual), the breaching of that pact through sin (individual or collective), divine punishment (often by military failure), and repentance (rewarded by miraculous assistance) was perhaps the most well-known model in Europe for describing the histories of peoples and military campaigns. Spacey does note that particularly in the case of contested or failed campaigns, narrators turned to miracles to indicate God's intervention, assistance, or chastisement of particular groups or individuals and to assign praise and blame. For example, while monastic chroniclers of the First Crusade tended to treat it as one slowly unfurling miracle, narrators of the Second Crusade (Otto of Freising, hagiographers of Bernard of Clairvaux, and Bernard himself) concluded that the crusaders' sins had sabotaged the divine assistance pledged in Bernard's preaching and miracles; while an abject military failure, the Second Crusade nonetheless enabled individual salvation. The most systematic version of this occurred in narrative accounts of the Fourth Crusade and translation accounts which sought to legitimize the transfer of relics from Constantinople to Latin Christendom. Here miracles demonstrated the transferred saints' acceptance of their new clients or confirmed the sanctity of the crusaders' sacrilegious and forcible transfer of relics.[8]

Perhaps the most innovative section of Spacey's book comes in the treatment of visions and dreams, prophecy and auguries. The discussion here is reminiscent of late medieval debates on the discernment of spirits. There were two main

---

[6] See Jessalynn Bird, Edward Peters, and James M. Powell, eds., *Crusade and Christendom: Annotated Documents in Translation from Innocent III to the Fall of Acre, 1187–1291* (Philadelphia, 2013).

[7] See Smith, *The Bible and Crusade Narrative*, also Elizabeth Lapina and Nicholas Morton, eds., *The Uses of the Bible in Crusader Sources* (Leiden, 2017); Philippe Buc, *Holy War, Martyrdom and Terror: Christianity, Violence, and the West* (Philadelphia, 2015).

[8] For example, David Perry, *Sacred Plunder: Venice and the Aftermath of the Fourth Crusade* (University Park, PA, 2015); M. Cecilia Gaposchkin, "Nivelon de Quierzy, the Cathedral of Soissons, and the Relics of 1205: Liturgy and Devotion in the Aftermath of the Fourth Crusade," *Speculum* 95/4 (2020): 1087–129.

sources of authorities for discussing visionary revelations: synthesizers of Platonic philosophy and Christian theology (such as Macrobius and Augustine), and biblical texts describing dreams and visions. Narrators drew on these to describe revelations and frame debates over their legitimacy, most famously in the visions of Peter Bartholomew and Stephen of Valence during the First Crusade. For narrators, visions could demonstrate divine approbation or condemnation, provide specific instruction, rationalize the validity and transfer of relics, and reveal the otherwise unknown fate of the deceased. Here Spacey enters the ongoing debate over whether deceased crusaders were considered to have earned martyr status.[9] She concludes that, while there appears to have been greater certitude regarding crusader martyrdom by the Third Crusade, nagging doubts remained as to which crusaders merited martyrdom and under what circumstances. Visions and dreams could therefore not only confirm individual or mass martyrdoms but could either critique or demonstrate the legitimacy of an entire campaign (either through their specific interpretation or through their presence or absence). Another interesting dynamic of visions less explored is how visions could empower both those within and/or traditionally outside the textual community (priests, women, commoners, warriors, non-Christians or eastern Christians) to add another "text" or witness statement to the authoritative corpus. This addition could transform the interpretation of, or supplement, key doctrines and practices (such as the extent of martyrdom, the validity of certain relics or liturgies, the crusaders' imitation of Christ's passion, or transubstantiation) and could either confirm or contest divine approval or redirection of the crusading enterprise.[10] Crucially, sometimes Latin authors deliberately assigned such visions to putatively ambivalent or hostile witnesses whose attestation of miracles or prophecies favoring the crusaders therefore felt all the more truthful to readers of the account. For example, captive Muslims were said to have witnessed a heavenly army assisting the Christians' capture of Damietta during the Fifth Crusade.[11]

Moreover, creation itself could speak as an authentic revelatory text. From Augustine onwards, creation was viewed as another "book" which supplemented the holy scriptures. Many medieval writers and audiences viewed signs and marvels as including both unusual but explicable events (comets and eclipses, volcanoes, floods) and overtly supernatural phenomena. Christian authors had to confront the perceived tendency of classical and non-Christian cultures to seek to interpret such phenomena through "illicit" means (such as horoscopes, misleading

---

[9] See, for example, Miikka Tamminen, *Crusade Preaching and the Ideal Crusader* (Brepols, 2018), esp. 169–73; Ane L. Bysted, *The Crusade Indulgence: Spiritual Rewards and the Theology of the Crusades, c.1095–1216* (Brill, 2015), 241–45; Caroline Smith, "Martyrdom and Remembering the Dead of Louis IX's Crusades," *Al-Masāq* 15/2 (2003): 189–96.

[10] See, for example, the visions of Elizabeth of Schönau on the Assumption of the Virgin Mary and of the peasant Pedro in: John Shinners, ed., *Medieval Popular Religion, 1000–1500: A Reader*, 2nd ed. (Toronto, 1997), 128–31, 152–56; Megan Cassidy-Welch, *War and Memory at the Time of the Fifth Crusade* (University Park, PA, 2019), 92–95.

[11] Cassidy-Welch, *War and Memory*, 78–79.

prophecy, or fatalist astronomy). Spacey convincingly argues that this concern was amplified with the translation of the Aristotelian *libri naturales* and their Arabic commentaries, which contained "scientific" rationalizations for unusual phenomena which potentially reduced the incidence and religious interpretation of the marvellous. However, this reviewer has also argued that Parisian treatise-writers turned to the *libri naturales* to defend both the goodness of nature itself and miraculous occurrences such as transubstantiation and host miracles from "heretical" or "infidel" attacks.[12] Spacey argues that in a similar fashion, crusade narratives often dramatized these tensions through episodes featuring characters depicted as "Other," such as Kerbogha's mother. Celestial signs presented particular temptations, as recourse to astronomy or astrology from the *libri naturales* could lead Christians into determinism, superstition, or augury. Crusade narratives, therefore, included both inferred and manifest discussions of signs to signal both licit and illicit means of determining divine plans and to firmly situate particular events within the context of sacred history. Thus, monastic chroniclers of the First Crusade enriched their narratives with signs and wonders to signal the apocalyptic context of that campaign. However, Spacey notes that wondrous phenomena signalling divine approval were relatively scarce in other crusade narratives (with the exception of the *De expugnatione Lyxbonensi*), although accounts of the Second and Third Crusade contain a different genre of miracles intended to warn or redirect crusaders.

Ever plastic and revisable, prophecies – whether attributed to an ally (Joachim of Fiore), an enemy (Kerbogha's mother), or a neutral third party (the Toledo letter) – also utilized the marvelous and could be "reset" to apply to future campaigns or invoked to retroactively justify events such as the crusader conquest of Constantinople (1204). Yet further work remains to be done to gauge how historical narrative, biblical exegesis, liturgy, and hagiography might have furnished many of the terms and contexts for medieval audiences' and authors' conceptions of the distinctions between dreams and visions, true and false prophets, revelation or fabrication.[13] Spacey's book nonetheless contributes much to the field of crusade studies by broadening the chronological and contextual scope for the study of the miraculous and the crusades. It is to be hoped that she and others will investigate the ways in which the language of the miraculous (or martyrdom) was used in other contexts. These contexts could include genres treating "proto-crusaders" such as Constantine, Heraclius, and Charlemagne, other campaigns seeking approbation as particularly "just" or "holy" wars, sharply contested campaigns (political crusades,

---

[12] See for example, Jessalynn Bird, "The Construction of Orthodoxy and the (De)construction of Heretical Attacks on the Eucharist in *Pastoralia* from Peter the Chanter's Circle in Paris," in *Trials and Treatises: Texts and the Repression of Heresy in the Middle Ages*, ed. Peter Biller and Caterina Bruschi (Woodbridge, 2002), 45–61.

[13] See, for example, Jean Flori, *L'Islam et la fin des temps: l'interprétation prophétique des invasions musulmanes dans la chrétienté médiévale* (Paris, 2007); Jay Rubenstein, *Nebuchadnezzar's Dream: The Crusades, Apocalyptic Prophecy, and the End of History* (Oxford, 2019).

anti-heretical crusades, crusades in the former Byzantine empire, the Baltic, Eastern Europe, and the Iberian Peninsula), and crusading imagery brought to bear in later conflicts (such as 9/11).

To conclude, the study of crusader narrative is being transformed by critical editions and studies of the regional reception of narratives of the First and following crusades. Important work is being done in studying the importance of the reception, transmission, and adaptation of crusader narratives in different locales and contexts for different purposes and audiences. Further crucial research is investigating the intersection of crusader narrative with other sources: literary, homiletic, liturgical, hagiographical, historical, prophetic, etc. Both Marcus Bull and Beth Spacey have focused on the techniques used in crusader narrative for the construction of individual and communal identity and memory. But as both authors note, much work remains and many more techniques could be applied to narrative construction and reception, in particular, to the rationalization and contestation of individual campaigns and to the concept of crusade itself and the ways in which communities negotiated memory. Further research should be undertaken, not only in applying similar narratological techniques to non-Latin sources to see if this form of memory formation and construction applies only to Latin traditions, but also in investigating the relationship between narratives and other sources in terms of reception. For example, crusader narratives in the Western tradition were often bound with pilgrim or debate literature, with prophecies and/or materials on the natural world and the marvelous, with universal chronicles or very local histories, with vernacular sources, and so on. How did these choices shape reader reception and how did local scribes adapt crusader narratives to appeal to their audiences?[14] Jay Rubenstein has investigated this recently for the influence of apocalyptic literature on the experience and narration of the First through Third Crusades.[15] Similarly, the influence of the representation and deliberate evocation of emotions,[16] gender,[17] family and communal memory,[18] and conceptions of the natural and unnatural[19] deserves to be examined not only in narratives, but in a wide range of sources. For example, the various ways in which papal crusade letters combined narrative,

---

[14] See, for example, the adaptation of Oliver of Paderborn's *Historia Damiatina* for English audiences in Thomas W. Smith, "Oliver of Cologne's *Historia Damiatina*: A New Manuscript Witness in Dublin, Trinity College Library MS 496," *Hermathena* 194 (2013): 37–68.

[15] See note 13 above, and Jay Rubenstein, *Armies of Heaven: The First Crusade and the Quest for Apocalypse* (New York, 2011).

[16] Stephen Spencer, *Emotions in a Crusading Context, 1095–1291* (Oxford, 2020); Susanna Throop, *Crusading as an Act of Vengeance, 1095–1216* (New York, 2011).

[17] Natasha R. Hodgson, Katherine J. Lewis, and Matthew M. Mesley, eds., *Crusading and Masculinities* (New York, 2019).

[18] Nicholas Paul, *To Follow in their Footsteps: The Crusades and Family Memory in the High Middle Ages* (Ithaca, NY, 2012); Anne E. Lester, "What Remains: Women, Relics and Remembrance in the Aftermath of the Fourth Crusade," *Journal of Medieval History* 40/3 (2014): 311–28.

[19] Jessalynn Bird and Elizabeth Lapina, eds., *Crusades and Nature* (Palgrave Macmillan, forthcoming).

exegesis and exhortation also merits further research.[20] Pioneering studies have already been published in many of these fields, as the footnotes to this review indicate, but much more remains to be done. Sometimes the most influential scholarly books are those which act as a stimulus to further investigations and reset paradigms, a task accomplished by both Bull and Spacey and many of the works cited in the footnotes here.

---

[20] Rebecca R. Rist, *The Papacy and Crusading in Europe, 1198–1245* (London, 2009). See also a series of important recent articles by Thomas W. Smith, for example: "Preambles to Crusading: The *arengae* of Crusade Letters Issued by Innocent III and Honorius III," in *Papacy, Crusade, and Christian-Muslim Relations*, ed. Jessalynn Bird (Amsterdam, 2018), 63–80.

REVIEWS

Baldric of Bourgueil, *"History of the Jerusalemites": A Translation of the* Historia Ierosolimitana, trans. by Susan B. Edgington, introduction by Steven Biddlecombe. Woodbridge: Boydell Press, 2020. Pp. 224. 5 ill. ISBN 9781783274802 (hardback), 9781787444539 (e-book).

Research into First Crusade narratives has flourished in recent years, and while previously scholars focused greater attention on the so-called "eyewitness" sources, new work has highlighted the importance of non-participant accounts as valuable cultural artefacts. Baldric of Bourgueil's *Historia Ierosolimitana* ("History of the Jerusalemites") is one such example, and Susan Edgington's translation – the first into a modern language – means that it can be fully centred as a key resource not only amongst scholars, but for students of medieval history who previously could not engage with the Latin. Edgington's translation is based on Steven Biddlecombe's 2014 edition and includes an introduction by the latter.

The *Historia* is a non-participant account of the First Crusade written in Latin prose, consisting of around 40,000 words, with the main body divided into four chapters of equal length. Composed in the first decade of the twelfth century in northern France, the *Historia* is commonly considered part of the so-called "Benedictine revision" of the expedition's history alongside Robert the Monk's *Historia Iherosolimitana* and Guibert of Nogent's *Gesta Dei Per Francos*. The narrative is bookended by discussions of Jerusalem: the prologue and first few paragraphs of Book I recount the divinely willed nature of the crusade, both the distant and contemporary history of the Holy City, and events leading to the expedition; the final sections of the text – following the *Historia*'s primary source document, the so-called "eyewitness" narrative of the First Crusade, the anonymous *Gesta Francorum* – describe the crusaders' successful capture of Jerusalem (July 1099) and the Battle of Ascalon (September 1099). As such, like his Benedictine contemporaries, Baldric recorded the history of the crusade for posterity, but also refined and embellished the *Gesta* narrative, firmly grounding these events in both their historical and theological contexts.

Baldric, as abbot of Bourgueil and later archbishop of Dol, was a renowned figure in his lifetime as well as a widely read author with an eclectic output. As discussed in the introduction to the translation, the value of this project is underscored by Baldric's impact both on how contemporaries understood "crusading," and on how later accounts repurposed his version of events. Indeed, prior to the 2014 edition it was believed that the *Historia* only existed in seven manuscripts, but following Biddlecombe's extensive manuscript search a further seventeen complete or near-complete witnesses were discovered across western Europe. Furthermore, as noted in the introduction to the text, Baldric's *Historia* influenced numerous contemporary and near-contemporary histories of the First Crusade, including Orderic Vitalis' *Historia Ecclesiastica*, as well as the histories of the lords of Anjou and Amboise, and the vernacular lyric song *Le siege d'Antioche ovesque le conquest de Jerusalem de Godefred de Boilion*. It also had an impact on the thinking of leading intellectuals such as Vincent of Beauvais and Humbert of Romans. As such, while not so great a "medieval bestseller" as Robert the Monk's *Historia*, the number of existing manuscripts, alongside the wide readership and repurposing of Baldric's account, demonstrates the impact his text had on the shaping of the First Crusade narrative as well as on "crusading" ideology across north-west Europe from the twelfth century onwards – thereby making Edgington's translation both timely and important.

The translation is vivid and engaging, making the *Historia* an especially interesting resource for undergraduate students as well as a useful point of entry for researchers less familiar with crusade histories. Reference markers associated with Biddlecombe's edition and with the much-cited earlier version in the *Recueil des historiens des croisades* are used throughout. This is particularly useful as it not only allows scholars to quickly check references, but also provides students of medieval Latin the opportunity to cross-reference their own translations and thus develop and improve upon vital skills. Furthermore, the translation is rich with meticulous contextual footnotes, highlighting a wide range of themes and exemplars; from biblical and classical texts to contemporary and near-contemporary sources, Edgington signposts a wealth of archetypes and accounts utilised by Baldric, thus furthering our knowledge not only of his own intellectual background, but also of shared cultural practices and processes of meaning-making in the medieval West.

Edgington's translation also includes two indexes, the first providing all the significant variations made by the author of Paris, BNF MS Latin 5513 (known as Manuscript G), the second offering a list of people and places named in the text as well as relevant historiographical references. Appendix 1 (Manuscript G) is of interest to those working closely with Baldric's text or indeed on the development of the First Crusade "story," as this witness contains many long and specific changes to the base text. Appendix 2 is also an excellent tool for students and scholars alike, introducing numerous topics, from biblical names and locations to key crusade participants. Moreover, the translation also contains five maps, one depicting medieval Europe and the routes taken by the crusading army, the remainder portraying key sections of the narrative, namely maps of the sieges of Nicaea, Antioch and Jerusalem, as well as the route taken during the crusader march south from Antioch towards the Holy City, which also includes a helpful timeline of events. Finally, Biddlecombe's introduction is a condensed version of that to the 2014 edition. While comparison between the two is recommended for scholars working closely with the *Historia*, the introduction to the translation is an excellent entry point both to the text itself and to the reception of crusading themes and ideologies in the early twelfth century.

KATY MORTIMER
ROYAL HOLLOWAY, UNIVERSITY OF LONDON

The Conquest of the Holy Land by Ṣalāḥ al-Dīn: A Critical Edition and Translation of the Anonymous Libellus de expugnatione Terrae Sanctae per Saladinum, ed. and trans. by Keagan Brewer and James H. Kane (Crusade Texts in Translation). Abingdon: Routledge, 2019. Pp. xx, 278. 3 maps, 5 figures. ISBN 9 781138 296855.

This is a welcome addition to Routledge's Crusade Texts in Translation, which, unlike many other titles in the series, also includes a facing-page critical edition from the extant manuscripts. As the editors explain in the comprehensive introduction, the *Libellus* has by no means been an overlooked source for the events following the death of Baldwin V in 1186, but its reliability and its relationship with other sources for the same period have frequently been contested.

The earliest and most important manuscript of the *Libellus* (MS C, described on pp. 67–81) is a compilation made at Coggeshall Abbey in Essex, England. The editors demonstrate that the first twenty-six chapters had an independent existence before being copied at the abbey, and they argue from internal evidence that the original author of this first part of the *Libellus* was present in Jerusalem during the siege in the autumn of 1187. This makes his account of the siege the most valuable of the three parts and hence it is the prime focus of the introduction as a whole. The Coggeshall copy of Part 1 was written in one hand; a twenty-seventh chapter, added by a different hand, takes the narrative forward and is a quite brutal précis of the version of the *Itinerarium peregrinorum* known as IP2. Chapters 28 and 29, written in a third hand, are letters, also taken from IP2, purporting to be from Frederick Barbarossa to Ṣalāḥ al-Dīn (28) and Ṣalāḥ al-Dīn to Barbarossa (29). The change in copyist is illustrated by reproductions of the folios (pp. 70 and 71). Apart from his probable presence in Jerusalem, very little can be conjectured with any certainty about the identity of the author of Part 1, even whether he was a resident of Outremer or a traveller caught up in events. He or his amanuensis used biblical, exegetical and liturgical phrases and references in a way that points to a churchman, although the Latin is imperfect and the editors have not identified any familiarity with classical authors, such as would be expected if the writer were educated in the schools of western Europe. The process by which the account reached Coggeshall is no better known, but the copy C was made during the first quarter of the twelfth century.

In addition to this essential information, the introduction is careful to provide the historical context for the action of the narrative and the content of Part 1 is summarised. The sources used by the anonymous writer are discussed at length. The continuations of William of Tyre known as the *Ernoul-Bernard* and the *Eracles* show close parallels, but no conclusion can be reached as to how the *Libellus* fits into their "complex web" (p. 37). There is attention to the reliability of the text as a source, a key question, but as so often it is unprovable. If it agrees with the William of Tyre continuations it may be informing or informed by them; where it has unique information it is uncorroborated. However, the editors have identified unique parallels with some of the Arabic sources, which encourages some confidence (pp. 31–36). Detailed manuscript descriptions and discussion of their relationship establish a simple stemma, and previous editions and translations are listed.

The Latin text of the edition has been established according to sound principles, outlined in the introduction (pp. 105–6). However, the critical apparatus is seriously overburdened: although the editors have successfully shown that C is the earliest manuscript and the exemplar for the other three medieval copies, they have chosen to include every tiny orthographical variant, inversion of word order, omission, and addition from the later manuscripts, none of which appears to be significant. It would have been enough to list such minor transmission quirks and errors when describing each of the manuscripts in the introduction. The English translation is accurate and reads well. However, as is invariably the case, the translation uses more words and more space on the right-hand page than the parallel edition on the left. The publishers have dealt with this by starting each chapter on a new page and by leaving space below the Latin where necessary, which results in a lot of white space and a disjointed reading experience. A better solution would have been to spread the historical notes, which are commendably full, across both pages. It is also good practice to key them to the Latin text as well as the English translation. Three appendices follow the *Libellus*. The first comprises entries from Ralph of Coggeshall's chronicle for 1187, distinguishing Ralph's sources including the *Libellus*. The second is a gazetteer identifying places in the translation, where they are in bold font. Appendix 3 is a list of minor biblical allusions arranged by chapter and translated (major quotations and references having been footnoted). It would be of use and interest to have all the biblical references tabulated by book of the Bible.

Most importantly, however, Keagan Brewer and James H. Kane are to be commended on producing a sound edition and a readable translation of this significant narrative.

SUSAN B. EDGINGTON
QUEEN MARY UNIVERSITY OF LONDON

Muslim Sources of the Crusader Period: An Anthology, ed. and trans. by James E. Lindsay and Suleiman A. Mourad. Indianapolis and Cambridge: Hackett Publishing, 2021. Pp. xxvii, 291. ISBN 978 1 62466 996 5 (hardback), 978 1 62466 984 2 (paperback), 978 1 62466 997 2 (e-book).

In recent years, greater emphasis within crusades scholarship and teaching has been placed on Muslim perspectives and responses, with new books and translations from the Arabic and more Muslim-authored texts appearing in general anthologies. Lindsay and Mourad have added to this trend with a source reader composed entirely of texts from the Islamic perspective, many of them here translated into English for the first time. This volume will find a receptive audience among educators and students who wish to consider the crusades, and Muslim-Christian interaction more broadly, in greater complexity and depth.

A brief introduction first situates the book within the context of crusades pedagogy and makes a strong case in favor of a source reader focused on Islamic texts. The argument in favor of such an anthology is that it expands the scope of consideration of the period, moving from a view of the crusades that emphasizes societal conflict between Muslims and Christians to one that also encompasses other types of interaction, such as indifference, collaboration, and alliance. The introduction then addresses the concept of jihad, arguing that in practice during the time period of the texts in this volume, it was always understood as meaning "warfare against infidels" (xvi). Finally, the introduction gives a brief description of Arabic naming conventions and explains the editorial choices about which texts to include and why. The guiding principles for the selection of texts are the following: the editors preferred texts that broaden the chronological scope of study; texts that show a wide variety of Muslim-Christian interactions; texts that represent eyewitness (or nearly so) accounts; and texts that have not been translated elsewhere. Not all the texts are translated here for the first time, but Lindsay and Mourad generally opted to include texts that are not otherwise available to Anglophone readers.

What the introduction does not provide is a chronological overview of the events of "the crusades." The presumption is that the volume will be used in the classroom in tandem with other textbooks, lectures, and primary source readers. Footnotes in the introduction direct readers to both general syntheses and specialized volumes for further reading. In making the choice to forgo a narrative overview, the volume is able to quickly advance to the main event, the texts themselves. This choice also suggests that the introduction is mostly aimed at the teachers who adopt the book in their classes, rather than at the student users themselves.

The selected texts are wide-ranging in genre, time period, and style. Students will thus gain access to accounts and perspectives that other anthologies cannot give them. Each text is preceded by a brief introduction to the author's life and work, and then followed by study questions for students to consider. The questions aim to lead students to think about matters of Muslim-Christian interaction and representation in ways that include, but are not limited to, warfare or civilizational clash. The questions emphasize authorial perspective and agenda, and the breadth of ways that Muslims and Christians regarded each other. The passages are rendered in clear, idiomatic English and filled with explanatory footnotes. The footnotes will be welcomed by scholars and educators, but perhaps less so by students.

The texts are divided into six chapters. The first chapter contains passages from geographical and travel accounts. The focus here is on how Muslim authors regarded the Christian-held territories of Syria-Palestine, and how they described the sacred spaces, the cities and villages under Christian control, and the varieties of interaction that they witnessed between the Muslim and Christian inhabitants of the region. Chapter 2 turns to juridical and theological texts concerning jihad. The effect in this chapter is to demonstrate to students that there were various perspectives on and legitimate targets of jihad, even showing that some thinkers found enemies of Islam residing within the broader Muslim community.

Chapter 3 is the longest chapter of the volume, containing chronicles, poetry, and memoirs. These sources provide both eyewitness accounts of selected events and an impression of the cultural, political, and intellectual riches of Muslim cultures during the period. The inclusion of several poems is most welcome; poetry shows students both the depth of medieval Islamic culture and some of the roles that art played in interactions among groups in the region. Chapters 4, 5, and 6 include biographies, diplomatic texts, and epigraphic inscriptions respectively. There are biographies of Muslim fighters, leaders, and prophets (Jesus), as well as Christian physicians. These collected biographies show different perspectives on people and events, teaching students to think and read critically. Letters between Muslim and Christian rulers, narrative accounts of diplomatic negotiations, and transcripts of oaths and truces all demonstrate the complexities of the political manoeuvrings in the twelfth and thirteenth centuries. Inscriptions found on fortifications, gates, churches and mosques, shrines, and walls are particularly fascinating for the glimpse they give into the self-presentations of the donors and patrons of these structures. Fighting for jihad is just one of the many ways that such people wanted to be memorialized. This selection of inscriptions also shows readers the variety of types of buildings they wanted to endow.

The anthology's apparatus contains four appendices: one explaining the Islamic calendar, another containing the Qur'anic verses about war and peace, a third that gives a helpful overview of the different genres of Arabic sources from the crusader period and brief descriptions of the major texts within each genre (noting which ones have been translated into English or French), and a fourth providing a glossary of Arabic terms and names used throughout the volume. The volume also contains two clear maps dated to the early twelfth century, a bibliography, and an index. Students and educators alike will find the volume easy to use and understand, and it will give students significant insights into medieval Muslim-Christian interactions that went beyond simply conflict, clash, and warfare.

SARAH DAVIS-SECORD
UNIVERSITY OF NEW MEXICO

Kenneth A. Goudie, *Reinventing Jihād. Jihād Ideology from the Conquest of Jerusalem to the End of the Ayyūbids* (*The Muslim World in the Age of the Crusades* 4). Leiden: Brill, 2019. Pp. ix, 221. ISBN 978 90 04 41069 5.

For obvious reasons, the last twenty years have seen significant scholarly interest in the key Islamic concept of jihad, and published works on the subject have examined it from a variety of places, times, and perspectives. Simultaneously, there has been increased research into the Muslim "side" of the crusades, kicked off by Carole Hillenbrand's famous 1999 book *The Crusades: Islamic Perspectives*. In a number of studies, these two arenas have intersected, resulting in the production of various works exploring jihad within the crusading period. This began as far back as Sivan's

1968 monograph *L'Islam et la croisade*, but, more significantly, includes various recent works such as Köhler's study of alliances and treaties between the two sides, recently translated into English and published in the same series. It is into this specific field that Kenneth Goudie's book – based on his PhD thesis and focusing on the period until the end of Ayyubid rule in Egypt – fits.

And yet, from another perspective, this study does not fit into the abovementioned research space at all because, as its author highlights, previous studies have almost exclusively examined how jihad was manifested *in practice* throughout the crusading period, and they have mainly been focused on the politico-military elites. Goudie's monograph takes a different approach, evident in two main ways. First, it traces how the concept of jihad was interpreted by members of the religious classes rather than the political rulers, as jihad in theory. As a result, the work steps back from conflating the notions of jihad and counter-crusade, providing further evidence for how these were separate concepts at the time. Secondly, through a lengthy first chapter, it traces the idea(s) of jihad from the very beginnings of Islam up to the crusading era, thereby situating the ideas from that period of conflict within the much broader history of jihad ideology. This contrasts with previous studies, which have tended to see jihad in the crusading period as almost a self-contained phenomenon.

The work is divided into four main chapters. The first is, as mentioned, a lengthy assessment of the concept of jihad in the centuries before the First Crusade. In this, Goudie underlines the importance of seeing it not as something concrete but as an ever-changing idea that was (and, by implication, still is) employed by Muslims largely in response to external circumstances. This is highlighted through an examination of three separate jihad discourses from these years: the juristic discourse, the Sufi discourse, and the frontier discourse. In the first of these, which examines the discourse as developed by the *'ulamā'*, the origins of jihad are described, as are its comparatively early links to apocalypticism, how it was redefined by the very important scholar al-Shāfiʿī – after whom one of the four main Islamic law schools was named – in the early ninth century, and the development of further ideas by the eleventh-century religious scholars al-Māwardī and Abū Yaʿlā. Within the Sufi discourse, as expounded especially by al-Ghazālī (d. 1111), Goudie highlights, crucially, how that group were not peace-loving individuals in search of mystical fulfilment but were instead among the most militantly aggressive jihad warriors; following recent work by scholars such as Neale, he unpacks how the modern Western perspective of Sufism as a peaceful movement is based on a fundamental (and wilful?) failure to correctly understand the greater/lesser jihad hadith (in which Muhammad is said to have commented, on returning from military campaigning to other religious activities: "I have returned from the lesser jihad to the greater jihad"). The final discourse, that of the frontier, highlights how ideas of jihad varied depending on geographical location through a comparison of how the concept was perceived in the Hijaz and in Syria. Using the writings of the eighth-century figure Ibn al-Mubarak, who composed a treatise on jihad and its merits, this section demonstrates that the discourse on jihad in Syria was particularly militant in nature as a result of it being on the frontier with Islam's most powerful adversary, the Byzantine Empire (this is contrasted with the more peaceful understanding of jihad as found in Hijazi works from the same time). What this opening chapter does, then, is underline that jihad was a multipronged, multifaceted concept long before the arrival of the crusaders in the late eleventh century, highlight that the lands of Syria were a core area in which all three jihad discourses had been developed, and provide contextualisation for the rest of the book.

The second chapter examines one of the most famous jihad writers from the crusading period – although he was of little importance in his own day – Abū al-Ḥasan al-Sulamī (d. 1106), who has previously been the focus of multiple studies by Christie. There is an in-depth investigation of the single, partially surviving manuscript of al-Sulamī's jihad treatise, including when it was read out, the place of composition, and the quite considerable corpus of modern scholarship on his work. Then, Goudie turns to the content, and, through highlighting how much of the work is based, for example, on the pre-existing juristic discourse and on Islamic concerns with *fitna* (strife) and eschatology, he argues convincingly that "the success of the First Crusade acts more as confirmation of ideas percolating in Damascus already, namely the need for religious revival, than it did as inspiration" (p. 87); this is a particularly crucial and significant departure from previous scholarship and, importantly, suggests that al-Sulamī was not as original a thinker as has previously been believed. Furthermore, he argues that the Damascene writer minimised the importance of the caliph for declaring jihad and shifted the meaning of the term from offensive to, essentially, defensive warfare. In so doing, al-Sulamī employed some aspects of pre-existing Sufi material, ignored others, and added new perspectives to create a unique viewpoint on jihad in response to the arrival of the Franks.

The third chapter explores the life and works of perhaps the most influential figure in the field of twelfth-century jihad propaganda, Ibn ʿAsākir, who has been the focus of a number of recent studies by Suleiman Mourad and James Lindsay. In this, there is a brief discussion of several now-lost works that Ibn ʿAsākir is reported to have composed, followed by a lengthy study of his extant work containing forty hadiths for inciting jihad, which has been edited by Mourad and Lindsay. This chapter focuses primarily on that text but examines it especially in the context of the aforementioned Ibn al-Mubarak by whom Ibn ʿAsākir was significantly influenced. In fact, it seems that the latter took several key concepts from the former and utilised them in his forty hadiths work, including the merits of the *mujāhid*, the significance of right intention, and martyrdom being the ultimate end of jihad activity. However, it is also underlined that Ibn ʿAsākir added several new points to the ideas of his predecessor, including that the jihad should be led by the ruler (in this case, of course, Nūr al-Dīn); thus, there is no place for the individual *mujāhid* who had been right at the heart of Ibn al-Mubarak's ideas. Ibn ʿAsākir's work was thus essentially a combination of the earlier juristic and frontier discourses of jihad.

The fourth chapter examines jihad in the Ayyubid period, and it begins by asking the question of whether that dynasty did carry out jihad. Goudie's view is negative: they did not. This contrasts markedly with the views of earlier writers such as Humphreys and Hillenbrand, both of whom see the Ayyubids as carrying out jihad internally; Goudie instead views their various acts of religious "cleansing" – founding madrasas and other religious buildings, for example – as part of the concurrent, linked, but still distinct phenomenon of Sunnī revivalism. This explains the criticism heaped on the dynasty by members of the religious classes, presented in this chapter through a brief overview of another forty hadith work – this one by Abū al-Faraj al-Wāsiṭī – and a discussion of the writings of ʿIzz al-Dīn al-Sulamī, a rather aggressive Damascene Shāfiʿī jurist who was eventually exiled to Egypt because of his outspoken criticism of the town's Ayyubid ruler. Having been banished, he composed two pieces on jihad that virulently criticised the ruling dynasty for their failures to confront the Franks militarily. Goudie highlights how these works continued to contribute to the ideological development of jihad even as its practice ossified under Ayyubid rule. Not only did they continue to criticise the rulers – thus, in this sense at least, continuing al-Sulamī's ideas – they also carried on highlighting the importance of eschatological aspects.

The conclusion provides a neat summary of the work, and in particular demonstrates that the normative counter-crusade model does not explain the development of jihad ideology in the twelfth and thirteenth centuries. However, questions remain over a significant number of issues. For example, the text is focused only on the Sunnīs, and thus wholly ignores the Shīʿī perspective (something which applies to much modern scholarship into the crusading period); it looks almost exclusively at how jihad ideology developed within the context of the city of Damascus; and, by focusing on three main authors, it neglects various other works which would certainly be relevant, such as the section on jihad by Sibṭ Ibn al-Jawzī in his Mirrors for Princes work *Kitāb al-jalīs*. These comments are only lightly meant as a criticism of the work under review here, however, as it was limited by design. Much more pertinently, they demonstrate that, despite the book's highly detailed nature, it should be regarded as but one step at the beginning of the process of understanding the dynamics of jihad ideology in the crusading period, along with its practice; much more work remains to be carried out.

Overall, this is an excellent study by a young scholar who has a very bright future ahead of him. It will prove invaluable for anyone studying Muslim perspectives on the crusades and should be on the reading list for all crusades courses. The level of detail provided, new methodology, and the fresh perspective on jihad in the medieval period that it supplies – *pace* Christie, Mourad and Lindsay, and Hillenbrand, among others – mean that this will be an essential text for years to come.

Alexander Mallett
Waseda University

Eivor Andersen Oftestad, *The Lateran Church in Rome and the Ark of the Covenant: Housing the Holy Relics of Jerusalem. With an Edition and Translation of the* Descriptio Lateranensis Ecclesiae *(BAV Reg. Lat. 712).* Woodbridge: Boydell & Brewer, 2019. Pp. 276. ISBN 978 1 78327 388 1.

There is something special about historical writing in twelfth-century Rome. During this period, several writers associated with ecclesiastical institutions wrote with a keen awareness of the city's visual and material culture; alongside archival documents, authors used images, objects, and archaeology to write and rewrite the history of their Rome. One of the lesser known and rarely examined texts of this ilk is the *Descriptio Lateranensis Ecclesiae* (hereafter the *Descriptio*). It is a complex source: a compilation of writings that circulated in several versions of which the best known is attributed to John the Deacon (c. 1159–81). This account describes the Lateran Basilica in Rome, its history, patronage, and relics including the basilica's twelfth-century claims to the Ark of the Covenant. It is these claims to the Jerusalem relic that form the focus of Eivor Andersen Oftestad's valuable study.

Oftestad is concerned with how medieval writers presented and understood the Ark at the Lateran, rather than undertaking a wholesale evaluation of the *Descriptio* or of the Ark itself. Her central hypothesis is that textual claims to the Ark by figures at the Lateran were "part of a theology shaped in the wake of the First Crusade" (p. 4). This holds new implications for interpreting the *Descriptio* and for dating the first version of this work, which has previously been placed at between 1073 and 1118 but – according to Oftestad – should be refined to *after* 1099.

The opening two chapters offer an accessible overview of the *Descriptio* and its treatment in past scholarship. Here, the author expands upon the concept of *translatio templi*, by which she means "legitimized sacerdotal authority" (p. 11) and presents it as crucial to understanding the motives of those at the Lateran who sought to position their basilica as the inheritor of the Temple in Jerusalem. I would advise the reader to examine the second chapter (a walk-through of the *Descriptio*) alongside Appendix 3 which is the author's edition and translation of one version of this text (taken from the manuscript Reg. lat. 712 in the Biblioteca Apostolica Vaticana). This is a useful inclusion, although a few amendments would have added much, namely: Latin and English facing one another, further commentary on the Latin terminology, and more detail about the author's editorial choices (see the gnomic reference at p. 35). The edition underscores how the Ark occupies a small, albeit significant, part of the *Descriptio*; it is just one of several facets to this most mutable of sources.

The subsequent chapters address the *Descriptio* in relation to a particular geographic context starting with Rome before turning to northern France and Flanders followed by Jerusalem. The Roman angle has been the traditional framework for previous scholarly discussions, but Oftestad is correct in arguing: "an internal Roman context fails to encompass the wider significance of the temple objects in the text" (p. 7). This is one of the most original emphases of the book.

Crucial to Oftestad's argument is the presence of several versions of the *Descriptio* in manuscripts relating to monastic communities in northern France and Flanders, and these form the focus of Chapter 4 and Appendix 1. The author shows that these manuscripts consistently included the *Descriptio* alongside several writings concerning the Holy Land and the crusades. These texts are drawn from various genres, including historical accounts of the crusades; descriptions of Jerusalem and the Holy Land; and catalogues of rulers. Oftestad contends that the associations fostered in these twelfth-century manuscripts positioned the *Descriptio* as "a strategic part of the interpretation of Jerusalem after the First Crusade" (p. 61). The chapter continues by exploring how the Lateran's claims to the Ark impinged upon the hierarchical relationship between Rome and Jerusalem. In this context, Oftestad refers to the writings of Bruno of Segni, Bonizo of Sutri, the Norman Anonymous and his *Tractatus Eboracenses*, Robert the Monk, and Fulcher of Chartres. The fifth chapter, concerning "the Jerusalem context," features Fulcher even more prominently; it maintains that passages in the *Descriptio* were influenced by twelfth-century accounts of Jerusalem and culminates with a refined dating of the *Descriptio* to after Fulcher of Chartres' *Historia* which is dated 1106 at the earliest (p. 119).

The final chapters pivot back to Rome and examine the Lateran's claims to the Ark in relation to liturgical practices and legitimization. The discussion of Nikolaus Maniacutius and John the Deacon is particularly rewarding. In several places, the sense of theological and textual archaeology builds in compelling ways with Oftestad tracing how certain texts informed one another. By way of brief illustration, take Oftestad's discussion of intertextuality and John the Deacon. In his prologue offering the *Descriptio* to Pope Alexander III, John decries his lack of eloquence: he terms his work to be merely "ram skin depicted and rubricated." His language is, of course, replete with knowing eloquence, but, as Oftestad astutely shows, it also invokes the gifts for the Tabernacle as cited in Exodus 25:5 and 26:14 (pp. 173–74).

There are occasions when more could have been done to unpack the literary and rhetorical complexities of the *Descriptio* as a whole – and especially in relation to other writings about relic collections and relic lists (a burgeoning topic of research in recent years). Equally, the references to the material culture of Rome prove fleeting and tantalizing: the many visual and material evocations of Jerusalem in and around the Lateran Basilica during this period would have added a further – and largely complementary – layer of discussion.

Ultimately, as the author rightly notes, the *Descriptio* is a text without "a constant meaning" (p. 11). Oftestad makes a strong case for reading the *Descriptio* in relation to the First Crusade. More importantly, this book will reanimate scholarly approaches to the *Descriptio* through its attention to different readerships and diverse theological frameworks.

WILLIAM KYNAN-WILSON
THE OPEN UNIVERSITY, UK

Mihai Dragnea, *Christian Identity Formation across the Elbe in the Tenth and Eleventh Centuries.* New York: Peter Lang, 2021. P. viii, 118. ISBN 978 1 4331 8431 4.

This is a book on an important area and an important people, the Wends north of the River Elbe in the tenth and eleventh centuries. It is also a book with some clearly formulated ideas and claims. Unfortunately, it is also a book with a lack of consistency in argumentation, which makes it confusing to read and less convincing as a result.

Wends were converted to Christianity during the reign of Otto I in the mid-tenth century, Mihai Dragnea claims. Later descriptions by Christian authors of Wendish paganism have nothing to do with the pre-Christian cult. Rather they should be considered a deliberate Christian construction ascribing to the Wends a blend of Classical Roman superstition and magic with some Christian practices. This is claimed throughout the book. At the same time, however, e.g., Thietmar is presented as one of the "most credible medieval sources regarding the Slavic pre-Christian religion, and the Wendish idolatry." Dragnea again and again describes pagan rituals using the same Christian sources that he criticises for misconstruing reality. Can we then believe the sources in this respect, or can we not?

The Wends fought against Christian lords – they rebelled in the medieval terms – according to Dragnea for political and economic reasons and not for religious ones. Nevertheless, in several instances Dragnea seems to stress the religious confrontation. The great uprising in 983 had a strong anti-clerical background (p. 46), but at the same time the uprising was a political decision (p. 47), and the contemporaneous medieval sources emphasised the connection between religion and political submission (pp. 46–47). Chapter 6 on horse divination has very little horse in it, especially considering that the cultic horse among the Wends is well described in contemporary sources. Some explanations seem over-pedagogical but not always clear, for example when a priest's ordination is explained as transmittal of grace. There are uncertainties in the Latin forms, *illiterates* for *illiterati* etc., and outright mistakes as when the Ottonians' *familiares* are understood as their relatives. There are only a few mistakes in the English, except in the first chapter which may have been added after the book was finished and perhaps escaped more careful proofreading as regards language.

A chapter on the highly complex political history of the region succeeds in giving succinct information into the ever-shifting alliances between various Wendish groups and their relations to neighbouring Christian rulers. Dragnea here demonstrates his thorough knowledge of the relevant source material.

Dragnea has written a book on an important topic, but it would have benefitted from a more thorough proofreading and a more consistent argumentation.

Kurt Villads Jensen
Stockholm University

Bridge of Civilizations. The Near East and Europe c.1100–1300, ed. Peter Edbury, Denys Pringle, and Balázs Major. Oxford: Archaeopress Publishing Ltd., 2019. Pp. 318. ISBN 978 1 78969 327 0.

A conference marking the 800th anniversary of the Hungarian crusade took place at Esztergom, Hungary in May 2018. Esztergom was the appropriate venue, having been the early medieval capital of Hungary. Of the papers published in the volume titled *Bridge of Civilizations, The Near East and Europe c. 1100–1300* the Hungarian connection is limited to a brief summary in the introduction describing the participation of King Andrew II in the Fifth Crusade and a single chapter at the very end of the volume dealing with two minor military orders in thirteenth-century Hungary. Nonetheless, a strong Hungarian link is established through the extensive coverage of the archaeological research carried out by the Syro-Hungarian Archaeological Mission (SHAM) in and around the Syrian coastal zone. The work of that mission is discussed, either exclusively or principally, in more than a third of the volume's chapters.

The title *Bridge of Civilizations* is appropriate, as indeed it would be to any study of the Near East under Latin rule. More exactly, this book is about the architecture and material culture of the Latin East and predominantly that of the two great Hospitaller fortresses – Margat (Marqab) and Crac des Chevaliers. A handful of contributions break from the overall theme of Syrian coastal fortresses, fortifications, and material culture, but each of these forms a valuable contribution. These contributions include: a paper on the impact of the crusades on the Mamluk architecture of Cyprus, a paper on the Western metalworkers of Cyprus, the above-mentioned paper on minor military orders in Hungary, and a chronicle describing the surrender of Jerusalem to Frederick II.

The volume is divided into three sections: "Castles and Warfare," "Architecture, Art and Material Culture," and "Historical Sources," though there is little to distinguish between the subject matter of the first two sections that constitute the majority of papers. The opening paper about Margat Castle is authored by the SHAM project director, Balázs Major. He discusses the construction of the fortress and outlines its development, following "a well-planned sequence" that, because of its proximity to enemy territory, was determined by the constant need to defend itself. This is indeed a situation that is repeated in many other Frankish fortresses. Best able to cope with these conditions were the great military orders that, despite the massive territorial and financial losses suffered in the aftermath of the battle of Hattin, were, thanks to their external resources, able to commit to major building campaigns, and these continued throughout the thirteenth century, right up to the time of the Mamluk conquests. A paper by Bendegúz Takáts considers the methodologies employed in archaeological and architectural documentation. In this regard, great strides have been made in the field, combining the application of traditional methods and modern technologies such as terrestrial and airborne laser scanning, 3-D object scanning, and Structure from Motion (SfM). A paper by

Marwan Hassan discusses national (Syrian) and international efforts to preserve, study, develop and manage major Frankish sites in Syria. This is a topic of particular relevance in the light of recent history and the major damage caused at Crac des Chevaliers and other sites in this war-torn region. Zsolt Vágner and Zsófia E. Csóka discuss Crac – its medieval water supply and management system consisting of cisterns, channels, basins, and latrines. Such installations were basic requirements of any castle. Indeed, the adequate supply of water was as fundamental as were the fortifications themselves, for no fortress could withstand a siege if its water supply was compromised. Erzsébet Bojtár considers the masons' marks of both Margat and Crac des Chevaliers, adding to the growing corpus of known marks in the Latin East. Teofil Rétfalvi discusses burials excavated in the courtyard at Crac in 2017, a useful addition to a topic that, along with ongoing research at other Frankish sites such as the vast cemetery at 'Atlit, expands our knowledge on this formerly neglected field. Anis Chaaya presents a useful description of the fortifications of the town of Giblet (Byblos/Jubayl), notably its remarkable castle, describing the phases of its construction. Although, other than the castle, only sections of the medieval fortifications can be traced today, a plan of the entire fortifications, even if fragmentary, would have been a useful addition to this paper. Micaela Sinibaldi discusses Karak Castle and its various phases of construction, from the time of Payen the Butler in 1142 to the repairs following damage caused by Saladin's sieges of 1183–84, and presents various hypotheses regarding its components, notably the location of the main entrance. A paper by Dávid Kotán on the effects of stone-throwing engines on the fortifications of Margat, Crac, and Saone supplies some interesting insights into the use of different-sized projectiles for various purposes, and the possible identification of the position of the siege engines based on the find location of hurled projectiles and their impact marks. Such information may be of considerable use at other battle sites and enable a reconstruction of the besiegers' positions during an attack. In the final chapter in the first section, Mayssam Youssef discusses baking ovens and cooking installations at Margat, adding to a growing body of work on the Frankish remnants of such activities in the Levant.

In the second section of this volume, Ibrahim Kherbek provides a reconstruction of the medieval coastal town of Latakia based on recent fieldwork of what are largely fragmentary remains. He discusses its ancient port, the castle, a number of churches, the al-Fārus monastery, and mosques. Júlia Sárközi discusses the impact of the crusades on Cairene architecture, which takes the form of imitation of such Western features as pointed-arch double windows surmounted by oculi, triple archways, basilica-like layouts and, perhaps most interestingly, the incorporation of spolia from crusader buildings from Jaffa, Acre, and perhaps elsewhere. Taking direction perhaps from the volume's title, Andrew Petersen presents an interesting paper on another much-neglected topic, that of bridges: in this case, nine bridges of Roman, medieval, and Ottoman date located along the Lebanese coast. With a comparatively large number of streams running laterally from the eastern mountain range to the Mediterranean, these bridges were crucial for the security, economy, and rule of settlements in the region. Even when they destroyed the coastal cities to prevent a return of the Franks, the Mamluks retained and repaired these bridges in order to maintain easy passage on the coastal road. Hany Kahwagi-Janho discusses eleventh- to thirteenth-century chapels in two north-Lebanese villages. Alongside the principal churches of these settlements, the large number of small chapels is evidence of intense rural communal life in the region of Mount Lebanon. Patricia Antaki-Masson discusses a specific ecclesiastical feature – the piscinae that are found in churches and chapels in the Latin East, noting that these are evidence of the Western Latin liturgy. Continuing the ecclesiastical theme, Nada Hélou discusses donor images found in twelfth- and thirteenth-century wall paintings in Lebanese churches, noting that the artists appear to have used conventional forms rather than actual portraits of donors, and that their depictions were intended as preserving the symbolic role of the donor rather than perpetuating a donor's individual appearance. Another paper by Zsófia Márk continues the discussion of wall painting, in this case describing the important murals of Margat Castle including those discovered comparatively recently, in 1978 in the northern oratory of the castle church, and in 2008 in the nave, along with those found in other parts of the castle and fragments from the suburbs and in the nearby watchtower (Burj al-Ṣabī). Nóra Buránszki describes a thirteenth-century pottery assemblage found in the excavations of the central courtyard at Margat. It includes Port Saint Symeon type sgraffito bowls, various monochrome glazed bowls, cooking vessels, unglazed storage and serving vessels, and unglazed vessels similar to the "Akko bowl" type found at Hospitaller sites. The author notes that there are some individual characteristics found in the latter group at Margat and suggests the existence of a "Margat type." This may be the case. "Akko bowls" found in an excavation that I directed at the Teutonic house in Acre, in 1999/2000, also differed somewhat in form from those recovered at nearby Hospitaller sites. These undecorated bowls were probably made specifically for use of the brothers in these military-order houses, and their simplicity and lack of decoration was in keeping with monastic ideals. The variant forms suggest that they had been produced by artisans working near or perhaps in the houses in which they were used. Every publication of material finds adds to the overall corpus, and a more detailed publication of the finds from Margat will certainly be an important contribution to Frankish ceramic studies.

In the final section of this volume, Nicholas Coureas presents an illuminating chapter on the Western metalworkers of Cyprus, based on the evidence from notarial deeds of the Genoese notary Lamberto di Sambuceto that record the presence of blacksmiths, steelworkers, weapon makers, and cutlers in Famagusta. Denys Pringle discusses the itinerary of an anonymous pilgrim travelling from Hungary to Jerusalem at the beginning of the crusader period, preserved in different versions, and in an appendix compares two of these: the *Via Hierosolimitana,* and the *Vision of Othmar the Priest.* Peter Edbury examines the surrender of Jerusalem by the Sultan al-Kāmil to Frederick II in 1229 as it is preserved in the thirteenth-century *Chronique d'Ernoul.* He understandably refers to this as one of the most extraordinary episodes in crusader history, and notes that the idea that a Muslim leader should hand over the Holy City to the Christians is even more remarkable at a time when the crusader threat seemed less formidable and the sultan had consolidated his position after the death of his rival, al-Mu'azzam. This paper focuses on the manner in which the two heroes of this event, al-Kāmil and Frederick II, are presented in Ernoul's account. The final paper by Dániel Bácsatyai is an account of two minor and hardly documented orders active in thirteenth-century Hungary: the Order of Saint Samson, possibly a military order that was originally established in Constantinople c. 1206/7, and the twelfth-century Order of Saint James (the Spanish Order of Santiago). Bácsatyai suggests that the presence of the Order of Saint Samson in Hungary probably dates to the time of the marriage of Andrew II and Yolanda of Courtenay, niece of Emperor Henry, in 1215 or sometime between 1217 and 1223 when the former empress, Margaret of Hungary returned to her homeland. That of Saint James he assigns to the mid-thirteenth century, around the time that Bela IV invited the Hospitallers to establish themselves in the southeast of the kingdom in order to contribute to its defence against the Mongols. The presence of both, Bácsatyai proposes, reflects the realpolitik of the time: in one case, the promotion of harmonious political relations with the Latin Empire of Constantinople, and in the other, the need to defend Hungary against the external threat of invasion by Mongol hordes.

Overall, this is an admirable collection, commendable for the range of topics, the level of scholarship, and the extensive use of excellent colour illustrations. One might contend that with the large percentage of papers dealing with a specific site, the Hospitaller fortress of Margat, or with the single geographical region of Syria/ Lebanon, the handful of papers discussing other sites, regions or topics almost seem out of place. But if their inclusion somewhat impairs the cohesion of this volume (a state of affairs not unusual in conference proceedings), in this case it is more than made up for by the quality of the individual contributions.

ADRIAN BOAS
UNIVERSITY OF HAIFA

The Military Orders Volume VII: Piety, Pugnacity and Property, ed. Nicholas Morton. London and New York: Routledge, 2020. Pp. xx, 366. ISBN 978 1 130 49683 5 (hardback), 978 1 351 02042 8 (e-book).

This seventh instalment of *The Military Orders* contains the proceedings of the conference held in Clerkenwell in 2016. Divided into seven sections, with twenty-nine chapters analysing property, piety, and pugnacity in the military orders from the twelfth to the twentieth centuries, it is an impressive volume in its breadth. Following the editor's preface, Helen J. Nicholson's introduction (pp. 1–4) outlines the book's contents, beginning with a dedication to Jonathan Riley-Smith († 2016) and describing how this book reflects his impact on the study of the military orders in their diversity and chronological span. Nicholson rightly notes the boom in scholarship on piety, in addition to visual media, and works produced by members of the orders, and concludes by highlighting the increasing interest of scholars on various other activities of the military orders, and studies focused on memory, economic activities, and other subfields (p. 4), pointing out areas for future research.

The first section, "Property: landholdings (Malta)," begins with George A. Said-Zammit's paper (pp. 7–21), analysing two Hospitaller *cabrei* from the National Library of Malta and using the framework of access-analysis to these sources to consider property ownership and management under the knights' rule (p. 21). Daniel Borg and Mevrick Spiteri (pp. 22–36) then consider land surveying practices in Malta in the seventeenth and eighteenth centuries based on surveyors' (*agrimensori*) documents, emphasizing how these show how space was perceived, valued, and represented. Spiteri's article (pp. 36–48) considers property and the architectural developments in Valletta in the eighteenth century.

"Property: landholdings (elsewhere)" is the subject of the second section. Claudia Cundari's discussion of settlements of the Templars in southern Italy (pp. 51–58) is followed by two papers on the Teutonic Order. The first, by Jerem van Duijl (pp. 59–74) considers the origins of the Teutonic Order's bailiwick in Utrecht in the context of social networks and regional crusade plans, while Shlomo Lotan's paper (pp. 75–84) examines the relationship between power, status, and property in the early years of the Teutonic Knights in the Holy Land. Simon Phillips' piece on piety and property in Rhodes (pp. 85–94) rounds out this section.

"Property and Piety: economic activity and material culture" is the title of the next section. Giampiero Bagni (pp. 97–105) uses an interdisciplinary approach combining local archival sources and pollen analysis to study wine production in the Bologna commandery of the Templars. Unpublished archival materials are used by Ana Cláudia Silveira (pp. 106–17) to examine the administration of properties and raising of livestock in Ourique, Portugal from the thirteenth to the fifteenth centuries. Emanuel Buttigieg and Adriana Mintoff's analysis of Hospitaller material culture in the seventeenth and eighteenth centuries (pp. 118–28) focuses on "treasured possessions" owned by individual members of the Order in central and southern Italy and individual piety. Theresa Vella (pp. 129–36) concludes the section by analysing the themes of individual works of art owned by Hospitallers.

"Property and pugnacity: serfs, slaves and slave-trading" forms the fourth section. Clara Almagro Vidal discusses the importance of language and terminology in attempting to understand Christian-Muslim relations in fifteenth-century Spain, and how the military orders administered their property – in this case, people (pp. 139–48). Nicholas Coureas, using a large body of archival sources, gives us an insight into the relations between the military orders, runaways, and female serfs, on Rhodes and Cyprus, and how these groups were able to gain emancipation in the fifteenth century (pp. 149–59). William Zammit then discusses different types of conversion, namely "conversion by crisis" and "conversion by conviction" (pp.

160–72), concluding with a remark on the importance of conversion as a tool to complement the Hospitallers' martial obligations as a military order.

We move from the Iberian Peninsula and the Mediterranean Sea to the northern frontiers of Christendom in the fifth section: "Property, piety and pugnacity: internal politics and vocations." Barbara Bombi investigates the Teutonic Order and networking with the papal curia in the fourteenth century (pp. 175–94), while Karl Borchardt provides an in-depth survey of the Hospitaller priory of *Alamania* through charters of the prior of that region (pp. 195–207). Rory MacLellan then discusses "new" military orders, offering an overview of a series of orders founded for a variety of different reasons, ranging from social to political (pp. 208–17). Indeed, MacLellan's paper is complemented nicely by that of Elizabeth Siberry on the foundation of the Order of Sanctissima Sophia by Harry Pirie-Gordon in the twentieth century (pp. 237–46). The final two papers focus on the military orders and internal conflicts/disputes. Maria Starnawska analyses the Hospitallers in Poland and Bohemia, particularly the *communication* between them and their headquarters in Rhodes, and the exchange of knowledge about the defence of the island from the Turks (pp. 218–26), while Victor Mallia-Milanes considers the disputes between the Hospitallers and Venice in the Early Modern Period (pp. 227–36).

"Piety: charity and spirituality" is the title of the sixth section. Jaime García-Carpintero López de Mota uses the charitable functions of the Order of Santiago in the fifteenth and sixteenth centuries as a case-study of its hospital at Alarcón, using visitation records which result in a reconstruction of the hospital itself (pp. 249–57). Relics and "relic politics" in Prussia form the topic presented by Karol Polejowski and Sobiesław Szybkowski, who provide a source edition concerning the donation of a piece of the True Cross to the bishop of Warmia, Henry III of Sorbom, from Charles V, King of France, in 1378 (pp. 258–66). Paula Pinto Costa, Raquel Torres Jiménez, and Joana Lencart provide the final paper (pp. 267–81) on patron saints of the military orders in Castile and Portugal in the fifteenth and sixteenth centuries, considering the role of the orders in popular piety and "evangelical traditions".

The final section of the book concerns "Pugnacity and property on the frontier." Andrew D. Buck examines the Templars' and Hospitallers' contribution to internal strife in the principality of Antioch (pp. 285–95), while Alan Forey discusses the emergence of the military orders in the so-called *Reconquista* (pp. 296–302) based on a document that has survived only in a fourteenth-century copy. Betty Binysh then presents a wonderful analysis on the role of the military orders in keeping *peace* in the mid-thirteenth century (pp. 303–21). Anthony Luttrell examines the concept of pugnacity in the Hospitallers from 1306 to 1421 (pp. 322–28). We stay on Rhodes with the paper by Michael Heslop (pp. 329–44), who addresses the itinerary of Bonsignore Bonsignori's record of his visit to the island on the way to the Holy Land in 1498. Matthew Glozier brings us to the final paper of the volume, an analysis of the Siege of Candia in 1648–69 (pp. 345–55), viewing the siege through concepts traditionally applied to the military orders in the Middle Ages, namely memory, and the question of "what is a crusade?".

The volume is heavy on content, but is divided into manageable sections with sharp, focused papers. The editor, Nicholas Morton, deserves great praise for his work here and for presenting the book in a highly approachable format. Some substantive questions emerge concerning Polejowski and Szybkowski's fascinating paper: why does it not discuss *other* pilgrimage shrines in the Teutonic Order's Prussian territories, such as Juditten (Mendeleevo, Kaliningrad oblast'), Arnau (Rodniki, Kaliningrad oblast') or Toruń, Elbląg, Brodnica, and others. These places had relics of the True Cross and were the target of local indulgences issued by the bishops of Prussia. Anthony Luttrell's reference to the "ongoing brutal warfare" of the Teutonic Order in Prussia which, apparently, did *not* depend "on joint action with other Christian powers" (p. 323) also stands out. What makes that frontier of crusading more brutal than the others? What should be said of the support of the Order from a variety of Christian powers (England, France, Bohemia, and the Holy Roman Empire) throughout the fourteenth and into the fifteenth centuries?

The book's contributions very much outweigh these minor critiques. It is an accessible collection of studies, varying geographically, chronologically, and thematically, setting forth the richness of current scholarship on the history of the military orders. Particular strengths include the increased focus on the Early Modern and even Baroque periods, as well as the contributions of new source editions in the volume and the consultation of archival sources. This opens the topic to researchers from a variety of different specialities. This book will be of great value to students and researchers alike, across disciplines from history, archaeology, and art history, while also pointing to future areas of research in the history of the military orders.

GREGORY LEIGHTON
NICOLAUS COPERNICUS UNIVERSITY

Legacies of the Crusades. Proceedings of the Ninth Conference of the Study of the Crusades and the Latin East, Odense, 27 June–1 July 2016. Volume 1, ed. Torben Kjersgaard Nielsen, and Kurt Villads Jensen (Outremer. Studies in the Crusades and the Latin East 11). Turnhout: Brepols, 2021. Pp. 304. ISBN 978 2 503 58788 2.

The Crusades: History and Memory. Proceedings of the Ninth Conference of the Study of the Crusades and the Latin East, Odense, 27 June–1 July 2016. Volume 2, ed. Kurt Villads Jensen, and Torben Kjersgaard Nielsen (Outremer. Studies in the Crusades and the Latin East 12). Turnhout, Brepols, 2021. Pp. 222. ISBN 978 2 503 58786 8.

These two volumes, products of papers presented at the SSCLE's Ninth Quadrennial Conference held at Odense in 2016, mark an ever-growing proliferation of works focused on the short- and long-term memories and legacies of crusading, as well as its global reach. Or, as the conference title put it: the "Diversity of Crusading." Indeed, across the twenty-three essays contained therein, there are contributions which range in topic from the role of Roman law in the Latin East to the crusades' representation in the *Encyclopaedia Britannica*, and which encompass regions from the Near East to Western Europe, Africa, the Baltic, Scandinavia, and Mexico. For those who adhere to the so-called "pluralist" model of crusading, therefore, these volumes perhaps represent one of the clearest (and no doubt most welcome) indications yet of the field's wider adherence to, and exploration of, this broad-spectrum approach.

The first volume, *Legacies of the Crusades*, begins with a discrete thematic section containing Alan V. Murray's adapted keynote "From Jerusalem to Mexico: Unity and Diversity in Crusading, Eleventh to Sixteenth Centuries," a broad-brush, wide-ranging sweep across some 500 years of crusading. Starting, of course, with the First Crusade, Murray charts the diverse aims, motives, organisational underpinnings, demographics, and targets of various expeditions, demonstrating the movement's evolution from rag-tag "popular" bands who, under Peter the Hermit's leadership, marched ahead of the noble crusading armies in 1096, through to the elite, professional fighters, and colonisers who came to predominate crusading activities and exercised their fervour (religious or otherwise) in theatres like Prussia, the eastern frontier with the Ottomans, Africa, and the Americas.

Parts II and III, "Crusades to the Holy Land" and "Societies in the Eastern Mediterranean," bring the reader's focus more squarely onto "the East." This begins with Ahmed M. Sheir's discussion of the role of Prester John in influencing crusader-Muslim conflict between 1144 and 1221. Sheir tracks how the fantasy of Prester John developed and how it reflected hopes for a united, two-front attack on Islam at a time when the security of the Holy Land was ever decreasing. Next, Betty Binysh considers the processes behind Muslim agreements to cease crusading conflict, seen here through Saladin's acquiescence to the Treaty of Jaffa in 1192. Comparing three Arabic accounts ('Imad al-Din al-Isfahani, Baha' al-Din ibn Shaddad, and Ibn al-Athir), Binysh points out efforts either to preserve Saladin's reputation by ensuring the treaty was religiously justified and in the Muslims' best interests, or simply to present him as a military pragmatist, and argues that, in the end, crusading peace *was* distinct from other forms of peace. Tomislav Karlović then traces Roman law in the Latin East, as seen through Usama ibn Munqidh's accounts of Frankish legal practices. Working from the (cautious) basis that Usama's account is factually correct enough to be used empirically, Karlović sees the potential for echoes of the Code of Justinian – one likely limited to the burgess classes – in the well-known episode of William Jiba's demand that Usama pay the ransom for an enslaved Muslim woman he had agreed to free but who had since escaped. Part II's final chapter is Jochen Burgtorf's study of refugees in the Latin East between 1168 and 1192. Focusing on the "nameless civilians" found fleeing in the narrative sources as conflict raged around the kingdom of Jerusalem, Burgtorf sees clear indications – ones often overlooked in modern historiography, leaving our picture of the past incomplete – of not only the prevalence of refugee status, but also behavioural patterns (freeze, flight, fight, and fright) that contribute to this.

Part III starts with Adam Simmons' discussion of Latin Christian moves to assimilate Nubians into the *Orbis Christianorum*, which argues that the disintegrating stability of the Latin hold over the East led – from the thirteenth century onwards especially – to ultimately unrealised attempts at promoting wider Christian unity; this was characterised by an increased awareness of Nubia and its peoples as an important and distinct community of the Holy Land. Shlomo Lotan then makes the case for better understanding the important roles played by the deputies of the frequently absent grand masters of the Teutonic Order, who defended and preserved the Latin East by enlarging their territorial commitments, especially following the Sixth Crusade. Departing the Levantine mainland, Nicholas Coureas next charts the evolution of the burgess class in Lusignan Cyprus from 1192 through to 1474. Coureas demonstrates the transferral and evolution of Western practices honed and adapted in the Latin East, as well as the role played by burgesses (including Latin and non-Latin communities) in securing, upholding, and contributing to Frankish dominion of the island. Lastly for Part III, Nicholas McDermott offers a study on the Hospitallers' role in the enslavement of peoples. It is argued that the order engaged in enslavement across the Mediterranean and the Americas not simply because of their access to, and role in subjugating, groups of so-called "outsiders," but because of their need for labour – including agriculturalists, rowers, builders, and manufacturers. Furthermore, their predilection for manumission is seen not simply as good will, but a demonstration of power.

Moving away from the eastern Mediterranean, Part IV, "New Polities and Societies in the Baltic Region," turns instead to north-eastern Europe. It commences with Mihkel Mäesalu's discussion on the role played by crusaders in the thirteenth-century subjugation of Livonia, as seen through the imposition of "Acceptance of Christianity" agreements made between invading and indigenous groups. Exploring seven such documents, their form and function, Mäesalu sheds light on an underappreciated method by which Christianisation – both spiritual and political – was achieved. Next, Anti Selart considers the existence of *connubium* (marriage) agreements during the crusader conquest of the Baltic. Asking the question "where did the wives come from?" for the hybrid conqueror-native noble elites of Livonia, Selart outlines and weighs the evidence for intermarriage and the survival of existing families. Raitis Simsons then offers a study on the inclusion of Baltic peoples in the Teutonic administration of Prussia and Curonia in the thirteenth and fourteenth centuries. Simsons describes most especially the varied means by which Prussian communities retained agency and social status, while noting how their example can serve as a useful comparator to Curonian materials, if not quite to fill the gaps. Sticking with Prussia, the volume's final chapter is Gregory Leighton's discussion of how its Teutonic state might serve as an example of a crusading landscape. Tracking the legacy of the crusading past (the Order's and more generally), as well as the Frankish presence in the Holy Land, over fourteenth-century Teutonic activities, Leighton argues that such memories did indeed deeply influence their engagement with the landscape.

Turning to the second volume, *The Crusades: History and Memory*, which is not divided into sections, but rather contains ten distinct – if still thematically interconnected – essays, we begin with Christoph T. Maier's attempt to pinpoint the first crusades history; or, more accurately, when a "historian" first used the *word* "crusade." Noting the lack of a strict pre-modern term for these ventures (albeit not for participants), Maier argues that no medieval crusade "history" exists; rather they first appeared in the sixteenth and seventeenth centuries. He suggests, therefore, that scholars turn to writing histories of crusaders and not, anachronistically, of crusades. Jonathan Phillips then discusses memories of Saladin and the crusades in the East between the fifteenth and nineteenth centuries. Exploring evidence from across this period, Phillips demonstrates that such memories, especially of the Ayyubid sultan, were far stronger and more complex than some scholars have previously thought – for instance the site where Baldwin I's entrails were buried was ritually stoned but retains the name "Baldwin's Lake" – and that they were woven into the region's political fabric. In a segue into the medieval period, Carol Sweetenham examines memories of miraculous events at Antioch in 1098. Honing-in on the depiction of the Holy Lance and saintly intervention in the earliest Latin texts through to the *chansons*, Sweetenham outlines not only how the First Crusade's numerous retellings recast such miracles according to authorial need, but also the influence their stories had over depictions of similar events. Next, Kurt Villads Jensen brings our attention to the entangled crusading careers of King Valdemar II of Denmark and Emperor Frederick II, the latter of whom seemingly helped to imprison the former and demanded they crusade together as the price for his release. In doing so, Jensen makes clear the fraught diplomatic worlds that existed around absent and aspirant crusaders. The circulation of the text known as *Eracles* within Italy at the end of the medieval period is the subject of Massimiliano Gaggero's chapter, which focuses on borrowings made from it in the *Chronicle* of Galeotto del Carretto. Here, Gaggero not only demonstrates *Eracles'* enduring popularity across the European Middle Ages, but he also situates del Carretto's *Chronicle* as a vehicle for preserving, crafting, and transmitting the crusading heritage of the lords of Montferrat.

The volume's final five contributions are largely, but not solely, modern in focus. The first is Mike Horswell's discussion of the evolving presentation of the crusades across the many iterations of the *Encyclopaedia Britannica*. Like an ice core, it is suggested, the articles on crusading found in various editions of the *Britannica* can offer a snapshot of the climate of the time – in this case the developing nature of crusader medievalism; while we can also use them partly to trace the (at times alarmingly circular) genealogy of crusading historiography. Aphrodite Papayianni then offers a summary of a historiographical debate that rages around a Greek folk poem that some – Papayianni included – feel is a near-contemporary echo of a legend surrounding the murder of Emperor Henry of Constantinople by his wife (an unnamed Bulgarian princess). Returning to the modern era, Adam Knobler introduces his "Paradigms for Understanding Modern Crusading": six specific scenarios where crusading rhetoric has been used in the recent past. Discussing each paradigm, which range from European dialogues surrounding nationalism and imperialism to those perpetuated by Islamists, we are once more reminded of the varied resonances these expeditions hold. Next, Elizabeth Siberry charts the use of crusade imagery in First World War memorials. Examining sculptures and stained glass, as well as the depiction therein of crusading heroes (especially Richard the Lionheart and Louis IX), Siberry reveals the great push to coat war losses with a chivalric gloss. Finally, Benjamin Weber returns to the topic with which this volume began: the earliest use of the word "crusade." *Contra* Maier, Weber asserts that it *is* medieval, even if a specific term only emerged – in writing, at least – in the thirteenth century. He maintains, moreover, that this is reflective not of a lack of contemporary belief in the concept of crusading, but of normative linguistic behaviour and the movement's growth outstripping existing terminology like *peregrinatio* or *sanctum bellum*.

Overall, then, these volumes represent a useful entry point for many areas of study relating to the legacies and memories of crusading. It has to be said that not all chapters are of equal quality (which is perhaps to be somewhat expected from the proceedings of such a large conference), and there are some editorial issues here and there which should have been ironed out given the price tag. Nevertheless, many contributions are truly stimulating, and the editors are to be congratulated for shepherding such a diverse set of essays into something like a coherent whole.

ANDREW D. BUCK
CARDIFF UNIVERSITY

Michael Heslop, *Medieval Greece. Encounters Between Latins, Greeks and Others in the Dodecanese and the Mani.* London: Routledge, 2020. Pp. 368, 111 b/w illustrations. ISBN 9780367859077 (hardback), 9781003015697 (e-book).

Wer sich wissenschaftlich mit Burgen, Befestigungen und Wachttürmen des 1307/09–1522 über Rhodos und die Dodekanes-Inseln herrschenden Johanniter-Ritterordens befasst kennt Michael Heslops substantielle Beiträge zu diesem Themenkreis. Als Forscher, der sich in verschiedenen britischen Institutionen wie der Society for the Promotion of Byzantine Studies (SPBS) und der Society for the Study of the Crusades and the Latin East (SSCLE) engagierte, wurde der jüngst verstorbene Heslop (†5.4.2022) 2002 Honorary Research Associate und 2019 Honorary Fellow in Byzantinistik am Hellenic Institute des Londoner Royal Holloway College. Mit dem hier besprochenen Buch legte er 2020 eine Sammlung von zwölf Aufsätzen vor; neun publizierte er bereits 2008–19 in verschiedenen Fachbüchern/-zeitschriften, einer (No. 9) befand sich in Vorbereitung für eine andere Publikation; die Kapitel 10 und 12 erschienen erstmalig.

Schwerpunkte der Darstellungen bilden die zum 1307/09 vom Papst etablierten Johanniter-Ordensstaat gehörigen Dodekanes-Inseln mit ihren Befestigungen, wobei sich Heslop neben Rhódos v. a. den Inseln Chálki, Kálymnos, Kós, Léros, Nísyros, Sými und Tílos sowie dem wichtigsten Brückenkopf des Ordens an der Küste Kleinasiens, der Festung St. Peter (Bodrum, Türkei), widmet. Darüber hinaus thematisiert er Versuche der Johanniter weitere Besitzungen in der Ägäis, auf der Peloponnes und in Kleinasien zu gewinnen. Heslop analysierte zudem bislang unveröffentlichte Archivalien, um daraus neue Erkenntnisse zu Verteidigungsmaßnahmen der Johanniter zu gewinnen; ebenso erforschte er die Beziehungen zwischen „Lateinern" und Griechen im Ordensstaat.

Außerhalb des Ordensstaatsgebietes galt Heslops Interesse der Lokalisierung von Guillaume II. de „Villehardouin's Castle of Grand Magne (Megali Maini)" (Kapitel 11), die laut der „Chronik von Morea" ca. 1248/50 auf der Halbinsel Mani erbaut wurde um den slawischen Stamm der Melingoi besser kontrollieren zu können.

Heslops gesammelten Aufsätzen wurden ein Vorwort von Jonathan Harris (S. xvi–xviii), eine Danksagung (S. xix) und eine Einführung (S. 1–3) vorangestellt. Kapitel 1: „The Search for the Defensive System of the Knights in Southern Rhodes": Mit der Aneignung der Dodekanes ab 1306 gewannen die Johanniter im Laufe der Jahrhunderte unter verschiedenen Maßgaben entstandene Wehrbauten, darunter byzantinische Befestigungen, von Byzanz zu Kástra ausgebaute antike Akropolen, aber auch inzwischen aufgegebene Höhenbefestigungen der „Dunklen Jahrhunderte" (7.–10. Jh.), während der islamisierte Araber das Byzantinische Reich und die Ägäis häufig überfielen. Infolge der Bedrohung durch Mamluken und das expandierende Osmanische Reich versuchte der Orden dann seit den 1440er Jahren durch Neu- und Ausbauten von Befestigungen zur Verteidigung mit und gegen schwere Feuerwaffen sowie die Installation eines Wachtturmsystems auf Rhódos ab der zweiten Hälfte des 15. Jh. sein Territorium zu sichern. Heslop stellt dies am Beispiel des von ihm so benannten „Defensive System" im Süden der Insel Rhódos dar, wobei ihm viele der dort existierenden mittelalterlichen Wehrbauten nicht bekannt waren, die erst innerhalb der letzten Jahre bei Surveys wiederentdeckt wurden, etwa um Kattaviá und am Akramítis-Gebirge an der rhodischen Westküste. Zudem schildert Heslop das Bemühen des Ordensmeisters Giovanni Battista Orsini (reg. 1467–76) und des Ordensrates um eine Verteidigungs- und Schutzstruktur, z.B. durch die Ausweisung bestimmter Burgen und Befestigungen als Fluchtorte für die ländliche Bevölkerung.

In Fortsetzung des 1. Kapitels widmet sich Heslop in den Kapiteln 2 und 3 („The Search for the Defensive System of the Knights in the Dodecanese [Part I: Chalki, Symi, Nisyros and Tilos]"; „[Part II: Leros, Kalymnos, Kos and Bodrum]") den wichtigen Funktionen dieser Inseln und ihrer Burgen und Befestigungen zur Kontrolle wichtiger Seewege in Sichtweite der kleinasiatischen Küste, wobei der Insel Kós – zusammen mit dem Brückenkopf St. Peter (Bodrum, Türkei) – eine besondere Bedeutung zukam. Auch auf den in diesen Kapiteln behandelten Inseln konnten seitdem durch Surveys weitere byzantinische und Ordens-Befestigungen aufgefunden werden.

Im 4. Kapitel „Hospitaller Statecraft in the Aegean" zeigt Heslop die Möglichkeiten der Ausprägung des Johanniter-Ordensstaates in der Ägäis während des 14. Jh. auf. Intensiv widmet er sich den Planungen des Ordens zur Brückenkopf-Ausbildung auf dem kleinasiatischen Festland gegenüber den Inseln Kós und Kálymnos und der Funktion der Burgen Kadı Kalesi und Strobilos.

„The Countryside of Rhodes and its Defences under the Hospitallers, 1306–1423" steht im Zentrum des 5. Kapitels, für das Heslop bislang unveröffentlichte Dokumente sowie Texte und Karten des italienischen Mönchs und Geographen Cristoforo Buondelmonti (1386–um 1430) nutzte; Buondelmonti lebte zweitweise auf Rhodos und bereiste die Dodekanes; aus dem Jahre 1420 stammt die erste Fassung seines Manuskripts *Liber Insularum Archipelagi*.

In Kapitel 6 „Defending the Frontier. The Hospitallers in Northern Rhodes" thematisiert der Autor die Versuche des Ordens zur Sicherung des Nordteils der Insel Rhodos, insbesondere während der Gefährdungen des Ordensstaates durch Mamluken und Osmanen seit dem 15. Jh. Er rekonstruiert Sichtlinien zwischen einzelnen Befestigungen und Wachtposten und stellt Fluchtorte für die Zivilbevölkerung vor.

Das Zusammenleben von Griechen und „Lateinern" analysiert Heslop in Kapitel 7 „Rhodes 1306–1423. The Landscape Evidence and Latin-Greek Cohabitation." Wichtig für die Burgenforschung ist dabei seine Darstellung des *castellania*-Systems: Zur Sicherung effektiver Verwaltung und zum Schutz der Bevölkerung bei Angriffen war der Ordensstaat in Burgdistrikte, eingeteilt, jeweils mit einer Burg oder befestigte Siedlung als Zentrum einer *castellania*, als regionaler Verwaltungssitz und Refugium für Einwohner umliegender Dörfer und Gehöfte.

Im 8. Kapitel „A Florentine Cleric on Rhodes. Bonsignore Bonsignori's Unpublished Account of His 1498 Visit" folgt die Präsentation und Analyse der Schilderung der Insel Rhodos des Klerikers und Reisenden Bonsignori, der sich 1498 zweimal – auf dem Weg zu und von seiner Pilgerreise ins Heilige Land – dort aufhielt und in seinem Bericht auf Maßnahmen zur Verteidigung der Insel eingeht.

Der Text des Kapitels 9 „The Defences of Middle Byzantium in Greece (Seventh–Twelfth Centuries). The Flight to Safety in Town, Countryside and Island" entstand in Kollaboration mit dem griechischen Archäologen und Burgenforscher Nikos D. Kontogiannis. Diesem Beitrag kommt innerhalb der griechischen Burgenforschung eine besondere Bedeutung zu, da sich die Byzantinistik lange Zeit vergleichsweise wenig mit Burgen und Wehrbauten befasste. Einen Schwerpunkt der Darstellung bilden Befestigungen auf den Dodekanes-Inseln Kálymnos und Télendos. Auch hier versucht Heslop, Sichtverbindungen zwischen verschiedenen Befestigungen auf den Dodekanes von Rhodos bis nach Léros zu rekonstruieren.

In den Kapiteln 10 („Prelude to a Gazetteer of Place-Names in the Countryside of Rhodes 1306–1423") und 12 („A Gazetteer of Place-Names in the Countryside of Rhodes 1306–1423") widmet sich Heslop einem wichtigen, bisher nur in Ansätzen erforschten Phänomen: der Zuordnung von Orts- und Flurnamen. Ausgehend von einer Auswahl an Dokumenten im Ordensarchiv in Malta, in denen Land- und Gütervergaben auf Rhodos an Griechen und Lateiner durch die Johanniter im Zeitraum 1306–1423 erwähnt werden, gelang Heslop offenbar die Lokalisierung von ca. 50% der in den Urkunden genannten Orte. Dies ist ein beachtlicher Anfang, doch bleibt darüber hinaus die Untersuchung zahlreicher Orts- und Flurnamen, die auf mögliche Befestigungen verweisen (z.B. *Kastrélia, Meroúgli, Pirgia*) ein Desiderat der Forschung, zu dem sich letztlich die Wissenschaftler/-innen, die dazu forschten zusammenfinden müssten; Heslop lieferte dazu eine Basis.

Während der 215-jährigen Herrschaft des Johanniter-Ritterordens über die Dodekanes (1307–1522) waren Burgen anfangs Instrumente seiner Expansion; er übernahm ältere Kástra und versuchte, durch Eroberung Brückenköpfe sowie durch Kauf und Verträge Burgen und Städte außerhalb seines 1307/09 begründeten Ordensstaates zu gewinnen, in der Ägäis, auf der Peloponnes und dem griechischen Festland. Ab dem frühen 15. Jh. waren die Johanniter zunehmend mamlukischen und türkischen Angriffen ausgesetzt; das expandierende Osmanische Reich entwickelte sich zur dauerhaften Bedrohung. Burgen und Befestigungen waren nun nicht mehr Instrumente der Expansion des Ordens, sie wurden zu Orten des Schutzes der Bevölkerung gegen zahlreiche türkische Überfälle auf Dörfer, mit der Absicht, Menschen zu versklaven. Gegen die effektive osmanische Artillerie baute der Orden viele Befestigungen zu Festungen aus, die zu den bedeutendsten ihrer Zeit in Europa gehörten. Michael Heslops Forschungen erbrachten zu ihren Erscheinungsterminen viele neue Aspekte zur Erschließung dieses international bedeutenden Objektbestandes. Leider konnte er seine Forschungsergebnisse nicht mehr aktualisieren, was auf Basis der inzwischen von Forschern/-innen aus verschiedenen Ländern gewonnenen zahlreichen neuen historischen, archäologischen und burgenkundlichen Erkenntnissen wünschenswert gewesen wäre.

Heslops Buch bietet über die substantiellen Texte hinaus wertvolle Materialsammlungen, z.B. die Auflistung der Besuche „westlicher" Reisender auf Rhodos 1480–1519 (S. 167). Zehn Übersichtskarten sowie zahlreiche Illustrationen und Fotografien vervollständigen das Werk. Unvollständig ist die Bibliographie, doch ist es ein allgemeines Manko der Johanniter-Burgenforschung, dass nicht-englischsprachige Publikationen oft nicht wahrgenommen werden; so fehlen z.B. die Arbeiten des tschechischen Kollegen Miroslav Plaček, aber auch Stephen C. Spiteris grundlegendes Werk *Fortresses of the Cross. Hospitaller Military Architecture (1136–1798)* (1994) im Literaturverzeichnis. Trotzdem ist Heslops Buch uneingeschränkt allen zu empfehlen, die sich mit Burgen und Befestigungen in Griechenland beschäftigen.

MICHAEL LOSSE
INDEPENDENT SCHOLAR, SINGEN

Rombert Stapel, *Medieval Authorship and Cultural Exchange in the Late Fifteenth Century: The Utrecht Chronicle of the Teutonic Order*. London: Routledge, 2021. Pp. vii, 440. ISBN 978 0 367 373227 6.

Rombert Stapel's comprehensive study of the Middle Dutch *Croniken van der Duytscher Oirden* (Chronicle of the Teutonic Order) uses the recent discovery of two copies of the chronicle, one in the Teutonic Order's central archive in Vienna (*We₁*) and the other in Ghent's city archive (*Ge*), to uncover the Low Countries connections to the Teutonic Order's extensive knowledge network. Claiming that *We₁* is in fact an authorial copy due to its dating in the late fifteenth century, Stapel argues that the *Croniken*'s author was motivated not only by the Teutonic Order's defeat in the Thirteen Years War (1454–66), but also by rising competition for funds and spiritual legitimacy with a Hospitaller commandery in Haarlem that had been aggressively disseminating news of their success against the Ottomans at the Siege of Rhodes in 1480. This book is the first in-depth study of the *Croniken* and as such it employs an array of techniques that range from traditional philology to digital research. Stapel's methodology is the book's greatest strength, as it painstakingly validates each of the author's arguments.

Stapel introduces the *Croniken* with an overview of the narrative tradition of military orders. While the Teutonic Order's written origin legends did not have the complexity of the Hospitallers', the rising prominence of the Haarlem commandery prompted the author of the *Croniken* to craft the Order's most sophisticated founding legend in the text's prologue. Despite the *Croniken*'s novel attempt to mix biblical history with the origins of the Teutonic Order, the vast number of the Order's chronicles and the labeling of the *Croniken* as the *Jüngere Hochmeisterchronik* (Younger Grand Master's Chronicle) in the first compilation of the Order's historical works, led the text to be unfairly considered by previous scholars as a mere "afterbirth of the Teutonic Order's chronicle tradition" (p. 16). Moving onto the *Croniken's* manuscripts themselves in the second chapter, Stapel notes the *Croniken*'s wide dissemination across libraries in the Low Countries, Livonia, and Prussia, paying particular attention to correlations between the German translations and *We₁* that do not exist in later Middle Dutch copies which were copied from *Ge*. This fact, *We₁*'s phased genesis from approximately 1480 to around 1496, its inclusion of editorial amendments, its closeness to its sources, and signs that only one person was responsible for the manuscript's production allow Stapel to credibly demonstrate that *We₁* is an authorial copy.

The most important sections of the book are the two following chapters on sources and composition, and sources in context. In Chapter 3, Stapel indicates that, although the *Croniken* owed a great deal to the Teutonic Order's previous tradition of chronicle-writing that had been established in the early fourteenth century by Peter von Dusburg, it did not simply copy Dusburg's format. Instead, its author made the first and only attempt to create a history that centered on the Holy Land and incorporated all the Teutonic Order's branches. This required the *Croniken* to include an extraordinarily wide array of sources which ranged from Middle Dutch religious texts and crusading histories written outside of the Order's historiography to Prussian and Livonian chronicles and archival sources. The Middle Dutch *Croniken*'s 800 chapters contained the prologue, a history of the Teutonic Order organized by the lives and genealogies of the grandmasters and occasionally interrupted by lists of privileges and indulgences, a history of the Utrecht bailiwick, and a list of Prussian and Livonian commanderies. While moments such as the Fall of Acre and the creation of the Teutonic Order's coat of arms necessarily required a range of sources not found in the narrative tradition crafted by Dusburg, even the *Croniken*'s description of Prussian and Livonian history made use of different sources such as letters, privileges, and court cases. The author's continued interest in the privileges and indulgences granted to the various branches of the Teutonic Order underscored his vision of the Order as an organization of nobles entitled to a high degree of autonomy. As discussed in the fourth chapter, the author's ability to combine various historiographical traditions with these archival documents required him to travel across much of Europe. Here Stapel masterfully maps out the wide expanse of the Teutonic Order's network of cultural and intellectual exchange, which connected Prussian and Livonian libraries to locations across the Holy Roman Empire.

The *Croniken*'s author's profile as a skilled writer interested in genealogy and able to travel outside of the Low Countries leads Stapel to argue in the fifth chapter that the former must have been Johan van Drongelen, the land commander of the Utrecht bailiwick from 16 July 1469 to 15 August 1492. He not only had the ability to cover the vast distances necessary to write the *Croniken* but was renowned for his knowledge of both noble genealogies and historical writing. A stylometric analysis of We_1, a statistical study of style, finds that although a scribe named Hendrik van Vianen physically wrote the *Croniken* and completed it after Drongelen's death, Drongelen was the principal author. Stapel concludes his work by reemphasizing the historical context which led to the creation of the *Croniken*, namely the Teutonic Order's defeat in the Thirteen Years War and the growing fame of the Hospitallers after the Siege of Rhodes. He also comments on how Grand Master Albrecht of Brandenburg-Ansbach's secularization of the Teutonic Order's lands in Prussia led to the *Croniken*'s wide dissemination as the Teutonic Order propagandized their claims in the Baltic, while Lutherans in Prussia and Livonia used Drongelen's *Croniken* to connect their local histories to a grand biblical narrative. Ironically, Drongelen's advocacy for regionalism within the Teutonic Order undermined the same networks that made the writing and dissemination of his *Croniken* possible. Stapel's excellent contribution to the study of the Teutonic Order's historiography bears consideration for anyone interested in the intersection of cultural history and the history of military orders in the Late Middle Ages.

PATRICK EICKMAN
UNIVERSITY OF WISCONSIN-MADISON

SOCIETY FOR THE STUDY OF THE CRUSADES AND THE LATIN EAST (SSCLE)

BULLETIN No. 42, 2022

Contents

Editorial

Firstly, I would like to thank the membership for submitting the forms that make this bulletin possible. The bulletin provides an introduction to the research carried out by our members across our field, and exists to stimulate discussion and cooperation between members new and old. The membership of the Society for the Study of the Crusades and the Latin East has grown considerably in the last year thanks to the efforts of our treasurer Dr Simon Parsons, and it is a sign of this success that this year's bulletin has grown accordingly. The number and quality of the entries this year is a strong signal of the strength of our field even in these difficult times.

At the time of writing, the SSCLE has just held its 10th Quadrenial Conference at Royal Holloway, University of London. As a member of the conference organising committee, it was a great pleasure to meet so many of our members in person and online. Following the success of the online event held for doctoral students and Early Career Researchers, held last summer at Royal Holloway, University of London, I am confident many papers and publications will emerge from this summer's meeting to fill the pages of future bulletins.

This marks my first solo effort as the new bulletin editor - eagle-eyed members will note that I have assisted Dr Nikolaos Chrissis for the past two years in compiling the bulletin. I would like to take this opportunity to thank Nikolaos for all of his support during the recent elections and the handover period. I hope that if the membership has any suggestions for improvements to the bulletin you will not hestitate to contact me.

This is an exciting time for the SSCLE, particularly as the journal moves online including the past issues. This development means that the bulletin will evolve beyond its current form in the coming years. The society's social media presence has increased dramatically thanks to the work of Dr Gordon Reynolds. As well as an online publication after the May deadline, bulletin entries could also inform the SSCLE's social media content to bring the exciting research of our membership in the form of new publications, book launches, and in-person and virtual papers to the attention of an even wider audience and in even more timely manner. I remind the membership that if you have any further suggestions for specific content for our social media platforms, please contact Gordon via sscle.socialmedia@outlook.com.

If you would like to be included in the next bulletin, please complete the Word document sent by the Treasurer when your membership is due. I draw your attention to the style guide included on the form, which I really appreciate members following since it does ensure a smoother editing process for the bulletin. Please continue to send your forms to the treasury email address: sscle123@gmail.com.

With many thanks and kind regards,

Dr Danielle E.A Park
Bulletin Editor

Message from the President

Dear Friends,

It is a real pleasure to write my first presidential message for the Bulletin. I am greatly honoured to have been elected to the post and very much look forward to holding office. Particular thanks to my immediate predecessor, Professor Adrian Boas, for his exemplary work as president from 2016 to 2021. I would also like to express my gratitude to the other members of the committee during that period, namely Nikos Chrissis, Danielle Park, Simon Parsons, Kyle Lincoln and François-Olivier Touati.

As I write, we have just completed the postponed 10th quadrennial SSCLE conference at Royal Holloway, University of London (27 June to 1 July 2022). After what seems an age of online only events it was a delight to share the energy and immediacy of a face to face gathering. We had over 190 people present in person as speakers and attendees with many more joining us online; the participation of six major publishers was also very welcome. I am happy to record that Kate Arnold of Nottingham Trent University won the prize for Best Paper by a Postgraduate/Early Career Researcher for her 'Pop and the Palästinalied: A Crusade Song Revived at the Turn of the New Millennium'. We were also very pleased to launch the SSCLE Best First Book Award, named in honour of our dear friend and colleague, Ronnie Ellenblum who passed away in January 2021. The winner, from an excellent field, was Dr Stephen Spencer's *Emotions in a Crusading Context, 1095-1291* (Oxford University Press, 2019). This prize will be awarded in alternate years, running between another new initiative, the SSCLE Best Book Award, which will be first presented in 2023. Details of both competitions can be found on the SSCLE website.

Finally, I am delighted to record that Crusades itself will, from 2023, have an online, as well as a physical form. We have signed a contract with Taylor and Francis (Routledge) which will mean two issues a year, a more streamlined editorial process and, crucially, a presence as a searchable online resource, including back issues, something that will bring far greater prominence both to the journal and the excellent research therein. This, along with a steadily rising membership, gives us all cause for optimism and excitement in our shared academic endeavours.

With all best wishes,

Jonathan Phillips, Professor of Crusading History,
Royal Holloway University of London
President of the SSCLE, July 2022

Practical Information

Dr Simon Parsons is the Treasurer of the SSCLE. If you have any queries concerning your subscriptions and payments, please contact him at the following address: **sscle123@gmail. com.**

The Bulletin Editor would like to remind you that, in order to avoid delays, she needs to have information for the Bulletin each year at an early date, usually by May. Please, conform the presentation of your information with the typographic model of this Bulletin. Use – if possible – the style of the last Bulletin in the presentation of your activities and publications. The best is to send them in attached document (via email), when you subscribe. The address of the Bulletin Editor is: **Dr Danielle Park**, Department of History, Royal Holloway, University of London, Egham, Surrey, TW20 0EX, UK; danielle.park@rhul.ac.uk.

I want to thank all members who provide bibliographical data. In order to make the *Bulletin* more useful for you, it would be helpful if those members who edit proceedings or essay volumes could let the Bulletin Editor know not only about their own papers but also on the other papers in such volumes. You are encouraged to supply any information via email.

Dr Kyle C. Lincoln is **webmaster** for the official website of the SSCLE (https:// societyforthestudyofthecrusadesandthelatineast.wildapricot.org/). There you will be able to find news about the SSCLE and its publications as well as bibliographical data and other information of interest to members.

Our journal entitled *Crusades*, now n° 21, 2022 allows the Society to publish articles and texts; encourages research in neglected subfields; invites a number of authors to deal with a specific problem within a comparative framework; initiates and reports on joint programmes; and offers reviews of books and articles.

Editors: Jonathan Phillips, Iris Shagrir and Benjamin Z. Kedar; Associate Editor: Nikolaos G. Chrissis; Reviews Editor: Torben Kjersgaard Nielsen; Archaeology Editor: Denys R. Pringle. Colleagues may submit papers for consideration to either Professor Jonathan Phillips or Professor Iris Shagrir. Information on the style sheet can be found in the back of this booklet.

The journal includes a section of book reviews. In order to facilitate the Reviews Editor's work, could members please ask their publishers to send copies to: **Professor Torben Kjersgaard Nielsen, Reviews Editor, *Crusades*, Dpt. of Politics and Society, Aalborg University, Fibigerstraede 1, 02, 9220 Aalborg N, DENMARK; tkn@dps.aau.dk.** Please note that *Crusades* reviews books concerned with any aspect(s) of the history of the crusades and the crusade movement, the military orders and the Latin settlements in the Eastern Mediterranean, but not books which fall outside this range.

Current subscription fees are as follows:
• Membership and Bulletin of the Society: Single £10, $12 or €12;
• Student £6, $7 or €7;
• Joint membership £15, $19 or €18 (for two members sharing the same household);
• Membership and the journal *Crusades*, including the Bulletin: please add to your subscription fees: £25, $31 or €29 for a **hard copy**, OR £15, $19 or €18 for an **electronic copy** of the journal.
• If a member wishes to purchase back issues of *Crusades*, each back issue costs £35, $43 or €41.

The cost of the journal to institutions and non-members is £115, US$140.

Cheques in these currencies should be made payable to SSCLE. For information on other forms of payment contact the treasurer.

Those members who do not subscribe to the journal will receive the Bulletin from the Bulletin Editor.

List of abbreviations

Crusading and Archaeology	*Crusading and Archaeology. Some Archaeological Approaches to the Crusades*, ed. Vardit R. Shotten-Hallel and Rosie Weetch, Crusades – Subsidia 14, London and New York, Routledge, 2021 [2020].
Chronicle, Crusade, and the Latin East	*Chronicle, Crusade, and the Latin East: Essays in Honour of Susan B. Edgington, Outremer. Studies in the Crusades and the Latin East 16* (Turnhout: Brepols, 2022).
De la Bourgogne à l'Orient	*De la Bourgogne à l'Orient: Mélanges offerts à Monsieur le Doyen Jean Richard*, ed. Jacques Meissonnier, *Mémoires de l'Académie des sciences, arts et belles-lettres de Dijon 148, Dijon, Académie des sciences, arts et belles-lettres de Dijon, 2020.*
Exploring Outremer Volume 2	*Exploring Outremer Volume 2: Studies in Crusader Archaeology in Honour of Adrian J. Boas*, Crusades – Subsidia, London: Routledge, forthcoming.
ICMS (following the year)	International Congress on Medieval Studies, Kalamazoo, USA.
IMC (following the year)	International Medieval Congress, Leeds, UK.
MO, 7	*The Military Orders, Volume VII: Piety, Pugnacity and Property*, ed. Nicholas Morton, London and New York, Routledge, 2019.
Settlement and Crusade	*Settlement and Crusade in the Thirteenth Century: Multidisciplinary Studies of the Latin East*, ed. Gil Fishhof, Judith Bronstein, and Vardit R. Shotten-Hallel, Crusades – Subsidia 15, London: Routledge, 2021.

1. Recent publications

ALVIRA-CABRER, Martín, Jean de Joinville, *Vida de San Luis*, Spanish translation, introduction, notes, appendices, maps, and indexes, Cáceres, Universidad de Extremadura, 2021 (Tempus Werrae, 7); [Edited] *"De fusta e de fierro"*. *Armamento medieval en la Península Ibérica*, Madrid, La Ergástula, 2021 (Guerra Medieval Ibérica, 3); [Edited with Miguel G. Martins] *"Fechos de Armas"*. *15 hitos bélicos de Medievo ibérico (siglos XI–XV)*, Madrid, La Ergástula, 2021 (Guerra Medieval Ibérica, 2); "Viajar a la cruzada a mediados del siglo XIII: el testimonio de Joinville", in *Viajes y viajeros en la Edad Media*, ed. Pilar Carceller Cerviño, Madrid, La Ergástula, 2021, pp. 203–223; "Conmemorando la victoria: la *Fiesta del Triunfo de la Santa Cruz*", in *Memoria y fuentes de la guerra santa peninsular (ss. X–XV)*, ed. Carlos de Ayala Martínez, J. Santiago Palacios Ontalva and Francisco García Fitz, Gijón, Trea, 2021, pp. 435–462; "Entre Alfonso X el Sabio y Jean de Joinville: el embajador García Pérez (*c.* 1253–1267)", in *El embajador: evolución, cambio e innovación en la Edad Media peninsular*, ed. Óscar Villarroel González and José Manuel Nieto Soria, Gijón, Trea, 2021, pp. 59–95; *"Dilecta consanguinea mea. A Donation of Fernando III to a Nun of Fontevraud"*, in *The Sword and the Cross. Castile-León in the Era of Fernando III*, ed. Edward L. Holt and Teresa Witcombe, Leiden, Brill, 2020, pp. 105–139; "Le traité de Millau (avril 1204)", in *Collection Heresis*, 1 (2020): *La vicomté de Millau au temps de la domination catalano-aragonaise. Rivalités et dissidences* [on line], https://circaed-heresis.com/?p=1657, pp. 53–83; "Simon et Pierre II d'Aragon : faits et mémoire", in *Simon de Montfort († 1218) : le croisé, son lignage et son temps*, ed. Martin Aurell, Laurent Macé and Gregory E.M. Lippiatt, Turnhout, Brepols, 2020, pp. 69–85; "La política occitana de Jaime I", *Desperta Ferro. Historia Antigua y Medieval*, 62 (2020: *La cruzada contra los cátaros II. Las hogueras de Montsegur*), pp. 20–25; "Conquista y reconquista en la Corona de Aragón (1162–1276)", *La Reconquista. Ideología y justificación de la Guerra Santa peninsular*, ed. Carlos de Ayala Martínez, J. Santiago Palacios Ontalva e Isabel C.F. Fernandes, Madrid, La Ergástula, 2019, pp. 187–229; "Le Siège de Beaucaire et les grands sièges de la croisade des Albigeois", in *Le Siège de Beaucaire, 1216. Pouvoir, société et culture dans le Midi rhodanien (seconde moitié du XIIᵉ – première moitié du XIIIᵉ siècle)*, dir. Monique Bourin, Toulouse, SHAB, 2019, pp. 169–206; "Presencia política y participación militar de las mujeres en la Cruzada Albigense", *Revista de Historia Jerónimo Zurita*, 94 (2019), pp. 27–66; "*Si possides amicum, in temptatione posside illum*. Alfonso VIII and Peter the Catholic", in *Regnans in Castella et in Toleto*, ed. Miguel D. Gómez, Kyle Lincoln and Damian J. Smith, Nueva York, Fordham University Press, 2019, pp. 185–203; "Jaque mate a la Gran Corona de Aragón. La batalla de Muret", *Desperta Ferro. Antigua y Medieval*, 65 (2019: *La Cruzada contra los Cátaros, I*), pp. 38–56.

BAGNI, Giampiero, *I Templari e San Michele Arcangelo: il caso bolognese*, Atti XXXIX Convegno Larti, P&P, 2022, pp. 67–82; Co-edited with F. Lanzi, *Le chiese templari e gli Ordini militari a Bologna: dedicazioni e legami politici nella città divisa tra guelfi e ghibellini*, Atti XXXVIII Convegno Larti, P&P, 2021, pp. 129–144.

BALARD, Michel, Co-dir: *Crusading and Trading between West and East. Studies in honour of David Jacoby*, Crusades – Subsidia 12, éd. Routlege, Londres–New York, 2019; "New Documents on Genoese Famagusta", dans, S. Menache, B.Z. Kedar et M. Balard (éd.), *Crusading and Trading between East and West. Studies in honour of David Jacoby*, London and New York 2019, p. 147–160; "David Jacoby, un passeur entre Orient et Occident", dans S. Menache, B.Z. Kedar et M. Balard (éd.), *Crusading and Trading between East and West. Studies in honour of David Jacoby*, London and New York 2019, p. viii–xi; "Les croisades par le prisme du XIXe siècle", dans F. Lacaille (dir.), Les salles des Croisades, Paris 2019, p.

11–37; "Colonization and population movements in the Mediterranean in the Middle Ages", dans N.G. Chrissis, A. Kolia-Dermitzaki et A. Papageorgiou (éd.), *Byzantium and the West. Perception and Reality (11th–15th C.)*, ed. Routledge, London and New York 2019, p. 22–37; Préface au livre de J. Richard, *La papauté et les missions d'Orient au Moyen Age (XIIIe–XVe siècles)*, Rome 2019, p. ix–xxi; "Caffa e il mondo tataro", dans *Imperia: Problemi Vnoutrennei i Vnchnei Kolonizatsii*, Moscou 2019, p. 41–74; "I Giustiniani: un modello degli alberghi?", dans *Ianuensis non nascitur sed fit. Studi per Dino Puncuh*, Genova 2019, p. 131–140; "David Jacoby et l'histoire de Chypre", dans Centre d'Etudes chypriotes. *Cahiers*, t. 49 (2019), p. 409–418; "Still a particular interest in the former 'Ountremer' – a (first) view from France", dans F. Hinz et J. Meyer-Hamme, *Controversial Histories – Current views on the Crusades*, London and New York (Routledge, 2020), p. 29–32; "Les Levantins de Gênes: de l'Ancienne à la Nouvelle Mahone de Chio", dans *De la Bourgogne à l'Orient*, p. 557–575; "Le emozioni di mercanti e pellegrini sul mare Mediterraneo", dans *Studi Genuensi*, 3ème s., t. III (2020), p. 6–15; "La population de Famagouste (XIIIe–XVe siècles)", dans G. Grivaud, A. Nicolaou-Konnari et C. Schabel (éd.), *Famagusta, t. 2. History and Society*, Turnhout 2020, p. 251–274.

BEREND, Nora, "Centrality of the Periphery in Crusade Rhetoric: the Afterlife of the Crusade of Andrew II of Hungary", *The Expansion of the Faith: Crusading on the Frontiers of Latin Christendom in the High Middle Ages*, Paul Srodecki and Norbert Kersken, eds, *Outremer: Studies in the Crusades and the Latin East* vol. 14 (Turnhout: Brepols, 2022), 281–290; 'The concept of Christendom: *christianitas* as a call to action'. In *Order into Action: How Large-Scale Concepts of World-Order Determine Practices in the Premodern World*, Christoph Mauntel and Klaus Oschema, eds, Cursor Mundi 40 (Turnhout: Brepols, 2022), 71–95; guest editor, *Minority Influences in Medieval Society*. Special Issue of *Journal of Medieval History* 45, no. 3 (July 2019), republished as a book: *Minority Influences in Medieval Society*. London: Routledge, 2021 (142 p.).

BINYSH, Betty, "Massacre or mutual benefit: The military orders' relations with their Muslim neighbours in the Latin East (1100–1300)", Jochen Schenk and Mike Carr (eds), *The Military Orders, Volume 6.1: Culture and Conflict in the Mediterranean World* (Abingdon, 2017), pp. 30–43; "Making Peace with 'God's Enemies': The Muslim Dilemma of Treaty-making with Christians in the Medieval Levant", Yvonne Friedman (ed.), *Religion and Peace: Historical Aspects* (London, 2018), pp. 98–114; "From Pugnacity to peace-mongers: The Military Orders protecting property and people in the Latin East", *MO, 7*, pp. 303–321.

BOAS, Adrian, "Acre – Gateway to the Holy Land and Teutonic Possessions in the Latin East", *Akkon – Venedig-Marienburg Mobilität und Immobilität im Deutschen Orden*, Conference proceedings for the International Historical Commission of the Deutschen Ordens in Venice, 2018, *Quellen und Studien zur Geschichte des Deutschen Ordens* 86 (312 pages), Weimar, 2022, pp. 1–15.

BORCHARDT, Karl, "Early Hospitallers in Latin Europe, 1122 and 1113/35", in *Crusades* 19 (2021), pp. 25–55; "Biebelried near Würzburg: a thirteenth-century Hospitaller castle in Franconia and its contexts", *Settlement and Crusade*, pp. 225–240; "Ablassbrief für Ingelfingen 1346", in *Württembergisch Franken* 105 (2021), pp. 237–242; "National Rivalry among Hospitallers? The Case of Bohemia and Austria, 1392–1555", in *Medievalista* 30 (Julho–Dezembro 2021), 203–245; "Das Mittelalterliche Kriminalmuseum und die Johanniterkomturei", in *100 Jahre Mittelalterliches Kriminalmuseum. Festschrift zum Museumsjubiläum*, ed. Markus Hirte, "Schriftenreihe des Mittelalterlichen Kriminalmuseum Rothenburg ob der Tauber 13" (Rothenburg ob der Tauber 2021), pp. 89–109; "Vom officium zum beneficium: Lokale Verwaltungsstrukturen im Johanniter-Priorat Alamania während des 13. und frühen 14. Jahrhunderts", in: *Ordines Militares. Colloquia Torunensia Historica. Yearbook for the Study of the Military Orders* 26 (2021), pp. 9–41; Johanna Maria van Winter, "Godschalk de Kruisvaarder, stichter van het Sint-Catharijneconvent?", *Oud-Utrecht, Tijdschrift voor geschiedeneis van stad en regio Utrecht,* februari 2022, pp. 4–8 [a comment on Borchardt, *Crusades* 19, pp. 25–55].

Buck, Andrew D., and Smith, Thomas W. (eds), *Chronicle, Crusade, and the Latin East: Essays in Honour of Susan B. Edgington,* Outremer. Studies in the Crusades and the Latin East 16 (Turnhout: Brepols, 2022) (350pp.); Buck, Andrew, "Remembering Outremer in the West: The *Secunda pars historiae Iherosolimitane* and the Crisis of Crusading in Mid-Twelfth-Century France", *Speculum* 97:2 (2022), 377–414; "Theorising the Religious Borders of the Latin East: Some Reflections on the Inter-Christian Landscape of Frankish Northern Syria", *Journal of Medieval History* 47:3 (2021), 317–31 – published as part of a special edition entitled *Landscapes of Conflict,* ed. by Beth C. Spacey and Megan Cassidy-Welch; "Castles and the Frontier: Theorizing the Borders of the Principality of Antioch in the Twelfth Century", *Viator* 50:2 (2021 for 2019), 79–108; "Women in the Principality of Antioch: Power, Status, and Social Agency", *Haskins Society Journal* 31 (2020 for 2019), 95–132; "Remembering Baldwin I: The *Secunda pars historiae Iherosolimitane* and Literary Responses to the Jerusalemite Monarchy in Twelfth-Century France", in A.D. Buck and T.W. Smith (eds), *Chronicle, Crusade, and the Latin East,* pp. 287–302; with Smith, Thomas W., "Introduction", in Andrew D. Buck and Thomas W. Smith, Ibid., pp. 19–24; Buck, Andrew "William of Tyre, Chronicle", in David Thomas (ed.), *The Bloomsbury Reader in Christian–Muslim Relations, 600–1500* (London: Bloomsbury, 2022), pp. 263–66.

Bysted, Ane, L., *"Historia de Profectione Danorum in Hierosolymam*: A Journey to the Lost Jerusalem" in *The Holy City: Tracing the Jerusalem Code. Christian Cultures in Medieval Scandinavia (ca 1100–1536),* ed. Kristin B. Aavitsland & Line Bonde, De Gruyter, Berlin/Boston 2021, pp. 132–139.

Carr, Annemarie Wehl, "The Lady and the Juggler: Mary East and West", *Dumbarton Oaks Papers* 75 (2022): 7–40; "Seeing Topographic Icons Hierotopically"; *Icons of Space. Studies in Hierotopy and Iconography A Tribute to Alexei Lidov on His 60th Birthday,* ed. Jelena Bogdanović, 199–213, London: Routledge, 2021; "Hell in the Sweet Land: Hell's Place in the Last Judgments of Byzantine and Medieval Cyprus", in *Damned in Hell in Cretan Frescoes,* ed. Angeliki Lymberopoulou, 1: 346–411, 2 vols, Cambridge: Cambridge University Press, 2021; "Orthodox Monasteries under Lusignan Rule: Relations with Others, Relations with Their Own", *Articles of Faith: Visual Culture in the Byzantine and Islamic Worlds. Essays in Honour of Erica Cruikshank Dodd,* ed. Eva Baboula, Lesley Jessop, Marcus Milwright, pp. 108–36. (London: Taylor and Francis, 2021); "The Portrait of a Lady", in *The Eloquence of Art, Studies in Honor of Henry Maguire,* ed. Rossitza B. Schroeder and A. Olsen Lam, pp. 71–90 (Leiden: Brill, 2020).

Carr, Mike, "Modifications to Papal Trade Licences at the Avignon Curia'", *Authority and Power in the Medieval Church c. 1000–1500,* ed. T.W. Smith (Turnhout: Brepols, 2020), pp. 205–215; "Between the Papal Court and the Islamic World: Famagusta and Cypriot Merchants in the Fourteenth Century", in *Famagusta Maritima: Mariners, Merchants, Pilgrims and Mercenaries,* ed. M. Walsh (Leiden: Brill, 2019), pp. 113–127; "Policing the Sea: Enforcing the Papal Embargo on Trade with 'Infidels'", in *Merchants, Pirates, and Smugglers: Criminalization, Economics and the Transformation of the Maritime World (1200–1600),* ed. P. Höhn et al. (Frankfurt: Campus Verlag, 2019), pp. 329–341.

Carraz, Damien, "Administration, délimitation et perception des territoires dans l'ordre de l'Hôpital: le cas du prieuré de Saint-Gilles (XIIe–XIVe siècle)", in *Ordres militaires et territorialité au Moyen Âge entre Orient et Occident* (Journée d'études de Montpellier, 20 octobre 2017), ed. M.-A. Chevalier, Paris, Geuthner, 2020, pp. 313–339; *L'Ordre du Temple dans la basse vallée du Rhône (1124–1312)*. *Ordres militaires, croisades et sociétés méridionales*, Lyon, Presses Universitaires de Lyon, 2020 (Collection d'histoire et d'archéologie médiévales, 17), 608 p.; *Un commandeur ordinaire? Bérenger Monge et le gouvernement des hospitaliers provençaux au XIIIᵉ siècle*, Turnhout, Brepols, 2020, 528 p. (Ecclesia Militans, 8); "La redécouverte de deux châteaux de l'Hôpital en Haute-Provence: Manosque et Puimoisson exhumés par les sources écrites", in Vardit Shotten-Hallel et Rosie Weetch (eds), *Crusading and Archaeology*, pp. 64–91; "L'Hôpital de Saint-Jean de Jérusalem en Gapençais. Les ressorts d'une implantation précoce entre Provence et Dauphiné (XIIᵉ–XIVᵉ siècle)", *Bulletin de la société d'étude des Hautes-Alpes* (2020), pp. 5–29; "Echoes of the Latin East among the Hospitallers of the West: the priory of Saint Gilles, *c*.1260–*c*.1300", *Settlement and Crusade*, pp. 241–253; "L'Hôpital de Saint-Jean de Jérusalem en moyenne montagne. Approche comparée des implantations en Haute-Provence et dans le Massif central (XIIᵉ–XIVᵉ siècle)", in Marina Gazzini et Thomas Frank (dir.), *Ospedali e Montagne. Paesaggi, funzioni, poteri nei secoli medievali (Italia, Francia, Spagna), Convegno internazionale di studi, Università degli studi di Milano, 25–26 settembre 2019*, Milan-Turin, 2021 (Quaderni degli Studi di Storia Medioevale e di Diplomatica), pp. 359–388; https://riviste.unimi.it/index.php/SSMD/issue/view/1710 ; "Note sur les pratiques sigillaires des hospitaliers en Provence (XIIᵉ–XIIIᵉ siècle)", *Ordens Militares, Identidade e Mudança, VIII Encontro Internacional sobre Ordens Militares, Palmela, 12 a 16 junho 2019*, dir. I. C. F. Fernandes., Palmela, GESOS-Município Palmela, 2021, vol. 1, p. 433–458.

CERRINI, Simonetta, Urbano II, papa; Urbano IV, papa, in *Dizionario Biografico degli Italiani*, Vol. 97, Roma, Istituto dell'Enciclopedia Italiana Treccani, 2020, pp. 550–556; pp. 558–563; with Franco Cardini, *Storia dei Templari in otto oggetti*, Milano, UTET, 2019; *Le dernier jugement des Templiers*, Paris, Flammarion, 2018 [avec un commentaire de la bulle *Vox in excelso* de 1312].

CHRISSIS, Nikolaos, "Tearing Christ's seamless tunic? The 'Eastern Schism' and crusades against the Greeks in the thirteenth century", in P. Srodecki and N. Kersken (eds), *The Expansion of the Faith: Crusading on the Frontiers of Latin Christendom in the High Middle Ages* (Brepols: Turnhout, 2022), 229–250; "Πνευματικές και ιδεολογικές εξελίξεις στη Μεσαιωνική Δυτική Ευρώπη και οι σταυροφορίες κατά των Βυζαντινών" [Intellectual and ideological developments in Medieval Western Europe and crusading against the Byzantines], in A. Markou, I. Mpakirtzis, A. Palikidis, and C. Papageorgopoulou (eds), *History, Society, Culture: Research Questions and Challenges. Anniversary Volume for the 30 Years of the Department of History and Ethnology of the Democritus University of Thrace* (Thessaloniki: Stamoulis, 2022), 579–602; "Western aggression and Greco-Latin interaction: A view from Greece", in F. Hinz and J. Meyer-Hamme (eds), *Controversial Histories: Current Views on the Crusades* (London and New York: Routledge, 2020 [2021]), 42–44; [Review of:] Dimiter Angelov, *The Byzantine Hellene: The Life of Emperor Theodore Laskaris and Byzantium in the Thirteenth Century* (Cambridge: Cambridge University Press, 2019), in *Speculum* 97/3 (July 2022), 778–779.

CLAVERIE, Pierre-Vincent, "Bertrand Du Guesclin avait-il les moyens de vaincre l'Égypte mamelouke? Essai d'uchronie raisonnée", *Egypt and Syria in the Fatimid, Ayyubid and Mamluk Eras, t. IX*, ed. K. D'hulster, G. Schallenberg (†) et J. Van Steenbergen, Louvain, 2019, pp. 237–249; "Une enquête pour sacrilège menée contre des Juifs d'Alexandrie sous le règne d'al-Nāṣir Muḥammad", *Egypt and Syria in the Fatimid, Ayyubid and Mamluk Eras, t. IX*, ed. K. D'hulster, G. Schallenberg (†) et J. Van Steenbergen, Louvain, 2019, pp.

251–263; "Starting Point of the Genoese Thalassocracy in Cyprus: An Unpublished Roll of Knights and Squires Imprisoned in Famagusta in 1374", *Famagusta maritima: Mariners, Merchants, Pilgrims and Mercenaries*, éd. Michael J.K. Walsh, Leiden, Brill, 2019, chapter 5 pp. 144–158; "*Ex Mari Lux*: The development of naval siege warfare in the crusading Levant", *Settlement and Crusade*, pp. 60–68; "La vision des ordres militaires dans les œuvres poétiques de Monaco dei Corbizzi et de Richard de Saint-Victor", ed. I.C. Ferreira Fernandes, *Ordens militares: identidade e mudança*, vol. I, Palmela, 2021, pp. 215–222.

Cobb, Paul M., "*Coronidis Loco*: On the Meaning of Elephants, from Baghdad to Aachen," in Sarah Davis-Secord et alii, eds, *Interfaith Relationships and Perceptions of the Other in the Medieval Mediterranean: Essays in Memory of Olivia Remie Constable* (London: Palgrave Macmillan, 2021), 49–77; "Hamdan al-Atharibi's *History of the Franks Revisited*, Again," Carole Hillenbrand, ed., *Syria in Crusader Times: Conflict and Coexistence* (Edinburgh: Edinburgh University Press, 2019), 3–20.

Coureas, Nicholas, "The Formation and Evolution of the Class of Burgesses in the Lusignan Kingdom of Cyprus, 1192–1474", in *Legacies of the Crusades*, eds T. K. Nielsen and K. Villads Jensen, Turnhout: Brepols, 2021, pp. 169–188; "Limassol from 1191 to 1300, its importance in the context of crusades, trade and settlement," in *Settlement and Crusade*, pp. 156–168; "The Grant of Safe-Conducts by the Hospitaller Order in the Fifteenth century to Recipients on Rhodes and Cyprus: Their Function and Effectiveness", *Ordines Militares*, XXV (2020) 185–204; "King Peter I of Cyprus and the Armenians" in *Haigazian Armenological Review*, 40 (2020), 201–210; "Crossing Cultural Boundaries in Merchants' wills from 14th Century Famagusta", *Perspectives on Culture*, 30 (3/2020), 47–62; "Food, Wine and the Latin Clergy of Lusignan Cyprus 1191–1473", in *Multidisciplinary approaches to food and foodways in the Medieval Eastern Mediterranean*, ed. Y. Waksman, MOM Editions, Lyon, 2020, pp. 87–95; "The Lusignan Kingdom of Cyprus 1192–1473," *The Encyclopedia of the Global Middle Ages*, ed. D. R. Messer, Arc Humanities Press, Bloomsbury Publishing 2019, http://dx.doi.org/10.5040/9781350990005,072; "The Non-Templar Clergy and the Trial of the Templars in Cyprus: Comparisons with other Countries", in *Gli Ordini di Terrasanta*, ed. M. Santanicchia and S. Merli, Perugia 2021, pp. 501–512; "The Phenomenon of the Divine in Medieval Cypriot Chronicles and Chronicles Referring to Cyprus", *The Medieval Chronicle*, 14 (2022), pp. 1–26; "Settlement on Cyprus after the Latin Conquest: The Accounts of Cypriot and other Chroniclers and the Wider Context," in *Ignatianum Yearbook of Philosophy*, 25/2 (2021) 13–30; The Greek Church in Lusignan and Venetian Cyprus 1191–1570," *Perspectives on Culture*, 35 (4/2021), 55–85; "The Manumission of Slaves in Fourteenth and Fifteenth Century Famagusta", in *Forms of Unfreedom in the Medieval Mediterranean, Biblioteca-Estudios & Coloquios-Publicacoes do Cidehus*, eds C. Almagro-Vidal and M. Filomena Lopes dos Barros, Evora, 2021, pp. 104–121; [Review of] *Byzantium and the West, Perception and Reality (11th–15th C.)*, eds N.G. Chrissis, A. Kolia-Dermitzaki and A. Papageorgiou, Routledge: London and New York, 2019, in *Byzantina Symmeikta*, 30 (202), 343–356; [Review of] *The Countryside of Hospitaller Rhodes, Original Texts and English Summaries*, eds A. Luttrell and G. O'Malley, Routledge: London and New York, 2019, in *Ordines Militares*, XXV (2020), 427–434; [Review of] *Venetian Cyprus (1489–1571) Reports by the Dominion's Supreme Administrative Officials*, ed. S. Birdachas, Epikentro: Thessalonica, 2019, in *Mediterranean Chronicle*, 10 (2021), 249–253.

Donnachie, Stephen, "The Predicaments of Aimery de Lusignan: Baronial Factionalism and the Consolidation of Power in the Kingdoms of Jerusalem and Cyprus, 1197–1205", in *Settlement and Crusade*.

Dragnea, Mihai, "Legitimate and Illegitimate Divination in Medieval Writings", *Croatica*

Christiana Periodica, vol. 46/89 (2022), pp. 41–57; "Shaping Religious Identity on the Northern Edge of the Christianitas: Portraits of Pagans and Idolaters in the Twelfth Century Pomerania", *Edinost in dialog*, vol. 76/2 (2021), pp. 241–271; "Constructions of Christian Identity in the Northern Periphery: The Sawley World Map in Twelfth-Century England", *The Journal of Ecclesiastical History*, vol. 72/4 (2021), pp. 726–750; "Crusade and Colonization in the Wendish Territories in the Early Twelfth Century: An Analysis of the So-called Magdeburg Letter of 1108", *Mediaevalia*, vol. 42 (2021), pp. 41–61; *Christian Identity Formation Across the Elbe in the Tenth and Eleventh Centuries*, (Peter Lang, Bern & New York, 2021); *The Romance-Speaking Balkans Language and the Politics of Identity*, eds. Annemarie Sorescu-Marinković, Mihai Dragnea, Thede Kahl, Blagovest Njagulov, Donald L. Dyer and Angelo Costanzo (Brill, Leiden, 2021); "The Cult of St. Olaf in the Latin and Greek Churches Between the Eleventh and Twelfth Centuries", *Hiperboreea*, 7/2 (2020), pp. 145–167

Echevarria, Ana, *Los mudéjares de la Corona de Castilla: Poblamiento y estatuto jurídico de una minoría*. Univ. de Granada ed. Granada, 2021. 304 pp.

Edbury, Peter, "The Crusader town and lordship of Ramla (1099–1268)", Andrew Petersen and Denys Pringle eds, *Ramla: City of Muslim Palestine, 715–1917* (Oxford, 2021), 7–17; "The Latin East and the English Crown" (Henry Loyn lecture) – posted on academia edu; "A Threat to Invade Cyprus: Pope John XXII, Walter of Brienne Duke of Athens, and the Latin East in 1331", *Frankokratia*, 2 (2021), 1–17; "Jerusalem and Cyprus: the Kingdoms of the Crusaders and the Military Orders", *Gli Ordini di Terrasanta: Questioni aperte nuove acquisizione (secoli XII–XVI)*, ed. Arnaud Baudin, Sonia Merli and Mirko Santaicchia (Perugia, 2021), 23–32; Review of Jane Gilbert, Simon Gaunt and William Burgwinkle, *Medieval French Literary Culture Abroad* (Oxford, 2020) in *Crusades*, 20 (2021), 279–82.

Edgington, Susan B., "Raymond of Aguilers, *History of the Franks who captured Jerusalem*", in *The Bloomsbury Reader in Christian Muslim Relations, 600–1500*, ed. D. Thomas (London: Bloomsbury, 2022).

Ekdahl, Sven, "Politik, Handel und dynastische Probleme der skandinavischen Königreiche in der ersten Hälfte des 14. Jahrhunderts", in *Monarchia, społeczeństwo, tożsamość. Studia z dziejów średniowiecza* [Book in honour of Sławomir Gawlas], Warszawa 2020, pp. 67–79; "Die Beschlagnahme der polnischen Getreidelieferung für Litauen in Ragnit durch Hochmeister Ulrich von Jungingen im Juni 1409. Ein Beitrag zur Vorgescbichte des "Großen Kriegs" 1409–1411", in *Von Hamburg nach Java. Studien zur mittelalterlichen, neuen und digitalen Geschichte. Festschrift zu Ehren von Jürgen Sarnowsky*, hg. v. Jochen Burgtorf, Christian Hoffarth, Sebastian Kubon (*Nova Medievalia. Quellen und Studien zum europäischen Mittelalter* 18), Göttingen 2020, pp. 393–408; *Locating the Battlefield of Tannenberg (Grunwald, Žalgiris) 1410 with Metal Detectors: A Polish-Scandinavian Research Project during the period 2014–2020*. 84 p.; "Moscow troops in the wars of Poland and Lithuania with the Teutonic Order in Prussia in 1414 and 1422. Two timeline questions", *Questiones Medii Aevi Novae* 25, Warszawa 2020, pp. 181–192; "Battlefield Archaeology at Tannenberg (Grunwald, Žalgiris): Physical Remains of the Defeat of the Teutonic Order in Prussia in 1410", in *The Art of Siege Warfare and Military Architecture from the Classical World to the Middle Ages,* ed. Michael Eisenberg and Rabei Khamisy. Scientific Editorial Denys Pringle, Werner Eck and Adrian Boas (Oxford & Philadelphia, 2021), pp. 213–225.

El-Merheb, Mohamad, *Political Thought in the Mamluk Period: The Unnecessary Caliphate*, Edinburgh Studies in Classical Islamic History and Culture (Edinburgh University Press, February 2022); with Mehdi Berriah (eds), *Professional Mobility in Islamic Societies (700–*

1750): New Concepts and Approaches, Handbook of Oriental Studies. Section One, the Near and Middle East (Leiden: Brill, August 2021).

FAVREAU-LILIE, Marie-Luise, "Der Deutsche Orden und der Fall Akkons 1291. Der Umzug des Haupthauses nach Venedig und die Folgen", in: Hubert Houben (ed.), *Akkon – Venedig – Marienburg. Mobilität und Immobilität im Deutschen Orden. Vorträge der Tagung der Internationalen Kommission zur Erforschung des Deutschen Ordens in Venedig 2018 (Quellen und Studien zur Geschichte des Deutschen Ordens*, vol. 86; *Veröffentlichungen der Internationalen Historischen Kommission zur Erforschung des Deutschen Ordens*, vol. 19), Ilmtal-Weinstraße 2022, pp. 55–69.

FILIPOVIC, Emir O., "Force Majeure, Act of God or Natural Disaster? Ottoman Military Threat as a Cause for Exemption from Contractual Liability During the Conquest of the Balkans". *Revue des Études Sud-Est Européennes* 59 (2021), 157–74; "Colluding with the Infidel: The Alliance between Ladislaus of Naples and the Turks". *Hungarian Historical Review* 8.2 (2019), 361–89.

FOLDA, Jaroslav, "Two Icons of the Virgin and Child Hodegetria from the Monastery of St. Catherine, Sinai: Byzantine or Crusader?," in *Art and Material Culture in the Byzantine and Islamic Worlds, Studies in Honour of Erica Cruikshank Dodd*, eds Evanthia Baboula and Lesley Jessop (Leiden/Boston: Brill, 2021), pp. 33–54; "The Restoration of the Nativity Church in Bethlehem, ed. Claudio Alessandri (London: CRC Press, Taylor & Francis Group, 2020) pp. 460.

GAPOSCHKIN, Cecilia, "Nivelon of Quierzy, the Cathedral of Soissons, and the relics of 1205: Liturgy and Devotion in the aftermath of the Fourth Crusade," *Speculum* 95/4 (October 2020), pp. 1087–1129. On-line appendixes for *Speculum* 95/4 article found at: https://doi.org/10.1086/710547, pp. 1–38; "Louis IX, Heraclius, and the True Cross at the Sainte Chapelle." For *Political ritual and practice in Capetian France*," ed. Jay Rubenstein and Cecilia Gaposchkin, (2021) 265–299; Between Historical Narration and Liturgical Celebrations: Gautier Cornut and the Reception of the Crown of Thorns in France, *Revue Mabillon* n.s. 30 (=v. 91)m 2019, 90–145.

HALLIBURTON, Ben & Minso Kang. "The Android of Albertus Magnus: A Legend of Artificial Being," *AI Narratives: A History of Imaginative Thinking about Intelligent Machines*, ed. Stephen Cave, Kanta Dihal and Sarah Dillon (Oxford: Oxford University, 2020), 72–94.

HARRIS, Jonathan, *Introducere în Istoria Bizanțului*, Romanian translation of *Introduction to Byzantium, 602–1453* by Mihai Moroiu (Bucharest: Baroque Books and Arts, 2021); *Bizans'ın Sonu*, Turkish translation of *The End of Byzantium* by Tevabil Alkaç (Istanbul: Alfa, 2021); "Refugees and international networks after the fall of Constantinople (1453–1475)", *English Historical Review* (April 2022).

HODGSON, Natasha, and Matthew Rowley, *Miracles Power and Authority in Medieval and Early Modern History* (Routledge, 2021); with John McCallum, Nicholas Morton, Amy Fuller eds, *Religion and Conflict in Medieval and Early Modern Worlds* (Routledge, 2020; and Katherine Lewis and Matthew Mesley eds *Crusading and Masculinities* (Routledge, 2019); "Bearded Ghosts and Holy Visions: Miracles, Manliness and Clerical Authority on the First Crusade" in Natasha Hodgson and Matthew Rowley eds, *Miracles Power and Authority in Medieval and Early Modern History* (Routledge, 2021); "Introduction" and "Leading the People 'as duke, count and father': the Masculinities of Abbot Martin of Pairis in Gunther of Pairis", Natasha Hodgson, Katherine Lewis and Matthew Mesley ed. *Crusading Masculinities*, Crusades – Subsidia 13 (Routledge, 2019) pp.1–17 and 199–221;

"Reputation, authority and masculine identities in the political culture of the First Crusaders: the career of Arnulf of Chocques" *History* 102 (2017) pp. 898–913.

HORSWELL, Mike, and Andrew B.R. Elliott, "Crusading Icons: Medievalism and Authenticity in Historical Digital Games", *History in Games: Contingencies of an Authentic Past*, eds Martin Lorber and Felix Zimmermann (Bielefeld: transcript Verlag, 2020), pp. 137–56; "Saladin and Richard the Lionheart: Entangled Memories", *The Making of Crusading Heroes and Villains: Engaging the Crusades, Volume Four*, eds Mike Horswell and Kristin Skottki (Abingdon: Routledge, 2021), pp. 75–94; Mike Horswell, "From 'Superstitious Veneration' to 'War to Defend Christendom': The Crusades in the *Encyclopaedia Britannica* from 1771 to 2018", in *The Crusades: History and Memory*, eds Kurt Villads Jensen and Torben Kjersgaard Nielsen, vol. 2 (Turnhout: Brepols, 2021), pp. 125–56.

IVASHKO, Roman, "The bishops of the Latin Metropolitanate of Lviv in Military on the Eve of the Florentine Union", *Ukraina Lithuanica: studies on the history of the Grand Duchy of Lithuania* 5 (Kyiv: Institute of History of Ukraine of the National Academy of Sciences of Ukraine, 2019): 15–27 http://resource.history.org.ua/publ/UkrL_2019_5_5; "The historical value of the indulgence of 1436 issued by the Council of Basel", *Schweizerische Zeitschrift für Religions- und Kirchengeschichte* 114 (Fribourg: The Association of Swiss Ecclesiastical History (ASCH), 2020): 229–236 DOI:10.24894/2673-3641.00060 https://www.schwabeonline. ch/schwabe-xaveropp/elibrary/media/E29277B10AD5BC16D41C0EEA131E1CAC/10_ 24894_2673-3641_00060_8177.pdf; "The early history of the Roman Catholic parish in Bibrka", *Annales universitatis Mariae Curie-Sklodowska section M Balcaniensis et Carpathiensis* 5 (Lublin: Publishing House of the Maria Curie-Skłodowska University in Lublin, 2020):123–131 DOI: 10.17951/bc.2020.5.123-131 https://journals.umcs.pl/bc/ article/view/11552; "Essay on policy of the Jagiellonians toward the Church Union on the eve of fall of Constantinople", *Academia Letters* (San Francisco: academia.edu, 2022): Article 4694 https://doi.org/10.20935/AL4694, https://www.academia.edu/s/ed8f9dd5ad.

JOSSERAND, Philippe, "La fabrique d'un diplomate: Jacques de Molay, grand-maître de l'ordre du Temple, et ses voyages en Occident (1292–1296)", *Revue Historique*, 696 (2020), p. 3–21;"The Crusade and its Fronts in French Historiography from the Interwar Period to 2020", *Crusades*, 20 (2021), p. 227–246; "Le Temple, le Portugal et l'Orient latin: un nouveau document pour un vieux débat", *Medievalista* [online], 30 (2021), p. 91–117; *L'histoire, l'ordre et le chaos. Une anthropologie de soi* (avec un avant-propos de Julien Théry et une postface de Patrick Boucheron), La Roche-sur-Yon, Dépaysage, 2021; "The Templar Order in public and cultural debate in France during the eighteenth and nineteenth centuries", in Helen Nicholson et Jochen Burgtorf (dir.), *The Templars, the Hospitallers and the Crusades. Essays in Homage to Alan J. Forey*, Londres–New York, Routledge, 2020, p. 137–151; "Au miroir de Palmela: trente ans de recherches sur les ordres religieux-militaires en France (1989–2019)", in Isabel Cristina F. Fernandes (dir.), *Ordens militares, identidade e cambio*, Palmela, Município de Palmela–GesOS, 2021 (2 vol.), t. I, p. 101–115; "La guerra en la Península Ibérica en la mirada de Jacques de Molay, gran maestro del Temple", in Carlos de Ayala Martínez, Francisco García Fitz et Santiago Palacios Ontalva (dir.), *Memorias y fuentes de la guerra santa peninsular (siglos X–XV)*, Gijón, Trea, 2021, p. 349–359; "Conclusions", in Marie-Anna Chevalier (dir.), *Ordres militaires et territorialité au Moyen Âge entre Orient et Occident*, Paris, Geuthner, 2020, p. 385–394; "Alle prese con la tormenta: Jacques de Molay, gran maestro del Tempio, nel mirino del potere capetingio (1307–1314)", in Arnaud Baudin, Sonia Merli et Mirko Santanicchia (dir.), *Gli ordini di Terrasanta. Questioni aperte, nuovi acquisizioni (secoli XII–XVI). Atti del Convegno internazionale di studi (Perugia, 14–15 novembre 2019)*, Pérouse, Fabbri, 2021, p. 513–530; "Face aux temps nouveaux.

Morimond et l'ordre de Calatrava au tournant des XIIIe et XIVe siècles", in Benoît Rouzeau et Hubert Flammarion (dir.), *Morimond 1117–2017. Approches pluridisciplinaires d'un réseau monastique*, Nancy, Presses universitaires de Nancy, 2021, p. 383–390.

KANE, James, (with Keagan Brewer), *"Ricardus explicit*: an elusive marginal note on the earliest manuscript of the *Libellus de expugnatione Terrae Sanctae per Saladinum"*, *Medium Ævum* 89:2 (2020), 374–80; "'Blood and water flowed to the ground': sacred topography, biblical landscapes, and conceptions of space in the *Libellus de expugnatione Terrae Sanctae per Saladinum"*, *Journal of Medieval History* 47:3 (2021), 366–80; "An early vernacular annal on the First Crusade from Christ Church, Canterbury", *Notes and Queries* 68:3 (2021), 248–51.

KEDAR, Benjamin Z., "Zwei bislang übersehene Frühwerke von Philipp Jaffé," *Deutsches Archiv* 76 (2020), 41–51; "World War I Aerial Photographs of Ramla", *Ramla: City of Muslim Palestine, 715–1917. Studies in History, Archaeology and Architecture*, ed. Andrew Petersen and Denys Pringle (Oxford, 2021), 74–79; "On Some Characteristics of the Second Kingdom of Jerusalem, 1191–1291," *Settlement and Crusade*, pp. 3–16; "Studying the 'Shared Sacred Spaces' of the Medieval Levant: Where Historians May Meet Anthropologists," *Al-Masāq* 34 (2022), 1–16.

KOLIA-DERMITZAKI, Athina, "Byzantium and the Crusades in the Komnenian Era", in: N. G. Chrissis, Athina Kolia-Dermitzaki and Angeliki Papageorgiou (eds), *Byzantium and the West: Perception and Reality*, Routledge, London and New York 2019, 59–83; "The multidimensional personality and varied oeuvre of Konstantinos Amantos. biographical approach", in: *Konstantinos Amantos: Mentor, Scholar, Citizen. Proceedings of the Scientific Symposium: Chios, 5–8 May 2016*, Athens 2020, pp. 29–61; "The attitude of the soldiers in warfare as reflected in the Byzantine sources (9th–12th centuries)", in: P. Cosme, J.-Chr. Couvenhes,S. Janniard, Michèle Virol (eds), *Le récit de guerre comme source d'histoire, de l'Antiquité à nos jours*, Presses universitaires de Franche-Comté, Besançon 2022, 337–353; "Euodios the Monk, Martyrdom of the forty-two martyrs", in: David Thomas (ed.), *The Bloomsbury Reader in Christin-Muslim Relations, 600–1500* (Bloomsbury 2022), pp. 143–146.

LENCART, Joana, "A guerra como condição de santidade: freires e mártires venerados entre as Ordens Militares (séculos XII–XVI)", *Via Spiritus*, 28 (2021), pp. 193–231; "A organização do fundo Gavetas da Torre do Tombo: ponto de situação bibliográfico", CEM, n° 13 (2021), pp. 283–300; "A governação de Braga no início do século XVI: o concelho, o arcebispo e o rei nas atas de vereação", *História. Revista da FLUP*. Porto. IV Série. Vol. 11 n° 2 2021, pp. 76–100; "O Porto visto pelo Doutor João de Barros em meados do século XVI", História. Revista da FLUP. Porto. IV Série. Vol. 11 n° 1. 2021, pp. 81–105; "Papeles tocantes al havito de Christo de Portugal": um códice português na Biblioteca Nacional de España, in *Vinculos de Historia*, 9, junio de 2020; "A Ordem de Cristo: imagens e retóricas (séculos XVI e XVII)", in Isabel Cristina Fernandes (ed.), *Ordens Militares, Identidade e Mudança*, Palmela, GEsOS, 2021, pp. 187–201; 2020, Costa, Paula Pinto; Torres Jiménez, Raquel; Lencart, Joana – "The Patrons saints of Military Orders churches in Castille and Portugal, 1462–1539", *MO, 7*, pp. 267–281; *Geographia d'Entre Douro e Minho e Tras-os-Montes por João de Barros*, Porto, Câmara Municipal do Porto, 2019; *Livro da Regra e Definições da Ordem de Cristo, por Pedro Álvares Seco*, in Paula Pinto Costa (dir.), Militarium Ordinum Analecta (n° 18), CEPESE 2018.

LUTTRELL, Anthony, "Les origines diverses des ordres militaires syriens," in *De la Bourgogne à l'Orient*, pp. 489–495; "Timur's Capture of Hospitaller Smyrna (1402)," in *Von Hamburg nach Java: Studien zur mittelalterlichen, neuen und digitalen Geschichte*, J.

Burgtorf *et al.* (eds) (Göttingen, 2020), pp. 337–347; "Confusion in the Hospital's pre-1291 Statutes," *Crusades*, xix (2020), pp. 109–114; "L'hospice Sainte-Catherine: Rhodes 1445," *Bulletin: Société de l'histoire et du patrimoine de l'Ordre de Malte*, xli (2020), pp. 15–24; "A Hospitaller *despropriamentum*: Dubrovnik 1396," *Ordines Militares*, xxvi (2021), pp. 341–347; "The Hospitaller Background of the Teutonic Order," reprinted in *Ordines Militares*, xxvi (2021), pp. 351–375; "'Liquid Frontiers': Hospitaller Rhodes 1306–1421," in *Ordens Militares: identidade e mudança*, I. C. Ferreira Fernandes (ed.), i (Palmela, 2021), pp. 209–214; "Linguistic Encounters: Hospitaller Rhodes after 1306," *Medioevo Romanzo*, xlv (2021), pp. 241–252.

MARVIN, Laurence W., "The Battle of Fariskur (29 August 1219) and the Fifth Crusade: Causes, Course, and Consequences," *The Journal of Military History* 85.3 (July, 2021): 597–618; "Raymond VI, Count of Toulouse," in *The Worst Military Leaders in History*, eds. John M. Jennings and Chuck Steele (London: Reaktion Books, 2022), 217–231.

MORTON, Nic, *The Crusader States and their neighbours: a military history, 1099–1187* (Oxford University Press, 2020); *Religion and Conflict in Medieval and Early Modern Worlds: Identities, Communities and Authorities* (Routledge, 2021). Edited collection (co-editors: Dr Natasha Hodgson, Dr Amy Fuller and Dr John McCallum).

NICHOLSON, Helen J., *Sybil, Queen of Jerusalem 1186–1190*, Rulers of the Latin East (London: Routledge, 2022: 978-1-138-63651-4); *The Knights Templar* (Leeds: Arc Humanities Press, 2021: ISBN 9781641891684), 96pp (series: Past Imperfect); "The Templars and 'Atlit", *Settlement and Crusade* (ISBN 9780367196745), pp. 71–90; "The trial of the Templars in Britain and Ireland", *The Templars: The Rise, Fall and Legacy of a Military Religious Order*, ed. Jochen Burgtorf, Shlomo Lotan, and Enric Mallorquí-Ruscalleda (London: Routledge, 2021: ISBN 9781138650626), pp. 209–33.

ORTEGA, Isabelle, "Γυναίκες ευγενείς και οικογενειακές στρατηγικές στην Φραγκοκρατούμενη Πελοπόννησο από τον 13° έως τον 15° αιώνα", *Women and Monasticism in the Medieval Eastern Mediterranean: Decoding a Cultural Map*, Eleonora Kountoura Galaki et Ekaterini Mitsiou (ed.), Athens, 2019, pp. 233–260; "Les lignages nobiliaires de la Morée latine aux XIIIᵉ et XIVᵉ siècles", *Miscellanea recordium, Cohésion sociale, identités, contestations et révoltes (XIIIᵉ–XVᵉ siècle)*, dir. Christiane Raynaud, préface Michel Pastoureau, Paris, Le Léopard d'or (Cahiers du Léopard d'or 19), 2021, pp. 121–144. ISBN: 978-2-86377-282-9.

PACIFICO, Marcello, (2021). "*Fideles coronae*: la Chiesa durante la reformatio pacis di Federico II in Europa e in Oltremare", in *Mediaeval Sophia*, vol. 23, p. 1–28; (2021). "*Fideles coronae*: la Chiesa nella costruzione del consenso al progetto imperiale di Federico II", in *Mediaeval Sophia*, p. 77–104; "Corrado IV di Svevia re dei Romani, di Sicilia e di Gerusalemme 1228–1254" in *Itineraria*, vol. 26, p. 1–182; "Il papato e l'idea di crociata" in (a cura di): Patrizia Sardina, Daniela Santoro, Maria Antonietta Russo and Marcello Pacifico, *Medioevo e Mediterraneo: incontri, scambi e confronti. Studi per Salvatore Fodale. vol. 2*, p. 423–442; "La crociata al tempo di Federico II: da bellum sacrum ad opus pacis", in *Mediaeval Sophia*, vol. 22, p. 13–28; "La politica mediterranea di Veneziani, Genovesi e Pisani al tempo di Federico II", in *Incontri*, vol. 1, p. 4–32; (2020). "Prefazione" in: (a cura di): Sardina P., Russo M., Santoro D. and Pacifico M., *Medioevo e Mediterraneo: incontri, scambi e confronti. Studi per Salvatore Fodale, vol. 2*, p. 1–3; Sardina P., Santoro D., Russo M. A. and Pacifico M. (a cura di) (2020). "Medioevo e Mediterraneo: incontri, scambi e confronti. Studi per Salvatore Fodale" in *Storia. Classici Fonti Ricerche*, vol. 2, Palermo: Palermo University Press.

PARSONS, Simon Thomas, 'Women at the Walls: Teichoscopy, Admiration, and Conversion on the First Crusade', in *Chronicle, Crusade, and the Latin East* (Brepols, 2022).

PAVIOT, Jacques, *Relation de la croisade de Nicopolis (XVᵉ siècle), suivie du Memoire du voyage de Hongrie fait par Jean comte de Nevers en l'an 1396, sa prison, sa rançon et son retour en France, par Prosper Bauyn (XVIIᵉ siècle)*, éd. Marie-Gaëtane Anton, Giovanni Palumbo et Jacques Paviot, Paris, Académie des Inscriptions & Belles-Lettres, "Documents relatifs à l'histoire des croisades, XXIV", 2021, 335 p.; *Jean Germain (v. 1396–1461), évêque de Chalon-sur-Saône, chancelier de l'ordre de la Toison d'or. Actes de la journée d'études, Chalon-sur-Saône, 27 octobre 2018*, dir. Delphine Lannaud et Jacques Paviot, Chalon-sur-Saône, Société d'histoire et d'archéologie, 2019, 173 p.

PINTO COSTA, Paula, "A Ordem do Templo e a construção do reino de Portugal", *Desmistificar alguns aspetos da História de Portugal*, ed. Jesus, Roger Lee de and Dias, Paulo M.,Ed. Desassossego (chancela da Saída de Emergência), 2022; with Sottomayor-Pizarro, José Augusto, "Fidalgos e freires-cavaleiros. Vidas sem fronteiras na Hispânia medieval", *Medievalista*, 31 (Janeiro–Junho 2022), pp. 47–71. ISSN 1646-740X. Available at: https://medievalista.iem.fcsh.unl.pt DOI: https://doi.org/10.4000/medievalista.5087; "Retóricas em torno da Relíquia de Vera Cruz de Marmelar: do poder devocional à apropriação sociopolítica", *Via Spiritus*, 28 (2021), pp. 55–69. DOI: https://doi.org/10.21747/0873-1233/spi28a2; "Património e recursos das comendas: sociabilidades, gestão de entradas e práticas fiscais (séculos XIII–XVI)", *Edad Media. Revista de Historia*, 2021, nº 22, pp. 179–208. E-ISSN: 2530-6448. Available at: https://revistas.uva.es/index.php/edadmedia/issue/view/278 DOI: https://doi.org/10.24197/em.22.2021.179-208; with Ferreira, Leandro Ribeiro, "Mobilizar para a Guerra: as Ordens Militares entre responsabilidades partilhadas", *Ordens Militares, Identidade e Mudança. Textos selecionados do VIII Encontro sobre Ordens Militares*, Vol. 2., Fernandes, Isabel Cristina F. (coord.), Palmela: GEsOS-Município de Palmela, 2021, pp. 1103–1110. ISBN 978-972-8497-83-5; "A Ordem de Cristo: incorporação e modelação de um passado templário e régio", *Ordens Militares, Identidade e Mudança. Textos selecionados do VIII Encontro sobre Ordens Militares*. Vol. 2. Fernandes, Isabel Cristina F. (coord.), Palmela: GEsOS-Município de Palmela, 2021, p. 657-671. ISBN 978-972-8497-83-5; with Costa, Paulo Sousa "Do conflito à soberania. Os forais em Trás-os-Montes no reinado de D. Dinis (1279–1325)", *Poder y Poderes en la Edad Media*, Martínez Peñin, Raquel e Cavero Domínguez, Gregoria (coords.), *Monografías de la Sociedad Española de Estudios Medievales*, nº 16. Múrcia, 2021, pp. 461–477. ISBN 978-84-17865-93-1; "Jerusalém: uma cidade épica", *Sacralidades Medievais: Textos & Temas*, Nascimento, Renata Cristina de Sousa (organizadora), Goiânia: Tempestiva, 2021, pp. 75–78. ISBN 978-65-992343-4-7.

PRINGLE, R. Denys, (with Ergün Laflı and Maurizio Buora) "Four Frankish Gravestones from Medieval Ephesus", *Anatolian Studies* 71 (2021), 171–84; (with Andrew Petersen, eds) *Ramla, City of Muslim Palestine, 715–1917: Studies in History, Archaeology and Architecture* (Archaeopress: Oxford, 2021), including chapters on "The Christian Buildings of Ramla", pp. 203–23, "Pilgrims' Graffiti of the Fifteenth to Seventeenth Centuries in the Franciscan Hospice in Ramla", pp. 276–82, and "Sites in the Crusader Lordships of Ramla, Lydda and Mirabel", pp. 286–93; "Itineraria Terrae Sanctae minora III: Some Early Twelfth-century Guides to Frankish Jerusalem", *Crusades* 20 (2021), 3–63.

RAGHEB, Fadi, "New Sources on the Memory of Saladin in Islamic History: An Explorative Essay in to the Arabic Chronicles of the Late Medieval and Early Modern Period." In *The Political and Cultural History of the Kurds*, edited by Amir Harrak, 201–37. New York: Peter Lang, 2022; "The City as Liminal Space: Islamic Pilgrimage and Muslim Holy Sites in Jerusalem During the Mamlūk Period (1250–1517)." In *The Friday Mosque in the City: Liminality, Ritual, and Politics*, edited by A. Hilâl Uğurlu and Suzan Yalman, 75–122. Chicago: Intellect, University of Chicago Press, 2020.

RODRIGUEZ GARCÍA, Jose Manuel, *Las Órdenes Militares de origen hispánico*. Dilema editorial. Madrid, 2021. 297 pp; "Las ligas santas y los planes de cruzada contra el Islam", *Muy Historia especial*, 141 (2021): 21–27; "La acción de las flotas de guerra en la época de Alfonso X el sabio" *Alcanate*, XII (2020): 163–182; "La cruzada en el mar: naves, logística y transporte marítimo", *Desperta Ferro*, 68 (2021): 46–50; "Que ben veya que la mar era sua et que non·l calia de res tembre La batalla de las Islas Formigues (1285)", en *Fechos de Armas. 15 hitos bélicos del medievo ibérico*. Laergastula ed. Madrid, 2021, pp. 101–114.

SCALONE, Alessandro, "La prostituta e la croce: adulterio e immoralità femminile nelle fonti della prima crociata", ("The prostitute and the cross: adultery and sexual immorality in the literary sources of the First Crusade"), *Collectana*, 52, 2020, pp. 331–346; "Memoria, crociata e diplomazia: un'analisi sui rapporti diplomatici tra Outremer e Europa Occidentale. 1149–1189" ("Memory, crusade and diplomacy: an analysis on the diplomatic relations between Outremer and Western Europe. 1149–1189"), in *Quarto ciclo di studi medievali. Atti del convegno. 4–5 giugno 2018 Firenze*, Firenze, EBS print, 2018, pp. 183–187.

SCHINDEL, Nikolaus, "Zu einem kreuzfahrerzeitlichen Münztyp aus Edessa", *Schweizer Münzblätter* 274, 2019, pp. 27–33; "Die kreuzfahrerzeitlichen Münzen im Wiener Münzkabinett. Erster Teil: Die Prägungen aus dem Heiligen Land. Zugleich ein Beitrag zur Forschungs- und Sammlungsgeschichte der Kreuzfahrernumismatik in ihrer Wiegenzeit" (together with Daniela Williams and Robert Kool), in: *Numismatische Zeitschrift* 125, 2019, pp. 259–282; "A New Assembly of Cut Gold Fragments from the Crusader Period" (together with Robert Kool and Issa Baidoun), in: *Israel Numismatic Research* 14, 2019, pp. 169–192; "Drei Notizen zur Münzprägung der kreuzfahrerzeitlichen Grafschaft Edessa", *Numismatische Zeitschrift*, 126, 2020, pp. 353–367; "Ein überprägter Follis aus Edessa", *Numismatische Zeitschrift*, 127, 2021, pp. 463–465.

SHEPARD, Jonathan, "Anna Komnena as a Source for the Crusades", ed. A. Mallett, *Franks and Crusades in Medieval Eastern Christian Historiography* (Outremer: Studies in the Crusades and the Latin East 10) (Turnhout, 2020), pp. 25–63; "Knowledge of the West in Byzantine Sources, *c.*900–*c.*1200", ed. N. Drocourt and S. Kolditz, *A Companion to Byzantium and the West, 850–1204* (Leiden, 2021), pp. 31–84; *Political Culture in the Latin West, Byzantium and the Islamic World, c. 700–c. 1500: A Framework for Comparing Three Spheres* (ed. with C. Holmes, J. Van Steenbergen and B. Weiler) (Cambridge, 2021).

SINIBALDI, Micaela, "The Crusader Lordship of Transjordan (1100–1189): Settlement Forms, Dynamics and Significance". *Levant* (1 April 2022, Open Access). Link to the online article: https://www.tandfonline.com/doi/full/10.1080/00758914.2022.2033016; The Crusader period, in *Pottery of Jordan Manual*, eds, Jehad Haron and Douglas R. Clark, ACOR publications, (Amman, 2021; The Late Petra Project: an archaeological study of settlement in post-urban Petra. Le Carnets de l'Ifpo. *La recherche en train de se faire à l'Institut français du Proche-Orient* (online from June 28th, 2021). Link to the online article: https://ifpo.hypotheses.org/11183; "Karak Castle in the Lordship of Transjordan: Observations on the Chronology of the Crusader-period Fortress", in P. Edbury, D. Pringle and B. Major, *"Bridge of Civilisations." The Near East and Europe c.1100–1300*, (Oxford, Archaeopress, 2019), pp. 97–114.

STANTCHEV, Stefan, "Formation and Refiguration of the Canon Law on Trade with Infidels (ca. 1200–ca. 1600)," in John D. Haskell and Pamela Slotte, eds, *Christianity and Public International Law* (Cambridge University Press, 2021), pp. 59–90; Stefan Stantchev and Benjamin Weber, "In Coena Domini: A Hierocratic Weapon or a Pastoral Staff?", *Bulletin of Medieval Canon Law* 38 (2021), pp. 361–419.

STAPEL, Rombert.J., *Medieval Authorship and Cultural Exchange in the Late Fifteenth Century: The Utrecht Chronicle of the Teutonic Order* (Abingdon/New York: Routledge, 2021); "Preußen und die frühe Verbreitung der "Jüngeren Hochmeisterchronik", Kulturelle Verbindungen zwischen Utrecht, Königsberg und Mergentheim (um 1480–1530)", in Heckmann, M.-L. and Sarnowsky, J. (eds) *Schriftlichkeit im Preußenland* (Osnabrück: Fibre, 2021) (Tagungsberichte der Historischen Kommission für ost- und westpreußische Landesforschung, 30), pp. 211–231.

TAL, Oren, with Shotten-Hallel, V., and Ashkenazi, D.; 2022 [early view] "Archaeometallurgical Analysis of Thirteenth-Century Bronze and Iron Construction Implements from the Walls of the Frankish Castle at Arsuf/Arsur", *Metallography, Microstructure, and Analysis*. [https://link.springer.com/article/10.1007/s13632-022-00838-x]; with Heidemann, S., and Nicolle, D. C. 2021, "An Inscribed Ballista Stone from Apollonia-Arsūf, Israel, and Stone-throwing Siege Machines in the Medieval Near East", *Journal of Islamic Archaeology* 8/2: 239–254; with Zeischka-Kenzler, A., Yohanan, H., Kenzler, H., Harpak, T., Yehuda, E., and Scholkmann, B., 2021, "The Crusader Town of Arsur by the Sea: A German-Israeli Collaborative Project (2012–2016)", Kamlah, J. and Lichtenberger, A., eds, *The Mediterranean Sea and the Southern Levant: Archaeological and Historical Perspectives from the Bronze Age to Medieval Times*. Abhandlungen des Deutschen Palästina-Vereins 48. (Wiesbaden: Harrassowitz), pp. 337–360; with Shotten-Hallel, V. and Yohanan, H., 2021; "The Castle Chapel of Arsur – New Evidence for Its Location and Architecture", Shotten-Hallel, V. and Weetch, R., eds, *Crusading and Archaeology*, pp. 369–400; with Jackson-Tal, R. E., 2021, "Crusader's Choice: Prunted Glass Beakers from the Latin Kingdom of Jerusalem", Ade, D., Frommer, S., Marstaller, T., Scholz, A., Terp-Schunter, M., Vossler-Wolf, C. and Wolf, M., eds, *Sachgeschichte(n): Beiträge zu einer interdisziplinär verstandenen Archäologie des Mittelalters und der Neuzeit. Festschrift für Barbara Scholkmann zu ihrem 80. Geburtstag.* (Universität Tübingen: Tübingen Library Publishing), pp. 133–141; with Shotten-Hallel, V., Yohanan, and H., Harpak, 2021. Apollonia: Arsur Castle. *Ḥadashot Arkheologiyot—Excavations and Surveys in Israel* 133. [http://www.hadashot-esi.org.il/Report_Detail_Eng.aspx?id=25908].

THORAU, Peter, "Herrschaft erbt man nicht – Herrschaft erobert man". Herrschaftserwerb, Nachfolgeregelungen und ayyūbidische Realpolitik im 12. und 13. Jahrhundert, in: Christian Vogel u.a. (Ed.): Frankenreich – Testamente – Landesgeschicht. Festschrift für Brigitte Kasten zum 65. Geburtstag (= Veröfflichungen der Kommission für Saarländische Landesgeschichte 53), Saarbrücken 2020, S. 401–420.

VILLADS JENSEN, Kurt, "Saxo and the Peoples to the East", *Authorship, Worldview, and Identity in Medieval Europe*, ed. Christian Raffensperger. London: Routledge 2022, 256–271; "Burning of Idols – Mission and Theology around the Baltic Sea", *The Expansion of Faith. Crusading on the Frontiers of Latin Christendom in the High Middle Ages*, eds Paul Scrodecki & Norbert Kersken. Turnhout: Brepols 2022, 99–111; "Once and Future Crusades. Past and Projected Plans of Emperor Frederick II and King Valdemar II of Denmark, c. 1214–1227", *The Crusades: History and Memory. Proceedings of the Ninth Conference of the Society for the Study of the Crusades and the Latin East, Odense, 27 June – 1 July 2016*, vol. 2, eds Kurt Villads Jensen and Torben Kjersgaard Nielsen. Turnhout: Brepols 2021, 77–94; Ibid.; "Jerusalem. Kampen om det hellige Sheikh Jarrah", *Politiken Historie* 18, 2021, 16–24; *Det Danske Imperium. Storhed of Fald*, Kurt Villads Jensen og Michael Bregnsbo, København 2021, e-book version; *Legacies of the Crusades. Proceedings of the Ninth Conference of the Society for the Study of the Crusades and the Latin East, Odense, 27 June – 1 July 2016*, vol. 1, eds Torben Kjersgaard Nielsen and Kurt Villads Jensen, Turnhout:

Brepols 2021. 304 pp.; "Valdemar 2. Sejr som hærfører", *Militært lederskap – Endring over tid?*, ed. Knut Arstad, Oslo: Forsvarsakademiet 2021, 9–35; "Jerusalem under medeltiden. Vallfartsort och prestigeprojekt", *Svenskarna och det heliga landet*, ed Kurt Almqvist, Louise Belfrage, Nathan Schachar, Stockholm: Stolpe 2021, 34–43; "The Dragon of Apocalypse: Sanctifying Portuguese History by Strong Emotions", *War, Diplomacy and Peacemaking in Medieval Iberia*, ed. Kim Bergqvist, Kurt Villads Jensen, Anthony John Lappin, Newcastle upon Tyne: Cambridge Scholars publ. 2021, 145–162; *War, Diplomacy and Peacemaking in Medieval Iberia*, ed. Kim Bergqvist, Kurt Villads Jensen, Anthony John Lappin, Newcastle upon Tyne: Cambridge Scholars publ. 2021. 286 pp; "1250. Handkvarnen", *År. Historiker berättar*, ed. Anna Götlind & Magnus Linnarsson, Stockholm: Appell 2020, 16–27; "The deplorable crusades – a view from Sweden", *Controversial Histories – Current Views on the Crusades*, ed Felix Hinz, Johannes Meyer-Hamme, London: Routledge 2021, 64–66; "Fra konge til korstog", *Helgener i nord. Nye studier i nordisk helgenkult*, ed. Magne Njåstad & Randi Bjørshol Wærdahl, Oslo: Novus 2020, 149–162; "Creating Cohesion in Dynastic Conglomerates. Identities in Comparison: Medieval Bohemia and Denmark", with Jana Fantysová-Matejková, *The Historical Evolution of Regionalizing Identities in Europe*, ed. Dick E.H. de Boer, Nils Holger Petersen, Bas Spierings, Martin van der Velde, Berlin: Peter Lang 2020, 63–121; *Conflict and Collaboration in Medieval Iberia*, ed. Kim Bergqvist, Kurt Villads Jensen, Anthony John Lappin, Newcastle upon Tyne: Cambridge Scholars publ. 2020. 328 pp.; "Knud Lavard – hertug og helgen", *St. Knudsgilde Flensborg 1170–2020*, udg. Knudsgildet, Flensborg: Knudsgildet 2020, 27–32; "I pestens tid. Ydre og indre fjender", *Sfinx* online; *Sfinx* 43:4 (2020), 16–23.; "Skandināvijas, Ziemeļvācijas un Livonijas kristianizācija, 1000.–1300. gads: Salīdzinošs skatījums", *Viduslaiku Livonija un tās vēsturiskais mantojums*, ed. Andris Levāns, Ilgvars Misāns, Gustavs Strenga (Riga 2019), pp. 42–63; "På Herrens vej – Middelalderens pilgrimsrejser", med Kirsi Salonen, *Veje & Kultur. forbindelser mellem kulturer fra antikken til i dag*, red. Pernille Carstens, København 2019, 50–53; "Rude. Zisterzienser", med Kirsi Salonen, Wolfgang Bauch, Katja Hillebrand, *Klosterbuch Schleswig-Holstein. Klöster, Stifte und Konvente von den Anfängen bis zur Reformation*, hrsg Oliver Auge & Katja Hillebrand, Regensburg: Schnell Steiner 2019, 500–532; *Ristiretket*. Toim & suom. Kirsi Salonen. Turku: Turun historiallinen yhditys 2019, 306 pp.; "Bjørne og biologi. Om sæd, ost og sikkerhedspolitik i Danmark omkring 1200", *Tidens landskap. En vänbok ill Anders Andrén*, red. Cecilia Ljung et al., Stockholm: Nordic Academic Press 2019, 245–247.

Villegas-Aristizábal, Lucas, "The Changing Priorities in the Norman Incursions into the Iberian Peninsula's Muslim–Christian Frontiers, 1018–1191", *Normans in the Mediterranean*, eds, Emily Winkler and Liam Fitzgerald, MISCS 9, Turnhout: Brepols, 2021, pp. 81–119. https://doi.org/10.1484/M.MISCS-EB.5.121958; "La guerra contra al-Ándalus: Una visión desde las fuentes narrativas ultramontanas (1064–1218)", *Memoria y fuentes de la guerra santa peninsular (ss. X–XV)*, eds, Carlos de Ayala, Francisco García Fitz y José Santiago Palacios Ontalva, Madrid: Trea, 2021, pp. 103–130; https://www.trea.es/books/memoria-y-fuentes-de-la-guerra-santa-peninsular-siglos-x-xv; "A Frisian Perspective on Crusading in Iberia as Part of the Sea Journey to the Holy Land 1217–1218", *Studies in Medieval and Renaissance History*, 3rd Series, 15 (2018) (Pub. 2021): 67–149; https://www.acmrs.org/journals/studies-in-medieval-and-renaissance-history/; with Dominic Alessio, "Re-thinking Religion and Empire: Non-State Organisations from the Knights Hospitallers to ISIS", *Journal of Balkan and Near Eastern Studies* 22 (2020): 1–17; "Was the Portuguese Led Military Campaign Against Alcácer do Sal in the Autumn of 1217 Part of the Fifth Crusade?", *Al-Masāq: Journal of the Medieval Mediterranean* 31:1 (2019): 50–67.

Voisin, Ludivine, *Les monastères grecs sous domination latine aux XIII*ᵉ*–XVI*ᵉ *siècles, Comme un loup poursuivant un mouton...*, Brepols, 2021, Turnhout, 452 p.

Wilskman, Juho, *Comparing Military Cultures: Warfare in the Aegean region from the Fourth Crusade to the Early Fifteenth Century*, PhD dissertation, University of Helsinki: Helsinki 2021. 455 pages. Accessible online (address https://helda.helsinki.fi/handle/10138/335952); "'Morean kronikka' – arvoitus ristiretkiajalta" [The Chronicle of Morea – A Mystery from Crusade Era], *Tuhannen vuoden kirjavuori, Kirjallisia näkökulmia Bysantin kulttuuriin*, ed. Pia Houni ja Kalle Knaapi. Acta Byzantina Fennica, Supplementa, 1. Bysantin tutkimuksen Seura (Helsinki 2021), pp. 93–123; Book Review: "Paavo Hohti: *Bysantti. Tuhat draaman vuotta*", WSOY: Helsinki 2021 [Byzantium. One Thousand Year of Drama] – *Skholion* 2/2021, pp. 13–15. "Väitöslektio. Comparing Military Cultures: Warfare in the Aegean Region from the Fourth Crusade to the Early Fifteenth Century" [*Lectio praecursoria* for the public defence of the PhD dissertation] – *Skholion* 2/2021, pp. 7–12.

2. Recently completed theses

Bagni, Giampiero, "Templars in Bologna: A multidisciplinary Approach", PhD, Nottingham Trent University, supervised by Nicholas Morton.

Battistelli, Daniele, "Il disciplinamento della violenza aristocratica nella Francia dell'anno Mille (secoli X–XII)" [Disciplining aristocratic violence in France around the year 1000 (cent. X–XII)]; BA in History, Anthropology, Religions (L-42), "La Sapienza" – University of Rome, 2021, supervised by Antonio Musarra.

Halliburton, Ben, "'Utriusque illorum illustrium regum, pari gradu consanguineus': The Marquises of Montferrat in the Age of Crusade, c.1135–1225', PhD, Saint Louis University, 2019, supervised by Thomas Madden.

Ivashko, Roman, "Formation of the structures of the Roman Catholic Church in the Kingdom of Rus' in the 14th century", Specialist (Master) degree in History Ivan Franko National University of Lviv, supervised by Modest Chornyi; "The requests for apology from St Pope John Paul II on behalf of the entire Catholic Church as an integral part of his pastoral service", Magister degree in Ecumenical Studies, The Ukrainian Catholic University, supervised by Taras Kurylets.

Lencart, Joana, Thesis: "Pedro Álvares Seco: a retroprojeção da memória da Ordem de Cristo no século XVI", PhD, Faculty of Arts and Humanities – University of Porto, 2018, supervised by Paula Pinto Costa. Grant: FCT SFRH/BD/94440/2013. Available in: http://catalogo.up.pt/F/?func=direct&doc_number=000872197&local_base=FLUP.

Lombardo, Simone, PhD in Medieval History, Title: "La croce dei mercanti. Genova, Venezia e la crociata mediterranea nella seconda metà del Trecento" [The merchants' cross. Genoa, Venice and the Mediterranean Crusade in the second half of the 14th century], Catholic University of Milan – Heidelberg University, 2022, supervised by Maria Pia Alberzoni (Milan) and Nikolas Jaspert (Heidelberg).

Roesch, Fabian, "Rechtskonstruktion und adeliger Herrschaftsanspruch im Königreich Jerusalem. Die Erfindung Jerusalems durch Recht.", PhD, Justus-Liebig-Universitaet Giessen, supervised by Stefan Tebruck and Verena Epp, 2018.

Scalone, Alessandro, "The Mongol conquest of Jerusalem: an analysis of an event that never happened", MA in Crusader Studies, Royal Holloway University, supervised by Jonathan Phillips, 2018; "Study on the diplomatic relations between the Latin East and the West between the Second and the Third Crusade", MA in Medieval Studies, University of Pisa, 2016, supervised by Duccio Balestracci.

SCHRADER, Jr., Stanley, "The Knights Templar: Knights of Christ", MA, Erskine Theological Seminary, 2020, supervised by Dale Johnson.

WILSKMAN, Juho, *Comparing Military Cultures: Warfare in the Aegean Region from the Fourth Crusade to the Early Fifteenth Century*, PhD, University of Helsinki, 2021, supervised by Björn Forsén and (after retirement of Hannes Saarinen) Heikki Mikkeli, awarded with Distinction.

3. Papers read by members of the Society and others

BALARD, Michel, "Genoese Caffa: Meeting Point of Orient and Occident (XIIIth–XVth)", communication présentée au colloque Crossing Boundaries, Cambridge, 10–12 avril 2019.

BYSTED, Ane, L., "Material and Non-material Aspects of Archbishop Anders Sunesen's Crusade Preaching", at IMC Leeds 2019.

CARR, Annemarie Wehl, "The Cave Church of St. Marina at Qalamoun: A Richly Rewarding Shared Project," 11 April 2022, Archarological Research Unit, University of Cyprus; "The Ziyareti of Kykkos: The Kykkotissa and the Ottomans," 8 April 2022, Yale Lectures in Late Antique and Byzantine Art and Architecture; "Reflections on the Dormition: Mary as Mother and Bride," 10 March 2022, The Virgin Beyond Borders, International Conference, National Hellenic Research Foundation; Center for Hellenic Studies – Harvard University; Simon Fraser University; The University of Oxford.

CARTER, Leo M., 'The Register of John de Pontissara, Bishop of Winchester, and the Voice of the Mamluk Sultan of Egypt in the Aftermath of the Fall of Acre (1291)', SSCLE 10th International Conference: Crusading Encounters (2022).

CERRINI, Simonetta, 2021 Troyes, 3–5 novembre, Colloque international: *D'Orient en Occident. Les Templiers des origines à la fin du XIIe siècle*, "Hugues de Payns, les 'proto-Templiers' et l'incipit de l'Ordre du Temple".

COUREAS, Nicholas, "The Regular Latin Clergy and Latin Lay Society in Lusignan Cyprus: The Evidence from the Notarial Deeds of Famagusta," in Orthodox and Latin Monasticism in the Eastern Mediterranean, 13th–16th c., International Digital Conference, National Hellenic Research Foundation, 1–2 October 2020; "Mamluk Naval Warfare against Cyprus, 1270 – post 1474," In Commerce and Crusade: The Mamluk Empire and Cyprus in a Euro-Mediterranean Perspective, 1–2 July 2021; "Women and the Hospitaller Order on Rhodes and Cyprus in the Fourteenth and Fifteenth Centuries," OM XXII, 22–24 September 2021.

EDGINGTON, Susan B., "After Ascalon: The *Gesta Francorum Ierusalem Expugnantium* on the Early Years of the Kingdom of Jerusalem" at 2021 IMC.

FAVREAU-LILIE, Marie-Luise, "Möglichkeiten und Grenzen eines Vergleichs, at Tagung der Internationalen Kommission zur Erforschung des Deutschen Ordens (IKEDO)", Gdansk/ Danzig, 21–22 June, 2021.

GAPOSCHKIN, Cecilia, "The Cross of War in the Age of the Crusades." October 2021, the 2nd International Seminar on Crusades and Military Orders, Conference organized by Latin American Society for the Study of the Crusades and Military. (online) Recorded talk streamed here: https://www.youtube.com/watch?v=YAa66BQJ1lo; "Louis IX and the Triumphal Cross of Constantine." Center for War and Diplomacy. Delivered virtually. March 18, 2021.

HODGSON, Natasha, "Wars in the Workshop: Digitizing manuscript rolls", *Schoenberg Institute for Manuscript Studies* (March 2022) online: available at https://www.youtube.com/watch?v=GhFtWSOKPCk; "Crusading Masculinities: past and present", University of Wisconsin (April 2021) online; "Diversifying the Crusades" *Teaching the Crusades* (Haskins Society, USA) (July 2020) online; "The Myth of the Knight Crusader" round table Leeds IMC (July 2019); "Contested masculinities and the crusades: two perspectives" University of Leeds *Contesting Medieval Masculinities* (May 2019); "An Examination of the Canterbury Roll" with Sotiria Kogou at European Research Infrastructure for Heritage Science (E-RIHS) Science and Heritage Interdisciplinary Workshop (March 2019); "Gendering the Later Crusades" Edinburgh University (February 2019); "No Future? Medievalists & Early Modernists, Interdisciplinarity and the Challenges of STEM in the context of Brexit", ANZAMEMS conference and Medieval Association of the Pacific (MAP) conference (January 2019); "The Canterbury Roll: Producing a Digital Edition for the Twenty-First Century", ANZAMEMS conference (January 2019); "(Re)defining the ideal crusader – gender and crusading ideals in the 'recovery treatises' of the early fourteenth century", ANZAMEMS conference (January 2019).

HORSWELL, Mike, March 2022, "The Last Crusade: The Use of Crusading Rhetoric and Imagery in Britain, 1914–45", *Ludlow Palmers, Shropshire*; June 2021; "'A Sleepy Topic' or Playing with Fire?: Wikipedia and the Reception of the Crusades Revisited", *SSCLE ECR conference*, RHUL; June 2021; "'Crusading' Knights in Jerusalem: Obliquely Remembering Allenby, Saladin & "Richard"', *Contested Histories, Swansea University*; May 2021; "Iconic Bastards and Bastardised Icons: *Plebby Quest*'s Neomedievalist Crusades", *Middle Ages in Modern Games,* online Twitter conference; May 2021; "Far-Right and White Supremacist Appropriations of the Crusades" for students of the crusades at Ursinus College, US; Feb. 2021; "Imagining the Crusades After 9/11 through Graphic Novels: Seagle's *Crusades* (2001–2) and Dufaux & Xavier's *Croisade* (2007–14)", *Historical Fictions Research Network*, annual conference, online; April 2019; "Crusading Unbound: Probing the Limits of Crusading through Fantasy after 1900", *King's College London and University of Notre Dame, London, Remembering the Middle Ages? Reception, Identity, Politics*; Jan. 2019; "Crusade Apologists: Exorcising and Embodying Crusaders", *IHR Medievalism Seminar, Senate House, London.*

JOSSERAND, Philippe, "Tres olhares sobre a Ordem do Templo em Portugal", à paraître dans *Medievalista*, 2022 (article écrit en collaboration avec Luís Filipe Oliveira et Paula Pinto Costa); "Manuel Zaccaria's Report on the Fleet in Outremer after the Fall of Acre (1292–3): Jacques de Molay, the War of Curzola, and Genoese-Cypriot Conflict", à paraître dans *Crusades*, 2022 (article écrit en collaboration avec Christopher D. Schabel et Antonio Musarra); "La croisade et ses fronts dans l'historiographie française de l'Entre-deux-guerres à aujourd'hui", à paraître dans *Revue Mabillon* en 2022; "Aux origines de l'ordre du Temple: histoire, écriture et historiographie", dans *D'Orient en Occident. Les Templiers des origines à la fin du XIIᵉ siècle. Colloque international du neuvième centenaire de l'ordre du Temple (1120–2020)*, éd. par Arnaud Baudin et Philippe Josserand, Heule, Snoeck, à paraître fin 2022; "Cruzada, idea de"; "Órdenes militares" (avec Carlos de Ayala Martínez); "Templarios", in Georges Martin (dir.), *Diccionario de historia medieval de la Península Ibérica*, Madrid, Akal, à paraître en 2022; "Templiers / templarisme", in Anne Besson, William Blanc et Vincent Ferré (dir.), *Dictionnaire du médiévalisme*, Paris, Vendémiaire, à paraître en 2022.

KANE, James, "A *swiðe mycel styrung*: the First Crusade in vernacular and Latin annals from Anglo-Norman England", 2021 IMC (Session 2204 – Historical Writing, the Crusades, and the Latin East, III: Reception, Emotion, and Gender).

KNOBLER, Adam, "Crusading Rhetoric and Ideology in the Long 19th century/Retórica e ideología de las cruzadas en el largo siglo XIX." Seminario de Posgrado: Las Cruzadas, entre la Península Ibérica y Tierra Santa, Madrid, Spain, October 2021.

KOLIA-DERMITZAKI, Athina, "Warfare in Byzantium: an outline of its ideology, practice and impact during the Middle Byzantine period", Medieval culture and War Conference, Athens 27–29 June 2019.

LEONARD Jr., Robert D., "Who Issued the "K Class" Imitation Venetian Ducats?," May 13, 2021, IMCS.

NICHOLSON, Helen J., 9 July 2021 (session 2304, "Historical Writing, the Crusades, and the Latin East, IV: After the Battle of Hattin") "The Silences of the *Itinerarium Peregrinorum* 1", IMC 2021; 23 September 2021: "*Dominus Jhesus novum genus militia constituit et elegit*: The Military Orders' Relations with Women in the Medieval Period" at the 21st conference on military orders in Torun, Poland, "Military Orders and Women. Donators – Affiliates – Sisters – Saints", 23–25 September 2021; 5 November 2021: "The reception of the *ordo novus* of the Temple", at the conference "D'Orient en Occident. Les Templiers des origins à la fin du XIIe siècle: colloque neuvième centenaire de l'ordre du Temple", Troyes, France, 3–5 November 2021.

PARK, Danielle E.A., "Melisende of Jerusalem: Female Lordship in the Kingdom of Jerusalem", GCMS Summer Symposium, University of Reading, online 2021; "Crusader Kingship in the Making: Fulk of Anjou's Angevin Origins", SSCLE ECR Conference, online, 2021.

PARSONS, Simon Thomas, "A Farewell to Tudebode: Does 'Tradition' Offer Us an Escape?", Keynote Lecture at Understanding the Sources for the Crusades: New Approaches, on 22 Jan 2022.

PERRY, Guy, https://fivebooks.com/best-books/the-crusades-guy-perry/ [online interview recommending books].

RAGHEB, Fadi, "New Sources on the Memory of Saladin and the Crusades in Pre-Modern Islamic History." Paper presented at the online lecture series, "Rethinking Memory and Historiography of the Crusades in the Middle East," organized by Dr. Ahmed M. Sheir, Uniiverrsiittät Marburg, March 31, 2022.

RODRIGUEZ GARCÍA, Jose Manuel, "La batalla de Tannenberg. Estableciendo un marco comparativo". Curo Grandes Batallas Medievales, UNED, Junio, 2021; "La memoria de las Órdenes Militares: los caballeros de la Orden Teutónica en España y Alemania". Curso La Construcción de la memoria en la sociedad Medieval. UNED, abril, 2021.

SCALONE, Alessandro, "The Recovery of Jerusalem and the relationship between the Mongols and the West", *Crusades* (approved for publication).

SINIBALDI, Micaela, "Settlement in Crusader Transjordan (1100–1189)", Public Lecture for the Faculty of Archaeology, University of Warsaw (February 24th, 2022); Workshop organised by Micaela Sinibaldi in July 2021: The history and archaeology of the Islamic and Crusader periods: some reflections on methods and methodologies of research. Organisation of a three-days international online workshop for the University of Shanghai (June 24–26 2021).

VILLADS JENSEN, Kurt, 22.24. september: deltog i konferencen *Die Ritterorden und Frauen: Stifterinnen – Affilierte – Schwestern – Heilige,* Torun, med foredraget "The Hospitallers in Scandinavia and Women – How Much Can We Actually Know?", og som moderator af to sessioner, 10.–12. september: deltog i konferencen *Danish-Estonian relations in the Middle Ages*, Tallinn, med foredraget "King Valdemar II and Tallinn 1219 – just another of his conquests or part of a grand plan?"; 4.–7. Juli 2022 IMC; med foredrag om "The Wilderness, at the End of the World. Missionizing around the Baltic", og som moderator af to sessioner, pr. zoom.

VILLEGAS-ARISTIZÁBAL, Lucas, July 9, 2021, "Warring against the Almohads during the Fifth

Crusade: Northern European Perspectives on its Legitimacy as a Crusade," (Online: Zoom) 2020 IMC; "Norman in the north-east of the Iberian Peninsula", *The Normans: A Story of Mobility, Conquest and Innovation*, (Online: Zoom) Reiss-Engelhorn-Museums, Mannheim, Germany; July 10, 2020 "Norman and Anglo-Norman Perspectives in the Iberian Frontier", Session v16-02, (Online: Blackboard) IMC 2019; "La guerra contra al-Andalus en las fuentes narrativas del norte de Europa (1064–1218)", Symposium: *Jornadas Internacionales: Memoria y fuentes de la guerra santa peninsular (ss. X–XV)*, Cáceres, Spain.

4. Forthcoming publications

ALVIRA-CABRER, Martín, "El *Llibre del Fets* de Jaime I de Aragón como manual militar", *Studia historica, Historia Medieval*, 40–41 (2022), pp. 35–62; "Un privilegio del rey Pedro el Católico a la villa de Reus (1207)", in *Homenaje al Profesor Salvador Claramunt Rodríguez*, Sociedad Española de Estudios Medievales; "Jaime I el Conquistador. *Tantas conquistas et tan grandes*", in *Comandantes medievales hispánicos. Siglos XII–XIII. Cuadernos de Historia Militar*, nº 5, Madrid, *Desperta Ferro*, 2022, cap. 10.

BAGNI, Giampiero, *The Sarcophagus of Templar Master Arnau de Torroja in Verona? Updated Results,* in *Crusades* 21 (2022).

BALARD, Michel, "The Black Sea Slavery", éd. F. Rozu, Brepols, end 2021; "Une économie insulaire: Chio (XIVe–XVe s.)", éd. J-A. Cancellieri, 2022.

BATTISTELLI, Daniele, "'Coment Jherusalem siet et l'estat de li'. La descrizione di Gerusalemme nella Cronaca di Ernoul" in *"Eurostudium 3W", Rivista trimestrale online del Dipartimento Storia, Antropologia, Religioni, Arte, Spettacolo (SARAS)*, (La Sapienza Università di Roma, 2022/3).

BERKOVICH, Ilya and RE'EM, Amit, "Broken, Hidden, Rediscovered: The Story of the Cosmatesque High Altar of the Holy Sepulchre", *Eretz-Israel* 35, (Forthcoming 2022).

BOAS, Adrian, *The Crusades Uncovered*, ARC Humanities Press, to be published in 2022; *Crusader Archaeology. The Material Culture of the Latin East*, third edition – Routledge, to be published in 2023; "Frankish Vernacular Architecture on the Levantine Mainland", "Informal Exchange of Objects: Gifts, Keepsakes, Relics, Plunder and Barter", "Preservation of the Frankish Past in Placenames", "The Franks' Engagement with Ancient Ruins" "Conclusion" – chapters in *Routledge Handbook of the Material Culture of the Crusader States*, eds Adrian Boas, Elizabeth Lampina and Nicholas Morton, Routledge, to be published in 2023.

BUCK, Andrew D., Kane, James H. and Spencer Stephen J., (eds), *Crusade, Settlement, and Historical Writing in the Latin East and Latin West, c. 1100– c. 1300* (Woodbridge: Boydell, under contract for 2022 submission); "Between *Chronicon* and *Chanson*: William of Tyre, the First Crusade, and the Art of Storytelling", in Andrew D. Buck, James H. Kane, and Stephen J. Spencer (eds), Ibid.; with James H. Kane and Stephen J. Spencer, "Introduction", Ibid.; "Antioch, the Crusades, and the West *c.*1097–*c.*1200: Between Memory and Reality", in Lean Ní Chléirigh and Natasha R. Hodgson (eds), *Sources for the Crusades: Textual Traditions and Literary Influences* (Abingdon: Routledge, forthcoming); "Relations between the Crusader States and Byzantium", Andrew Holt (ed.), *Religion and World Civilizations: How Faith Shaped Societies from Antiquity to the Present* (Santa Barbara: ABC-Clio, 2022/3) (in press); "The Byzantine-Crusader Split at the Siege of Antioch (1098)", Andrew Holt (ed.), *Religion and World Civilizations: How Faith Shaped Societies from Antiquity to the Present* (Santa Barbara: ABC-Clio, 2022/3) (in press).

CARR, Annemarie Wehl, "Art Historical Notes on the Wall Paintings of St. Marina, Qalamoun", *Dévotion et sainteté au féminin. Les peintures murales médiévales de sainte*

Marina de Qalamoun au Liban Nord. Ed. Lina Souad Fakhoury and May Davies. Tripoli: Balamand University, forthcoming; "Saint Luke and the Lady: The Substance of Things Half-Seen." In *Byzantine Materiality*. Ed. Evan Freeman and Charles Barber. New York: Cambridge University Press, forthcoming; "Epithet and Emotion: Reflections on the Quality of *Eleos*: The Epithet of the Mother of God Eleousa." In *Managing Emotion: Passions, Affects and Imaginings in Byzantium*. Ed. Margaret Mullett and Susan Ashbrook Harvey. London: Routledge, forthcoming; "Inscriptions in Cyprus." In *Medieval Texts on Byzantine Art and Aesthetics, vol. 3. From Alexios I Komnenos to the rise of Hesychasm (1081 – ca. 1330)*. Ed. Charles Barber and Foteini Spingou. Cambridge: Cambridge University Press, forthcoming.

CARR, Mike, "Cyprus and the Crusades between the Fall of Acre and the Reign of Peter I", *Crusading, Society, and Politics in the Eastern Mediterranean in the Age of King Peter I of Cyprus*, ed. A. Beihammer and A. Nicolaou-Konnari (Turnhout: Brepols, c.2022), pp. 107–117; Carr, M., Christ, G. and Sänger, P. (eds), *Military Diasporas and the Building of Empire in the Euromediterranean from Antiquity to the Middle Ages* (London: Routledge, c.2022); Carr, M. and Grant, A., "The Catalan Company as a Military Diaspora", *Military Diasporas*, as above; Carr, M., "Maritime Crusading, 1095–1291", in *The Cambridge History of the Crusades: Vol. 1*, ed. J. Phillips, M. Bull, A. Jotischky and T. Madden (Cambridge: C.U.P.); "Pius II, Letter to Mehmed II", in *Christian-Muslim Relations, Primary Sources, Vol. 1 (600–1500)*, ed. D. Thomas (London: Bloomsbury); Carr, M., Chrissis, N. and Raccagni, R. (eds), *Crusading Against Christians in the Middle Ages* (London: Palgrave, c.2022); "Crusades against the Catalans of Athens", in *Crusading Against Christians*, as above.

CARRAZ Damien, "Un hospitalier provençal et ses réseaux au XIIIᵉ siècle: le commandeur Bérenger Monge", in *Relationships, Nobles, Orders, Networks. Europe and Mediterranean, Cahiers de la Méditerranée*, ed. A. Brogini et *alii*; "Le tropisme d'une ville neuve: templiers, hospitaliers et antonins à Montferrand (vers 1150–vers 1312)", in D. Carraz, J. Picot et L. Viallet (eds), *Identités montferrandaises, de la ville neuve au quartier (1120–2020)*, Clermont-Ferrand, Presses Universitaires Blaise-Pascal, published in 2023; "The Occupation of Belvoir by the Hospitallers: Chronological and Written Sources", *The castle of Belvoir (Israel) and the fortified architecture of the Hospital of Saint John of Jerusalem, Medievalista*, n° 33, Janeiro-Julho 2023; "Two thirteenth-century hospitaller castles in Provence: Manosque and Puimoisson according to written sources", *The castle of Belvoir (Israel) and the fortified architecture of the Hospital of Saint John of Jerusalem, Medievalista*, n° 33, Janeiro–Julho 2023.

CARTER, Leo M., 'Fall of Constantinople (1453)', *Religion and World Civilizations: How Faith Shaped Societies from Antiquity to the Present*, ed. by Andrew Holt (Santa Barbara, CA: ABC-CLIO, publication date pending).

CHRISSIS, Nikolaos, "Gregory IX and the Greek East", in C. Egger and D. Smith (eds), *Pope Gregory IX (1227–1241)* (Amsterdam: Amsterdam University Press, forthcoming 2022/2023); "Frankish Greece", in J. Phillips et al. (eds), *The Cambridge History of the Crusades* (Cambridge: Cambridge University Press, forthcoming 2022/2023); (with Marie-Hélène Blanchet) "Accusations of Heresy between East and West", in R. Flower (ed.), *The Cambridge Companion to Christian Heresy* (Cambridge: Cambridge University Press, forthcoming 2022/2023); "Crusades against the Byzantines", in M. Carr, G. Raccagni, and N. Chrissis (eds), *Crusading against Christians in the Middle Ages* (London: Palgrave Macmillan, forthcoming 2022/2023).

CLAVERIE, Pierre-Vincent, *Saint Louis en sa croisade*, Paris, Académie des Inscriptions et Belles-Lettres, 2023.

COBB, Paul M., "Contemplating Books with Usama ibn Munqidh's *Book of Contemplation*," Heather Blurton and Dwight Reynolds, eds, *Bestsellers and masterpieces: the changing medieval canon* (Manchester: University of Manchester Press, 2022), 25 pages.

COUREAS, Nicholas, "Success or Failure?" The Case of Multicultural Education on Lusignan Cyprus, an Island Kingdom at the Crossroads of Several Cultures", *Perspectives on Culture, Cyprus-A Cultural Mosaic*, 39 (4/2022); "The Churches of Famagusta and their Secular Congregations (1448–1474)", *Exploring Outremer Volume 2*; "The Papal Embargo and Cyprus 1291–1360", in *Economic Warfare and the Crusades*, ed S. Stanchev, Presses Universitaires du Midi, 2023; "All Christians are Equal but some are more Equal than others: Heresy, Orthodoxy and inter-community Relations in Lusignan Cyprus," in *Heresy and Deviance in Medieval Europe and Japan*, ed. L. Chollet, Editions Alphil, PUS 2022; "The Regular Latin Clergy and Latin Lay Society in Lusignan Cyprus: The Evidence from the Notarial Deeds of Famagusta," in *Orthodox and Latin Monasticism in the Eastern Mediterranean, 13th–16th c.*, Athens, 2022; (with Demetra Papanikola-Bakirtzi) "Glazed Table Wares on Medieval Cyprus: Parameters of Diffusion and Market Forces", *Convivium*, BAR International Series, 2023; "Armenian Soldiers on Lusignan Cyprus, 1191–1473," PULM Editions, 2022.

DOUROU-ELIOPOULOU, Maria, *Western Europe and eastern Mediterranean. A survey of the Franks in Romania during the crusades (13th–15th centuries)*, monograph, Herodotus, 2022 (in press); "Problems of methodology in the study of latin dominions. The case of the principality of Achaea and angevin Corfou", in *Latin dominions in Greek lands*, ed. K. Lambrinos, Academy of Athens, 2022 (in press); "Byzantium and the West (1258–1328)", Chapter in By*zantium. History and civilization. Research conclusions*, ed. T. Lounghis, t. 7, Herodotus 2022 (under publication); "Women in Frankish Achaea", *Charisma, Volume in honour of Nikos Moschonas*, National Research Foundation, Athens 2022 (under publication).

DRAGNEA, Mihai, *The various faces of Islamic radicalization in the Balkans after the fall of Communism*, eds. Mihai Dragnea, Adriana Cupcea, Darko Trifunovic, John Nomikos, Joseph Fitsanakis, (Peter Lang Bern & New York, 2022); "Entre obéissance et apostasie. La conversion des Poméraniens au christianisme (XIIe siècle)", *Cahiers de civilisation médiévale* (2022); "Cistercian abbeys in Pomerania and their impact on colonization in the second half of the twelfth century", *The Estonian Historical Journal* (2022); "The Christian Attitude to Hippomancy in Twelfth-Century Szczecin", *International Journal of Divination and Prognostication* (2022).

EDBURY, Peter, "The Colbert-Fontainebleau Continuation of William of Tyre, 1184–1247: Structure and Composition", *Chronicle, Crusade, and the Latin East*; "The Nobility of Cyprus and their Rural Residences" *Exploring Outremer Volume 2*; "The development of cities and urban life in the Crusader States", Routledge Handbook of the Material Culture of the Crusader States, 1099–1291, eds Nicholas Morton, Adrian Boas and Elizabeth Lapina.

EDGINGTON, Susan B., "The Attempted Assassination of Lord Edward of England at Acre, 1272", *Exploring Outremer Volume 2*; "Echoes of the *Iliad*: The Trojan War in Latin Epics of the First Crusade", in *Sources for the Crusades: Textual Tradition and Literary Influences*, ed. Léan Ní Chléirigh and Natasha Hodgson (Routledge, n.d.); "After Ascalon: 'Bartolf of Nangis' and the Early Years of the Kingdom of Jerusalem", in *Crusade, Settlement, and Historical Writing in the Latin East and Latin West*, ed. A. Buck, J. Keagan, T. Smith (Boydell, 2022); *Gesta Francorum Ierusalem expugnantium: The Deeds of the Franks who Conquered Jerusalem, 1095–1106*, ed. and tr. with T. W. Smith (Oxford Medieval Texts,

2023/4); "Josephus and the First Crusade", in *Josephus and the West*, BCCT series, ed. Paul Hilliard and Karen Kletter (Brill, 2023).

FILIPOVIC, Emir O., "Converting Heretics into Crusaders on the fringes of Latin Christendom. Shifting Crusading Paradigms in Medieval Bosnia", *Infidels, Heretics, Schismatics. Crusading on the Frontiers of Latin Christendom in the Later Middle Ages*, edited by Paul Srodecki and Norbert Kersken. Turnhout: Brepols, 2022; "Crusading on the Eastern Adriatic Coast and its Hinterland in the Late Middle Ages", *Handbook on the Later Crusades*, edited by Emir O. Filipovic and Magnus Ressel. Berlin: De Gruyter, 2023; Ibid, edited by Emir O. Filipovic and Magnus Ressel.

FOLDA, Jaroslav, "The Crusader Templum Domini: Fact and Fiction," for the symposium volume, *Marking the Sacred: The Temple Mount/Haram al-Sharif in Jerusalem*, ed. Joan Branham, Penn State Press, 20 pp. (forthcoming in 2022); "Figural Art of the Crusaders in the Holy Land, 1099 – 1291", Cambridge University Press History of the Crusades project, ed. Jonathan Phillips, et al. (expected publication in 2023).

GAPOSCHKIN, Cecilia, "Louis IX and the Triumphal Cross of Constantine." Accepted at *French Historical Studies* (2022?)

HARRIS, Jonathan, *Byzantium and the Crusades*, third edition (London and New York: Bloomsbury, late 2022); (Trans. with Georgios Chatzelis), *Byzantine Sources for the Crusades, 1095–1204*, Crusade Texts in Translation (Abingdon and New York: Routledge, 2023).

HODGSON, Natasha, "Legitimising authority in the *Historia Ierosolimitana* of Baldric of Dol", *Chronicle, Crusade and the Latin East.*

HORSWELL, Mike, *Nationalising the Crusades: Engaging the Crusades, Volume Nine*, ed. Mike Horswell (Abingdon: Routledge, 2022); "Historicising *Assassin's Creed* (2007): Crusader Medievalism, Historiography and Digital Games for the Classroom", in *Using, Modding and Creating Games for Education and Impact*, ed. Robert Houghton (Berlin: De Gruyter, 2022); with Andrew B.R. Elliott, "Pulling Ranke: The Inevitability of Presentism in Teaching Medievalism", *Decoding the Medieval: Teaching the Medieval in the Modern Age*, eds Claire Kennan and Emma Wells (Turnhout: Brepols, 2022); with Andrew Jotischky, Thomas Simpson and Astrid Swenson, "Modern Memories of the Crusader States", *The Material Culture of the Crusader States: A Handbook*, eds Elizabeth Lapina, Adrian Boas and Nicholas Morton (Abingdon: Routledge, forthcoming 2022); "New Crusaders and Crusading Echoes: The Modern Memory and Legacy of the Crusades in the West and Beyond", *The Cambridge History of the Crusades, Volume II: Expansion, Impact and Decline*, eds Thomas Madden and Jonathan Phillips (Cambridge: Cambridge University Press, forthcoming); with Felix Hinz, "Playing Crusaders: Crusading Literature, Art, Performance, Films and Games", Ibid.

IVASHKO, Roman, The Latin Metropolitanate of Lviv and encounters of the Crusade of Varna (in review process).

JOSSERAND, Philippe, *1460 – Une université pour le duché de Bretagne*, Portet-sur-Garonne, Éditions midi-pyrénéennes ("Cette année-là... à Nantes"), à paraître en juin 2022 (co-écrit avec Jean-Luc Sarrazin); *D'Orient en Occident. Les Templiers des origines à la fin du XIIe siècle. Colloque international du neuvième centenaire de l'ordre du Temple (1120–2020)*, Heule, Snoeck, à paraître fin 2022 (co-direction avec Arnaud Baudin); *Les ordres religieux-militaires dans le royaume de Castille au Moyen Âge (XIIe–XVe siècle)*, Toulouse, Presses universitaires du Midi, à paraître en 2022 (avec une préface de Carlos de Ayala Martínez); *Croisades et ordres militaires dans l'espace latin (XIe–XXIe siècle)*, Lyon, Presses universitaires de Lyon, à paraître en 2023 (avec une préface d'Alain Demurger); *A Companion to the Templars*, Leyde, Brill, à paraître en 2024 (co-direction avec Jochen Schenk).

KANE, James, (ed. with Keagan Brewer), *The Latin Continuation of William of Tyre: A Critical Edition and Translation*, Crusade Texts in Translation (Abingdon and New York: Routledge, 2023); (ed. with Andrew D. Buck and Stephen J. Spencer), *Crusade, Settlement, and Historical Writing in the Latin East and Latin West, c.1100–c.1300*, Crusading on Context (Woodbridge: Boydell, 2023); "History and Politics", *A Cultural History of the Bible in the Medieval Age*, ed. Daniel Anlezark (London: Bloomsbury, 2024).

KNOBLER, Adam, "Neuformulierung der Vergangenheit – Neuausrichtung der Gegenwart: Kreuzzugsrhetorik und -ideologie im 'langen' 19. Jahrhundert" in *Historische Dimensionen der religiösen Gewalt*, eds Dorothea Weltecke and Jorg Rettroth, (forthcoming, 2022).

KOLIA-DERMITZAKI, Athina, "The Rhetoric of Victory in Byzantine Texts of the 10th to 12th Centuries: Historiography and Panegyrics in a Comparative Context", *Victors and Vanquished in the Euro-Mediterranean Cultures of War in the Middle Ages*, Mainz (forthcoming 2022).

LENCART, Joana – "A coleção *Gavetas* do Arquivo Nacional da Torre do Tombo: construção da memória e conservação do património escrito do século XII ao século XXI", Leonor Zozaya-Montes (ed.): *Los archivos y documentos de la Edad Media a la Contemporánea en Europa y América (estudios de caso)*, Trea, Gijón, 2022 (forthcoming).

LOMBARDO, Simone, "A Turkish issue in the Fourteenth Century, Transformations within the idea of Crusade through the papal letters (1352–1378)", in: *Crusades*.

LUTTRELL, Anthony, "Dragonetto Clavelli: Magistral Procurator on Rhodes 1382–1415"; "Fr. Domenico de Alamania: a Career on Hospitaller Rhodes"; "Pilgrim Trafficking on Hospitaller Rhodes after 1309"; "Déodat de Gozon and the Serpent: Rhodes 1346/1366"; "English Hospitallers in Holy War and Papal Schism: 1378–1417"; "Hospitaller Lodgings and Auberges on Rhodes after 1309"; "Hospital and Temple: 1291–1314"; "A Hospitaller Crusade Treatise Reviewed"; "Philibert de Naillac Master of Rhodes: 1396–1421".

MAIER, Christoph T., "When was the first history of the crusades written?", *The Crusades: History and Memory. Proceedings of the Ninth Quadrennial Conference of the Society for the Study of the Crusades and the Latin East, Odense, 27 June–1 July 2016*, Vol. 2, eds. K. V. Jensen and T. K. Nielsen (Outremer 12; Turnhout: Brepols, 2021; "Crusaders and Jews: the York massacre of 1190 re-visited", *Anglo Norman Studies XLV: Proceedings of the Battle Conference 2021* (Volume 45), ed. Stephen D. Church (Woodbridge: Boydell & Brewer, 2022); "Crusade Propaganda and Attacks against Jews: A Breakdown of Communication?", *Journal of Medieval History*, 48 (2022); "Historiography of the Crusades", *The Cambridge History of the Crusades*, eds. J. Phillips, M. Bull et al., Cambridge; Cambridge University Press.

PAVIOT, Jacques, *Pero Tafur: Aventures et voyages*, intr. et notes J. Paviot, trad. Julia Roumier et Florence Serrano, Toulouse, Presses universitaires du Midi, April 2022.

PRINGLE, R. Denys, *Three Pilgrimages to the Holy Land: Saewulf, John of Würzburg, Theoderic: Introduction, Translation and Notes*, Corpus Christianorum in Translation 41 (Brepols: Turnhout 2022); "Hospitaller Castles and Fortifications in the Kingdom of Jerusalem, 1136–1291", *Medievalista* (2022); "The Confraternity and Chapel of St Edward the Confessor in Acre (1271/2–1291)", *Exploring Outremer Volume 2*; (with Benjamin Z. Kedar) "The Site of the House of St Mary of Mountjoy, near Jerusalem", *Revue biblique* (2022). "Obituary: Michael Hamilton Burgoyne (1944–2021)", *Levant* 54.1 (2022); "Churches in the Crusader Kingdom", *The Cambridge History of the Crusades, 1: Sources, Conquest and Settlement*, ed. Marcus Bull and Andrew Jotischky (Cambridge University

Press: Cambridge); "Jerusalem 1099: From Muslim to Christian City", *Medievalista* 31 (July 2022); "Itineraria Terrae Sanctae minora IIIA: A Revised edition of *Descriptio Ierusalem* (Group E2), based on British Library, Royal 6.A.I, fols. 134r–135r", *Crusades* 21 (2022).

RAGHEB, Fadi, "Mamlūk-Timurid Embassy Exchanges and the Gifting of a Mātūrīdī tafsīr: A Historical and Bio-Bibliographical Inquiry." In *Proceedings of The Third Conference of the School of Mamlūk Studies*, edited by Marlis Saleh. Leuven: Peeters Publishers, 2022 (forthcoming July 2022).

ROESCH, Fabian, *Die Rechtsbücher im Königreich Jerusalem. Politische Ansprüche und Sicherheitsinteressen von Krone und Hochadel in Jerusalem und Zypern (12.–14. Jahrhundert)*, Publisher: Didymos-Verlag, Expected date of publication: 2022.

SCALONE, Alessandro, "The Recovery of Jerusalem and the relationship between the Mongols and the West", *Crusades* (approved for publication).

SHEPARD, Jonathan, "Adjustable Imperial Image-Projection and the Greco-Roman Repertoire: Their Reception among Outsiders and Longer-Stay Visitors", ed. J. Stouraites, *Identities and Ideologies in the Medieval East Roman World* (*Edinburgh Byzantine Studies* Series), (Edinburgh, forthcoming); "Laws of Nations, Border Treaties and Roman Override", ed. W. Brandes, H. Reimitz and J. Tannous, *Legal Pluralism and Social Change in Late Antiquity and the Middle Ages* (*Recht im ersten Jahrtausend* Series) (Frankfurt am Main, forthcoming); "The Workings of Byzantine Soft Power, and Abbot Leontios' Progress", ed. A. Jusupović, A. Paron and A. Vukovich, *Christian Rus in the Making* (*The Worlds of the Slavs* 1), (Leiden, forthcoming)

SIROTENKO, Anastasiia, *Erinnern an Herakleios: Zur Darstellung des Kaisers Herakleios in mittelalterlichen Quellen / Remembering Heraclius: On the Representation of the Emperor Heraclius in Medieval Sources*, to be published by Utzverlag in the series "Münchner Arbeiten zur Byzantinistik" (series editor Albrecht Berger), approximately in 2023.

TAL, Oren, with Shotten-Hallel, and V.R., Yohanan, H., In press/2022 "Et domus sua cuique est tutissimum refugium: Jean II of Ibelin, Arsur Castle and the Hospitallers", *Exploring Outremer Volume 2*.

TSURTSUMIA, Mamuka, *De velitatione bellica* and the Georgian Art of War During the Reign of David IV – *Journal of Medieval Military History*, XX, 2022.

VILLEGAS-ARISTIZÁBAL, Lucas, "Norman Holy Warriors and Settlers in the North-Eastern Frontier of the Iberian Peninsula (1064–1130)", *Norman Connections – Normannische Verflechtungen zwischen Skandinavien und dem Mittelmeer*, eds Viola Skiba, Nikolas Jaspert, and Bernd Schneidmüller, Regensburg: Schnell & Steiner, 2022. https://www. schnell-und-steiner.de/artikel_10517.ahtml.

VOISIN, Ludivine, "Between West and East: the Monastic 'Order of St Basil' in Sixteenth-Century Cyprus", M. Koumanoudi, Z. Melissakis (dir.), *Orthodox and Latin Monasticism in the Eastern Mediterranean, 13th–16th centuries*, National Hellenic Research Foundation, 24 p. (2022); "*et se chantoit si hault que cestoit merveille*: the church of the Panagia Hodegetria in the Greek episcopal 'archipelago' (13th–16th centuries)", M. Olympios (dir.), *Historic Bedestan. Articulating Greek Visual Identity in the "Long" Middle Ages: an Ecclesiastical, Social and Architectural History of the Bedestan in Nicosia*, Ca'Foscari (Studi Ciprioti), 55 p. (2022).

5. Work in progress

ALVIRA-CABRER, Martín, Rubrique "La guerre dans la Péninsule Ibérique au Moyen Âge", website *Ménestrel. Médiévistes sur le net: sources, travaux et références en ligne*, www. menestrel.fr.

AMOUROUX, Monique, La seconde croisade d'après un auteur grec et deux auteurs latins.

BAGNI, Giampiero, a new volume in the *Military Orders Series* titled "Templars in Bologna: A Multidisciplinary Approach".

BALARD, Michel, *Poivre et gingembre. Une histoire des épices au Moyen Age* for publication in 2022.

BATTISTELLI, Daniele, monograph: *Questione d'onore. Ragioni, forme e disciplina della violenza nella Francia dell'anno Mille (secoli X–XII)* [*A Question of Honor. Reasons, forms and discipline of violence in France around the year 1000 (X–XII centuries)*]; and an article on the use of topographical description and its function in the *Chronicle of Ernoul*.

BUCK, Andrew D., "William of Tyre, *Translatio Imperii*, and the Genesis of the First Crusade: Or, the Challenges of Writing History" (under review with journal); with Edgington, Susan B., "The Anonymous *Historia regum Hierusalem Latinorum ad deplorationem perditionis terrae sanctae accomodata*: A Critical Edition, Translation, and Commentary" (to be submitted to journal in 2022); *Creating Outremer: William of Tyre and the Writing of History in Twelfth-Century Jerusalem* (monograph to be proposed to publisher in 2022/23); "Rebellion and Political Negotiation in the Principality of Antioch", *Noble Rebellion in Medieval Europe, c. 1150–c. 1350*, ed. Adrian Jobson and Fernando Arias (to be proposed to publisher summer 2022); "Solving the Riddle of the 'L' Manuscript: On the Transmission and Transformation of Fulcher of Chartres' *Historia* in the Twelfth Century" (to be submitted to journal in 2023); Article on two manuscripts British containing William of Tyre/the Latin Continuation of William of Tyre and their role as vehicles for memory of the Latin East (to be submitted to journal in 2023/24).

CARLSSON, Christer, Aslackby Templar Preceptory, Lincolnshire, UK.

CARR, Annemarie Wehl, monograph on the Mother of God Kykkotissa at Kykkos Monastery on Cyprus.

CARR, Mike, "Crusading in the Eastern Mediterranean, 1291–1500", *The Oxford Illustrated History of the Crusades*, ed. J. Harris (Oxford: O.U.P.); "Trade Embargoes against the Turks in the Fourteenth Century", in *Economic Warfare and the Crusades*, ed. S. Stantchev (Toulouse: Presses Universitaires du Midi); Carr, M. & Banister, M., "Religious Authority", *Handbook of Mediterranean History (300–2020): Volume II (1000–1500)*, ed. F. Bauden, A. Beihammer, N. Jaspert & R. Salicrú i Lluch.

CARRAZ Damien, the Epigraphy of the Military Orders – a database for France.

CERRINI, Simonetta, Nouvelle édition augmentée de *La Révolution des templiers*, basée sur les 10 manuscrits de la Règle du Temple, Paris, Perrin.

CHRISSIS, Nikolaos, "Crusades against Christians, 1200–1500", in J. Harris (ed.), *The New Oxford Illustrated History of the Crusades* (Oxford: Oxford University Press, in progress).

COBB, Paul M., Edition and translation of: Muhammad ibn Mangli, *The Hunter's Companion* for the Library of Arabic Literature (New York, NYU Press).

COUREAS, Nicholas, *King Henry II of Cyprus*, part of the series Rulers of the Latin East, ed. by N. Morton and J. Phillips.

DE LA TORRE, Ignacio, The Templars' banking activities and their potential connections in the demise of the Order.

EDBURY, Peter, (with Massimiliano Gaggero) continues work on *The Chronique d'Ernoul and the Colbert-Fontainebleau Continuation of William of Tyre* (Brill – to be submitted in 2021); *King Hugh III of Cyprus: Politics in the Latin East, 1254–1291* (for Routledge 'Rulers of the Latin East' Series).

EDGINGTON, Susan B., Anonymous *Historia regum Hierosolymitanorum Latinorum ad deplorationem perditionis terrae sanctae accomodata*: A New Edition, Translation, and Commentary with Andrew D. Buck.

FAVREAU-LILIE, Marie-Luise, *Italien und der islamische Orient zur Zeit der Kreuzzüge* (book).

FOLDA, Jaroslav, Research continues on a study of the çintamani ornament in the Book of Kells and the impact of eastern icon painting on the image of the Virgin and Child enthroned with angels on fol. 7v.

HODGSON, Natasha, *Gender and the Crusades* (Palgrave Macmillan, 2023).

HORSWELL, Mike, with Elizabeth Siberry, "Receiving and Reviewing the Crusades: Revealing Perceptions of the Crusades through Reviews and Periodicals in Nineteenth- and Twentieth-Century Britain", *Medievalism and Reception*, eds. Ika Willis and Ellie Crookes (Woodbridge: Boydell & Brewer, forthcoming); "Crusading Today: Historians, Historiography and the Crusades in Britain and the US Twenty Years After 9/11", for *The Mediæval Journal*; "Crusading Unbound: Imagining Success in Fantasies of the Crusades", for *Postmedieval*; "'We come with Passports instead of Swords': Unpacking The 1926 Mediterranean Pilgrimage of the Order of St John", for *Historical Research*.

KANE, James, *The Crusading Cross: Ideology and Practice, c.1095–c.1300* (single-authored monograph; provisional title only).

KEDAR, Benjamin Z., A socio-cultural history of the Frankish Kingdom of Jerusalem 1099–1187.

KNOBLER, Adam, *Shaping the Present, Reinventing the Past: Crusading in the Long 19th Century, 1798–1928*. Under contract with Routledge.

LEONARD Jr., Robert D., Numismatics of the Crusades, to Fifteenth century.

MAIER, Christoph T., [with Nicole Bériou (Paris)] Sermones contra hereticos. Sermons preached for the fight against heretics by Philip the Chancellor and Eudes of Châteauroux from the years 1226 and 1231 (Oxford Medieval Texts).

MARVIN, Laurence W., A military history of the Fifth Crusade.

MORTON, Nic, *The Mongol Storm: Making and Breaking Empires in the Medieval Near East* (Basic Books).

NICHOLSON, Helen J., The Knights Templars' English and Welsh Estates, 1308–13, transcription and analysis of the inventories and accounts of the Templars' properties in England and Wales during the trial of the Templars (documents at Kew, The National Archives of the UK) – as described in bulletin no. 29; *Women and the Crusades*, a trade book for Oxford University Press: as described in Bulletin no. 37.

ORTEGA, Isabelle, Publication toujours en cours: "Philippe de Gonesse, l'ascension d'un officier dans l'espace angevin durant le règne de Charles Ier", *Gouverner le royaume: le roi, la reine et leurs officiers. Les terres angevines au regard de l'Europe (XIIIe–XVe siècle)/ Governare il regno: il re, la regina e i loro ufficiali. I territori angioini nel quadro europeo (secoli XIII–XV)*, École française de Rome et Academia d'Ungheria in Roma; Publication en cours: *L'ingouvernabilité en questions* (Europe chrétienne méridionale et orientale, XIIe–première moitié du XVIe siècle), Isabelle Mathieu, Isabelle ORTEGA (dir.), Rennes,

PUR, 2022; *"Anciens homs, sachans homs* et autres *vieillarts*: la participation des plus âgés au pouvoir dans la principauté de Morée (XIIIe–XIVe siècles)" lors de la journée d'étude organisée par Emmanuelle Santinelli-Foltz et Gilles Lecuppre sur *Vieillesse et pouvoir dans l'Occident médiéval: la gérontocratie à l'épreuve*, Université de Valenciennes (à distance). Publication en cours aux *Médiévales*.

PARK, Danielle, Still engaged on Fulk and Melisende for the *Rulers of the Latin East* series (Routledge).

PERRY, Guy, Still engaged on *Cross and Crown: Church and State in the Middle Ages and the Making of the Modern World* (monograph); early/preparatory work for *The Emperor Frederick II and the Crusader States* for the *Rulers of the Latin East* series (Routledge).

PRYOR, John, has been engaged for the past 12 years on a study of the ecclesiastical corpus of texts for the First Crusade: The *Gesta Francorum*, Peter Tudebode, the *Historia de Via* (Bongars & St Catharine's 3), and the *Belli Sacri Historia* (Mabillon & BnF Lat. 5051A). He has copies of all known manuscripts and editions and expects to be able to prove that it was Peter Tudebode who was the originator of the corpus. The volume is expected to be completed in 2023.

RAGHEB, Fadi, "Early Military Experience of 'Imad al-Din Zengi Against the Crusaders in Syria (505–509/1111–1115): A Blueprint for His Later Anti-Damascene Strategy?" (book chapter); "Medieval Muslims and Crusaders in Modern Arabic Cinema: Arab Nationalism, Muslim-Christian Parallels, and Personal Cinematic Didacticism in Youssef Chahine's Film *al-Nāṣir Ṣalāḥ al-Dīn (The Victorious Saladin)*" (article/book chapter).

RODRIGUEZ GARCÍA, Jose Manuel, Crusade Preaching in the Iberian Peninsula, 13th century. Still engaged on the book on the Teutonic Order in Spain (13th–16th centuries).

SCHRADER, Jr., Stanley, Currently researching the Teutonic Knights and the Baltic Crusade.

SINIBALDI, Micaela, *Settlement in Crusader Transjordan (1100–1189): a Historical and Archaeological Study,* monograph to be published by Archaeopress, Oxford.

SIROTENKO, Anastasiia at the Friedrich-Meinecke-Institut, Freie Universität Berlin – "Auf der Suche nach historischer Selbstvergewisserung: Konstantin, Helena und Herakleios im sozialen Gedächtnis des lateinischen Königreichs Jerusalem (1099–1187)" / "In search of historical self-reassurance: Constantine, Helena and Heraclius in the social memory of the Latin kingdom of Jerusalem (1099–1187)"; Research article planned on the liturgical commemoration of Constantine, Helena and Heraclius in the Latin kingdom of Jerusalem in 12th century.

TAL, Oren, In preparation. *Apollonia-Arsuf: Final Report of the Excavations. Volume III: Crusader Arsur.* Tel Aviv University, Monograph Series of the Institute of Archaeology. University Park/Tel Aviv.

VILLADS JENSEN, Kurt, Sacred war and the senses c. 1050 – c 1300 – why was it necessary to change all physical to change the religion of others?

VILLEGAS-ARISTIZÁBAL, Lucas, "Contextualising *De itinere frisonum* as a Source for Seaborne Pilgrimages to the Holy Land 1217–1218"; "A Question of Loyalty in the Temporary Alliances between the Normans and Iberians in the Wars against the Andalusi", Book Chapter for Festschrift in honour of Prof Michael C. E. Jones (2023); *The Normans in the Iberian Sacralised Wars against Al-Andalus,* 2024; *De expugnatione Lyxbonensi: La conquista de Lisboa,* Traducción al español. 2024.

VOISIN, Ludivine, In collaboration with Katèrina Korrè and Philippe Trélat, *Entre Venise et Rome: l'archevêché latin de Nicosie à la fin du XVe siècle. Documents concernant la* *succession et l'administration de l'archevêché sous les archiépiscopats de Vittore Marcello (1471–1484) et Benedetto Soranzo (1484–1495)*, Brepols ("Mediterranean Nexus 1100–1700"), end of 2023; Historiography of the Latinocracy.

6. Theses in progress

BATTISTELLI, Daniele, MA degree in Historical Sciences (LM-84), "La Sapienza" – University of Rome Supervisors: Antonio Musarra, professor of Medieval History and Serena di Nepi, professor of Modern History.

BINYSH, Betty, PhD. "Representations of Muslim Approaches to Peace-making with the Crusaders, Franks and Military Orders in the Latin East from Saladin to Qalawun", Cardiff University. Supervised by Helen Nicholson.

CARTER, Leo M., "Interest in the Dioceses of Winchester and Chichester of the Kingdom of England for the Support of the Holy Land, Byzantium and the Crusade During the Late Thirteenth to Late Fifteenth Centuries", Royal Holloway, University of London, supervised by Andrew Jotischky.

DUARTE, Tadeu Duarte Barros dos Santos, "As relações entre Portugal e a Santa Sé no reinado de D. João I", MA. Faculty of Arts and Humanities of the University of Porto. Supervised by Cristina Cunha and Paula Pinto Costa.

FERREIRA, Leandro Filipe Ribeiro, "A prática da guerra em Portugal do final da reconquista à batalha de Toro: o papel das Ordens Militares", PhD thesis. Faculty of Arts and Humanities of the University of Porto. Supervised by Paula Pinto Costa and Miguel Gomes Martins.

IVASHKO, Roman, "The Lviv Latin Archdiocese in the Union Processes with Eastern Christianity in 1410s–1460s", PhD, Ivan Franko National University of Lviv, supervised by Oleg Faida.

MILSTEIN, Eleanor, "Mason's Marks in the Holy Land: GIS Application for Their Mapping in 12th and 13th Frankish Architecture (tentative title)", MA, Tel Aviv University, co-supervised by O. Tal and R.G. Khamisy.

PEREIRA, Nuno Miguel dos Santos Silva *"Cura animarum: entre a essência carismática e o confronto com a hierarquia"*, MA, University of Porto, supervised by Paula Pinto Costa.

RUDOLPH, Theresa, "Zwischen Providenz und Kontingenz. Akteure, Modi und Praktiken des Entscheidens im Kontext des Ersten Kreuzzugs" ["Between Providence and Contingency. Actors, Modes and Practices of Decision-Making in the Context of the First Crusade"], PhD, Westfälische Wilhelms-Universität Münster, supervised by Professor Jan Keupp.

SCHRADER, Jr., Stanley, Master of Theology (ThM) program Fall 2022 at Erskine Theological Seminary, supervised by Dale Johnson. I intend to complete the ThM with a second consecutive graduate thesis on the Military Orders, this one on The Teutonic Knights.

7. Fieldwork planned or undertaken recently

BAGNI, Giampiero, 2022: GPR survey at Cortina d'Ampezzo, Italy to verify possible hidden structures.

BATTISTELLI, Daniele, in 2021, in the context of the ongoing project for the Restauration of the pavement of the Holy Sepulchre, supervised by the Department of Antiquities, "La Sapienza" – University of Rome, I joined the workshop "Laboratorio medievistico sul Santo Sepolcro", led by prof. Antonio Musarra. The aim of the workshop is to support the archaeological mission by collecting and studying descriptions of Jerusalem and the Basilica of the Holy Sepulchre from the beginning of Christianity to the end of Middle Ages. In particular, I worked on the *Monachi anonymi Scaphusensi de reliquiis sanctissime Crucis et dominici Sepulchri* (RHC, Occ. v. V, pp. 335–339), the *Historia Vie Hierosolimitane* of Gilo of Paris and the *Chronique d'Ernoul et Bernard le Trésoriers*.

CARLSSON, Christer, is continuing work on Archaeological research excavations of Aslackby Templar Preceptory, Lincolnshire, UK.

IVASHKO, Roman, Middle Ages, the Church Union, interfaith relations in the Late Medieval Rus', Late Medieval crusades.

TAL, Oren, Apollonia-Arsuf, Season XXX, May–June 2022 [https://en-humanities.tau.ac.il/apollonia-arsuf-excavation-project].

8. News of interest to members

a) Conferences and seminars

Alessandria, 26–29 agosto 2021, Festival internazionale dei Templari. Evento storico-artistico ideato e diretto da Simonetta Cerrini e Gian Piero Alloisio. Relatori: Michel Balard, Philippe Josserand, Julien Théry; con interventi in video di Alessandro Barbero e Franco Cardini. Con il Patrocinio dell'Università del Piemonte Orientale.

VILLEGAS-ARISTIZÁBAL, Lucas, "Temporary loyalty? Crusading co-operation in the conquest of Lisbon, 1147", 2022 IMC; "*De itinere Frisonum*: The Frisian crusading itinerary to the Holy Land 1217–1218: A Frisian Perspective on Crusading as Pilgrimage to the Holy Land", *Tenth Quadrennial conference of the SSCLE*, Royal Holloway, London, UK; "Did Savary of Mauleon participate in the failed siege of Caceres in 1218?", Mercenaries and Crusaders (1202–1480) An Interdisciplinary Conference, Debrecen, Hungary; 6 Feb 2023 Exhibition: *Die Normannen, The Normans: A German-French exhibition project* at The Reiss-Engelhorn-Museen, Mannheim, Germany.

VOISIN, Ludivine, "Du Cange, la papauté et la francocratie du Moyen Âge à l'époque moderne", Journée d'études "Charles du Fresne du Cange" (Rouen, 28 October 2022), French School of Athens-University of Rouen; "*per miracholo de dio*: les monastères grecs de la région de Paphos dans les sources écrites (1191–1570)", Colloquium *Nea Paphos III* (Athens, 8–10 November 2022), French School of Athens-University of Sydney.

b) Other news

The final text of the Revised RRH for the years 1245–1260 (ca 820 documents) is currently being prepared for publication as a supplement to the existing material. The team is still working on the years 1261–1292.

HODGSON, Natasha, Teaching resources relating to the Crusades: 2 x Historical Association podcasts "The Near East and the Italian Maritime States" and "Women and the Crusades" (March 2022); BBC World Histories Magazine "Queen Melisende of Jerusalem" (June 2020); BBC History Extra Podcast "Women and the Crusades" (June 2020); with LEWIS, Katherine and PARK, Danielle BBC Radio 4 In Our Time "Melisende, Queen of Jerusalem", 21st November 2019.

Northern Network for the Study of the Crusades (NNSC). The Network provides an inter-disciplinary regional hub for scholars at all stages of their career with a view to fostering cross-institutional interaction and collaboration, sharing news and announcements, and promoting the study of the history of the crusades and all its related fields of investigation. For more information https://www.northernnetworkforstudyofcrusades.com/ or contact Dr Jason T. Roche on J.T.Roche@mmu.ac.uk.

Jonathan Riley-Smith's *Röhrichts Regesta Revised* (RRR) database [http://www.crusades-regesta.com/]. This project aims to compile a calendar of all the charters, other legal or formal documents and letters that were composed between 1098 and 1291 in the Latin kingdoms of Jerusalem and Cyprus, the principality of Antioch and the counties of Edessa and Tripoli or were addressed to individuals in those settlements. The new calendar is based on Reinhold Röhricht's *Regesta Regni Hierosolymitani* (1893–1904). Every RRR entry has been carefully rechecked against the latest or best edition of the original document and has been redrafted and rendered in English. The RRR database is also fuller than the original, as many newly discovered documents have been added, and all the protocols of the rulers of the settlements and references to all eleemosynary grants were included. This resource will be of the greatest importance for scholars as well as a tool to introduce students to the valuable range of material from the Latin East. It currently contains 2,457 entries ranging from 1098 to 1244.

New book series at Peter Lang: "Christianity and Conversion in Scandinavia and the Baltic Region, c. 800–1600", edited by Mihai DRAGNEA. This is a single-blind peer reviewed series which provides an opportunity for scholars to publish high-quality studies on the culture, society and economy of Scandinavia and the Baltic region under the influence of Christianity. It welcomes submissions in various formats, including monographs, edited volumes, conference proceedings, and short form publications between 30,000 to 50,000 words (Peter Lang Prompts) on subjects related to: Christian kingship, Christian and pagan identity, cultural encounters, otherness, barbarians, missionary strategy, canonical aspects of missionary work, forced conversion, clerical involvement in warfare, military orders, Holy War, martyrdom, sacralisation of a landscape, pilgrimage, shrines of gods, relics of saints, icons, and war banners, pagan war rituals, diet and fashion, rural area and the concept of town life, intragroup and intergroup relations, linguistic interactions, narratives gesta episcoporum, saga studies, colonization, ethnography, mental geographies, political relations, dynastic marital alliances, media and communication, trade, exploration, mappae mundi, art history, architecture, numismatics, and all archaeological sub-disciplines. More details at https://www.peterlang.com/view/serial/CCSB

DŹWIGALA, Bartłomiej, would like to invite members of SSCLE to submit articles in English, French, German or Italian to an academic journal of the Institute of History at Card. Stefan Wyszyński University in Warsaw entitled: *Saeculum Christianum*. If any questions, please contact via e-mail b.dzwigala@uksw.edu.pl; bartlomiej.dzwigala@gmail.com. More details at: https://czasopisma.uksw.edu.pl/index.php/sc/index.

c) Annual *Bernard Hamilton Essay Prize*

In honour of the former president and current honorary president of the SSCLE, Professor Bernard Hamilton, and in recognition of his enormous contribution to the society and support of young scholars, the SSCLE will award an annual essay prize.

The Rules

The essay should be on any aspect of history, art history or archaeology of the Crusader period or otherwise relating to Crusader studies.

Any current doctoral student, or an individual who is within two years of receiving their doctorate is eligible to enter the competition.

The essay, excluding references and bibliography must not normally exceed 6,000 words and must conform with the editorial requirements of the SSCLE journal *Crusades* (available on the SSCLE webpage and in the Bulletin/Journal).

Essays submitted elsewhere for competitions or publication will not be eligible for the prize.

The essays must be submitted as electronic copies as an e-mail attachment, to Professor William PURKIS and Dr Anna GUTGARTS (email: sscle.pgecr.officer@gmail.com) the SSCLE Postgraduate Officers, by **31 December**.

Essays should be accompanied by details of the author's name, address (including email address), institutional affiliation and degree registration.

The Decision

The essays will be read by a jury consisting of a panel drawn from the Committee of the SSCLE and the editors of *Crusades*.

The jury panel reserves the right not to award a prize in any particular year.

The jury decision will be announced in **April**.

The decision of the jury is final.

The winner of the essay competition will have their paper put forward to *Crusades* where, subject to the normal procedures of satisfactory reports from two anonymous external referees (and, if required, the chance to modify, amend or improve the piece on their advice), it will be published under the title '*Bernard Hamilton Essay Prize*'.

Names of prize winners will be posted on the SSCLE webpage and announced in the Bulletin.

9. Members' queries

EDBURY, Peter, The late David Jacoby, in his article "Migration, Trade and Banking in Crusader Acre" (in L. Mavromatis (ed.), *Βαλκάνια και Ανατολική Μεσόγειος* / *The Balkans and the East Mediterranean, 12th–17th centuries* (Athens, 1998), 105–119), noted that in April 1291 (i.e. just as the siege was beginning) the local representatives in Acre of a Sienese banking house "allied to the Buonsignori" (named as Giacomo Franchi and Maso Bosi) loaned 50,000 deniers to the patriarch of Jerusalem and the masters of the three military orders for the defence of the city. He acknowledged the help of Dr Mario Borracelli who he said (p. 119 n. 55) was going to publish the text. Does anyone know whether Borracelli did in fact publish this material and, if so, where? If not, does anyone know where the document in question is? Any suggestions will be most gratefully received Peter Edbury (edbury@ cf.ac.uk).

Nicholas MORTON is the co-editor of two book series and he would be interested to hear from members interested in submitting proposals for either. They are: 1. Rulers of the Latin East (Routledge, co-editor Dr Jason Roche); 2. The Military Religious Orders: History – Sources – Memory (Routledge, co-editor Professor Jochen Burgtorf).

10. Financial Statement 2022 (1 July 2021–7 June 2022)

This is my first financial statement as Treasurer, and I pay tribute to the excellent work, guidance, and support of my predecessor in the role, Dr Danielle Park. I am happy to report that the Society is financially stable and has acquired a surplus over the year.

By way of explanation of the accounts below, I should note that the Society's finances have been simplified since the last set of annual accounts. This is due to the closing of our US dollar account and EU account balance by Barclays, our banking provider, on the 30th November 2021, without warning, on the basis that the Society has become ineligible to hold foreign currency accounts with them. This is due to the non-commercial nature of our Society. As Treasurer, I am hoping to be able to reinstate some form of foreign currency account in the future, with a different banking provider. Until then, payments in various

	UK accounts	US account	EU account	Total
Opening Funds 01-07-21	**£15,744.05**	**£4,327.63**	**£10,847.52**	**£30,919.20**
Income				
Interest	£1.18			£1.18
Subscriptions	£11,562.51			£11,562.51
Back Copy Journal Orders	£835.15			£835.15
Total	**£12,398.84**			**£12,398.84**
Transfers				
Transfers from other accounts	£14,240.05			
Transfers to other accounts		£3,392.53	£10,847.52	
Expenditure				
Back Copy Journal Orders	£972.85			£972.85
Administration Costs	£143.52			£143.52
Journal Bulk Order	£630.00			£630.00
Honoraria	£500.00			£500.00
PayPal Fees	£522.66			£522.66
Wild Apricot Fees		£935.10		£935.10
Total	**£2,769.03**	**£935.10**	**0.00**	**£3,704.13**
Closing Funds 07-06-22	**£39,613.91**	**0.00**	**0.00**	**£39,613.91**
Surplus 01-07-21 to 07-06-22				**£8,694.71**

currencies can be accepted through PayPal. This means that the balances from the dollar and Euro accounts were transferred in November 2021 into the Society's sterling bank account, and represent together £14,240.05 of the increase in the total sterling funds over the year. All of the Society's financial assets are now in pounds sterling.

In summary, the Society remains in good financial health compared with this time last year. The total funds the Society has access to on 7 June 2022 constitute £39,613.91, an increase of £8,694.71 on the £30,919.20 of 1 July 2021. Significantly, this excludes the separate bank account for the London conference, which is managed separately by the conference organisational team, and which is founded upon the sum allotted by my predecessor in previous financial statements. The conference is not expected to require further subsidisation from the Society's central funds.

One further note for those comparing these accounts with last year's: the sterling figure given on 1 July 2021, £15,743.05, was in error by £1, and the true figure was £15,744.05.

There has been a significant increase in membership over the past year: we currently sit at 429 members. Disregarding potential future subscriptions this year, this would be an increase of around 122 members on my predecessors' estimate dating to the last financial statement in mid-2021 (307 members). I anticipate putting in a journal order for 2022, for *Crusades* 21, for at least 256 members. This will already be a substantial increase on the 214 journal orders for *Crusades* 20 (2021), the 141 for *Crusades* 19 (2020), and exceeding the pre-pandemic *Crusades* 18 (2019), for which there were 222 orders. For administration purposes, memberships now run annually in alignment with the calendar year, but members' status is not removed until a full year without payment has elapsed.

The main outgoing costs for this year beyond the standard journal distribution have been: honoraria paid to our outgoing and incoming bulletin editors (£500), PayPal fees (£519.04) and fees for the website with WildApricot (£935.10). In terms of expected future outgoings, the Society ought to be liable for some invoices for journal distribution, which are pending with Taylor & Francis, but these will not seriously alter the picture of a substantial surplus over the year. A prize of £250 will be awarded for the Ronnie Ellenblum 'Best First Book' prize imminently, and will be paid from the Society's account.

Many thanks to all members for your support, generosity, and courtesy over the past year.

Respectfully submitted,
Dr Simon Thomas Parsons

11. Officers of the Society (2021-2022)

President: Professor Jonathan Phillips.

Honorary Presidents: Professor Benjamin Z. Kedar, Professor Michel Balard, Professor Adrian Boas.

Secretary: Dr Nikolaos G. Chrissis.

Conference Secretary: Professor Jonathan Phillips.

Editor of the Bulletin: Dr Danielle E.A. Park.

Officers for Postgraduate Members: Professor William Purkis and Dr Anna Gutgarts.

Treasurer: Dr Simon Parsons.

Webmaster: Dr Kyle C. Lincoln.

Crusades: Guidelines for the Submission of Papers

The editors ask contributors to adhere to the following guidelines. Failure to do so will result in the article being returned to the author for amendment, or may result in its having to be excluded from the volume.

1. Submissions. Submissions should be sent as email attachments to one of the editors (contact details below). Papers should be formatted using MS Word, double-spaced and with wide margins. Times New Roman (12 pt) is preferred. Remember to include your name and contact details (both postal and email addresses) on your paper. If the author is not a native speaker of English, it is their responsibility to have the text checked over and polished by a native speaker prior to submission.

2. Peer Review. All submissions will be peer reviewed. The manuscript will be scrutinized by the editors and sent to at least one outside reader. Decision on acceptance or rejection of the submitted article will normally be made by the editors after two rounds of revision.

3. Length. Normally, the maximum length of articles should not exceed 6,000 words, not including notes. The editors reserve the right to edit papers that exceed these limits.

4. Notes. Normally, notes should be REFERENCE ONLY and placed at the end of the paper. Number continuously.

5. Style sheet. Please use the most recent *Speculum* style sheet (see: http://www.medievalacademy.org/?page=stylesheet). This sets out the format to be used for notes. Please note that this is not necessarily the same format as has been used by other edited volumes on the crusades and/or the Military Orders. Failure to follow the Speculum format will result in accepted articles being returned to the author for amendment. In the main body of the paper you may adhere to either British or American spelling, but it must be consistent throughout the article.

6. Language. Papers will be published in English, French, German, Italian and Spanish.

7. Abbreviations. Please use the abbreviation list on pp. ix–xi of this journal.

8. Diagrams and Maps should be referred to as figures and photographs as plates. Please keep illustrations to the essential minimum, since it will be possible to include only a limited number. All illustrations must be supplied by the contributor in camera-ready copy, and free from all copyright restrictions.

9. Italics. Words to be printed in italics should be italicised if possible. Failing this they should be underlined.

10. Capitals. Please take every care to ensure consistency in your use of capitals and lower-case letters. Use initial capitals to distinguish the general from the specific (for example, "the count of Flanders" but "Count Philip of Flanders").

11. Summary of Article. Contributors will be required to provide a 250 words summary of their paper at the start of each article. This will be accompanied by the author's email address. The summary of the paper is to be in English, regardless of the language of the main article.

Submission of papers to either of the editors:

Professor Jonathan Phillips
Department of History
Royal Holloway, University of London
Egham, Surrey, TW20 0EX,
England, UK
j.p.phillips@rhul.ac.uk

Professor Iris Shagrir
Department of History, Philosophy and
 Judaic Studies
The Open University of Israel
1 University Rd., POB 808, Raanana,
 Israel 4353701
irissh@openu.ac.il

SOCIETY FOR THE STUDY OF THE CRUSADES AND THE LATIN EAST
MEMBERSHIP INFORMATION

The primary function of the Society for the Study of the Crusades and the Latin East is to enable members to learn about current work being done in the field of crusading history, and to contact members who share research interests through the information in the Society's Bulletin. There are more than 300 members from 41 countries. The Society also organizes a major international conference every four years, as well as sections on crusading history at other conferences where appropriate.

The committee of the SSCLE consists of:
Professor Jonathan Phillips, *President*
Dr Nikolaos Chrissis, *Secretary*
Dr Simon Parsons, *Treasurer*
Dr William Purkis and Dr Anna Gutgarts, *Officers for Postgraduate Members*
Dr Danielle Park, *Bulletin Editor*
Dr Kyle C. Lincoln, *Webmaster*

Professor Iris Shagrir, *Crusades* journal representative

Advisory Councilors:
Dr Jessalynn Bird
Professor Kurt Villads Jensen
Dr Antonio Musarra
Dr Caroline Smith

Honorary Presidents:
Professor Benjamin Z. Kedar, Professor Michel Balard, Professor Adrian Boas

Current subscription fees are as follows:
*   Membership and Bulletin of the Society: Single £10, $12 or €12;
*   Student £6, $7 or €7;
*   Joint membership £15, $19 or €18 (for two members sharing the same household);
*   Membership and the journal *Crusades*, including the Bulletin: please add to your subscription fees: £25, $31 or €29 for a **hard copy**, OR £15, $19 or €18 for an **electronic copy** of the journal;
*   If a member wishes to purchase back issues of *Crusades*, each back issue costs £35, $43 or €41.

The cost of the journal to institutions and non-members is £115, US$140.